Well Advised™

Your Guide to Total Health Care

Well Advised™

Your Guide to Total Health Care

With 95 Illustrations

The material in this publication is for general information only and is not intended to provide specific advice or recommendations for any individual. Your doctor or other health professional must be consulted for advice with regard to your individual situation.

Mosby Consumer Health
263 Summer St.
Boston, MA 02210
800-729-5285

Institute for Research and Education
HealthSystem Minnesota
3800 Park Nicollet Blvd.
Minneapolis, MN 55416
800-372-7776

International Standard Book Number: ISBN 1-56066-777-X

97 98 99 00 / 9 8 7 6 5 4 3 2

Introduction

Well Advised: Your Guide to Total Health Care is a unique self-care reference manual written specifically for people like you, who get their health care through health maintenance organizations (HMOs) and other managed care systems. This book provides valuable information about common health emergencies, and also covers a wide range of self-care steps you can take to stay in the best possible health.

About Well Advised

When you have managed care coverage, you become more involved in your health care decisions than when using a traditional fee-for-service health insurance plan. Traditional insurance plans rely heavily on the physician as the sole decision maker for your medical care. Managed care health plans depend on that same relationship, but encourage you to work in partnership with your primary health care provider and to share responsibility for your treatment plan. *Well Advised* was designed to enhance and support that sense of shared responsibility by educating you about many of your health care needs. The more informed you are about your health and well-being, the more actively involved you can be with the decisions your physician and other health care providers make. Understanding what you need from your health care is the key to making sure that it happens.

Based on information gathered originally by the Park Nicollet Medical Foundation, a national leader in health care research, *Well Advised* includes national guidelines from the American Academy of Pediatrics, the American College of Obstetricians and Gynecologists, the National Institutes of Health, the Centers for Disease Control and Prevention, and national leaders on managed care procedures, including the National Commission on Quality Assurance (NCQA) and Health Plan Employer Data Information Set (HEDIS). The material in this guide was updated and reviewed by experts in their fields, and has been checked for accuracy.

How to Use This Book

Whether you're dealing with a medical emergency, a chronic condition, or simply a question about a general health concern, you want to find the information quickly and easily. *Well Advised* is designed to help you do that. To search for a specific category, you can thumb through the pages, using the tabs along the right edge as your guide, refer to the index, or check the table of contents. The *Emergencies and Urgent Care* section page tabs are highlighted in yellow for quick access.

Specific topics within each section are in alphabetical order. When reviewing information about a particular health concern, read the description of the condition and then refer to the self-care steps. Finally, review the decision guides. For reference, a key to symbols that appear in the decision guides is on page 60.

Section One: Your Guide to Managed Care

This section provides you with up-to-date information about how to use your managed care health benefits, and how to choose a primary care physician. It also provides a glossary of managed care terms.

Section Two: A Healthy You

This section contains information you can use every day to stay healthy. Health prevention advice about topics such as regular checkups, weight control, quitting smoking, and improving your fitness level are outlined here, along with tests you can take to learn about your own health and lifestyle choices. You can use the Personal Health Record on page 37 for yourself; you may also want to copy and share it with your friends and family members. Preventive care guidelines (the recommended treatments and screening guidelines for children, teenagers, and adults of all ages) are shown in easy-to-read charts. Because preventive care guidelines may differ among managed care health plans, the guidelines used in this book reflect the prevailing national protocols developed by the NCQA.

Section Three: Emergencies and Urgent Care

This section covers emergency and urgent care situations such as cuts and scrapes, fractures, insect bites, and poisoning. The beginning of this section contains information about when to go to an emergency room, what first aid supplies you should stock in your home, and how to perform CPR, or cardiopulmonary resuscitation.

Section Four: Self-Care for Common Problems

This section is where you will find information about general health concerns such as the common cold, sore throats, and muscle and joint problems. This section also contains guides to women's health and men's health, as well as a chapter about mental health.

Section Five: Living With Chronic Health Problems

This section is for people who have a chronic health condition such as asthma, diabetes, and high blood pressure. If you have a friend or family member who has a chronic health problem, you will also find this section helpful.

Resources

This section, starting on page 291, is a list of national information clearinghouses, such as the American Association of Retired Persons, the American Heart Association, and the American Cancer Society. The list is organized alphabetically by topic. You will find addresses and, in many cases, toll-free numbers for organizations that can provide you with more detailed material.

Well Advised, Your Guide to Total Health Care, is a unique self-care guide. This book, originally developed by the Institute for Research and Education, HealthSystem Minnesota, was revised in cooperation with Mosby Consumer Health, the country's leading expert on managed care communications.

Table of Contents

Section Four

Section Five

Section One

Your Guide to Managed Care

Getting your health care through a managed care plan can save you a lot of time and work. You have a built-in advocate in the health care system: Your primary health care provider coordinates your care, keeps track of your medications and medical history, and helps you choose a specialist when you need one. What's more, you can focus on your care rather than on paperwork. Most managed care organizations cover all of your care—hospitalizations, prescriptions, office visits, and tests—for only a small fee.

You can also count on your plan to take an active role in improving your well-being. Your health plan may offer special programs—to help you quit smoking, manage a risky pregnancy, or learn to handle stress—that can help keep you healthy. Some health plans offer members reduced rates at health clubs and gyms.

Getting to Know Your Plan

Whether you are a new member or have been with your health plan for a long time, you should be familiar with your benefits. Your plan will give you a membership packet that includes a list of providers participating in the plan, a detailed description of your benefits, and other related information. Read these materials, as well as the information on your member ID card. Becoming familiar with your health plan's policies will help you avoid unexpected claim denials in the future.

Once you've read everything, you may still have questions. Call your member services representative. He or she will be your guide in learning the ins and outs of your health plan. Your member services representative is the person to call for information about choosing a primary health care provider, changing your health care provider, and getting a referral to see a specialist. Member services can also help you if you have concerns about the quality of care you're getting, if you've lost your member ID card, if you need to add a dependent to your coverage, or if you have a new address or phone number.

You and Your Health Care Provider

Your managed health care plan stresses the importance of your relationship with a primary care provider. Establishing and maintaining that relationship is a valuable way for you to participate in your health care.

Choosing a Health Care Provider

As a member of your health plan, you'll need to choose a primary health care provider. Your plan has taken some of the hassle out of this process. Although you'll still have to find a health care provider who is a good match, every provider in your plan has gone through an extensive screening process. Your plan reviews the credentials, practice history, and office standards of all health care providers before hiring them—and continues to review the quality of care that physicians provide after they're hired. Since your plan has certified the quality of its physicians, you can concentrate on choosing a physician based on your personal preferences.

Finding a provider who clicks with you has a lot to do with chemistry. Like everyone else, health care providers vary widely in their communication skills and in the value they place on the personal aspects of your relationship. It's important to establish a relationship with a provider who matches your needs and values. See the decision guide below for steps to take in getting to know your health care provider and his or her practice.

Decision Guide for Choosing a Health Care Provider

Get a list. You will receive a list of health care providers who practice in your plan. To narrow it down, take the following steps:

- Check to see whether your current health care provider is on the list.
- Decide what you're looking for in a primary health care provider. Make a list of qualities that are important to you. A few things to consider: Is the location of the provider's office important to you? Is the hospital where the provider admits patients important to you? Is the age, sex, race, or religion of the provider important to you?
- Ask your health plan whether the provider is accepting new patients.
- You can choose a general practitioner or family practitioner as a primary care provider. A woman may decide to choose a gynecologist as her primary care provider. Pediatricians generally serve as primary care providers for children.
- Ask friends and family who share your values for the names of providers they like and trust.

Call the provider's office. Before you make an appointment to see a health care provider, talk to the receptionist in his or her office. Identify yourself as a member of your health plan. Your impression of the office staff is important, because their attitude tends to reflect the attitude of the doctors, nurses, and other staff members. A good receptionist will take the time to answer your questions in a friendly manner. Tell the receptionist you are thinking of choosing the doctor as your primary care provider and would like to ask some questions, such as the following:

- How many patients does the doctor usually see in one day?
- For routine visits, how far in advance must I make an appointment?
- How do I reach the doctor in an emergency?
- Who cares for patients after hours or when the doctor is away?
- With which hospitals is the doctor affiliated? Are they close to my home?
- What kind of educational materials or programs are available through the office to help patients learn more about diseases, treatments, and prevention?

(continued)

Decision Guide for Choosing a Health Care Provider (continued)

- Is a brochure or pamphlet about the doctor's background, schooling, or specialties available? If not, where did the doctor go to medical school? What kind of postgraduate training did he or she have?
- How long has the doctor been practicing?

Check out the office. If you are satisfied with the interview you have with the receptionist, make an appointment to talk personally with the health care provider. Some charge a fee for this appointment, while others do not. Check with your health plan and see if they cover introductory visits. When you arrive at the office, pay attention to the following:

- Note the facilities. Are they clean and pleasant? Are many patients waiting?
- How are you greeted? Is the staff pleasant?
- Is the provider friendly, professional, and treating you like an adult, not a child?

Ask the doctor the following questions:

- How do you keep up with the latest developments in the medical profession? Are you on the teaching staff of any hospital?
- What are your usual office hours? If I need your help after office hours, what should I do?
- If I have a concern that is not an emergency, when is the best time to call you?
- How do you help your patients stay well?
- What do you include in your periodic physical exams?
- How would you feel about my obtaining a second opinion on your diagnosis or recommended treatment?
- Are you a specialist in any other area of medicine?
- How do you handle "living wills" and would you honor an advance directive (a legal document that covers the kind of medical treatment you want if you cannot make your wishes known)?

Ask yourself the following questions:

- Is this provider a caring person?
- Will he or she take the time to get to know me?
- Does the provider explain complicated things in a way I can understand?
- Would I feel comfortable asking the provider a "silly question"?
- Would I trust this provider to be my advocate if I were to become disabled or develop a complicated health condition?

If you're happy with what you've learned about this provider, it's probably a good match. If you have doubts, don't be shy about making an appointment with another one of your candidates. You might work better with someone else.

If you've chosen a health care provider already but decide you'd like to change for any reason (for example, the office turns out to be in an inconvenient location, or you feel the provider's services are below par), the member services department of your health plan can help you. So that the plan can monitor member satisfaction, the representative will probably ask you why you want a new primary care provider.

Schedule an appointment. Once you've chosen a provider, you should make an appointment to see him or her—even if you are not sick. Getting to know your provider is good medicine. That way, if you develop health problems, you'll be cared for by someone who knows you and understands your medical history.

During a routine visit, the provider can probably spend only a few minutes with you. To make the most of this time, you should gather your thoughts and concerns before your visit and then state them clearly. You want to be sure that you and your health care provider understand each other.

How to Talk With Your Provider

Though people may feel nervous or uncomfortable talking with a health care provider, it's important to ask questions and tell your provider what concerns you have. This may get easier over time, and you can take steps to get the most out of these conversations. Be prepared and try to relax.

Write down your most important concerns. Before your visit, make a list of the things you want to discuss. Review your symptoms, including when each one began; the history of the problem, including whether you've had the problem before; and any treatments you have tried. List these things in order of importance so that you get your most pressing concerns answered.

Bring related records. Before you see your new health care provider for the first time, have your medical records transferred. Give your previous provider's staff the name and address of your new provider and they can send your records. You may need to sign a release form. If you are taking any medication or have allergies or other health problems, bring these records if you are seeing a provider for the first time. If your appointment is with a provider you have been seeing for a while, be sure to let him or her know what over-the-counter remedies you are using and whether you are taking medicine prescribed by another provider.

Be brief and clear. As you describe your symptoms to your provider, avoid vague statements such as "I've been feeling sick lately." Be specific: "I've had a headache and nausea for the past week, and I don't know what's causing it."

Be honest. It may be tempting to mask the truth about how much fat you eat or how much you smoke, but your provider needs to know your real habits in order to give you the best treatment.

Ask questions. Asking questions is key to getting what you want from a visit. Ask questions if you don't know the meaning of the word, or when instructions aren't clear. It may help to repeat in your own words what you think the provider means and ask, "Is this correct?"

Share your point of view. Your provider can't read your mind. Speak up if you feel rushed, worried, or uncomfortable. Try to voice your feelings in a positive way. For example, say, "I know you have many patients to see, but I'm really worried about this. I'd feel much better if we could talk about it a little more."

Take notes. It can be hard to remember what your provider says, so take along a notepad and pencil, and write down the main points.

Get written or recorded information. Whenever possible, have your provider or his or her staff provide written advice and instructions. Ask for any brochures, cassette tapes, or videotapes about your health conditions or treatments.

Beyond Office Hours

Your health care provider or a physician on call is available 24 hours a day, seven days a week, for emergency or urgent care (see *Emergencies and Urgent Care*, page 53). You should also be able to get an appointment in a reasonable amount of time.

When you call to schedule an appointment, be prepared to provide details about your condition or other reasons for your call. That way, your health care provider's staff can help you decide whether you need care right away, and determine how much time you need for a visit.

If you're calling for immediate medical advice, the same rule applies: Be as detailed about your symptoms as possible. Depending on your condition, your provider may recommend that you come in for a visit, go to an emergency room immediately, or go to an urgent care facility or clinic. Your provider may also prescribe medication for you over the phone so that you can take care of your condition at home.

When the office is closed, an answering machine or answering service will give you instructions for contacting your provider or the provider on call.

Getting a Referral

Except in life- or limb-threatening conditions, you should call your health care provider before seeking treatment—even after hours and on weekends. Consult your provider before getting care, to ensure that your care is covered at the maximum benefit level. Most health plans will also require a referral from your primary care provider before they cover specialist visits, visits for second opinions, or a hospitalization. If your primary care provider determines that you need to see a specialist, he or she can write or phone in the referral—or may even make it by computer. Some referrals must also be authorized by the plan.

Keeping Your Own Records

No matter how good your memory is, you probably can't keep all the details of your medical history—and your family's—in your head. That's why it's important to keep up-to-date records of both on hand. Make copies of the *Family Medical History* on pages 5 and 6 and *Your Medical History* on page 7, and complete one for yourself and each member of your family. Keep them with your medical records and update them as necessary. Make a copy of the *Medical Resources* form on page 8 and complete it. Keep a copy in your wallet and one near your telephone at home.

Family Medical History

Blood Relative	Significant Health Problem	If Deceased: Cause of Death	Age at Death
Mother			
Father			
Brothers and Sisters			
Mother's Side:			
Grandfather			
Grandmother			
Aunts and Uncles			

(continued)

Family Medical History (continued)

Blood Relative	Significant Health Problem	If Deceased: Cause of Death	Age at Death
Father's Side:			
Grandfather			
Grandmother			
Aunts and Uncles			

Have any of your blood relatives (mother, father, brothers, sisters, grandparents, aunts, uncles) had any of the following diseases or conditions?

Condition	Name/Relationship
☐ Allergies	
☐ Anemia or other blood disorder	
☐ Arthritis	
☐ Asthma	
☐ Bowel disorder	
☐ Cancer	
☐ Cataracts	
☐ Diabetes	
☐ Eczema	
☐ Emphysema	
☐ Epilepsy	
☐ Glaucoma	
☐ Heart disease	
☐ High blood pressure	
☐ High blood cholesterol	
☐ Liver disease	
☐ Lung disease	
☐ Nervous system disorder	
☐ Stroke	
☐ Thyroid disorder (type)	
☐ Ulcer	
☐ Other	

Your Medical History

Name ______________________

Date of birth ______________________

Blood type ______________________

Acute Diseases	Date of Illness
☐ Chicken pox	
☐ Ear infection	
☐ German measles (rubella)	
☐ Hepatitis	
☐ HIV/AIDS	
☐ Mononucleosis	
☐ Measles	
☐ Mumps	
☐ Polio	
☐ Scarlet fever	
☐ Sexually transmitted disease	
☐ Sinus infection	
☐ Strep throat	
☐ Whooping cough	
☐ Other	

Chronic Disorders	Date Diagnosed	Treatment
☐ Arthritis		
☐ Asthma		
☐ Blood disorder		
☐ Cataracts		
☐ Diabetes		
☐ Epilepsy		
☐ Gastrointestinal disorder		
☐ Glaucoma		
☐ Heart disease		
☐ High blood pressure		
☐ High blood cholesterol		
☐ Kidney disease		
☐ Ulcers		
☐ Other		

Medical Resources

Doctor	
Clinic	Telephone
Doctor	
Clinic	Telephone
Hospital	Telephone
After-hours medical care center	Telephone
Pharmacist	Telephone
Poison control center	Telephone

Taking Medication

Some people may need to take medicine every day. Others rarely take any over-the-counter or prescription medications. Knowing what to do will make it easier to take care of yourself whenever you need medication.

Choosing a Drugstore

Whether it's near your home or in your clinic, you should select one drugstore that suits your needs. Go to that drugstore consistently so that the pharmacist has all your medications on file. That way, he or she can check your records for possible drug interactions and allergies whenever a new prescription is filled. (Most drugstores have a computer program that does this.)

Look for a drugstore where pharmacists will take the time to answer your questions thoroughly, either in person or over the phone. Some drugstores offer special conveniences such as 24-hour emergency service, computerized records of the drugs you purchase, senior citizen discounts, and delivery service. Consider cost, helpful service, and convenience when deciding which drugstore to use. Your health plan may also have a list of pharmacies in its network.

Managing Your Medicine

Medications can interact with one another and with certain foods, and must be taken correctly to be effective. You can make sure your medicines work for you—instead of against you—by following a few simple steps whenever you get a new prescription.

Whenever you visit your health care provider, bring a complete list of any prescription or over-the-counter drugs you are taking. Over-the-counter medications include aspirin and other pain relievers, antacids, laxatives, cough and cold medicines, and vitamin supplements, to name a few. If you have more than one health care provider, be sure each one knows what the others have prescribed.

Tell your provider and pharmacist about any past reactions to specific drugs. If you are allergic to a certain drug, such as penicillin, your provider needs to know this. Make sure this information is in your medical record.

You should also keep your own record of the medications you take. Use the *Personal Medication Record* on page 10 to list drugs you take now and past drug reactions. Refer to this record when discussing a new prescription with your health care provider or pharmacist. Update your records whenever you receive a new prescription. You'll be more likely to take your medicine as directed—and you may avoid a bad reaction.

Here are some questions to ask your health care provider or pharmacist when you begin taking a new medication.

- If I miss a dose, should I double up next time?
- Does this medication have any serious side effects? If I notice side effects, which should I report to you and which can I ignore?
- Is it OK to drink alcoholic beverages while I'm using this medication?
- I have another health problem and want to use an over-the-counter medication. Is it OK to use with my current prescription?
- Are there specific foods I should avoid?
- Are there ways to treat my condition that don't involve medication?
- If I think I might be pregnant, or am planning on becoming pregnant, is it OK to take this medication?

What Is a Drug Formulary?

Some health plans have drug formularies, which are lists of safe and effective brand-name and generic drugs covered by the plan. This list is usually developed by a committee of physicians and pharmacists who review all available drugs and select safe, effective, and quality drugs to include in the formulary. This committee also reviews new drugs that come on the market and decides whether to add them to the formulary. Hospitals, clinics, and HMOs have been using formularies for years to promote proper treatment and keep drug costs down.

When you receive a prescription from your health care provider, ask him or her whether the drug is on the formulary. If it is not, he or she may prescribe an alternative that is on the formulary. If your provider believes it is necessary for you to take a drug that is not on the formulary, he or she can contact the plan to request an exception.

Making Your Medicine Work for You

Your medication will be most effective if you carefully follow all the instructions for taking it. Use the *Prescription Drug Worksheet* on pages 11 and 12. Taking a pill at the wrong time of day can affect how some drugs work, and over-the-counter drugs, certain foods, or alcohol can interfere with the action of many medications. To get the most out of your medicine, follow these steps.

Take all your medication, in the proper dosage, at the proper times. If you don't understand the instructions or if you have a question, ask your health care provider or pharmacist. Just because you are starting to feel better doesn't mean you can stop taking your prescription—unless your provider tells you that you can. Always talk with your health care provider before making any changes in how you take your medications.

Personal Medication Record

Make copies of this record as needed.

PRESCRIPTION DRUGS

List any prescription drugs you've taken in the last 2 to 4 weeks, as well as any you have on hand to use as needed, but that you haven't taken recently. Add new drugs as they are prescribed.

Drug (brand or generic name) ______

Purpose ______

Dose ______

Instructions ______

Date started ______

NONPRESCRIPTION DRUGS

Make a similar list for nonprescription drugs.

Drug ______

Purpose ______

Dose ______

Instructions ______

Date started ______

DRUG ALLERGIES AND PAST REACTIONS

List any drugs you know you are allergic to and those to which you have had a bad reaction in the past. You may also include the names of prescription drugs that haven't worked for you.

Drug ______

Purpose ______

Drug ______

Purpose ______

Drug ______

Purpose ______

What happened to make you think you are allergic to this drug?

______

______

______

______

Always follow the directions on the label. Some drugs must be taken with food, and others work best on an empty stomach. You may also need to avoid alcohol or stay out of the sun while taking certain drugs. Even instructions such as "shake first" or "refrigerate" can make a big difference in the drug's effectiveness. Repeat the instructions on your prescription in your own words to the pharmacist before you leave the pharmacy. This way you will understand how to take your medicine.

Chewable medications should only be chewed. Coated tablets must be swallowed whole. The purpose of the coating is to allow for release of the medication at a certain point in the digestive tract. Some medications may require you to take half a tablet. Your pharmacist should be able to give you a tool to use for splitting pills.

Ask about side effects and report reactions promptly. Some side effects are common and are not dangerous. Others can signal that a drug isn't right for you. If you don't feel right, call your provider or pharmacist. Report the name of the drug you're taking and the reaction(s) you're having.

Take your prescription drugs only. Never take another person's prescription, even if you're certain it will help your condition.

Know whether you can drink alcohol when taking a medication. Alcohol may react with medications you are taking. There are about 100 prescription medications that cause problems when combined with alcohol—some severe, some even fatal. Ask your pharmacist or your health care provider whether your medications are affected by alcohol.

Be consistent. Remember to take your medication regularly and on time. If you miss a dose, check with your provider or pharmacist. You might be told to double the next dose, but at times that could be harmful. Don't make the decision on your own.

Prescription Drug Worksheet

NAME OF DRUG AND DATE

What was prescribed and when? ______

What type (class) of drug is this? ______

PURPOSE

Why am I taking it? ______

______

What does it do? ______

______

How does it work? ______

______

How long does it take to work? ______

(continued)

Prescription Drug Worksheet (continued)

DOSAGE

How much should I take?

When and how often should I take it?

What should I do if I miss a dose?

COURSE OF TREATMENT

How long should I take this drug?

Is it all right to quit when symptoms stop?

SPECIAL INSTRUCTIONS

Take with food or on an empty stomach?

Any other precautions?

SIDE EFFECTS/REACTIONS

What are the most common side effects or allergic reactions?

What should I do if I have an allergic reaction?

Will side effects decrease after routine use?

DRUG/FOOD/ALCOHOL INTERACTION

What other drugs, foods, or activities should I avoid while taking this medication?

FOLLOW-UP

When should I report back to the doctor?

Are lab tests necessary to monitor changes?

REFILLS

How many and when?

STORAGE

What is the expiration date?

How should I store this drug?

Does my household require childproof or easy-to-open caps?

COST

How much does it cost?

Is there a less expensive generic form?

Find a way to remember to take your medicine. Try to link taking medicine with other activities that are part of your daily routine, such as meals or bedtime. Here are some examples:

- Once a day: watching the evening news.
- Twice a day: brushing your teeth. (Turn the bottle upside down in the morning and right side up in the evening.)
- Four times a day: at three meals and at bedtime. (If the medicine should be taken on an empty stomach, take one hour before meals.)

To help you make the right decision, use the *Nonprescription Drug Worksheet* on page 14 as a reminder of what to consider when choosing an over-the-counter drug. You may want to list a summary of options and compare the uses, dosages, costs, and side effects of medicine you commonly use. Photocopy the *Pain Medication Chart* on page 15 and keep it in a convenient place for times when you may need to use one of these common medicines. This table will help you decide which type of pain reliever is the right choice for your condition.

Over-the-Counter Medicine

Even though you don't need a prescription to buy them, over-the-counter medications are drugs that should be taken with care. In fact, some over-the-counter drugs were once available only by prescription. Over-the-counter drugs can cause overdoses, allergic reactions, and dangerous interactions with other medications, just as prescription drugs can. People with certain chronic illnesses can't take some over-the-counter medications.

Over-the-counter drugs can also interfere with your prescription drugs. For example, a seemingly innocent antacid can destroy the effectiveness of certain antibiotics. The side effects of cough or cold medicines can be serious if you're taking medicine for high blood pressure, diabetes, or glaucoma.

Choose over-the-counter drugs with care, making sure to take the right medication for your symptoms. Not all over-the-counter drugs recommended for treating a specific condition have the same active ingredients. Read the label to make sure you're taking medicine that will treat the symptoms you have, or ask your pharmacist for a recommendation.

Storing Your Medicine Safely

Storing a medicine improperly—where it is exposed to extreme temperatures or dampness, for example—can make it less effective or even dangerous. Follow these tips to keep the power in your prescription and over-the-counter medications:

- A cabinet in a dry environment is better for storage than the medicine cabinet in the bathroom.
- Store medication in a locked cabinet that is out of the reach of children.
- Store your medication properly. Some need to be refrigerated, and others must be kept away from the light. All medication containers should be tightly sealed to keep the medication from spoiling. If it is hard for you to open child-resistant tops, ask your pharmacist for easy-to-open tops.
- Check expiration dates on over-the-counter medications. Aspirin that smells like vinegar has gone bad and should be thrown away. Throw out unused or expired medications. Flush pills and liquids down the toilet.
- Rinse out and discard bottles. Never use them to store other medications.

Nonprescription Drug Worksheet

Keep copies of this worksheet available so that family members can use it whenever they consider taking a nonprescription drug.

EVALUATE

What symptoms do you want the medication to relieve?

Can home remedies do the job?

Are you supposed to avoid certain drugs for any reason (pregnancy, breast-feeding, drug interactions, allergies)?

CONSULT

Ask your pharmacist or provider, or check a reference book for help in choosing the proper product. Write any information here that you'll want to remember.

INVESTIGATE

Read the label thoroughly. What are the ingredients?

Do they conflict with any other drugs you are taking?

Are you allergic to any of the ingredients?

What does the drug do?

What is the recommended dosage for you?

Do any warnings or cautions apply to you?

CONFIRM

Ask your pharmacist about possible interactions with food, alcohol, or your other medicines. Write any information here that you'll want to remember.

DECIDE

What is your reason for buying this drug?

Are you being influenced by recommendations, price, or advertising?

Pain Medication Chart

DRUG Examples of brand names	**ACETAMINOPHEN** Tylenol, Tempra	**IBUPROFEN** Advil, Nuprin, Motrin IB	**ASPIRIN** Coated aspirin such as Ecotrin prevents stomach upset.
When to use	First choice for fever, headache, mild burns, stings	Sports injuries, acute trauma, menstrual cramps headache, tendon/joint inflammation	Stroke/heart attack prevention; fever in adults
Dose	Children by weight Adults: two 325 mg tablets	Take with food. Adults: one or two 200 mg tablets	**Don't use for children.** Adults: one or two 325 mg tablets
Use for pain?	Yes	Yes Increasing dose will increase relief; take up to 3,200 mg/day.	Yes Increasing dose will not increase relief.
Use for fever?	Yes	Yes, small doses	Yes
Use for muscle/ joint pain?	No	Yes, higher doses of 2,400-3,200 mg/day	Yes
Use for blood thinning?	No	Some	Yes
Side effects	Safe for short-term use (large overdose can be dangerous)	Can irritate stomach	Ulcers, gastrointestinal bleeding; easy to overdose

PLEASE NOTE: You should be careful of combination products; some may have caffeine and some mix the drugs listed here. Do not use more than one pain reliever at a time. Do not take with cold medicines, which may already contain a pain reliever.

Taking Medication

Deciding About Surgery

When a health care provider recommends surgery, you should take an active role in deciding whether to go through with it. You'll have to consider the risks and benefits of surgery. Sometimes it is clear that surgery is the only way to go, while in other cases an alternative to surgery may be the wisest choice. Learning to ask the right questions to get the information you need will help you decide whether surgery is right for you. The first step is to find out whether the surgery your health care provider is recommending is nonelective or elective.

Nonelective surgery. When surgery is needed to save a person's life (such as to remove a ruptured appendix) or must be done immediately to prevent permanent disability (such as to surgically repair a badly broken bone), it is considered nonelective. That means you have little or no choice but to have the operation. And you probably do not have time to explore other options. Fortunately, few surgical procedures are truly nonelective.

Elective surgery. Most surgical procedures involve some degree of choice for the patient. In some cases, alternatives to surgery exist, such as drugs or other ways of dealing with the problem. In other cases, surgery may be the only option for correcting a particular problem, but the symptoms don't merit the risk that surgery presents. For example, many people who have gallstones have no pain, discomfort, or other symptoms and do not need surgery. For some conditions (such as an enlarged prostate or gallstones), your health care provider may opt for watchful waiting. This involves following your symptoms carefully to make sure your condition isn't worsening.

Surgery is appropriate if it is needed to do any of the following:

- Relieve or prevent pain.
- Restore or preserve normal function.
- Correct a deformity.
- Save or prolong your life.

Make an appointment with your health care provider to discuss your concerns (see *Questions to Ask Before Surgery*, page 17). Write down the answers. If you feel anxious or nervous, take a friend or relative along for moral support. Then weigh the information and decide what you want to do. You and your provider can make this decision together. Don't let yourself be pressured into having surgery you don't need. Ask your provider if he or she has any information on your condition and the surgery. That way you can review the material at home. Later, you can ask your provider any further questions you may have.

Asking for a Second Opinion

Getting more information can help when you're deciding about surgery. One way to do this is to get a second opinion (also called a "review of treatment"). Some health plans require second opinions before they will cover certain procedures. Call your health plan to find out what steps you need to take to get a second opinion.

You might feel uncomfortable asking for a second opinion, but most health care providers today are used to this and may even encourage you to do so. Don't be timid. A provider who dismisses your request may not have your best interests at heart.

Although a second opinion isn't needed in every instance, you would be wise to seek one in the following situations:

- The procedure is experimental or poses a high risk, such as an organ transplant.
- Your symptoms aren't severe and it isn't clear whether the surgery will help.
- The procedure has a reputation for being performed when not absolutely needed.

Getting a second opinion is a good idea if your health care provider recommends any of the surgeries listed below. These procedures tend to be performed more often than is medically necessary.

- tonsillectomy (removal of tonsils)
- hysterectomy (removal of uterus and sometimes ovaries)
- coronary bypass
- radical mastectomy (removal of the breast)
- orthopedic surgery (back, bones, or joints)
- cholecystectomy (removal of the gallbladder)

Learning more about the pros and cons of any recommended procedure is the best way to decide whether the risk outweighs the benefits, given your personal preferences. Other controversial procedures that warrant discussion include:

- fixing a fracture of the femur (the thigh bone), internally or externally
- transurethral resection of the prostate (TUR)
- delivering a baby with a vacuum instrument or instrument for a baby low in the vagina (vacuum extraction or low forceps delivery with episiotomy)
- balloon angioplasty
- unilateral thyroid lobectomy
- total knee or hip replacement

To find a second surgeon, ask your primary health care provider, your health plan, or a local hospital for a recommendation. If you ask the first surgeon to recommend someone, you are less likely to get an unbiased second opinion.

When you go for a second opinion, you should do several things. Avoid the expense of repeating tests and procedures by bringing your medical records and X-rays, if any, along with you. If this is not possible, you can have them sent to the second surgeon before your appointment by signing a records release form. Ask the second surgeon the same questions you asked the first. If the second surgeon disagrees with the first, find out why. You may find that one surgeon's philosophy and reasoning fit with your own more than the other's.

Questions to Ask Before Surgery

Take this list of questions when you visit your provider to discuss surgery.

- What operation are you recommending?
- Why do I need the operation?
- Are there alternatives to surgery?
- What are the benefits of having the operation?
- What if I don't have the operation?
- Where can I get a second opinion?
- Where will the operation be done?
- What kind of anesthesia will I need?
- How long will it take me to recover?

If Your Health Care Provider Recommends Hospitalization

These days, many procedures that once required a hospital stay can be done at outpatient surgical clinics. Surgeries and rehabilitation that once demanded days and even weeks in the hospital can now often be taken care of in a few hours at the hospital.

If your health care provider advises hospitalization, ask why your condition can't be treated at home or an outpatient clinic. Going into the hospital can disrupt your life a great deal, and the cases in which hospitalization is truly necessary are becoming more rare.

To get your questions answered efficiently, make a copy of the questions below and take it with you when you visit your health care provider. Write down or tape-record the answers. For some people, it helps to bring a friend or relative who can help remember the details of the discussion with the provider.

If your provider recommends hospitalization, ask the following questions:

- Why is hospitalization necessary?
- What tests and/or procedures will be done?
- Must the tests and/or procedures be done at the hospital?
- What other choices do I have?
- How much will I be involved in deciding about my treatment?
- Are there any risks involved with any of the tests or procedures? What are they?
- How long will I be in the hospital?
- How soon can I return to normal activities?
- How long will I be away from work?

Glossary of Managed Care Terms

ambulatory care: Medical care given outside a hospital, or within the hospital without the patient being admitted

ancillary services: Services during your hospital stay other than room, board, and nursing. Examples are prescriptions, operating room services, and laboratory tests.

appeal: The procedure by which you can question and attempt to reverse a decision made by your health plan or primary care physician, such as denial of coverage for a certain procedure

benefits package: The services you are entitled to by being part of your health plan

board certified: A physician who has completed medical school, internship, and residency in a medical specialty and who has passed an examination given by a group of physicians in that specialty

case management: Process of review by a case manager of conditions that require complex treatment; case manager ensures that a patient is getting the proper services and making the most of his or her benefits.

certificate of coverage: A document describing the benefits you receive as a member of your health plan

claim: The bill your health plan pays for any health care you receive

coinsurance: The percentage of covered medical bills that you pay once an annual deductible is met. This percentage is set by your health plan.

coordination of benefits: When you are covered by more than one health insurance company, your primary health plan works with your other health insurance companies to ensure that you are covered by both plans at the maximum benefit level.

copayment: The set amount you pay at the time of you go for an office visit or receive other health care services

covered benefits: Services that are paid for by your health plan, such as regular office visits with your primary care physician

credentialing: The review of a health care provider's education, licensing, training, and performance to determine whether he or she is eligible to be on a hospital's medical staff or part of a health plan's network

deductible: Set amount of money you must pay for health care coverage, above which your health plan coverage kicks in

dependent: Any person you support, such as your spouse or child

drug formulary: List of generic and brand-name medications covered by a health plan

durable medical equipment: Equipment such as wheelchairs, crutches, walkers, and other assistive devices that are usually rented for temporary use rather than purchased

employee assistance program: A service offered by some companies to help employees deal with emotional or physical health problems or substance abuse issues that are affecting job performance

formulary: See drug formulary.

health care provider: The people and facilities within the network or your area of coverage that provide health care, including physicians, nurses, physician's assistants, pharmacists, therapists, social workers, ambulance services, hospitals, nursing facilities, respiratory therapists, and physical therapists

health maintenance organization (HMO): A type of health care plan that provides health care services from providers in a network to its members

individual practice association (IPA) model: A health maintenance organization in which physicians provide health care services from their private practices

identification (ID) card: Cards for you and each covered family member that show that you are part of a health plan. ID cards list important phone numbers at the health plan, your primary care physician's name and phone number, and your member ID number. Always carry your ID card. Show your ID card whenever you seek medical services.

managed care: A health care system in which care provided is reviewed and authorized by the health care plan

NCQA accreditation: Certification that a managed care organization has been reviewed by the National Committee on Quality Assurance and has demonstrated quality performance in preventive health care, health promotion, and other areas

network: A group of physicians and other health care providers who are contracted with your health plan to provide health care services in a geographic area

out-of-network care: Medical services or supplies that you do not receive—or for which you are not referred—by your primary health care provider or another provider in the network

out-of-pocket costs: Any money paid by the member for health care services that are not covered by your health plan

participating provider: A primary care physician, specialist, hospital, or other group that is part of a network within a health maintenance organization

point-of-service plan: A type of coverage that requires you to pay a deductible for using out-of-network services

preadmission certification: Sometimes called preauthorization. This is an approval required by many health plans before any scheduled hospital stays and in some cases, before some scheduled outpatient procedures.

preferred provider organization (PPO): A network of providers (including physicians and hospitals) that have a contract with a health plan to provide health care services at a discount for members

primary care physician: A physician who participates in the network of health care providers and who is responsible for providing, prescribing, and coordinating all your health care and treatment

prior authorization: See preadmission certification.

provider: See health care provider.

provider network: See network.

referral: When your primary care physician determines that you need to see a specialist in the network to receive specialty care for a medical condition. A referral may be written, phoned in, or made via computer, depending on the guidelines set by your health plan.

service area: The geographic area served by your health plan's networks

staff model: A health maintenance organization (HMO) that employs the physicians and other health care providers who work at the health care centers operated by the HMO

Section Two

A Healthy You

Everyone has different health concerns, and these can change throughout a person's lifetime. Your family history, gender, weight, habits, and diet can determine whether you are likely to develop certain diseases. For example, if you have relatives who have had breast cancer or heart disease, your chances of eventually having one of these conditions may be higher.

But you can do many things to stack the odds in your favor. Quitting smoking, eating less fat, getting regular exercise, and reducing your stress levels are all positive changes that can help you live a longer, healthier life. If you are at risk for a disease, screening tests can help your health care provider detect the disease earlier when it is easier to treat. You can also learn the early warning signs of illnesses such as cancer so you'll know whether your symptoms need to be checked out by your health care provider.

This section includes several quizzes that can help you assess your health, as well as the health and safety of your family. The section also discusses individual health risks by age and gender. Suggestions on beginning and sticking to an exercise routine, eating healthy, and quitting smoking are also included.

Children's health is also addressed in this chapter, with a list of the immunizations your child should have and why, and some sample questions to ask your child's health care provider during well-child visits as well as when your child is sick. There's also a list of tips that will help you make your home as safe for children as possible.

Above all, remember that it's important for you and your children to see your providers when you're healthy, not just when you're sick. You can do more to protect your health than all the doctors, hospitals, new medical equipment, and scientists in the world. It's up to you to prevent future health problems by learning more about prevention, taking care of yourself, and getting all the screening tests and care you need.

Weighing Your Health Risks

Taking a careful look at your health habits and risks, reviewing them with your provider, and setting goals for changing your lifestyle are the first steps toward taking charge of your health. The following health assessments will help you examine how well you're taking care of yourself in terms of exercise, diet, safety, and substance use.

Reading across each row, mark the one box in each row that is closest to your current situation.

Health Assessment One: Lifestyle Choices

COLUMN 1 (1 POINT)	COLUMN 2 (2 POINTS)	COLUMN 3 (3 POINTS)
☐ I am a nonsmoker or I quit smoking more than 12 months ago.	☐ I smoke 1 to 9 cigarettes per day or quit within the past 12 months.	☐ I smoke 10 or more cigarettes per day.
☐ I regularly eat a well-balanced diet that includes all the food groups.	☐ I sometimes eat a well-balanced diet, but do not consistently eat foods from all the food groups.	☐ I rarely or never eat a variety of foods in a well-balanced diet.
☐ I do aerobic exercise—such as brisk walking, swimming, biking, jogging, or aerobics—3 or more times a week.	☐ I do aerobic exercise once or twice a week.	☐ I seldom or never do aerobic exercise.
☐ I am within 10 pounds of the weight recommended for me.	☐ I am 10 to 20 pounds over or under the weight recommended for me.	☐ I am more than 20 pounds over or under the weight recommended for me.
☐ I seldom or never drink more than 2 alcoholic beverages per occasion. I am not concerned about how much alcohol I drink, nor are the people who are close to me.	☐ I sometimes drink more than 2 alcoholic beverages per occasion and/or sometimes I am concerned—or people close to me are concerned—about how much alcohol I drink.	☐ I often drink more than 2 alcoholic beverages per occasion and/or I am often concerned—or people close to me are concerned—about how much alcohol I drink.
Column 1 total: ______	**Column 2 total:** ______	**Column 3 total:** ______

Add your points from columns 1, 2, and 3 together to arrive at your "Lifestyle Choices" total and enter it here. **Total Points:** ______

Key: 6 or less: Healthy choices 7-11: Somewhat risky choices 12 or more: Risky choices

Reading across each row, mark the one box in each row that is closest to your current situation.

Health Assessment Two: Personal Safety

COLUMN 1 (1 POINT)	COLUMN 2 (2 POINTS)	COLUMN 3 (3 POINTS)
☐ I always wear my seat belt when driving or riding in a car.	☐ I sometimes wear my seat belt.	☐ I rarely or never wear my seat belt.
☐ I always wear a helmet when riding a bicycle.	☐ I sometimes wear a helmet when riding a bicycle.	☐ I rarely or never wear a helmet when riding a bicycle.
☐ I never ride in a car with a driver who has been using alcohol or other drugs.	☐ I sometimes ride in a car with a driver who has been using alcohol or other drugs.	☐ I often ride in a car with a driver who has been using alcohol or other drugs.
☐ I always follow safe sex practices or don't have intercourse.	☐ I sometimes follow safe sex practices.	☐ I rarely or never follow safe sex practices.
☐ I always or almost always use sunblock to protect my skin from the sun.	☐ I sometimes use sunblock to protect my skin from the sun.	☐ I rarely or never use sunblock to protect my skin from the sun.
Column 1 total: ______	**Column 2 total:** ______	**Column 3 total:** ______

Add your points from columns 1, 2, and 3 together to arrive at your "Personal Safety" total and enter it here. **Total Points:** ________

Key: 6 or less: Healthy choices 7-11: Somewhat risky choices 12 or more: Risky choices

Weighing Your Health Risks

Reading across each row, mark the one box in each row that is closest to your current situation.

Health Assessment Three: Home Safety

COLUMN 1 (1 POINT)	COLUMN 2 (2 POINTS)	COLUMN 3 (3 POINTS)
☐ I have a working smoke detector in my home that I check regularly.	☐ I have a smoke detector at home but rarely check to see whether it's working.	☐ I do not have a home smoke detector or do not check on it.
☐ I keep all possibly poisonous items in my home locked and stored away from children.	☐ I have some or most poisonous items in my home locked and stored away from children.	☐ I do not keep poisonous items locked and stored away from children.
☐ To prevent burns, my water heater is no higher than 120 degrees.	☐ I do not know the temperature setting of my water heater.	☐ My water heater is set above 120 degrees.
☐ I do not have firearms or weapons at home, or I keep them locked, stored, and unloaded, where children can't get them.	☐ I keep firearms or weapons stored and locked most of the time.	☐ I do not keep firearms and weapons stored away from children.
☐ To prevent slips and falls, I always keep electrical cords and carpets secured.	☐ I sometimes check to be sure cords or carpets will not cause slips and falls.	☐ I rarely or never check cords or carpets to prevent slips and falls.
Column 1 total: ______	**Column 2 total:** ______	**Column 3 total:** ______

Add your points from columns 1, 2, and 3 together to arrive at your "Home Safety" total and enter it here. **Total Points:** ________

Key: 6 or less: Healthy choices 7-11: Somewhat risky choices 12 or more: Risky choices

Reading across each row, mark the one box in each row that is closest to your current situation.

Health Assessment Four: Personal Health Decisions

COLUMN 1 (1 POINT)	COLUMN 2 (2 POINTS)	COLUMN 3 (3 POINTS)
☐ I rarely or never feel overwhelmed with problems.	☐ I sometimes feel overwhelmed with problems.	☐ I often feel overwhelmed with problems.
☐ I rarely or never feel afraid in my relationships.	☐ I sometimes feel afraid in my relationships.	☐ I often feel afraid in my relationships.
☐ I have a complete and current living will that states my wishes for care if I should become unable to make my own decisions.	☐ I have a living will that needs updating.	☐ I do not have a living will.
☐ I have many social contacts and do not feel isolated from others.	☐ I have some social contacts but sometimes feel isolated from others.	☐ I have few social contacts and often feel isolated from others.
Column 1 total: ______	**Column 2 total:** ______	**Column 3 total:** ______

Add your points from columns 1, 2, and 3 together to arrive at your "Personal Health Decisions" total and enter it here. **Total Points:** ______

Key: 6 or less: Healthy choices 7-11: Somewhat risky choices 12 or more: Risky choices

Weighing Your Health Risks

Children and Teenagers

Keeping children safe and healthy is a main concern as we watch them cut new teeth, hit growth spurts, and struggle through adolescence into adulthood. The health risks children and teenagers face are as varied as the interests and skills they learn as they grow up. From infections to falling out of trees to experimenting with sex, some health issues facing children and teenagers will always stay the same, while others are new and unnerving.

You need to weigh many factors when deciding how often to bring your children and teens to their health care provider. Questions about a child's developmental stages, a family history of certain health problems, or significant changes in a child's environment or behavior are all reasons to take your child to see his or her provider.

Planning for a Visit to Your Child's Health Care Provider

Whether you're seeing a health care provider for a well-child visit or because your child is sick, it's a good idea to think ahead of time about the questions you want to ask. If you're not sure whether your child needs medical care, you can call his or her provider's office at any time of day or night. A staff member or doctor on call can tell you if your child needs to be seen in the office or at an urgent care clinic or emergency room (see *Using the Emergency Room*, page 53).

The following are sample questions you might want to ask when visiting your child's provider.

Well-Child Exam

- What are the office hours?
- How can I contact my child's health care provider in an emergency or when the office is closed?
- If I have a minor question, when is the best time to call?
- If the provider isn't available, who can answer my questions?
- Is there anything the provider needs to know about my family?
- What immunizations does my child need, and when?
- How often does my child need a well-child exam?
- What else can I do to keep my child safe and healthy at home or with a caregiver?
- Should I be concerned about my child's weight or activity level?
- How can I encourage my child to exercise?
- How can I be sure my child eats a nutritious diet?
- How can I help my child cope with a recent divorce, death, or emotional or behavioral problems?

When Your Child Is Sick

- What isn't working, and why?
- What caused the problem?
- When will my child start feeling better?
- Are there signs or symptoms I should watch for?
- How can I make my child comfortable?
- Will my other children catch this illness?
- Can I do anything to prevent this illness or injury from happening again?
- Is this related to any past medical conditions?
- Does my child need to stay home from school?
- When can my child start doing normal activities again?

- Is it OK for my child to play with other children now?
- What is the plan for my child's treatment?
- Does my child need to be on a special diet?
- What is this medication for? When is the best time to give it?
- How long will it take this medication to work?
- Is it OK for my child to take vitamins or over-the-counter medications with this prescription?
- What are the side effects of this medication? Can I do anything about them? Will they go away?
- How long should my child take this medication?
- Are there organizations or support groups that can give me more information about this condition?
- Does the doctor need to see my child for a follow-up visit?

The table on pages 28 and 29 summarizes the preventive health care schedules for children and teenagers. The schedules are mainly for children without symptoms of health problems and who do not have special health risks. If you have a family history of certain illnesses, ask your child's health care provider to recommend a schedule of preventive care visits that is appropriate for your child.

Childhood Immunizations

Among the greatest achievements in modern medicine, vaccines protect children from serious diseases, including mumps, measles, diphtheria, and polio. Some immunizations work by giving a very weak dose of the disease—strong enough to prompt the body's immune system to develop antibodies against the disease but not strong enough to cause it. The following section describes each of the major vaccines.

Diphtheria/pertussis/tetanus (DPT). The DPT shot combines all three vaccines to protect against these life-threatening diseases. Most children should have five DPT shots before they enter kindergarten. Babies should have three shots by the time they reach 6 months of age—at 2, 4, and 6 months—plus one at about 15 months.

Oral polio vaccine (OPV). Since becoming available in the 1950s, this vaccine has nearly wiped out polio. Experts warn, however, that without continued vaccination,

Your Child's Immunization Record

Use this chart to keep track of your child's immunizations.

Child's Name ____________ Date of Birth ____________	Date of Dose 1	Date of Dose 2	Date of Dose 3	Date of Dose 4	Date of Dose 5
DPT (Diphtheria/pertussis/tetanus)					
OPV (Oral polio vaccine)					
HIB (*Haemophilus influenzae* type B)					
MMR (Measles/mumps/rubella)					
Hepatitis B vaccine					
Chicken pox (Varicella) vaccine					

Preventive Care Recommendations for Children

PREVENTION STEP	SCREENING RECOMMENDATIONS
Birth to Age 23 Months	
Lab Tests	
Hemoglobin or hematocrit	Once during infancy
Cholesterol	Not recommended for healthy children
Urinalysis	Not recommended for healthy children
Tuberculin skin test	Not recommended for healthy children[1]
Lead screening	Recommended for children at high risk[4]
Immunizations	
Haemophilus influenzae type B (HIB)	2, 4, 6, and 12 to 15 months
Oral polio vaccine (OPV)	2, 4, and 6 to 15 months
Diphtheria/pertussis/tetanus (DPT)	2, 4, 6, and 15 months
Measles/mumps/rubella (MMR)	15 months
Hepatitis B	Birth, 1 and 6 months or 2, 4, and 10 months
Examinations	
Hearing exams	Special hearing tests given by primary caregiver if child is at risk[2]
Ages 2 to 6	
Lab Tests	
Cholesterol	Recommended for children at high risk[3]
Urinalysis	Not recommended for healthy children
Tuberculin skin test	Not recommended for healthy children[1]
Lead screening	Recommended for children at high risk[4]
Immunizations	
Oral polio vaccine (OPV)	4 to 6 years old
Diphtheria/pertussis/tetanus (DPT)	4 to 6 years old
Examinations	
Blood pressure	Every 2 years
Eye exam	Once by age 5
Hearing exam	Only if hearing ability is questioned[2]
Ages 7 to 12	
Lab Tests	
Cholesterol	Recommended for children at high risk[3]
Urinalysis	Not recommended for healthy children
Tuberculin skin test	Not recommended for healthy children[1]

(continued)

Preventive Care Recommendations for Children (continued)	
PREVENTION STEP	**SCREENING RECOMMENDATIONS**
Immunization	
Measles/mumps/rubella (MMR)	12 years old
Examinations	
Blood pressure	Every 2 years
Vision and hearing exams	If problems are suspected[2]
Scoliosis screening	Not recommended for healthy children
Ages 13 to 18	
Lab Tests	
Urinalysis	Not recommended for healthy teens
Pap smear	At age 18 or after first sexual activity
Immunization	
Tetanus/diphtheria	Once at 14 to 16 years old[5]
History/Counseling	
Sexual practices	Weigh risks and provide appropriate information/advice
Tobacco/alcohol/drug use	Weigh risks and provide appropriate information/advice
Examinations	
Blood pressure	At all visits
Pelvic exam (women)	At age 18 or after first sexual activity

Risk Factors

1 Children suspected of having tuberculosis, children who live in households with cases of tuberculosis, or children who are new immigrants from areas known to have high rates of tuberculosis should be tested.

2 Vision and hearing tests given at school do not need to be repeated by the health care provider. Special hearing tests should be given to children with infections at birth, family history of hearing problems, low birth weight, low Apgar scores, or malformation of the head or neck.

3 Children over age 2 who have a family history of heart disease before the age of 55 or who have a parent with cholesterol readings of over 300 may need to have their blood cholesterol checked.

4 Children at high risk include those who live in—or often visit—housing built before 1950 that is run down or undergoing renovation; those who come into close contact with other children who have high lead exposure; those whose parents work in lead-related occupations; or children who live near hazardous waste sites, busy highways, or lead processing plants.

5 If the child has a serious wound, a tetanus booster may be recommended if he or she has not had one in the past 5 years.

the risk of contracting this crippling, potentially fatal disease could return. Children should receive four doses of oral polio vaccine by age 6. In most cases, this provides protection for life.

***Haemophilus influenzae* type B (HIB).** HIB is a dangerous bacterium that can cause meningitis, pneumonia, and other infections. The HIB vaccine protects almost all children who receive the full four doses. It is given by injection three times before a child is 7 months old, followed by a booster at 12 to 15 months.

Measles/mumps/rubella (MMR). The MMR vaccine is given by injection once at 15 months and again at age 12 to guard against these common childhood infections. For most people, these two doses provide protection for life.

Hepatitis B vaccine. Hepatitis is an inflammation of the liver that can damage the liver and result in cancer or cirrhosis. Hepatitis can even cause death. Hepatitis B is considered to be the most serious form of hepatitis. It is transmitted most frequently through sexual contact or from mother to child during or shortly after birth. The hepatitis B vaccine is given three times before age 1. Teenagers may also be vaccinated if they weren't vaccinated earlier.

Chicken pox (varicella) vaccine. Chicken pox is seen most often in children under the age of 10. This contagious infection is caused by the varicella-zoster virus. Children between 12 months and 12 years of age who have not had chicken pox should be vaccinated, which takes only a single dose. Healthy adolescents past their 13th birthday who have not been immunized previously and have not had chicken pox should be immunized with two doses of vaccine, 4 to 8 weeks apart.

Safety in the Home

Accidents are the leading cause of death and disability for children and young adults. Here are several tips for making your home safer for everyone.

Child Safety—Inside and Outside

- Guard all electrical outlets with safety covers.
- Put childproof locks wherever poisonous substances (including alcohol) and sharp utensils or tools are stored.
- Set water to 120 degrees or lower to prevent scalding.
- Use plastic dishes and cups for toddlers.
- Keep all cribs and beds away from windows.
- Keep pins, paper clips, and other small, swallowable objects out of the reach of young children.
- Dispose of or properly store plastic bags to prevent suffocation.
- Put up fences around pools, spas, and ponds.
- Make sure kids wear helmets when biking or skating.
- Mark sliding glass doors so that they are visible.

Fire Safety

- Install smoke detectors in hallways and outside all bedroom doors, and replace batteries at least once a year.
- Keep a fire extinguisher in a central location and make sure that the whole family knows how to use it.
- If a fire starts when you are cooking, put it out by turning off the burner and smothering the flame with baking soda, a pan lid, or a fire extinguisher.

- Teach all the members of your family how to "stop-drop-roll" if their clothes catch on fire.
- Have a household fire drill and plan emergency escape routes.
- Make sure that second-floor rooms have escape ladders.
- Have your fireplace inspected annually for creosote buildup. Make sure that the fire screen closes completely. Keep newspaper and upholstery a safe distance from your fireplace.
- Never leave a fire unattended.
- Keep flammable objects away from space heaters, and use space heaters with care.
- If your efforts to put out a fire aren't effective after one minute, it's too big. Leave the house right away and call 911.

Preventive Health Care for Adults

Part of taking care of yourself is getting the screenings that are recommended for you at your age. Although these tests are an important part of your health care, that doesn't mean that it will make you healthier if you get every possible screening. But there are other steps you can take to put yourself on the road to good health.

Your health care provider can help you weigh the pros and cons of various screenings. If it is unclear to you whether a particular screening is necessary, ask your provider the following questions:

- If the results of a screening test are unclear, is it likely that I will need other tests and exams?
- How effective is the test at detecting this disease?
- Could this test harm me? If so, what is the risk of having the test? What is the risk of not having the test?
- Given my age and health history, how effective is the treatment for the disease this test may detect?

The answers to these questions will help you and your health care provider to decide whether the test is appropriate for you.

The Best Prevention Years: Ages 19 to 39

While you're building a career, starting a family, establishing a home—or even all three—paying attention to your health habits may not be a high priority. After all, the odds are in your favor. Your chances of falling victim to a major illness such as heart disease or cancer are remote before the age of 40.

But the habits you establish now can affect how you feel and what health problems you may have in the future. For example, during these years you tend to gain weight faster than at any other time in your adult life. And although the combined effects of smoking, extra calories, or lack of exercise may be reversible, habits of 10 or 20 years are tough to change. Now is the time to invest in a healthy future by making positive health choices—like regular exercise and a low-fat, low-salt diet.

Besides shaping your personal health habits, you should also develop a schedule of preventive health care exams that fits your health history. It's also important to build a good relationship with your health care provider.

What to watch out for. Although it may seem that physical ailments are a problem

Preventive Care Recommendations—Ages 19 to 39	
PREVENTION STEP	**SCREENING RECOMMENDATIONS**
Lab Tests	
Cholesterol and HDL	Every 5 years (test more often if risk factors are present[1] or if total cholesterol is higher than 240)
Blood pressure	Every 2 years (test more often if risk factors are present[4] or if blood pressure is higher than 130/85)
Chest X-ray	Not recommended for healthy adults
Urinalysis	Not recommended for healthy adults
Rubella titer	Women lacking evidence of immunity to rubella
Immunizations	
Tetanus/diphtheria	Every 10 years[7]
Influenza	Yearly if at risk[2]
Pneumonia vaccination	At least once if at risk[3]
Hepatitis B	Once if at risk[3]
For Women	
Breast examination	Professional exam: Every 3 years, beginning at age 20 (test more often if risk factors are present[8]) Self-exam: Monthly
Mammography	Age 35 if at risk[8]; otherwise, age 40
Pelvic exam/Pap smear	Annually beginning at age 18 (or at age of first intercourse); then every 3 years after 3 normal exams in a row[6]

Risk Factors

1 High blood pressure; elevated cholesterol; smoking; fat stored above or near waist

2 Residents of chronic care facilities such as nursing homes; people with diabetes or chronic lung or kidney disease; health care workers who see patients at high risk

3 Chronic heart, kidney, or lung disease; diabetes; alcoholism; Hodgkin's disease; cirrhosis; sickle cell disease

4 Male; smoking; high blood pressure; African-American; diabetes; obesity; sedentary lifestyle; family history of heart disease

5 Regularly scheduled visits are recommended for those with a history of ulcerative colitis, severe dysplasia (abnormal changes in cells), or Crohn's disease; mother, father, sister, or brother with colon cancer; obstruction in flow of urine.

6 Yearly if at risk due to history of sexually transmitted disease; first intercourse before age 18; history of several sexual partners or of a sexual partner who has had several other partners; smoker

7 If the person has a serious wound, a tetanus booster may be recommended if he or she has not had one in the past 5 years.

8 Mother, sister, or daughter with breast cancer; previous breast biopsy; personal history of cancer

only for people who are older than you, no one is invincible before age 40. But you can do a number of things to prevent injury and illness. To stay safer and healthier, wear your seat belt, do not drive when you have been drinking, stay within the speed limit, use a helmet when you ride a bicycle, and practice safe sex.

This is also the time to identify your risks for diseases you may get later in life and adjust your health habits to lower those risks. Talk about these risks with your health care provider. The two of you can put together a game plan to monitor your health. One important strategy is to have regular blood pressure checks and cholesterol screenings. For women, regular Pap smears and pelvic exams are important to detect cervical cancer early. Men should have regular screenings for prostate cancer.

The Early Detection Years: Ages 40 to 64

After you turn 40, your body may remind you that middle age brings physical changes. But this does not have to be a time of physical decline. Studies show that staying active can slow the decreases in stamina and strength that are commonly associated with aging.

For many, the middle years are a time of self-renewal. You may be more ready to deal with personal health goals you postponed during your 20s and 30s. If you smoke, now is the time to quit—before cancer, heart disease, or shortness of breath begin. And if you've been putting off improving your eating habits, it's time to get on track.

If you haven't exercised routinely in years, start soon but start slowly. Be sure to check with your health care provider before you start, especially if you haven't been working out regularly. Exercise, a balanced diet, and stress reduction are very important for many health conditions—such as hypertension or diabetes—that begin to show up during middle age. Slowly changing your routine is safest, and you will be more likely to stick with new habits if you add them gradually.

What to watch out for. Heart disease is the major killer of adults in midlife. But you can cut your risk of heart attack and stroke by controlling your cholesterol levels and blood pressure. Know your cholesterol level—less than 20 percent of Americans do. Now is also a good time to check your weight and see whether you need to drop a few pounds. Obesity is a major risk factor for both high blood pressure and high cholesterol. (To learn more about diet, fitness, and cholesterol, read the sections later in this chapter.)

Lung cancer remains the most common cause of cancer-related death for men, and the incidence of lung cancer among women is increasing at an alarming rate. It has more than doubled in the last two decades. Cigarette smoking accounts for at least 75 percent of these deaths. Although breast cancer is the most common cancer among nonsmoking women, lung cancer is by far the leading cause of cancer among women who smoke. In fact, lung cancer is now the most prevalent cancer for women in general. Talk with your health care provider about classes to help you quit smoking, or check with your health plan to see if it offers them.

The table on page 34 highlights recommendations for preventive health care that you should discuss with your health care provider. He or she will suggest a schedule that is tailored to your needs. But blood pressure checks every two years are recommended for everyone.

Preventive Care Recommendations—Ages 40 to 64	
PREVENTION STEP	**SCREENING RECOMMENDATIONS**
Lab Tests	
Cholesterol and HDL	Every 5 years (test more often if risk factors are present[1] or if total cholesterol is higher than 240)
Rubella titer	Women lacking evidence of immunity
Urinalysis	Not recommended for healthy adults
Chest X-ray	Not recommended for healthy adults
Immunizations	
Influenza	Yearly if at risk[2]
Pneumonia vaccination	At least once if at risk[3]
Tetanus/diphtheria	Every 10 years[7]
Examinations	
Health counseling	Every 3 years for women, every 5 years for men
Blood pressure	Every 2 years (test more often if risk factors are present[4] or if blood pressure is higher than 130/85)
Blood-stool test	Beginning at age 50, optional[5]
Sigmoidoscopy	Every 5 years beginning at age 50[5]
For Men	
Prostate-specific antigen (PSA)	Not recommended for healthy males
For Women	
Breast examination	Professional exam: Yearly Self-exam: Monthly
Mammography	Every 2 years beginning at age 40, and yearly if at risk[8]; yearly for all women beginning at age 50
Pelvic exam/Pap smear	Every 3 years after 3 normal exams[6] (yearly if risk factors present)

See page 32 for **Risk Factors.**

The Health Maintenance Years: Age 65 and Older

Some people believe that disease prevention is for younger people and that by age 65 chronic illnesses have already developed. Although it's true that 4 out of 5 persons age 65 and older have arthritis, heart disease, diabetes, or other chronic conditions, preventive health care is still important. As you get older, it's important to renew your focus on prevention and keep existing health problems from getting worse.

Advice you followed—or ignored—about diet, exercise, and use of alcohol and tobacco is as important now as ever. For example, exercise remains one of the most effective ways to become or stay vital, even for the frail elderly. The following suggestions can help you make the most of your health care:

- If you see more than one health care provider, make sure each one knows what drugs another provider has prescribed for you. Drugs can interact dangerously with one another and with foods, so it's important for your providers to know everything that you're taking, including over-the-counter medications. Whenever you see your provider, bring all the original bottles of any medications you are taking.
- Tell your provider about any ailment, even if you think it's not that important. Not all aches, pains, and discomforts are normal parts of aging; yours may be treatable, and the quality of your life may improve.
- If you become ill and can no longer live independently, remember that a nursing home isn't your only option. Hospital social workers and area agencies may be able to help you find support services so you can remain at home.

What to watch out for. If you have a chronic illness, the main threats to your physical health may be related complications. But even simple cases of influenza or pneumonia can also become life-threatening. Fortunately, you can get vaccines to eliminate both risks. Preventing falls is more important than ever, particularly for women, who are more likely than men to have osteoporosis, which makes them more likely to break bones.

Depression is common among older adults because of the many losses they often experience, including the death of friends and loved ones and loss of health or independence. Fortunately, depression can be treated with prescription medication, counseling, support groups, or a combination of these. (See *Depression*, page 260.)

The following table highlights recommendations for preventive health care services you should discuss with your provider. It is unclear how effective several screening tests are after the age of 75 or 80. Your health care provider can help you decide whether you will benefit from having certain exams that may have been routine for you in the past.

Preventive Care Recommendations—Ages 65 and Older	
PREVENTION STEP	**SCREENING RECOMMENDATIONS**
Lab Tests	
Cholesterol	Every 5 years (test more often if risk and HDL factors are present[1] or if cholesterol is higher than 240)
Urinalysis	Not recommended for healthy adults[2]
Chest X-ray	Not recommended for healthy adults
Immunizations	
Influenza	Yearly
Pneumonia vaccination	Once, at age 65
Tetanus/diphtheria	Every 10 years[5]
Examinations	
Blood pressure	Yearly at physical exam (test more often if risk factors are present[3] or if blood pressure is higher than 130/85)
Hemoccult test (for "hidden blood" in stool)	Periodically, optional
Sigmoidoscopy	Every 5 years until age 80
Vision/hearing exams	Starting at age 65
For Women	
Breast exam	Professional exam: Yearly Self-exam: Monthly
Mammography	Yearly
Pelvic exam/Pap smear	Every 3 years (optional if low risk)[4]

Risk Factors

[1] High blood pressure; elevated cholesterol; smoking; waist measure greater than hip measure

[2] Routine urinalysis is recommended only for male smokers over age 65.

[3] Male; smoker; high blood pressure; African-American; diabetes; obesity; sedentary lifestyle; family history of heart disease

[4] Pelvic exams are not effective for detecting ovarian cancer. Patients may consider discontinuing Pap smears after age 65 if there are no high risk factors. Risk factors include history of sexually transmitted disease, first intercourse before age 18, history of several sexual partners or of a sexual partner who has had several other partners, and smoking.

[5] If the person has a serious wound, a tetanus booster may be recommended if he or she has not had one in the past 5 years.

This table provides a way to chart your screening tests and immunizations. Use the following letters to record what happened during your last visit. Enter (A) if you met with your health care provider but took no tests; (B) if a test was completed and passed with no problems; or (C) if tests indicated health problems.

Your Personal Health Record

Test Age:	20	22	24	26	28	30	32	34	36	38	40	42	44	46	48	50	52	54	56	58	60	62	64	66 or over
Blood pressure Every 2 years, more often if at risk																								
Cholesterol Every 5 years, more often if at risk																								
Tetanus/diphtheria Every 10 years																								
Influenza Yearly from age 65																								
Pneumococcal vaccine Once, at age 65																								
Hearing Every 2 years from age 65																								
Vision/glaucoma tests Every 3 years from age 65																								
Hemoglobin																								
Urinalysis																								
Rubella titer																								
Rectal exam and stool blood test																								
Sigmoidoscopy																								
Women																								
Pap smear and pelvic exam																								
Professional breast exam Every year from age 40																								
Mammography Every 2 years from age 40; yearly from age 50																								

A Healthy Lifestyle

Eating a healthy diet, exercising regularly, and quitting smoking (if you smoke) will do wonders for your well-being. By being aware of what you eat, you can cut down on the amount of fat you consume and reduce your risk of heart disease and stroke. If you eat right and exercise, you can lose weight or maintain your weight at a healthy level. Read on for tips on eating right, beginning an exercise program, and quitting smoking.

Diet

A well-balanced diet does you a world of good, from helping to prevent disease to making it easier for you to manage stress. One of the keys to eating right is variety. You need more than 50 nutrients from food each day, including those that supply calories (carbohydrates, protein, and fat) and those that help with various body functions (vitamins, minerals, and water).

The Food Guide Pyramid (see *The Food Guide Pyramid*, page 44) was developed by the U.S. Department of Agriculture to show the range of servings and variety of the foods we should eat each day. Look over the pyramid and think about your eating patterns. Then you can set goals that will bring you closer to eating the amounts of foods suggested. Overall, the pyramid supports eating less fat, getting more of your calories from complex carbohydrates, and eating more fiber.

- Choose foods daily from each of the five major groups shown in The Food Guide Pyramid.
- Include a variety of different foods from each group to balance calorie and nutrient needs.
- Choose low-fat foods most often.
- Go easy on sweets, salt, and alcoholic beverages.

The amount of food you need depends on your age, gender, physical condition, and activity level. Most people should have at least the minimum recommended number of servings from each food group daily. Many men, women, and older children—and most teenagers—need more. When grocery shopping, as well as planning and preparing meals for yourself and others, use this guide to maintain a healthy weight.

Cutting Fat, Adding Fiber

Eating the typical high-fat American diet can increase your risk of heart disease, certain cancers, and obesity. Since fat is the most concentrated calorie source, you can

Diet Recommendations to Reduce Blood Cholesterol

This chart summarizes the current National Cholesterol Education Program Step I and Step II diet recommendations. The Step I diet emphasizes reducing total fat intake, especially major saturated fat and excess calories. The Step II diet calls for even less saturated fat and cholesterol, depending on the response to the initial changes. The guides on pages 40 and 41 will translate these recommendations into changes in lifestyle and eating patterns.

NUTRIENT	RECOMMENDED INTAKE	
	Step I Diet	**Step II Diet**
Total fat	Less than 30% of total calories	Less than 30% of total calories
Saturated fat	Less than 10% of total calories	Less than 7% of total calories
Polyunsaturated fat	Up to 10% of total calories	Up to 10% of total calories
Monounsaturated fat	10 to15% of total calories	10 to 15% of total calories
Carbohydrates	50 to 60% of total calories	50 to 60% of total calories
Protein	10 to 20% of total calories	10 to 20% of total calories
Cholesterol	Less than 300 mg/day	Less than 200 mg/day
Total calories	To achieve and maintain healthy weight	To achieve and maintain healthy weight

reduce your calorie intake by reducing the amount of fat you eat.

Saturated fat (found in animal products and some vegetable oils) contributes to high blood cholesterol levels. Polyunsaturated and monounsaturated fats (found in olive, canola, corn, sunflower, safflower, and soybean oils) can actually lower your blood cholesterol when substituted for saturated fat. However, since both types of fat are high in calories, you should limit your intake of unsaturated fat as well.

Cutting down on total fat will help you reduce the amount of saturated fat in your diet. The U.S. Department of Agriculture recommends that adults and children over the age of two get no more than 30 percent of their calories from fat. (Never limit fat or calories for children under age two, unless your child's health care provider advises you to do so.) You can reduce your risk of heart disease even further by eating less fat. See the guidelines above from the National Cholesterol Education Program about trimming fat from your diet, and the *Low-Fat Food Choices Guide* that starts on page 40.

Getting fewer calories from fat means you'll need to increase your carbohydrate-rich choices: beans, breads, grains, pasta, rice, fruits, and vegetables. Carbohydrates include simple sugars and complex carbohydrates, also known as starches and fibers. Most foods contain a combination of these carbohydrate sources. Although simple sugars pose no health risks other than tooth decay and excess calories, getting more complex carbohydrates will give you a better balance of vitamins, minerals, and fiber.

Studies have shown that eating foods high in fiber may help lower blood cholesterol, reduce the risk of heart disease, and protect against certain cancers and digestive diseases. Fiber is found in all plant foods. Whole grains are also an excellent source of fiber.

Low-Fat Food Choices Guide

MEATS

- Limit intake of lean meat, chicken, turkey, and fish to 6 ounces or less each day (cooked weight).
  - A good rule of thumb is that 3 ounces of cooked meat is equal to 4 ounces of raw meat.
  - A 3-ounce portion of cooked meat is the size of a deck of cards.
- Choose lean meats (with no more than 3 grams of fat per ounce).
  - Chicken, turkey, fish, and shellfish (without skin or added oil)
  - Lean, trimmed cuts of beef, pork, and lamb such as beef or veal tenderloin, sirloin tip, round steak, rump roast, flank steak, pork-loin chops, tenderloin, center-cut ham, Canadian bacon, lamb-loin or lamb-leg roasts, and chops
- Limit high-fat, high-cholesterol meats.
  - High-fat, processed meats such as bacon, bologna, salami, sausage, and hot dogs
  - High-fat cuts of beef, pork, and lamb such as prime-grade steaks, roasts, ribs, and veal cutlets
  - High-cholesterol meats such as liver, sweetbreads, brains, and kidneys

EGGS

- Limit egg yolks (including those used in baked goods and cooking) to no more than 3 per week. The yolk of 1 large egg has about 5.12 grams of fat and 213 milligrams of cholesterol.

DAIRY

- Have at least 2 servings of nonfat or low-fat dairy products per day. Children under age 2 should eat whole-milk dairy products to get essential nutrients and calories needed for growth and development. A serving size equals:
  - One 8-ounce glass of milk
  - 1 ounce of cheese
- Choose nonfat (skim) or low-fat dairy products.
  - Skim or 1% milk and milk products such as skim or 1% evaporated milk or yogurt
  - Nonfat or low-fat dairy desserts such as sherbet, sorbet, frozen yogurt, in moderation
  - Nonfat or low-fat cheese (any cheese that has no more than 5 grams of fat per ounce) such as low-fat cream cheese, low-fat or nonfat cottage or cream cheese, part-skim mozzarella, farmer cheese, or string cheese
- Limit high-fat dairy products.
  - Regular and 2% milk and milk products such as regular evaporated milk or yogurt
  - Whole milk; processed and natural cheeses such as cheddar, Swiss, brick, Brie, Monterey Jack, Colby, American, and cream cheese
  - Rich dairy desserts such as (or containing) ice cream, whipped toppings, sour cream, and half-and-half

(continued)

Low-Fat Food Choices Guide (continued)

FATS AND OILS

- Cut back on all fats, especially sources of saturated fat, to no more than 3 to 8 servings per day. One serving contains 4 to 5 grams of fat. It's important to understanding serving sizes. If you know how much a serving size is, it's easier to limit your fat intake and avoid extra calories.
  Examples of one serving of fat:
  - 1 teaspoon butter, margarine, or oil
  - 2 teaspoons salad dressing
  - 2 teaspoons peanut butter
- Choose unsaturated fats (in limited quantities, as recommended above), including oils such as olive, canola, corn, safflower, sesame, soybean, and sunflower.
  Examples of foods with unsaturated fat:
  - nuts or seeds
  - black or green olives
  - fresh or canned salmon
- Limit saturated fats.
  Examples of foods with saturated fat:
  - butter, lard, bacon fat, coconut oil, palm oil, and cocoa butter
  - hydrogenated oil (found in shortening, some margarines, and salad dressings)
  - avocados, whole milk and whole milk products

FRUITS AND VEGETABLES

- Eat 2 to 4 servings of fruit and 3 to 5 servings of vegetables per day.
  One serving equals:
  - 1/2 cup cooked or 1 cup of raw vegetables
  - 1/2 cup or 1 small piece of fresh fruit

STARCHES, GRAINS, AND LEGUMES

- Eat 6 to 11 servings per day, especially whole-grain products. The type of fiber found in oat, rice, and barley bran, along with beans, peas, and some fruits and vegetables has been shown to lower blood cholesterol.
- Choose low-fat starches (containing no more than 2 grams of fat per serving).
  - Angel food cake, low-fat cookies and crackers, bagels, English muffins, yeast breads
  - Cereals, rice, pasta, corn, potatoes, peas, beans, lentils, pretzels, bread sticks
- Limit high-fat baked goods and snacks.
  - Pies, cakes, doughnuts, pastries, croissants, muffins, quick breads, high-fat cookies and crackers
  - Granola, potato chips, tortilla chips, french fries

Losing Weight

Obesity is another health risk you can control by watching your diet and exercising more. Being overweight increases your risk of developing non-insulin-dependent diabetes, high blood pressure, high blood cholesterol and triglycerides, and some cancers, as well as other health problems.

Even though an increasing number of people are aware of the importance of maintaining a healthy weight, the number of obese Americans is growing, too. About one third of the nation's adults are obese, which is defined as being approximately 20 percent above one's desired weight, according to a recent study by the Centers for Disease Control and Prevention.

A combination of many factors adds up to a healthy weight, including how much weight is fat, where the fat is stored, and any medical problems that would benefit from more or less weight. Take a look at the accompanying chart to help determine your healthy weight range. If you or a relative have had elevated blood pressure, cholesterol, or blood sugar levels (all health problems related to weight), a weight in the lower end of the range may be best for your health. Ask your health care provider what weight is best for you.

Your Fat Limits

If your planned daily calorie intake is:	Your daily fat intake should be less than:
1,200 calories	40 grams
1,500 calories	50 grams
1,800 calories	60 grams
2,400 calories	80 grams

You also need to know if you carry too much fat tissue, and how the fat is distributed. Studies show that fat stored above the waist is linked with an increased risk of diabetes and heart disease. One way to identify your level of health risk is to find your waist-to-hip ratio. Divide your waist measurement by your hip measurement. The resulting figure is your risk ratio. A ratio of more than 1.0 for men and more than 0.8 for women may mean a higher health risk.

Example:
Waist (38 inches) / Hip (42 inches) = Risk ratio (0.9)

Suggested Weights for Adults

HEIGHT*	WEIGHT IN POUNDS†	
	19-34 yrs	35+ yrs
5′ 0″	97-128	108-138
5′ 1″	101-132	111-143
5′ 2″	104-137	115-148
5′ 3″	107-141	119-152
5′ 4″	111-146	122-157
5′ 5″	114-150	126-162
5′ 6″	118-155	130-167
5′ 7″	121-160	134-172
5′ 8″	125-164	138-178
5′ 9″	129-169	142-183
5′ 10″	132-174	146-188
5′ 11″	136-179	151-194
6′ 0″	140-184	155-199
6′ 1″	144-189	159-205
6′ 2″	148-195	164-210
6′ 3″	152-200	168-216
6′ 4″	156-205	173-222
6′ 5″	160-211	177-228
6′ 6″	164-216	183-234

* without shoes † without clothes

The right way to shed pounds. Just as there are no simple explanations for how weight problems start, there are no simple solutions. Weight loss requires a combination of fewer calories taken in, more calories used up, and behavior changes.

Dangers of fad diets. If there were a simple way to take off extra pounds, no one would have a weight problem. And although most people know that fad diets aren't the answer, the short-term reward of rapid weight loss is hard to resist. These quick weight-loss plans cost American consumers up to five billion dollars annually.

However, very low-calorie diets or diets that restrict certain foods can be dangerous and should never be used without medical supervision. In fact, there is growing concern that long-term use of very low-calorie diets may actually make lasting success more difficult to maintain. Instead of enduring a "diet" you can hardly wait to go off, focus on developing better eating and exercise habits.

Your calorie needs. Remember that eating and exercise aren't the only factors that affect your weight, but they are the ones you can control. Your basal metabolic rate (the energy your body needs to carry on its functions at rest) and body composition (the amount of fat versus muscle you have) help determine the number of calories your body burns at rest, and these tendencies are often inherited.

The number of calories you need depends on how many calories your body burns. People burn calories at different rates, depending on many factors, including activity, body size, genetics, age, health, and gender. The more muscle you have, the higher your metabolism.

Losing at a healthy rate. To lose weight you need to burn an extra 3,500 calories for each pound you would like to lose; this is the approximate number of calories in 1 pound of body fat. To lose 1 pound per week, you need 500 fewer calories per day than the calories required to maintain your weight. It's best to cut back on the calories you usually eat and increase your activity level. Try eating 250 fewer calories per day and adding 250 calories in activity to lose that pound of fat. (See the following chart for average calorie needs.)

Your current eating habits took years to develop. That's why it's important to remember that you can't change the habits of a lifetime overnight. Don't get upset when you slip. Fortunately, you don't need to make dramatic changes in your eating habits for them to work.

Your Calorie Needs

Typical Daily Calorie Needs for Maintaining Weight

	CALORIES/DAY
Women	1,800 to 2,100
Men	2,100 to 2,400

Recommended Daily Calorie Ranges for Losing Weight

	CALORIES/DAY
Women	1,200 to 1,500
Men	1,500 to 1,800

The Food Guide Pyramid

Build your diet from the bottom up. Grains, fruits, and vegetables should make up the bulk of your diet. These foods supply energizing carbohydrates, help replace unwanted fat calories, and supply fiber.

Don't count on one food group to do it all. You need more than 50 different nutrients. Have at least the minimum number of servings from each group. Eat regularly to keep energy flowing. Don't go longer than five hours without food.

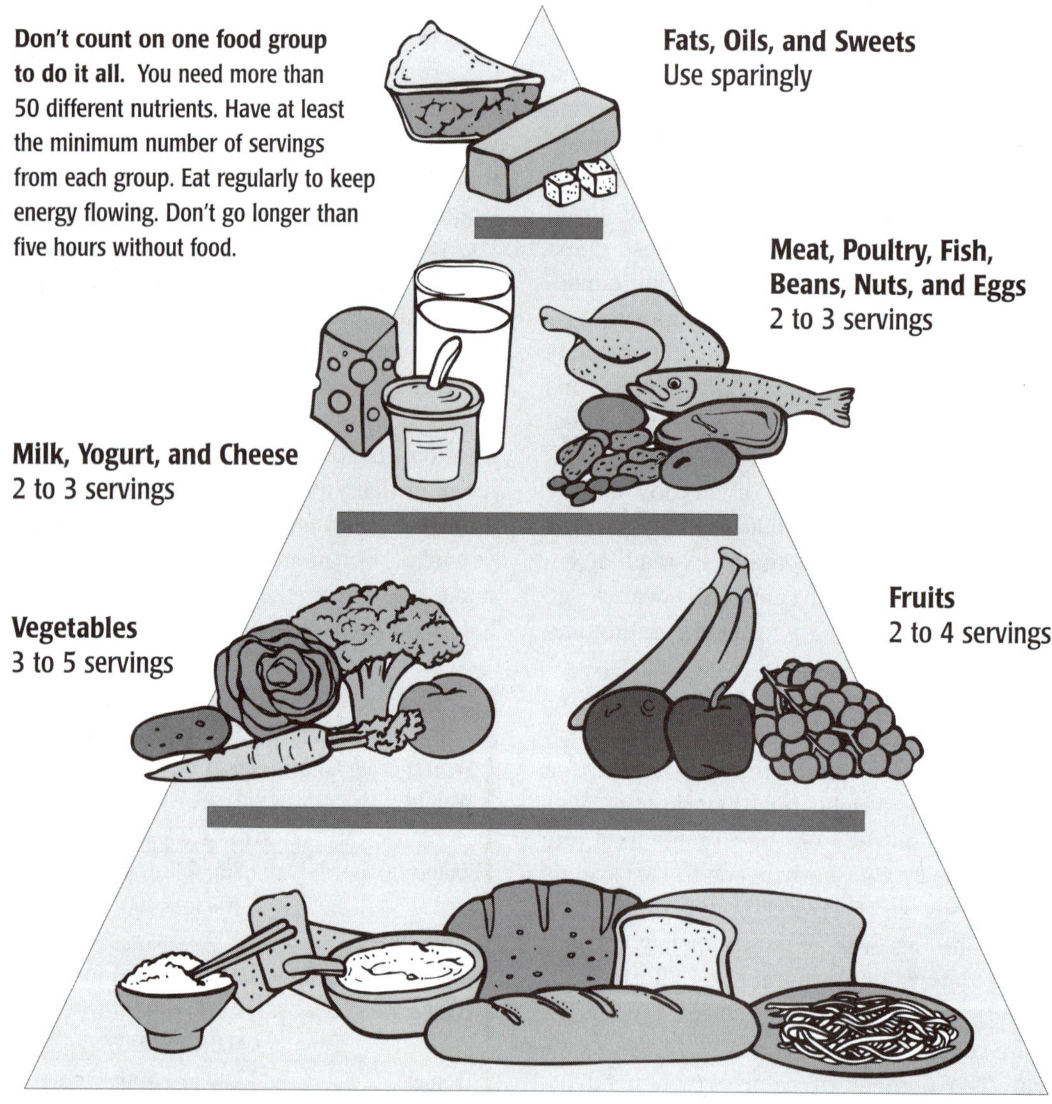

Develop an eye for portion size. The number of servings from each food group may sound like a lot, but it's really not. For example, a cup of pasta is the equivalent of two bread servings. One serving of meat is the size of a deck of cards. Don't feel guilty about an occasional treat. But remember, occasional doesn't mean daily.

Exercise

Exercise lengthens life, improves the quality of your life, and reduces the risk of heart disease, diabetes, hypertension, and osteoporosis. Increasing your activity level will help you deal with stress, and may help lower your blood pressure and cholesterol. While people's health and stamina often decline during middle age, those who stay physically active have nearly twice as much endurance as those who are not active.

How much exercise is enough? Two recent studies may have the answer. A review of the 25-year exercise history of almost 17,000 Harvard alumni revealed that those who were more active lived up to two years longer than their couch potato counterparts. Health improvements resulted from burning even 500 calories per week through exercise. However, burning 2,000 calories provided the best health benefits.

In another study, 13,000 men and women were divided into five fitness groups. The least-fit group had, by far, the highest number of deaths. But surprisingly, the most dramatic drop in death rate occurred in the second-least-fit group. This group exercised moderately—the equivalent of 30 to 60 minutes of walking per day—and burned a weekly total of 1,000 to 2,000 calories.

These studies dispel the idea that activity has to be intensely aerobic (meaning it makes your heart and lungs work harder to meet your muscles' demand for oxygen) to produce a health benefit. There is convincing evidence that lower-intensity activities like walking, gardening, and golfing have very favorable health benefits. Ultimately, doing any activities that use up to 2,000 calories per week is a healthy goal. At the very least, get in at least 30 minutes of moderate exercise three times a week. Use the *Exercise and Calories* chart below to estimate how your various calorie-burning activities are adding up to better health.

What You Can Do

For nearly everyone, the risks of not exercising far outweigh the risks of exercise. Still, for those with existing chronic illness such as diabetes, heart disease, or high blood pressure, completing an exercise test would be a good idea before you start an exercise program.

You don't have to endure the rigors of a runner who is training for a marathon. Competitive athletes often suffer sports injuries, but moderate activity rarely leads

Exercise and Calories

EXERCISE ACTIVITIES	CALORIES BURNED*
Biking (5 1/2 mph)	210
Walking (2 1/2 mph)	210
Gardening	220
Golf	250
Swimming	300
Walking (4 mph)	300
Tennis, doubles	300
Biking (10 mph)	415
Tennis, singles	420
Aerobics	445
Jogging	585
Running (8 1/2 mph)	700
Cross-country skiing	900

* Average calories burned for a 150-pound person in an hour of activity

Source: *Lifetime Fitness and Wellness, 4th Edition*, by Werner W.K. Hoeger and Sharon A. Hoeger. Copyright 1995 Morton Publishing Co., Englewood, CO. Reprinted with permission.

The Activity Pyramid

Each week, try to increase your physical activity using this guide. Here's how to start.

If you are inactive (rarely active), increase daily activities at the base of the pyramid by:

- taking the stairs instead of the elevator
- hiding the TV remote control
- making extra trips around the house or yard
- stretching while standing in line
- walking whenever you can

If you are somewhat active (active some of the time, but not regularly), increase activity in the middle of the pyramid by:

- finding activities you enjoy
- planning activities in your day
- setting realistic goals

If you are often active (active most of the time, or at least four days each week), include activities from the whole pyramid by:

- changing your routine if you start to get bored
- exploring new activities

Cut Down on

- Watching TV
- Computer games
- Sitting for more than 30 minutes at a time

2 to 3 Times a Week

Leisure Activities

- Golf
- Bowling
- Softball
- Yardwork

Flexibility and Strength

- Stretching and yoga
- Push-ups and curl-ups
- Weight lifting

3 to 5 Times a Week

Aerobic Exercise (20+ minutes)

- Brisk walking
- Cross-country skiing
- Bicycling
- Swimming

Recreational (30+ minutes)

- Soccer
- Basketball
- Martial arts
- Dancing
- Hiking
- Tennis

Every Day (or as much as possible)

- Walk the dog.
- Take longer routes.
- Take the stairs instead of the elevator.
- Walk to the store or the mailbox.
- Park your car farther away and walk.
- Add extra steps to your day.

to injury if you build up slowly. In fact, intense exercise—the kind that leads to injuries related to wear and tear on the joints—is simply not necessary to achieve long-term health benefits.

How to Get Started

- Get off to a slow start. If you are just beginning, 30 minutes of walking three times a week is plenty. Move slowly toward a daily routine of 30 minutes of activities you enjoy. But increase your activity only when you feel your present level is getting too easy.
- Keep a diary of your activity. As your entries build so will your commitment.
- Try a variety of activities to keep exercise fresh and interesting.
- Exercise at the same time every day. If you can't lock into a regular time, then schedule your exercise in advance—as an appointment to keep with yourself. There is some evidence that people are more successful at sticking with a morning routine.
- Join a club or start a regular routine with friends to add a social element to your activity.

There is no secret formula for deciding how much exercise is enough or which types of activities are best. The Activity Pyramid was developed to show the value of different types of exercise. In general, when it comes to activity, the more, the better. Examine *The Activity Pyramid* on page 46 to help think about your current activities and set goals.

Kicking the Habit

Years ago, smokers were left alone to enjoy their habit. Those days are gone. It's getting to be more and more of a hassle to be a smoker. And given the overwhelming evidence that tobacco use causes serious health problems, most smokers want to quit. In fact, an estimated 80 percent of smokers want to quit and most have tried several times. The good news is that, even if you haven't quit, each attempt puts you one try closer to reaching your goal of becoming a nonsmoker.

The reasons to keep trying to quit are more compelling than ever. According to the Centers for Disease Control and Prevention, 1 out of every 6 deaths in the United States is related to smoking. About 18 percent of cases of low birth weight, premature deliveries, respiratory distress syndrome, and sudden infant death syndrome (SIDS) are linked to smoking during pregnancy. And 1 in 4 deaths from home fires are related to smoking.

Lung cancer isn't the only cancer caused by smoking; others include cancer of the larynx, esophagus, kidneys, pancreas, and stomach. Although many people believe that smokeless (chewing) tobacco poses fewer health hazards than do cigarettes and other smoking tobacco, it can cause cancer of the mouth. Tobacco—of any kind—is one of the most potent cancer-causing agents for humans.

More than 50 million Americans—slightly less than one quarter of the population—smoke, and another 10 million use smokeless tobacco. Because tobacco is both physically and psychologically addictive, quitting is often hard, but it's not impossible.

Where smoking is concerned, quitters do win. The health benefits of quitting are tremendous. After 5 to 15 years of not smoking, ex-smokers' risks of developing heart and lung diseases, cancer, and lung problems drop to the same—or nearly the same—levels as if they had never smoked. Obviously, if you don't smoke, don't start. But if you do smoke, here are some tips to help you quit.

Steps to Quitting

The following steps can help prepare you to stop smoking and may make you less likely to light up in the future.

Talk with your health care provider. Find out whether your health plan offers programs to help you quit smoking. If the plan doesn't, it still may cover programs offered by other groups.

Set your goal. Pick a date on which to stop smoking and plan to quit completely and for good. Switching to a lower-tar brand or cutting back just doesn't work.

Take it one day at a time. Focus on making it through today without a cigarette, rather than worrying about how you will go without one for the next week. If you do falter and light up, don't give up. Forgive yourself and work on resisting the next cigarette.

Find support. Tell your friends that you are quitting, then take advantage of as much encouragement and prodding as they can give you. Check in with your health care provider for support as well. He or she may be able to prescribe a nicotine substitute to help you. Organizations such as the American Lung Association and the American Cancer Society offer classes and support groups for people trying to quit smoking. Many employers and health care providers also offer such help.

Find a substitute. By finding other things to keep your mouth and hands busy, you can avoid the temptation to smoke. Try sugarless gum, hard candy, or flavored toothpicks. Try woodworking, needlework, snapping a rubber band on your wrist, or playing with fidget toys.

Exercise to avoid weight gain. If you're afraid of gaining weight, keep in mind that the average weight gain after quitting smoking is only 5 pounds. Only 3 percent of those who quit smoking gain 20 pounds or more. While you are quitting, eat a well-balanced diet and avoid excess calories in sugary or fatty foods, drink six to eight glasses of water a day, and exercise. By walking just 30 minutes a day or doing some other activity, you can prevent weight gain and ease some of the tension of tobacco withdrawal. To learn more about exercise and diet, see the sections earlier in this chapter.

Avoid smoking situations. Go to places where smoking isn't allowed, such as a movie theater or the nonsmoking section of a restaurant. Take your work breaks with nonsmoking coworkers. After eating, take a walk or do the dishes instead of lighting up a cigarette. When you can't avoid a smoking situation, plan in advance for ways to curb the desire to smoke, such as having sugarless gum or a healthy snack close by.

Cancer Prevention and Treatment

On your way to work you notice the American Cancer Society billboard, and one of the seven warning signals of cancer leaps out at you: a nagging cough or hoarseness. You've been thinking your dry morning cough is caused by allergies or too many cigarettes or not enough humidity—but now you fear the worst. Should you?

Don't fear the worst, but do something about your fears. Now is the time to make an appointment with your health care provider to find out the source of your cough. (And maybe it's time to get help and quit smoking.) Many symptoms that indicate cancer may be signs of a less serious illness. But the earlier that cancer is detected, the easier it is to treat. So see your health care provider if you have any of the following symptoms:

- a change in bowel or bladder habits
- a sore that does not heal
- unusual bleeding or discharge, especially from the rectum or vagina
- a thickening or lump in a breast or elsewhere
- indigestion or difficulty in swallowing
- an obvious change in a wart or mole
- a nagging cough or hoarseness

Other possible signs of cancer include a constant, low-grade fever, fatigue, unusual and persistent headaches with changes in vision or behavior, nagging and unexplained pain in the bones or elsewhere, easy bruising, loss of appetite, and sudden, unexpected weight loss. (See *Breast Cancer*, page 232; *Cervical Cancer*, page 231; *Ovarian Cancer*, page 244; *Colon Cancer*, page 51; *Prostate Cancer*, page 229; *Skin Cancer*, pages 223 and 224; and *Testicular Cancer*, page 227.)

Preventing Cancer: Risk Factors You Can Control

Despite the odds, you can take steps now to greatly decrease your chances of developing cancer. It's not just a throw of the dice, but a combination of your hereditary risk factors and the type of lifestyle you lead. For detailed information on any of these topics, check the table of contents or the index.

Quit smoking. Smoking causes two thirds of all lung cancer deaths. It increases the risk of cancers of the mouth, pharynx, larynx, esophagus, pancreas, uterus, cervix, kidney, and bladder. (Research also shows that the smoke blown your way from others' cigarettes can endanger your health.) As soon as you quit smoking, your lungs begin healing themselves, and some changes that might lead to cancer can be totally reversed. Check with your health care provider or health plan to find out about classes that can help you kick the habit.

If you drink, drink in moderation. Heavy drinkers may have a twofold to sixfold risk of developing throat or mouth cancer. The chances of developing cancer of the pancreas, liver, breast, stomach, and rectum are also greater if you drink alcohol. The news is even worse for drinkers who smoke. The risks of throat and mouth cancers are 15 times greater, and the risks of esophageal cancer are up to 25 times greater. Heavy drinking may keep the liver from breaking down potentially cancer-causing substances. Alcohol may also irritate tissues of the mouth, throat, and esophagus, making them more prone to cancer.

Eat less fat. Scientists are finding that a high-fat diet may be linked to an increased risk of breast and colon cancer. It may also contribute to prostate and ovarian cancer. Fat may cause the body to make some bile acids that promote cancer, and it definitely increases production of hormones. This tends to trigger the growth of some tumors in overweight people. Several suspected cancer-causing chemicals are first stored in animal fat and then in the body fat of people who eat meat.

Eat more fiber. Research from the National Cancer Institute shows that if most people had 20 to 30 grams of fiber daily, their risk of colon cancer would be cut in half. The insoluble fiber found in wheat bran, whole-grain cereals and breads, and vegetables and fruits, as well as the soluble fiber in such foods as oat bran and beans, flushes possibly cancer-promoting waste through the intestines and colon. It also flushes out fats and bile acids.

Protect your skin from the sun. Most skin cancers are caused by too much exposure to the sun's ultraviolet rays and to the high-energy bulbs in tanning parlors. It's easy to protect yourself from this threat: Avoid direct sunlight between 10 A.M. and 2 P.M., wear clothing such as hats and long-sleeved shirts that block the sun, and use sunscreen year-round. Make sure you use one that has a sun protection factor (SPF) of at least 15 (see *Skin Cancer*, page 223).

Maintain a healthy weight. Overweight women have higher death rates from cancer of the uterus, gallbladder, cervix, ovaries, and breast. More overweight men die from colon, rectal, and prostate cancers. Eating healthy foods in moderation and exercising regularly will help you tone up and lose weight. (Read about *Diet*, on page 38, and *Exercise*, on page 45.)

Avoid dangerous chemicals. Workplaces are now regulated so that hazardous materials are not routinely released into the air, but if you work around chemicals or dust, tell your health care provider during your next physical examination. Whenever you use paint, varnish, or any other chemical indoors, leave windows open. Have your house checked for radon leakage. Use pesticides and herbicides carefully, and wash fruits and vegetables before eating them.

When the Diagnosis Is Cancer

Cancer is a single name for many diseases, all of which occur when abnormal cells grow and multiply unchecked in any of the body's tissues or organs. Treatments involve attempting to stop cell growth.

After cancer is detected and confirmed, several treatment options or combined options may be available. Surgery, radiation, and chemotherapy are the most common treatments. Antihormone therapy, immunotherapy, and regional perfusion are less common.

Surgery. The oldest form of cancer treatment, surgery involves removing a tumor or cancerous growth.

Radiation therapy. Radiation kills cancer cells by exposing them to high doses of X-rays.

Chemotherapy. Taken by mouth or injected into the bloodstream, these drugs interfere with cancer cell growth.

Hormone therapy. Various hormones are used to stop certain types of cancer cells from growing. Hormone therapy is commonly used for prostate cancer.

Immunotherapy. Drugs are used to boost your ability to fight cancer in the same way the body wards off infections. The best known of these, interferon, has been successful in treating a rare form of leukemia but less successful against other cancers.

Regional perfusion. Chemotherapy drugs are delivered only to the part of the body that has cancerous tissue. Damage to healthy tissue is minimal, the drugs may be more effective, and there are fewer side effects.

Support is available. Learning that you have cancer and looking ahead to an uncertain future can be frightening. Many cancer patients and their families find it helpful and reassuring to talk with others who are also dealing with cancer. For more information on how to locate a support group, ask your health care provider or contact your local chapter of the American Cancer Society (see *Resources*, page 292).

Colon Cancer

Colon cancer is a common cancer that can be detected and prevented in many people if they follow simple steps. The rate of colon cancer among men and women is about the same, with 6 percent of women and 5 percent of men getting this disease during their lifetime.

Colon cancer ranks second in prevalence only to lung cancer, with more than 152,000 new cases reported each year. The earlier the cancer—or any changes in the colon that might lead to cancer—is found, the better the chance for cure. Indeed, if detected early, the cure rate is about 91 percent. But the death rate among people in the late stages of colon cancer at the time of diagnosis is high—about 60 percent—and the statistics are not improving.

No one knows for sure what causes colon cancer, but we do know some of the risk factors. Your chance of developing colon cancer is higher if you have a history of ulcerative colitis, severe dysplasia (precancerous changes), or Crohn's disease, or if your mother, father, sister, or brother has had colon cancer. Age plays a role, too. Most cases occur among people over age 65. Less than 2 percent of cases occur in those who are under age 40.

Screening tests. The three tests most commonly used for colon cancer screening are the digital (finger) rectal exam, stool blood test (also called fecal occult blood test), and sigmoidoscopy (described on page 52).

The American Cancer Society and other national medical organizations recommend annual digital rectal exams for adults over

Preventive Steps for Colon Cancer

Since cure by early detection is the goal of colon cancer screening, your quick response to warning signs is critical. If you have a change in your bowel habits (black stools, thin stools, blood in your stools, or intermittent or persistent diarrhea or constipation) talk with your health care provider about whether you need an examination of your colon to find the cause, regardless of your age. Cancer, however, is just one of the many possible causes of these symptoms.

Several dietary factors are thought to play a role in colon cancer. In both animal and human research, obesity, total calorie intake, and high-fat diets have been implicated in causing cancer. A diet high in fiber may be helpful in preventing colon cancer. Foods high in fiber include whole-grain cereals and breads, beans, potatoes, brown rice, fruits, and vegetables. (For healthful ways to improve your diet, see *Diet*, page 38.)

40, annual blood-stool testing starting at age 50, and sigmoidoscopy every three to five years beginning at age 50. Given the inconvenience and uncertainty about the effectiveness of colon cancer screening, you and your health care provider may decide that it is unnecessary for you. People with a history of cancer are obvious candidates for regular screening. Remember, these are only screenings, and if you have symptoms that persist you should see your provider regardless of what your last screening showed.

Screening exams can be mildly uncomfortable, but these tests are usually safe and easy to do. If any test results are abnormal, your provider will probably order more tests. He or she can help you decide whether you need any of these tests.

Stool test for blood. Because polyps (growths in the colon) and cancers produce small, unnoticeable amounts of blood that are carried away in the stools, blood-stool tests are used to detect bleeding. (These are also known as "Hemoccult" or "guaiac" tests.)

Digital rectal exam. Using a finger, the health care provider feels for lumps (polyps) in your colon that could be cancer. The effectiveness of this screening method is limited because less than 13 percent of colon cancers are located in the lower colon.

Sigmoidoscopy. For this test, a slender, lighted tube called a flexible sigmoidoscope is inserted into your rectum after you have had an enema. About 80 percent of cancers and polyps (growths) that might become cancer can be found this way, because they tend to build up at the lower end of your bowel. Patients are given tranquilizers before the test to ease discomfort.

Section Three

Emergencies and Urgent Care

When you or someone you love is sick, it isn't easy to wait for relief. People often rush to the hospital emergency room with the flu, sore throats, earaches, colds, and similar problems. But you may end up waiting hours to treat a condition that could have been remedied with a call to your health care provider and a quick trip to the pharmacy. This chapter will tell you when a trip to the emergency room is in order, and when you can handle a problem by calling your provider, visiting a clinic, or taking self-care steps at home.

Two types of medical conditions require immediate care: emergencies and urgent situations. Your health plan will cover you for both, but you may need to follow different procedures. It's important that you know how to tell the difference.

Using the Emergency Room

Emergencies. An emergency is a condition that will cause loss of life or permanent or severe disability if it isn't treated right away. Examples of emergencies include the following:

- chest pain
- shortness of breath
- severe abdominal pain (except for constipation or menstrual cramps), especially after an injury
- uncontrollable bleeding
- confusion or loss of consciousness, especially after a head injury
- poisoning or suspected drug overdose
- serious burns or cuts
- inability to swallow
- seizure
- slurred speech or sudden onset of paralysis
- broken bones

In an emergency, go to the nearest emergency room. Your health plan may require you to notify your health care provider as soon as possible.

Urgent care. Urgent conditions aren't life-threatening. However, delaying treatment for urgent conditions could cause serious problems. Examples of urgent situations include the following:

- ear infections
- sprains
- urinary tract infections
- vomiting
- high fever

Heading for the emergency room usually isn't the best choice in these situations. Urgent conditions can usually be treated at home, at a clinic, or with a visit to your health care provider. Call your provider to find out what you should do. He or she can give you advice on how to reduce discomfort and arrange for you to see a doctor if necessary; an on-call doctor or a clinic nurse can do the same. Your health plan may also provide an emergency number you can call to ask a health care provider about the best treatment for your condition or situation. You can reach your health care provider or a physician on call 24 hours a day, even after normal business hours. Call your provider's office and either a recording or an answering service will tell you how to reach the physician on call.

Keep a list of emergency phone numbers near your phone—for your provider, the poison control center, and any emergency help line your health plan may offer—along with fire and police numbers.

Emergencies and First Aid

Along with first aid advice, these guidelines will help you decide whether to go to an urgent care center or the emergency room. Review this information before an accident occurs so that you are prepared to make the best decision possible.

All true emergencies need to be treated by an appropriate medical professional. The self-care guidelines in this section are appropriate for use only when medical professionals are not immediately available and before you can get to an emergency room. These guidelines describe how to assess what an accident victim needs, how to offer life support if needed, and when to offer first aid.

You may also find it helpful to take a first-aid class and learn cardiopulmonary resuscitation, or CPR. The more you know about first aid, the more likely you are to stay calm when helping yourself or someone else after an accident. In many areas the American Red Cross offers first-aid and CPR classes. And first-aid instruction is often available through community education programs, hospitals, or local colleges and universities. These courses teach you how to identify medical emergencies, understand the causes, symptoms, and signs of injuries, and apply first aid.

Before trying to help someone who is hurt, you should always ask his or her permission or the permission of a guardian. You are legally protected for trying to help someone if you do so in good faith and are not guilty of willful misconduct. You can assume that you have the victim's consent to help if the victim is unconscious or so badly hurt that he or she cannot give permission.

You should also take care to protect yourself when offering emergency help. Many diseases can be spread through contact with blood. These infections do not penetrate skin that is intact, but you may have cracked or scratched skin that is vulnerable. Latex gloves offer the best protection. Otherwise, keep plastic wrap, several layers of gauze pad, or other barriers (such as a towel or dry clothing) between you and the blood of the victim.

Cardiopulmonary Resuscitation (CPR)

These guidelines are meant to help you review your skills. Reading them is not a substitute for taking an American Heart Association-certified CPR class.

Stocking Your Own First-Aid Kit

To assemble your own complete first-aid kit, place a copy of this book in a small tote bag or a sturdy box that's easy to carry, along with the following items:

DRESSINGS

- adhesive bandage strips (assorted sizes)
- butterfly bandages
- elastic bandages, 2 or 3 inches wide
- adhesive dressing tape
- sterile cotton balls
- sterile eye patches
- sterile gauze pads, 4 by 4 inches
- sterile nonstick pads for use with sterile gauze pads
- stretchable gauze, one roll
- triangular bandage for sling or dressing cover

INSTRUMENTS

- bulb syringe to rinse eyes or wounds
- sharp scissors
- tweezers

MEDICATION

- antiseptic ointment
- antihistamine tablets for allergic reactions
- aspirin or acetaminophen. Do not give aspirin to children or teenagers. Aspirin has been linked to a severe illness called Reye's syndrome in young people.
- syrup of ipecac to induce vomiting in some poisoning cases. Call a poison control center or health care provider and follow directions.

MISCELLANEOUS ITEMS

- airtight packages of hand wipes
- candle and waterproof matches
- instant chemical cold packs
- cotton swabs
- disposable latex gloves
- flashlight (remove batteries to prevent corrosion and/or accidental discharge)
- paper and pen or pencil
- soap
- tissues
- safety pins
- blanket
- sterile eyewash and/or plastic cup

SPECIAL NEEDS ITEMS

- adrenaline or epinephrine, insulin and sugar, or nitroglycerin

EVERYDAY ITEMS TO USE IN AN EMERGENCY

- disposable or regular diapers for compresses, bandages, or padding for splints
- sanitary napkins (same uses as above)
- magazines, newspapers, or umbrella for use as a splint
- a clean dish towel, scarf, or handkerchief for bandages or slings

Cardiopulmonary resuscitation (CPR) is a basic life-support technique that is used when the victim is not breathing and the heart may have stopped. CPR allows you to manually perform the functions of the heart and lungs, which send blood and oxygen to all parts of the body.

All of the body's cells, especially the brain cells, need a steady supply of oxygen. CPR opens and clears the victim's airway, and restores breathing and blood circulation through mouth-to-mouth breathing and repeated pressure on the chest.

CPR for Adults and Children Ages 8 and Older

Check for consciousness. Gently shake the victim and shout, "Are you OK?" If there is no response or if the victim is not breathing, shout for help and ask someone to call 911 immediately. The order of action to take in an emergency can be remembered as the ABCs—Airway, Breathing, and Circulation.

AIRWAY: OPEN THE AIRWAY
(Head Tilt/Chin Lift)

1. Tilt the victim's head back if no neck or spinal injuries are suspected.
2. Place your hand on the forehead and apply firm, backward pressure to tilt the head back.
3. Push down on the forehead and, with your other hand, lift the victim's chin.
4. Place 2 fingers of your other hand on the bony part of the victim's chin. Pull the victim's chin forward and support the jaw, helping to tilt the head back.

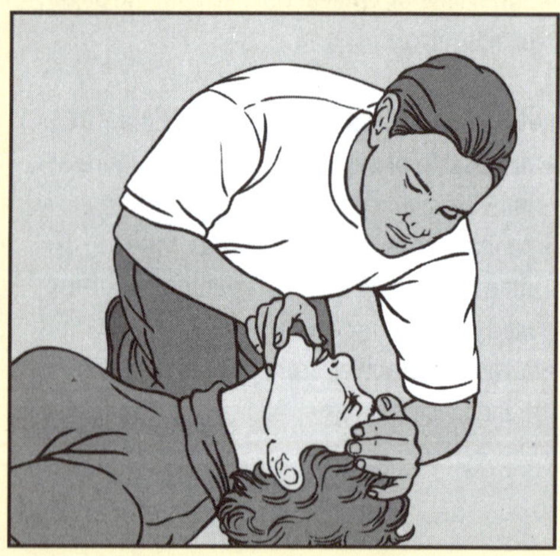

BREATHING: CHECK BREATHING/PERFORM RESCUE BREATHING

Place your ear over the victim's mouth and nose while keeping up an open airway. Look for the chest to rise and fall. Listen for air escaping during exhalation, and feel for the flow of air. Watch

for 5 seconds. If there is no sign of breathing, perform rescue breathing as follows:

1. Keep the airway open by using the head tilt/chin lift maneuver described above. Gently pinch the victim's nose shut using your thumb and index finger on the forehead.
2. Take a deep breath and seal your lips tightly around the victim's mouth.
3. Give 2 full breaths—1 1/2 to 2 seconds per breath, 10 to 12 breaths per minute. Take a breath for yourself after each 2 breaths for the victim. Watch for the victim's chest to rise with each breath. Let the victim's chest fall between breaths.

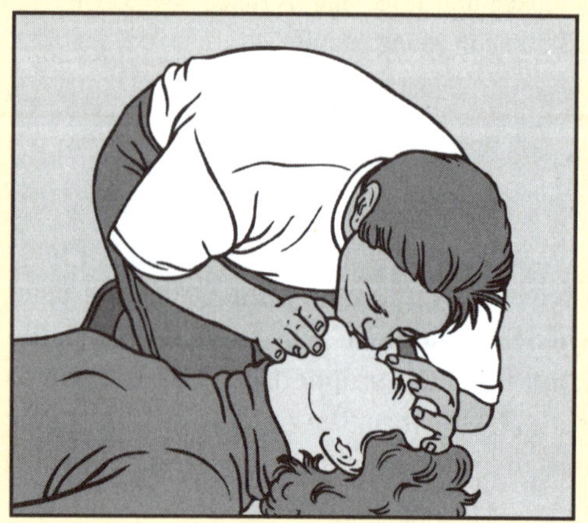

(continued)

CPR for Adults and Children Ages 8 and Older (continued)

CLEARING A BLOCKED AIRWAY FOR AN UNCONSCIOUS VICTIM

If the victim's chest doesn't rise during rescue breathing, the airway is blocked. Retilt the victim's head and try again. If the airway is still blocked, perform the Heimlich maneuver (steps 1 and 2) as follows:

1. Kneel and straddle the victim, placing the heel of your hand on the victim's stomach above the navel and below the ribs.
2. Place your other hand over your fist. Keeping your elbows straight, give 4 quick, downward thrusts toward the chest.

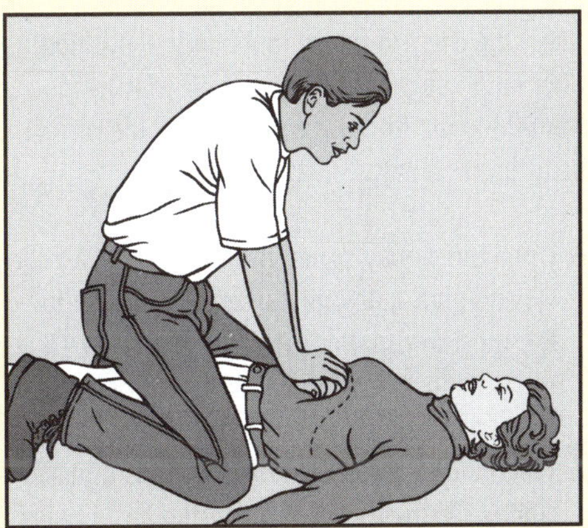

3. Open the victim's mouth by grasping both the tongue and lower jaw between your thumb and fingers, and lift. This will draw the tongue away from the back of the throat and away from any object that might be lodged there. Look to see if an object is visible in the back of the throat.
4. Next, perform the finger-sweep maneuver as follows: Insert the index finger of the other hand down along the inside of the cheek and deeply into the throat to the base of the tongue. Use a hooking action to dislodge the object, and move it into the mouth so that you can remove it.

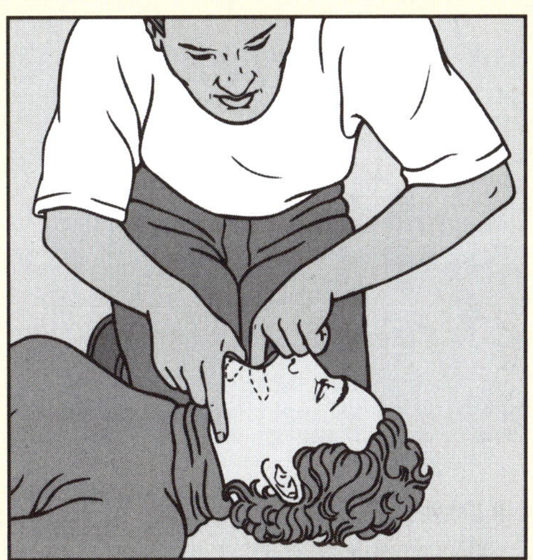

5. Attempt rescue breathing again. If you are still unable to breathe air into the victim's lungs, reposition the head and try again. Repeat the sequence of Heimlich maneuver, finger sweep, and rescue breathing. Perform this cycle until the object is dislodged, and you are able to continue rescue breathing.

(continued)

CPR for Adults and Children Ages 8 and Older (continued)

CIRCULATION: CHECK FOR PULSE

1. While keeping the head tilted, move 2 fingers from the Adam's apple to the side of the neck between the windpipe and the neck muscles. Press down gently and gradually for 5 to 10 seconds. A pulse shows that the heart is beating.

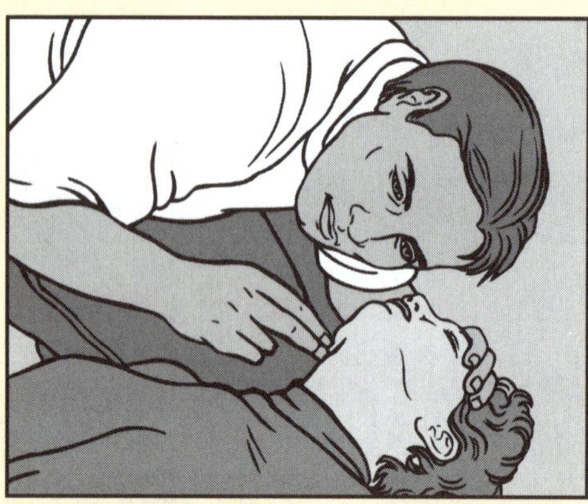

2. If the victim has a pulse but is not breathing, continue rescue breathing at a rate of 10 to 12 times per minute, or once every 5 or 6 seconds. If the victim has no pulse and is not breathing, begin CPR.
3. Find the notch where the victim's ribs meet the breastbone in the center of the chest. Place the heel of your hand 2 finger-widths above the notch. Place your other hand on top of this hand, interlocking your fingers.

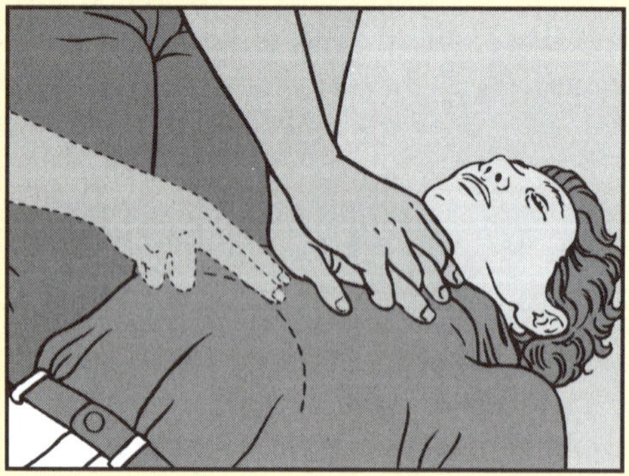

4. Lean forward until your shoulders are directly over your hands. The weight of your body falling forward provides the force to depress the breastbone.
5. Do 15 chest compressions (at a rate of 80 to 100 per minute), continuing to lean over the victim so your shoulders are over your hands.

NOTE: Don't rock back and forth or pause between compressions. Lock your arms straight and press hard on the breastbone 1 1/2 to 2 inches or one third of the chest depth.

Count out loud, "one and, two and, three and, four and," as you push straight down. Allow the chest to return to its normal position after each compression. Do not lift your hands from the chest or change position, or the correct hand position may be lost.

6. Open the airway again using the head tilt/chin lift and give 2 slow rescue breaths. Watch for the chest to rise. Repeat this sequence of 15 compressions and 2 breaths for 4 cycles. Recheck for pulse.
7. When the victim is breathing and has a pulse, stop performing CPR. If the victim has a pulse but is not breathing, continue rescue breathing. Recheck the pulse every 60 seconds. Start CPR again if pulse stops. If the victim has no pulse and is not breathing, repeat sequence of 15 compressions and 2 breaths, checking for pulse every 4 cycles. Continue until the victim is revived or help arrives.

CPR for Children Under 8 Years Old

Shout for help and ask someone to call 911 immediately. Then provide the basic ABC's (Airway, Breathing, Circulation) of life support.

AIRWAY: OPEN THE AIRWAY

If no neck or spinal injuries are suspected, open the airway by placing your hand on the child's forehead and tilting the head back into a neutral position. Place the fingers of your other hand under the bony part of the lower jaw at the chin and lift upward and outward.

BREATHING: CHECK BREATHING/PERFORM RESCUE BREATHING

1. After the airway is opened, check to see if the child is breathing. Look for a rise and fall of the chest and abdomen, listen for exhaled air, and feel for exhaled air flow at the mouth.
2. If no spontaneous breathing is detected, begin rescue breathing while keeping the chin lifted. If the victim is less than 1 year old, place your mouth over the mouth and nose. If the victim is 1 to 8 years old, make a mouth-to-mouth seal and pinch the child's nose tightly with your thumb and forefinger, maintaining head tilt.
3. Give 2 slow breaths (1 to 1 1/2 seconds per breath) to the child. Pause to take a breath after the first breath. If the air enters freely and the chest rises, the airway is clear. If air does not enter freely or if the chest does not rise, either the airway is blocked or more breath pressure is necessary.

NOTE: Improper opening of the airway is the most common cause of airway blocks. Reattempt to open the airway and try rescue breathing again. If you suspect an object is blocking the airway, see *Choking*, page 66. If a child loses consciousness or has more difficulty breathing, have someone call 911 immediately and perform the Heimlich maneuver (see page 67 or page 68).

CIRCULATION: CHECK FOR PULSE

Spend only a few seconds checking a pulse in an infant who is not breathing before starting chest compressions.

1. In infants less than 1 year old, gently press your index and middle fingers on the inside of the upper arm, between the infant's elbow and shoulder. In children 1 to 8 years old, find the Adam's apple with 2 or 3 fingers. Slide your fingers into the groove on the side of the neck between the windpipe and neck muscles.

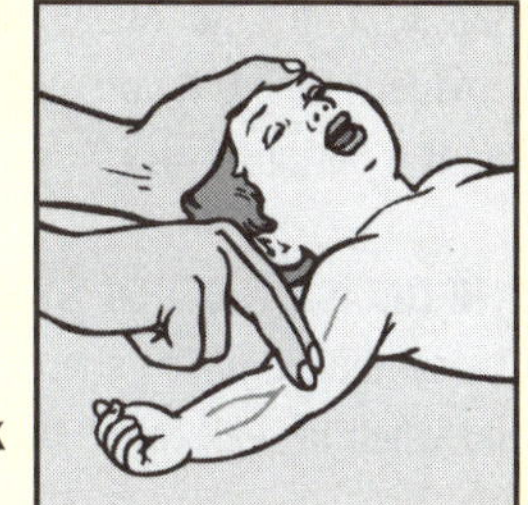

2. If a pulse is present but the child is not breathing, do rescue breathing at a rate of 20 breaths per minute (once every 3 seconds) until spontaneous breathing resumes. After giving 20 breaths, call 911.
3. If there is no pulse, do chest compressions as follows:
   - Use one hand to maintain the infant's head position. Use your other hand to compress the chest.
   - Place your index finger just below the level of the infant's nipples. Place your middle fingers on the breastbone next to the index finger.
   - Using 2 or 3 fingers, compress the breastbone by about one third to one half the depth of the chest—about 1/2 inch to 1 inch.
   - Do compressions at a rate of at least 100 per minute.
   - Coordinate with rescue breathing by doing 5 compressions to each breath.
   - Continue until medical help arrives. If the infant starts breathing, place the victim in the recovery position (on one side with the arm supporting the head).

How to Use the Decision Guide

The decision guides found throughout this book can help you make decisions about the best course of treatment when you are ill or injured. If you still have doubts after using the guides, seek medical advice.

DECISION GUIDES ARE NOT FOR INFANTS.
The decision guides do not apply to infants less than 3 months old. Always seek your health care provider's advice if you are concerned that your infant is seriously sick.

THE DECISION GUIDE SYMBOLS
The symbols offer a general guide as to how and when to seek care:

Use self-care
Symptoms can usually be treated at home. If symptoms persist you should call your health care provider for advice.

Call provider's office
Symptoms may be treated at home or by your health care provider. You and your provider usually need to share additional information about your condition to decide what is best for you.

See provider
Symptoms need to be evaluated by a health care provider. As you call to make an appointment, your provider will help you determine how soon you need to be seen.

Seek help now
Symptoms in this category are serious and should usually be seen within 2 hours. Depending on your health plan, you may choose to call your health care provider to determine whether you should be seen in his or her office, in an urgent care center, or in the emergency room.

Emergency: call 911
Symptoms in this category are life-threatening and require immediate medical treatment.

Allergic Reactions

In rare cases, someone may be so severely allergic to something—usually an insect bite or an injected drug—that a sting or a shot causes a life-threatening reaction called anaphylactic shock. In anaphylactic shock, blood pressure drops, swelling in the lungs restricts breathing, and the tongue and throat swell. If you have ever had an anaphylactic reaction, you should carry a syringe of epinephrine with you. An injection of this drug could save your life. A health care provider can prescribe epinephrine and show you how to use it. It's also a good idea for you to wear a bracelet or carry a card that alerts others to your allergy.

If you suspect that someone is having anaphylactic shock, call for emergency medical assistance immediately. Until help arrives, lay the victim down and raise his or her legs to keep blood flowing to the heart and brain. Use cardiopulmonary resuscitation if the person's heartbeat or breathing stops (see *CPR for Adults and Children Ages 8 and Older*, pages 56-58, or *CPR for Children Under 8 Years*, page 59). For more information on less severe allergic reactions, see *Allergic Reactions*, page 60. To treat insect bites, see *Insect Bites*, page 83.

Bites

For *Insect Bites*, see page 83; for *Snakebites*, see page 90.

Animal bites. More than two million dog bites resulting in cuts or puncture wounds are reported each year. Half of the victims are children. Millions of bites and nips from other animals are believed to go unreported. Animal bites raise three concerns: bleeding, the possibility of viral infections such as rabies, and the possibility of bacterial infections including tetanus. Animal bites that break the skin often cause bacterial skin infections.

The best way to prevent injury from such bites is to avoid animals in the first place. Don't get too close to wild animals. Don't pester an unfamiliar dog or cat, or attempt to pet an animal that appears unfriendly.

Self-Care Steps for Animal Bites

- Wash an animal bite vigorously under running water with soap for 5 minutes, even if it has not bled. Apply an antibacterial ointment to shallow wounds, and watch for signs of infection (see *Cuts, Scrapes, and Wounds*, page 69). Deep puncture wounds, especially cat bites, carry a greater risk of infection and should be treated immediately by your health care provider.
- The main carriers of rabies are wild animals—especially skunks, raccoons, bats, and foxes. Rabid animals act strangely, attack without provocation, and may drool or foam at the mouth. If a pet has bitten you, the animal must be confined and watched for 10 days to see if it develops rabies symptoms.
- If possible, catch and confine any wild animal that has bitten you so it can be evaluated for rabies. (Call the animal control office or the police or sheriff's department for help with animals.) Capture the animal alive if you can safely do so without risking further injury. If necessary, kill the animal, but do not damage its head. Save the carcass in a plastic bag in the refrigerator (or freezer) until you can turn it over to health department officials for examination. For information after hours, check to see whether there is a 24-hour rabies hotline in your area.

Call your health care provider if any of the following things happen:

- Any wild animal bites you.
- A strange dog or any cat bites you.
- The animal owner has no vaccination records.
- You are concerned that the animal is ill, or the bite was not provoked.
- You haven't had a tetanus shot in the past 10 years.
- Any sign of infection appears (see *Decision Guide for Cuts, Scrapes, and Wounds*, page 71).
- The bite is severe, especially on the face or hand.

Human bites. Human bites happen more often than you think. Because of the amount and kind of bacteria in the mouth, an infection can result. The possibility of the human immunodeficiency virus (HIV) being spread through the bite of an HIV-infected person is considered extremely unlikely. (HIV is the virus that causes acquired immunodeficiency syndrome, or AIDS.) To date there have been no documented cases of HIV transmission through biting.

Self-Care Steps for Human Bites

- If the wound is bleeding, apply direct pressure and try to raise the wound above heart level. Wash it vigorously with mild soap and a washcloth under running water for at least 5 minutes.
- Check with your health care provider to be sure you've received a tetanus booster within the last 10 years.
- Watch the wound site closely for signs of infection (see *Cuts, Scrapes, and Wounds,* page 69), and see your health care provider immediately if the skin is broken or if you have any of the signs or symptoms listed in the *Decision Guide for Cuts, Scrapes, and Wounds* (see page 71).

Burns

Burns are the second most frequent cause of accidental death in the United States. Each year, 1 out of every 100 Americans will seek medical help for a burn. About 100,000 people will be hospitalized and 12,000 will die as a result of burns.

Fortunately, most burns are minor, and many can be treated successfully at home. But because burns can be serious, it's important to be able to recognize the different types of burns and know when to seek medical care.

Most burns happen in and around the home. Some of the most common causes of burns follow:

- contact with hot objects
- overexposure to the sun
- scalding from hot water, other liquids, or steam
- Contact with caustic chemicals such as household cleaners and drain cleaners (this includes swallowing them, which can burn the mouth, esophagus, stomach, and intestines)
- explosions
- electrical burns

Burns are classified according to degree, as follows:

First-degree burns. These are the mildest burns, affecting the outer layer of skin. Symptoms include pain, reddened skin, and possibly swelling. Most first-degree burns can be treated with self-care, but there are exceptions.

Second-degree burns. These are deeper and more serious burns. They are painful, often wet or seeping, and can be bright red and/or blistered. Second-degree burns require professional medical care.

Third-degree burns. These burns are very serious. They damage the skin deeply and may affect muscles, tendons, and bones. These burns are usually not painful because nerve endings have been destroyed. Third-degree burns are dry and brown or black in color. Third-degree burns require professional medical care.

Chemical burns. Chemical burns happen when someone is doused or splashed with a harsh acid or alkaline chemical. These chemicals can burn the skin in exactly the same way fire can.

Electrical burns. Electrical burns are serious medical emergencies. Such a burn is often deep, and although it may not look threatening, a small skin burn can indicate extensive internal damage. Electricity can also cause the heart to stop beating or to beat unevenly.

Take great care when aiding a victim of electrical burn. Never approach the victim of an electrical injury until you are certain the power has been shut off. If possible, turn off the electric current by flipping the main breaker or removing the fuse.

Do not touch someone who is being electrocuted, and do not get within 20 yards of a high-voltage electrocution victim. This electricity can leap across gaps and strike you. Don't try to rescue the victim until the current has been shut off. If someone has been struck by lightning, you can approach him or her right away. Unless there is immediate danger, do not try to move the victim. Since electric shock can stop the heart or cause it to beat unevenly,

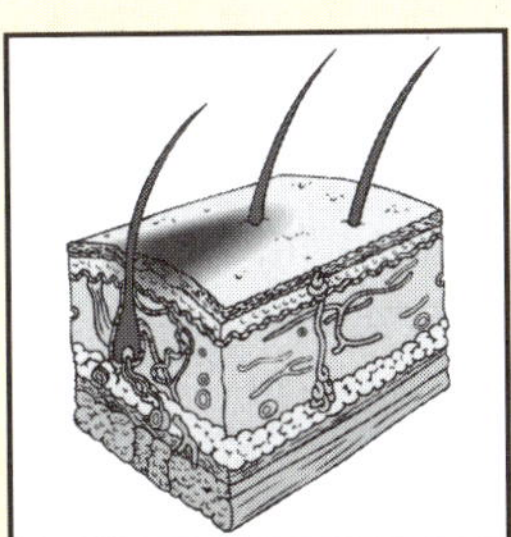

FIRST-DEGREE BURN

Minor burns injure the epidermis, or outside skin layer. The skin will be red, dry, or swollen. These burns may peel and are usually painful. Examples include mild sunburns or slight scalding. Medical attention is not needed unless a larger area of skin is damaged. Such burns usually heal within 5 to 6 days without permanent scars.

SECOND-DEGREE BURN

Some of the skin layers beneath the surface are injured by second-degree burns. These burns are marked by blisters, local swelling, clear fluid discharge, and mottled skin. The pain may be severe. If the burn covers an area larger than 1 square inch, get medical attention. Second-degree burns can be fatal if more than 50 percent of the body is involved. Healing takes 3 to 4 weeks and may leave scars.

THIRD-DEGREE BURN

Third-degree burns destroy all of the skin layers and any or all of the nerves, muscles, bones, or fat underneath. These burns have a charred appearance. The tissues surrounding or beneath the burn may be white or look waxy. Third-degree burns are either very painful or painless, depending on nerve damage. Medical attention is crucial. Even if the burn is in one spot, treatment by a specialist and skin grafts will be necessary. Scars may occur, depending upon the severity of the burn.

Decision Guide for Burns

Symptoms/Signs	Action
First-degree burn	Use self-care
Second-degree burn	Call provider's office
Third-degree burn (see *Shock*, page 88)	Seek help now
No tetanus booster received within last 10 years	 Seek help now

For more about the symbols, see page 60.

For minor burns: Soak burned area in cold water, use bacitracin to prevent dehydration, apply a light gauze bandage, and tape where skin is not burned.

Self-Care Steps for Minor Burns

- Cool the burned area with cool water for several minutes. This relieves pain and helps prevent swelling.
- For a chemical burn, rinse the area thoroughly with cool water until the chemical is removed.
- Wash the area and apply antibiotic ointment to minor, first-degree burns. Do not apply ointment to more serious burns that require medical attention.
- Never put butter or other grease on a burn.
- Do not break blisters. They protect the burned area from infection.
- Take nonprescription antihistamines, if needed, to relieve itching as the burn heals.
- Avoid the sun. Burned skin can be sensitive to the sun for up to a year.
- Trim a burned child's fingernails to keep him or her from scratching the burned skin.
- Do not use anesthetic sprays designed to treat sunburn pain.

Self-Care Steps for Severe Burns

- Do not use ice or very cold water to cool a burn. This could damage burned tissue and cause hypothermia or shock if burns are extensive.
- Apply a sterile dressing. Gauze is best, but a clean bedsheet will do if nothing else is available. Do not use cotton balls or similar materials, which will stick to the wound.
- Do not wipe the burn. This may damage the skin.
- Keep the person quiet and warm. For more serious burns, elevate the feet and legs to reduce the effects of shock.

check the victim's pulse and administer CPR if necessary. (See *CPR for Adults and Children Ages 8 and Older*, page 56, or *CPR for Children Under 8 Years Old*, page 59. These guidelines are intended as a review, and are not a substitute for American Heart Association CPR training.)

Self-Care Steps for Chemical Burns

SKIN BURNS

- Flush the burned area with a gentle, constant spray of water for at least 10 minutes using a hose, bucket, or shower. Remove all clothing on the burned area and keep flushing until you are certain all the chemical has been washed away.
- After flushing, call the local poison control center or your health care provider for more instructions. Dry the wound site and cover with a clean cloth or dressing.
- Do not apply first-aid ointments, antiseptics, or home remedies to chemical burns. Cool, wet dressings work best to relieve pain.

EYE BURNS

- Speed is vital in removing a chemical from the eye. Before calling your health care provider, flush the eye right away with a constant stream of cool, clean water for at least 20 to 30 minutes. Or have someone call for you while you do this. A stream of water can't harm the eye and thorough washing can reduce the risk of permanent eye damage. Use milk if water is unavailable. Do not bandage the eye before seeing a health care provider.
- To flush the eyes, hold the victim's head under a faucet or use a pitcher of water, a plastic squirt bottle, a drinking fountain, or shower spray. Hold the eyelids open for proper flushing. Make sure the water runs from the inside corner of the eye (near the nose) outward, so that the contaminated water doesn't flow into the unaffected eye.
- If both eyes are affected, let water flow over both, or quickly alternate flushing each eye. Make sure water reaches all parts of the eye by lifting and separating the eyelids. Another method is to submerge the top half of the victim's face in a large bowl or sink. Have the victim open both eyes and move the eyelids up and down. This technique should not be used with people (especially young children) who are upset or who cannot hold their breath.
- Advise the victim not to rub his or her eyes. After rinsing the eye, seek immediate medical care at the nearest hospital emergency room. Bring the chemical container with you for analysis.

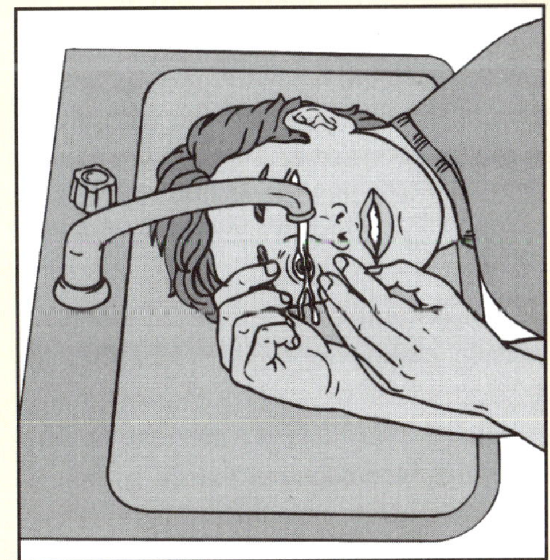

Carbon Monoxide Poisoning

Carbon monoxide is a colorless, odorless gas made when carbon or materials containing carbon (such as gasoline, kerosene, natural gas, and wood) are burned. Poisoning may occur from exposure to gas appliances that are improperly vented (such as a furnace, hot-water heater, or oven), or from automobile exhaust or smoke inhalation from a fire.

Unconsciousness resulting from carbon monoxide poisoning is a life-threatening emergency. If you suspect carbon monoxide poisoning, call 911 or take the victim to a hospital right away. Carbon monoxide can cause death by reducing the blood's oxygen-carrying capacity and depriving the tissues of necessary oxygen.

Carbon monoxide gas does not smell, so the victim may not be aware of being exposed to it until he or she is ill. The gas also does not change the color of blood, so the victim's skin color looks normal.

Carbon monoxide poisoning should be suspected in situations where gas is trapped in a contained area, such as a car with a running engine or a fire in a poorly ventilated area. Symptoms include severe headache, confusion, agitation, tiredness, stupor, or even coma.

Many gas and electric utilities offer inexpensive carbon monoxide detectors to their customers or will promptly check your house if you suspect a gas leak or carbon monoxide poisoning. Check to see if your local utility provides this service. However, detectors are not fail-safe.

Self-Care Steps for Carbon Monoxide Poisoning

- Do not remain in the room if carbon monoxide poisoning is suspected. Move the victim into fresh air as quickly as possible before beginning first aid.
- Check for breathing and pulse. If the victim is not breathing, call 911. Start mouth-to-mouth resuscitation, also called rescue breathing (see page 56 for adults and older children; page 59 for children under 8), and continue until the victim starts breathing or trained medical assistance arrives.
- If pulse is absent, begin massaging the heart (see page 58 for adults and older children; page 59 for children under 8) and continue until trained medical assistance arrives.

Choking

Choking occurs when a piece of food or another object becomes lodged in the throat, blocking the flow of air. Choking victims may react by coughing hard in an effort to dislodge the object. A person whose airway is completely blocked is unable to speak, breathe, or cough, and may clutch his or her throat.

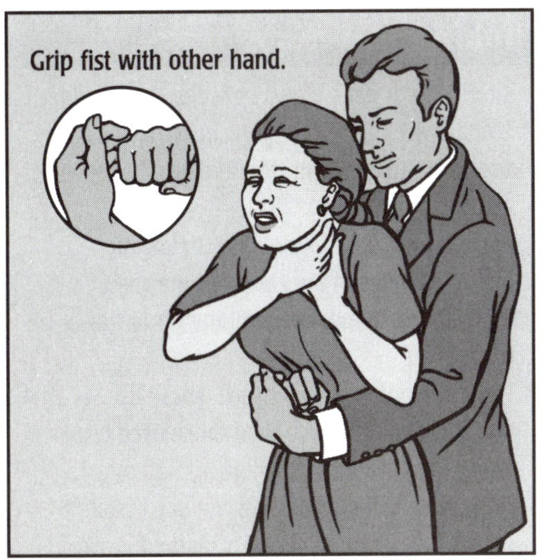

Heimlich maneuver while standing up

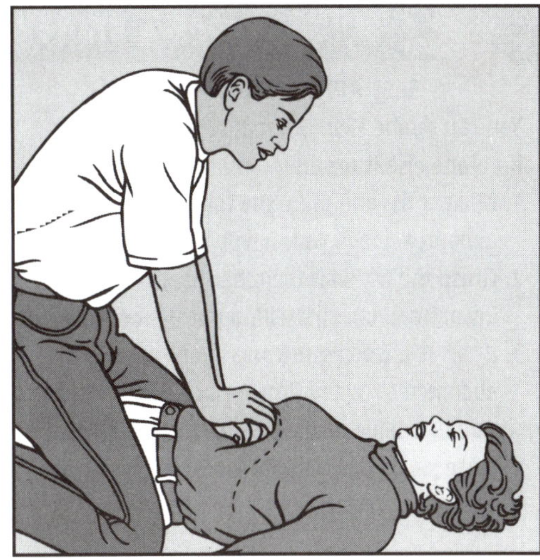

Heimlich maneuver while lying down

Self-Care Steps for Choking

Choking is life-threatening and requires immediate action. If the victim can speak, cough, or breathe, this means air is still passing through the airway. Do not interfere in any way with the victim's efforts to expel the object. Reassure the victim, and advise him or her to breathe deeply and slowly. This will help relax the muscles surrounding the windpipe.

Heimlich Maneuver for Adults or Children When the Victim Is Standing or Sitting

If the victim is unable to breathe or make sounds, have someone call 911. Meanwhile, perform the Heimlich maneuver:

1. Stand behind the choking victim and wrap your arms around the victim's midsection. Place the thumb side of your fist against the victim's stomach, slightly above the navel.
2. Grip your fist with your other hand and press the doubled fist into the victim's abdomen with a quick upward thrust. Repeat the thrusts until the object is expelled from the airway or the victim loses consciousness.
3. Do not squeeze the victim's ribs with your arms. Use only your fist in the abdomen. Each thrust should be a separate and distinct movement.

Heimlich Maneuver for Adults or Children When the Victim Is Lying Down

1. If the victim is lying down and still conscious, turn him or her onto the back.
2. Kneel and straddle the victim, placing the heel of your hand on the victim's stomach above the navel and below the ribs. Place your other hand over the fist.
3. Keeping your elbows straight, give 4 quick, strong, downward thrusts toward the chest.
4. Repeat this procedure as needed until the object is cleared from the airway or the victim loses consciousness.

(continued)

Self-Care Steps for Choking (continued)

SELF-APPLICATION

You can do the Heimlich maneuver on yourself if no one else is around.

1. Make a fist and place the thumb side on the abdomen above your navel.
2. Grasp the fist with the other hand. Press inward and upward with a quick motion.
3. If this is unsuccessful, press your upper abdomen over any firm surface such as the side of a table or the back of a chair. Repeat these single thrusts until the object is cleared from your airway.

HEIMLICH MANEUVER FOR INFANTS

Follow these guidelines with an infant who is small enough to be supported on your forearm, or is up to 1 year old.

1. Ask someone to call 911 immediately. Meanwhile, place the infant face down on your forearm. Support the infant's head by firmly holding the jaw.
2. Give 4 quick back blows between the shoulder blades with the heel of your hand. If this is unsuccessful, perform the Heimlich maneuver as described below.
3. Place 2 fingers 1 finger-width below the infant's nipples in the center of the chest on the breastbone, avoiding the tip of the breastbone.
4. Push forward and downward. These thrusts should be more gentle than those used on an adult. Repeat both procedures if necessary.
5. If the Heimlich maneuver is not successful, follow CPR instructions for a blocked airway (see *Airway: Open the Airway,* page 56).

NOTE: After receiving the Heimlich maneuver, a person who was rescued should call his or her health care provider. Some internal injuries can result from the thrusting motion; however, the risk of injury is lower if you positioned your hands correctly.

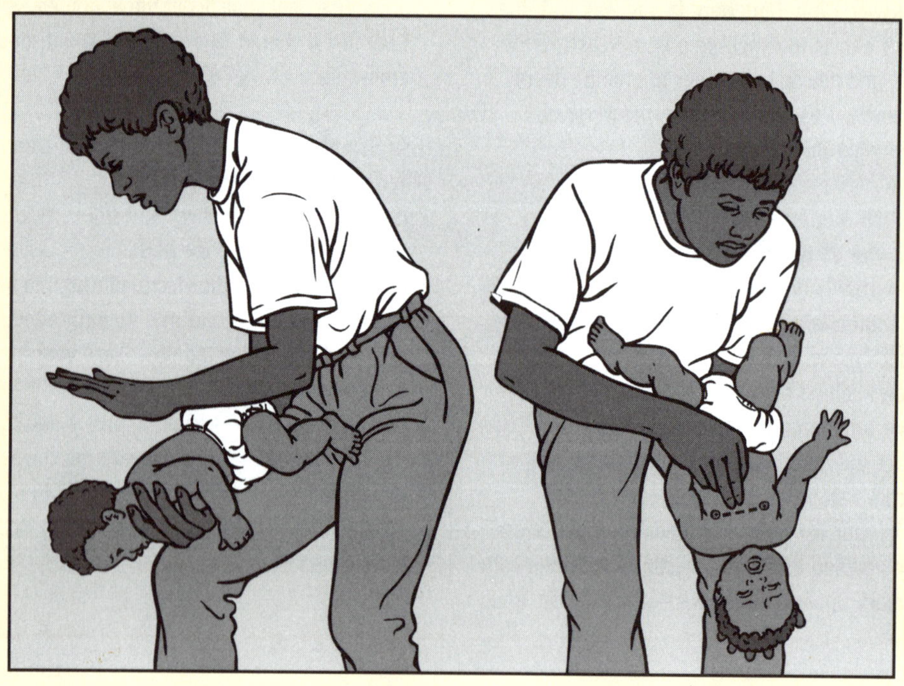

Cuts, Scrapes, and Wounds

To help prevent simple cuts from becoming complicated infections, you should know how to treat cuts properly. The outermost layers of skin are part of the body's defense against the environment. They keep out germs and dirt and keep in body fluids. Your injured tissues will repair themselves over time. How fast a wound heals depends on the blood supply to the area, the type of wound, how good your general health and nutrition are, and how much daily use that part of your body gets.

Infection can delay the healing process. While tissues are healing, they don't act as a barrier, so infections can enter. The blood supply to an area plays an important role in defending against infection as well as in the healing process itself. There is a low risk of infection in places with a rich blood supply, such as the scalp and face. Because the blood supply to the legs and feet is poor, wounds there have a high risk of infection.

Puncture wounds (usually deep, small wounds caused by animal bites, stepping on a nail, or by a sharp object puncturing the skin) require special care to avoid infection.

Self-Care Steps for Cuts, Scrapes, and Wounds

The next time you get caught on a nail, sliced by a knife, or even cut by a piece of paper, follow these steps:

STOP THE BLEEDING

- Cover the wound with a gauze pad or a thick, clean piece of cloth. Use your hand if nothing else is available.
- Press on the wound hard enough to stop the bleeding. Don't let up on the pressure even to change cloths. Just add a clean cloth over the original one.
- Raise the wound above heart level, unless this movement would cause pain.
- Get medical help immediately if blood spurts from a wound or bleeding does not stop after several minutes of pressure.

CLEAN THE WOUND

- Wash the cut with soap and water or use hydrogen peroxide (3 percent solution). Don't use Mercurochrome, Merthiolate, or iodine. They are not necessary and can be very painful.
- Make sure no dirt, glass, or foreign material, remains in the wound.

BANDAGE THE WOUND

- Bandage a cut (rather than seeing a health care provider for stitches) when its edges tend to fall together and when the cut is not very deep.
- Use butterfly bandages, strips of sterile paper tape, or adhesive strip bandages. Change them daily.
- Apply the bandage crosswise, not lengthwise. This will bring the edges of the wound into firm contact and promote healing.

STAY COMFORTABLE

- Keep an arm or leg wound elevated for 24 hours to reduce swelling.
- Keep the wound dry with a bandage for the first few days. Change the bandage if it gets wet.
- Take aspirin, acetaminophen, or ibuprofen to relieve pain from incisions or wounds. (Do not give aspirin to children or teenagers because of the risk of Reye's syndrome.) Prescription pain relievers may be prescribed after surgery.

(continued)

Self-Care Steps for Cuts, Scrapes, and Wounds (continued)

SHOULD YOU SEE YOUR PROVIDER?

See your health care provider for stitches or other care as soon as possible if:

- The wound is deep and gapes widely, is very dirty or irregular, or can't be held together with a bandage.
- A deep cut is located on an elbow, knee, finger or other area that bends.
- The cut is on the finger or thumb joint, palm of the hand, face, or other area where you want to avoid scars.
- The wound damages bones or muscles or feels numb.
- The victim is a young child who is likely to pull off the bandage.
- Bleeding cannot be controlled after applying pressure for 20 minutes.
- Any part of your body doesn't work as well as it did before you were wounded. There may be damage to nerves, blood vessels, ligaments, or tendons that should be repaired as soon as possible.
- The cut was caused by an obviously dirty object, or if a foreign object is embedded in the wound. If you get dirt, soil, or clay in a wound, you have a greater chance of infection. That means any cuts you get in swamps, standing water, or excavations can be quite dangerous. Sand and blacktop debris, however, don't usually cause infections.
- You have not had a tetanus booster within the last 10 years.

For puncture wounds:

- Allow the wound to bleed freely unless a lot of blood has been lost or the blood is spraying out. Bleeding will cleanse the wound and help prevent infection. After several minutes, stop the bleeding by applying pressure to the wound and raising it above the level of the heart.
- Next, clean the area around the wound with soap and warm water. For the next 4 to 5 days, soak the wound in warm water for 15 minutes every 1 or 2 hours. This will clean the wound from the inside. Cover the wound with a sterile or clean dressing and tape in place.
- Do not tape the wound closed or apply antibiotic ointment. Sealing off the wound can increase the risk of infection. Signs of infection usually take more than 24 hours to develop. Call your health care provider if redness, swelling, or pus appears around the wound; if you have pain or fever; or if the wound doesn't heal within 2 weeks.

For scrapes and abrasions:

- On the scalp or a fingertip, you may apply an ice pack wrapped in a towel to constrict the blood vessels and stop the bleeding. Apply the ice pack for no more than 15 minutes or until the wound begins to feel numb. After a 10-minute rest, you may reapply the ice pack. You can repeat this 15 minutes on, 10 minutes off procedure several times.
- Within 24 hours, remove the bandage and wash the area with mild soap and running water. The wound should be washed daily with plain tap water and soap. Change bandages 2 to 3 times daily. Watch for signs of infection (see page 71).

Decision Guide for Cuts, Scrapes, and Wounds

Symptoms/Signs	Action
Bleeding stops within 10 minutes with direct pressure	Use self-care
Wound is shallow	Use self-care
Wound doesn't heal in 10 to 14 days	Call provider's office
Signs of infection are present (see box at right)	See provider
Cut or scrape cannot be adequately cleaned, or debris may be in the wound	See provider
Person has not had a tetanus booster in the last 10 years	See provider
Wound is deep or irregular, or the edges of it cannot be held together easily with a bandage (see box at right)	See provider
Wound is deep and located on the face, chest, abdomen, back, palm, finger, knee, or elbow	See provider
More than 2 to 3 tablespoons of blood has been lost in 24 hours	See provider
Numbness or weakness occurs	Seek help now
Bleeding cannot be controlled	Seek help now
Person is unable to move fingers or toes normally	Seek help now

Decision Guide for Signs of Infection

Symptoms/Signs	Action
Increased pain at the wound site	Call provider's office
Redness or swelling around the cut or wound	Call provider's office
Swollen lymph nodes (see page 127)	Call provider's office
Fever over 100.5 degrees	See provider
Red streaks spreading from the wound site toward the heart	See provider
Pus draining from the cut or wound	See provider

For more about the symbols, see page 60.

Drowning

Drowning is the fourth leading cause of accidental death in the United States. People who are revived after being submerged underwater for a long time are said to be victims of "near drowning." The near-drowning victim may be awake, semiconscious, or unconscious, with little or no breathing or heartbeat. Vomiting, cold skin, and bluish-white paleness are common signs.

Near drowning is a very upsetting experience. Stay with a near-drowning victim to provide support and help keep the person calm. Any near-drowning victim should be taken to the nearest hospital for intensive care, even if he or she has regained consciousness. Complications or death from heartbeat disturbances can occur as long as 24 to 48 hours after the accident.

Self-Care Steps for Near Drowning

Rescue the near-drowning victim if you can do so without endangering yourself. If head and spinal injuries are suspected, follow the steps listed below. Immediately establish an airway and begin CPR if necessary, even before the person is removed from the water.

WHAT TO DO UNTIL HELP ARRIVES

- Look, listen, and feel for breathing. Look to see if the victim's chest is rising and falling.
- If the victim is not breathing, see *CPR for Adults and Children Ages 8 and Older,* page 56, or *CPR for Children Under 8 Years Old,* page 59.
- Stay with the victim and have someone call 911 for emergency medical help. Check for a pulse by moving 2 fingers along the victim's throat to the Adam's apple. Then move fingers off to the side of victim's throat between the windpipe and the muscles at the side of the neck. Firmly press down until you feel a pulse (as described on page 58 for adults and page 59 for children).
- A pulse indicates that the heart is beating. If there is no heartbeat, begin external cardiac massage.
- Hypothermia—lowering of body temperature—often afflicts near-drowning victims, especially when incidents involve submersion in icy water. Therefore, it is extremely important that CPR be continued until medical help arrives. Complete recovery has been reported after prolonged resuscitation of hypothermia victims.

Fever

From shivers and shakes to sweating and aches, your body's temperature is an important barometer of how well you are dealing with germs, stress, exertion, or extreme changes in weather. For good health, the body works best at a temperature of about 97 to 99 degrees.

Although your body temperature rises slightly during the day, this change is not important unless your temperature is higher than 100.4 degrees. In fact, many people have a temperature that is always a little above or below 98.6 degrees, which is considered "normal."

By itself, a high temperature is not necessarily cause for concern—it can actually be a perfectly normal way for your body to defend itself against infection. A fever is a special cause for concern with infants under 3 months of age, and for the elderly and those with a history of heart and lung disease. But for most people, there is no medical reason to try to reduce a fever unless other symptoms of illness are present.

Self-Care Steps for Fever

- When you have a fever and no other symptoms, drugs are not necessary. But if the fever makes you uncomfortable, take aspirin or acetaminophen. For children, use acetaminophen, not aspirin (see *Special Concerns for Children,* page 74).
- Drink 8 glasses of fluid a day. When you have a fever, your body loses fluids, so it's important to prevent dehydration. Avoid drinking coffee or tea, which can also cause fluid loss.

Decision Guide for Fevers

Symptoms/Signs	Action
Fever for up to 3 days without other symptoms	Use self-care
Oral temperature of 100.4 degrees or less	Use self-care
Fever with sore throat, earache, or frequent cough	Call provider's office
Fever that lasts 3 days or longer	Call provider's office
Fever with vomiting	See provider
Shaking, teeth-chattering chills	See provider
Fever with back pain or painful urination	See provider
Oral temperature higher than 100.4 degrees	See provider
Fever in an older person, who is suddenly confused	Seek help now
Fever with stiff neck	Seek help now
Lower abdominal pain and fever for more than 2 hours	Seek help now

For more about the symbols, see page 60.

How to Take a Child's Temperature

Since most children under 2 years of age cannot keep their mouths closed or remain still for an oral temperature, it is best to take their temperature rectally. Apply petroleum jelly to the thermometer for comfort, and insert it about an inch into the rectum (until you can no longer see the silver end) for about three minutes. Be certain to hold onto the thermometer while it is in the child's rectum so that the child doesn't roll over or move and puncture his or her colon. If you seek medical advice, tell your child's health care provider the temperature and whether it is an oral or rectal temperature. A rectal temperature is normally 1 degree higher than an oral temperature.

Special Concerns for Children

Fever is not necessarily harmful, nor does it mean serious illness. Be more concerned about coughing, pain, changes in eating or sleeping habits, or other marked changes in a child's behavior.

- Fluids are very important for children so be sure to give plenty of soups, juice, or water.
- Because a dangerous condition called Reye's syndrome can result when children or teenagers take aspirin, use acetaminophen.
- In children between 6 months and 5 years of age, seizures sometimes result from fever. These seizures are seldom harmful. During a seizure, try to protect your children from hurting themselves. Keep them away from nearby objects, and make sure they are breathing freely.
- When a child under 3 months of age has a rectal temperature over 100.4 degrees, call your health care provider.

Fishhook Wounds

A fishhook caught in the body is a common injury. On most fishhooks, the biggest problem is the barb. Although fish sometimes free themselves quite easily, people often stay hooked.

When only the point of the fishhook has entered the skin, it can be removed easily by backing the fishhook out the way it went in. If the fishhook is so deeply embedded that the barb has entered the skin, there are these two options:

- If medical care is available nearby, take the victim to a health care provider to get the hook extracted. A local anesthetic may be administered to the area around the hook before removing it.

Decision Guide for Fishhook Wounds

Symptoms/Signs	Action
Barb is not embedded	Use self-care
Hook with barb is embedded, and not easily removed	See provider
Signs of infection are present (see page 71)	See provider
Stitches are needed	See provider
No tetanus shot has been received within the last 10 years	See provider
Hook is embedded in eye or near major artery	Seek help now

For more about the symbols, see page 60.

- If the victim is in an area far from medical care, the fishhook can be dislodged by using either pliers or fish line, as shown below. If the fishhook cannot be taken out easily, seek medical care.

NOTE: Do not try to remove a fishhook that is embedded in the eye. Get medical attention immediately!

Self-Care Steps for Fishhook Wounds

Use these methods only if you cannot see a health care provider within 24 hours.

PLIERS METHOD

- Before beginning, try to cut through an extra hook with your pliers to ensure that the pliers work well enough. Use ice, cold water, or hard pressure to numb the area temporarily before beginning.
- Gently push the embedded hook deeper into the skin until the point and barb come out through the skin. Using the pliers, cut off the barb and back the hook out the way it entered or cut off the other end of the hook and pull it through. Although this method can be painful, it works if the proper pliers are available and the barb is not too deeply embedded to be pushed through to the surface of the skin.

FISH LINE METHOD

- Loop or tie a piece of fish line to the embedded hook, near the skin surface. Hold the area where the hook is embedded so that it can't move, and use ice, cold water, or hard pressure to numb the skin temporarily.
- With one hand, press down about 1/8 inch on the eye of the hook to take out the barb. While still pressing the hook down, jerk the line parallel to the skin surface so the hook shaft leads the barb out of the skin.

After the hook has been removed by either method, wash the wound thoroughly with mild soap and running water if possible. Cover the wound with an adhesive bandage and seek follow-up medical cares (see *Decision Guide for Cuts, Scrapes, and Wounds,* page 71).

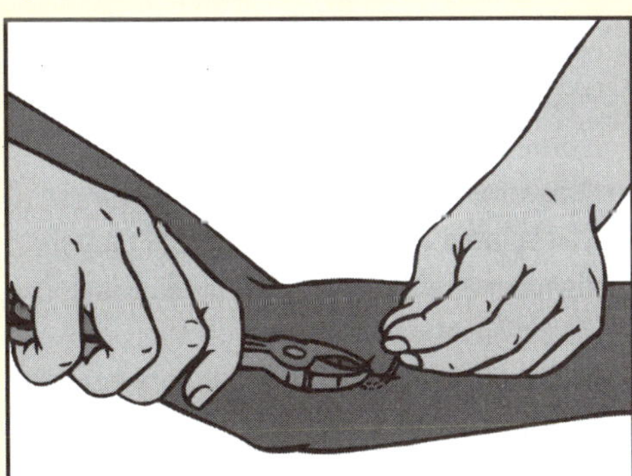

Pliers method

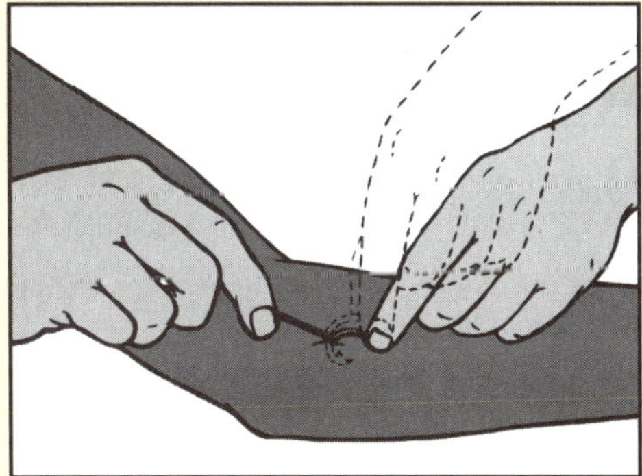

Fish line method

Fishhook Wounds

Fractures

A broken or cracked bone is a fracture. There are two types of fractures. A closed fracture means that the bone isn't poking through the skin. An open (or compound) fracture, in which the skin is broken and bone is visible, is more dangerous and may involve severe bleeding. Open fractures are also more likely to get infected.

A fracture may show one or both of the following symptoms:

- pain with motion or pressure
- a grating sensation of the ends of bones rubbing together

Bone fragments in many fractures are still in the proper place, so setting is not required. A fracture that injures nearby nerves or arteries may make the limb cold, blue, or numb. Ultimately, the person could lose the ability to use the limb. Fractures of the pelvis or thigh can be particularly dangerous.

Decision Guide for Fractures

Symptoms/Signs	Action
Fracture is suspected	Call provider's office
Limb is crooked	See provider
Person is unable to use limb or bear weight on limb	See provider
Limb or portion of limb is cool, blue, or numb	Seek help now

For more about the symbols, see page 60.

A crooked limb, a lot of swelling or discoloration, and an inability to bear weight after an injury or fall are reasons to have your health care provider check for a fracture. Call your provider if pain prevents any use of the injured limb. When great force is involved in an injury, such as in a car accident or a fall from a roof, the possibility of a broken bone increases. In these situations, look closely for signs of fractures.

Self-Care Steps for Fractures

- Apply ice packs to the injury. For open fractures, use clean, preferably white, wrappings. Dye in colored cloth can enter the bloodstream. Apply cold immediately to help decrease swelling. If you suspect that a bone is broken, protect and rest the injured limb immediately.
- Splints are used to hold a suspected fracture in one position to prevent further injury until treatment is completed (this also applies to ribs or collarbones). A fracture can be held steady by wrapping something around the injured limb or by fixing the limb to some other part of the victim's body. It is best to immobilize the joint (keep it from moving) above and below the injured area.
- Magazines, cardboard, or rolled newspaper can be used as a splint. Do not wrap too tightly or circulation will be cut off. A limb that cannot be used at all is probably broken and should be seen by a health care provider.
- Minutes and hours are not crucial unless the limb is crooked, arteries or nerves are injured, or the injury is causing great pain. A fractured limb that is protected and rested is likely to mend well, even if casting or splinting is delayed.

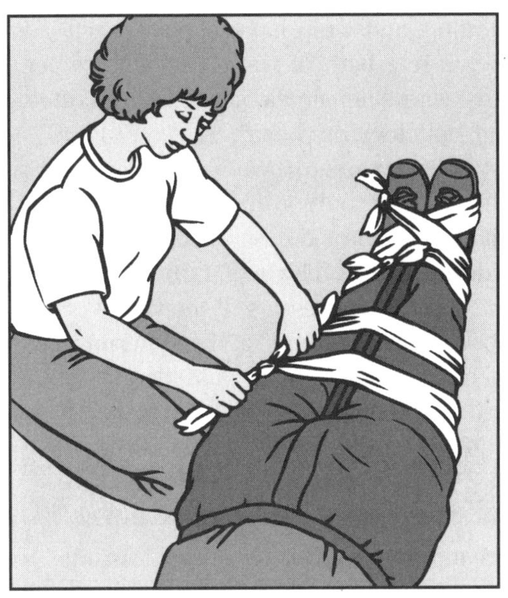
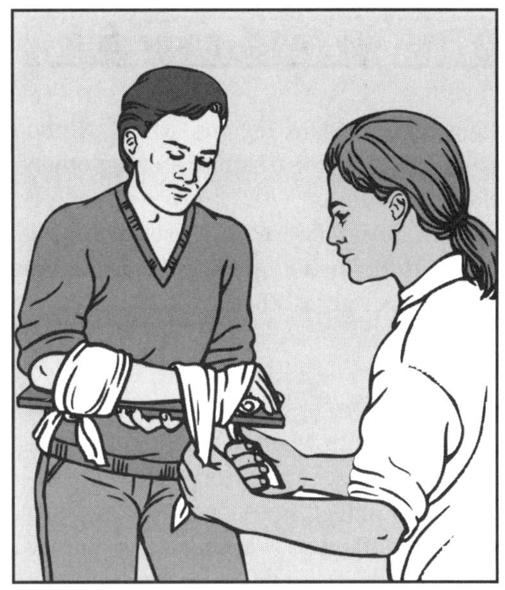

Applying a rigid splint—Use a board or anything stiff to immobilize a broken limb. Take care not to cut off circulation by tying too tight. Check for feeling, warmth, and color.

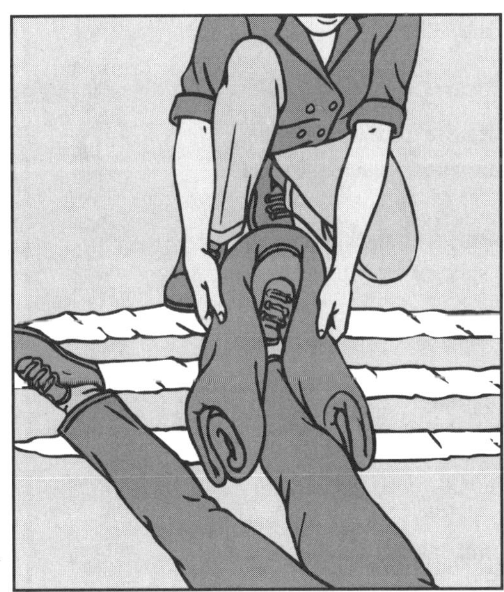
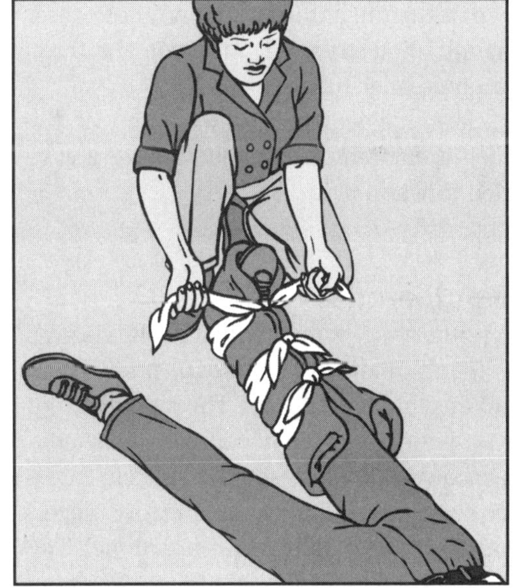

Applying a soft splint—Use a blanket, pillow, or any soft object to support the injured area. Check for feeling, warmth, and color after tying bandages.

Frostbite and Hypothermia

Many of us live in regions where winter brings the threat of frostbite and hypothermia (the loss of vital body heat). Fortunately, most cold weather risks are easily managed by using good judgment and wearing the right clothes.

Frostbite

Frostbite occurs when the skin and tissues freeze after exposure to very cold temperatures. Hands, feet, nose, and ears are most commonly affected. Warning signs include tingling and then numbness in the skin. Frostbitten areas become cold, white, or grayish-yellow, and hard to the touch. As the area thaws, it becomes red and painful.

If you suspect frostbite, get out of the cold immediately. Warm the affected area by putting it in barely warm, not hot, water (about 100 degrees). Do not rub the frostbitten area, or rub snow on it.

Seek medical help immediately if the frostbitten area remains numb after you've tried to warm it.

Hypothermia

Hypothermia happens when the body's temperature drops due to exposure to cool and/or damp conditions. The symptoms of hypothermia include uncontrollable shivering; cold, pale skin; slurred speech; memory lapses; fumbling, stumbling, or staggering; and abnormally slow breathing. The victim may feel tired or apathetic. The condition becomes grave when shivering stops, muscles stiffen, and skin turns bluish.

To treat hypothermia, get the victim out of the cold and remove any damp or wet clothing. Dress the victim in warm, dry clothing and wrap in blankets. Or put the victim in a bath of warm (not hot) water. Give warm, nonalcoholic drinks like coffee, tea, hot cider, or cocoa.

Call the person's health care provider for advice if the only symptoms are shivering and cold, pale skin. Someone on the provider's staff can tell you if a trip to the clinic or hospital is necessary. If the victim develops other symptoms of hypothermia, get medical help as soon as possible.

Decision Guide for Frostbite and Hypothermia

Symptoms/Signs	Action
Numb skin	Use self-care
Blistered skin	Call provider's office
Headache	Call provider's office
Nausea, dizziness, vomiting, or uncontrollable shivering	Call provider's office
Pale, cold, clammy skin, or cold, white, or grayish-yellow skin	Seek help now
Rapid pulse and breathing	Seek help now
Unconsciousness	Emergency: call 911
Stiff muscles and bluish skin	Emergency: call 911
Confusion and slurred speech	Emergency: call 911

For more about the symbols, see page 60.

Head Injuries

Although most are minor, any head injury can lead to a more serious problem. Head injuries can range from a concussion, which is usually not serious, to bleeding inside the head, a condition that can be life-threatening.

Concussion. This is a brief loss of consciousness caused by a blow to the head. The most common symptom of concussion is a constant headache that may get worse and is sometimes accompanied by vomiting. Other symptoms include blurred vision, sleepiness, and memory problems.

Cerebral hemorrhage. This is bleeding caused by broken blood vessels in the brain, and is more serious than a concussion. Symptoms of cerebral hemorrhage include headaches, vomiting, confusion, weakness, and difficulty staying awake or being awakened. Athletes who have had a head injury should not return to their sport without a medical evaluation.

People taking anticoagulants (drugs prescribed to prevent blood clotting) need to take special precautions to prevent falls because they could bleed more easily from a blow to the head. In older people, a fall—even without a direct blow to the head—can cause life-threatening head injury complications.

Call 911 if a head injury results in unconsciousness, breathing difficulty, or a neck injury. Every person with a head injury should be watched for 24 hours for the symptoms listed above.

Decision Guide for Head Injuries in Adults

Symptoms/Signs	Action
Bleeding from the scalp lasts more than 10 minutes with pressure	 See provider
Person appears dazed or confused or is hard to awaken	 Seek help now
Person has difficulty walking or talking	 Seek help now
Headaches increase in severity	 Seek help now
Vomiting persists	 Seek help now
Person has blurred vision or pupils are not equal in size	 Seek help now
Person has severe headache or neck pain	 Seek help now
Breathing is difficult	 Seek help now
Blood drains from the person's nostrils or ears	 Seek help now
Person's temperature rises above 100 degrees	 Seek help now
Person loses consciousness	Emergency: call 911
Person has seizures	Emergency: call 911

For more about the symbols, see page 60.

Head Injuries in Children

Every year more than 80,000 children in the United States are admitted to hospitals with head injuries. Children's large head-to-body ratios and developing brains and muscles put them at great risk for head injuries. These injuries require prompt attention because they can be life-threatening and can affect growth and development.

Quick action is required if a head injury results in unconsciousness, breathing difficulty, or a neck injury. Head injuries may also cause a lot of bleeding from the scalp, which is not necessarily serious. Even without these symptoms, be sure to watch the child closely for 24 hours, since some symptoms may develop over time. Careful observation, which in most cases can be done at home, is the best way to diagnose a head injury (see definitions of *Concussion*, and *Cerebral hemorrhage*, page 79). Check the decision guide on page 81 to see when you should contact your child's health care provider.

Preventing Head Injuries

ADULTS

- Wear a helmet when riding bikes, horses, or motorcycles, or when using in-line skates.
- Use seat belts in automobiles.
- Wear a hard hat at an industrial site.
- Never dive into shallow water.

CHILDREN

- Childproof your home (see page 24-31).
- Do not use baby walkers and never leave infants alone on beds, changing tables, or other high places.
- Supervise outside play.
- Teach children to cross streets safely.
- Have children wear helmets when biking, riding horses, or wearing in-line skates.
- Have children wear seat belts or sit in car safety seats when they are in vehicles.
- Teach children not to dive into shallow water.

For head, spine, or neck injuries, move the victim only if it is absolutely necessary. Immobilize the head. Stay with the victim until help arrives, making sure that the airway is not blocked.

Self-Care Steps for Head Injuries

- If the head is bleeding, apply pressure to control bleeding.
- Clean and bandage the wound. Apply an ice pack for swelling.
- Check to see if the victim's pupils are equal in size. If they are not, call for medical help.
- Check skin color every few hours. Wake a child every 2 hours to observe breathing and to be assured of consciousness. Wake an adult every few hours to check breathing and level of consciousness.
- Question an adult (or a child who is old enough) about name, age, and address to check his or her level of confusion.
- Do not give any medicine without talking to the person's health care provider.
- Limit activity for 24 hours after the injury.

Self-Care Steps for Neck and Spinal Injuries

- Call 911 and then stay with the victim. Do not move the victim if you suspect head, neck, or spinal injuries unless the victim is in immediate danger from fire, drowning, explosion, or gas. If possible, wait for professional help. Neck and spinal injuries may result in permanent paralysis if not treated carefully.
- If the victim has to be moved for safety reasons, immobilize the head and neck first, using a backboard, table leaf, or door, or have several people move as a team to support the head and neck and keep both level with the victim's back.
- When using a board or other flat, rigid surface, it should extend from the head to the buttocks.

Decision Guide for Head Injuries in Children

Symptoms/Signs	Action
Child doesn't lose consciousness but appears dazed	 Call provider's office
Bleeding from scalp lasts more than 10 minutes with pressure	 See provider
Child has difficulty walking or talking	 Seek help now
Child is confused or disoriented	 Seek help now
Headaches increase in severity	 Seek help now
Child vomits 3 times or more	 Seek help now
Vision is blurred or pupils are unequal sizes	 Seek help now
Blood drains from nostrils or ears	 Seek help now
Child has severe headache or neck pain	Seek help now
Child is difficult to awaken or loses consciousness	Emergency: call 911
Child has seizures	Emergency: call 911

For more about the symbols, see page 60.

Heat-Related Problems

Many of us live in regions where sunburn, heat exhaustion, and heatstroke are summer health risks. If you live in a hot region, the weather can affect your health year-round.

Heat Exhaustion

Heat exhaustion typically occurs when people work or exercise in hot, humid conditions. The symptoms are as follows:

- cool, pale, and clammy skin
- heavy sweating
- dilated pupils
- headache
- nausea
- dizziness
- vomiting
- faintness
- rapid pulse and breathing

Heatstroke

Heatstroke is life-threatening. It requires immediate medical attention. In heatstroke, the mechanism that regulates the body's temperature stops working and body temperature rises rapidly to 104 degrees or higher. A heatstroke victim's skin is bright red, dry, and hot. There is a strong, rapid pulse. The victim may be confused or unconscious.

If someone is suffering from heatstroke, call for an ambulance immediately. While waiting for help, undress the victim and

Self-Care Steps for Heat Exhaustion

- When heat exhaustion strikes, have the victim lie on his or her back in a cool, quiet place with feet slightly raised. The person should drink salt water every 15 minutes. (Mix a quarter teaspoon of salt per pint of water.)
- Call a health care provider's office for advice if you don't notice an improvement within 30 minutes. Stay alert to signs of heatstroke.

Decision Guide for Heat-Related Problems

Symptoms/Signs	Action
Headache	Use self-care
Heavy sweating	Use self-care
Mild sunburn	Use self-care
Nausea, dizziness, vomiting	See provider
Blistered skin	See provider
Bright red, dry, hot skin (can be a sign of heatstroke, which requires immediate attention)	Seek help now
Unconsciousness	Emergency: call 911
Stiff muscles and bluish skin	Emergency: call 911
Confusion, slurred speech	Emergency: call 911
Rapid pulse and breathing	Emergency: call 911

For more about the symbols, see page 60.

wrap him or her in wet sheets, and fan the body with your hands or an electric fan. Give the victim water if he or she is able to drink.

Hyperventilation

Hyperventilation means breathing faster and deeper than normal, due to anxiety or stress. Physical conditions such as oxygen deprivation or uncontrolled diabetes can also cause hyperventilation. Breathing too quickly causes the carbon dioxide levels in the blood to fall quickly. To the victim, it feels as if not enough air is getting into the lungs. Feeling the need for more air, the victim breathes faster and makes the symptoms worse. Slowing down the victim's breathing will restore the normal balance of oxygen and carbon dioxide in the blood.

These symptoms may accompany hyperventilation:

- rapid breathing
- difficulty getting a deep, satisfying breath
- light-headedness
- numbness or tingling in the hands and feet and around the mouth
- muscle twitching
- convulsions or fainting

Rapid breathing, shortness of breath, or light-headedness may also be signs of other, more serious conditions such as kidney failure or lung problems.

Self-Care Steps for Hyperventilation

- Encourage the victim to breathe more slowly and calmly. Reassure and calm the victim by talking to him or her. Your goal is to break the cycle that begins when hyperventilation makes the victim anxious, which then makes him or her breathe even more rapidly.
- Because hyperventilation is caused by breathing too deeply and rapidly, have the victim close his or her mouth and slow down the breathing rate. Tell the victim to hold his or her breath and silently count, "one-one-thousand, two-one-thousand, three-one-thousand." Then the victim should take a shallow breath (mouth still closed) and repeat this. Within several minutes, the symptoms should begin to go away.
- If you are unable to calm the victim and slow his or her breathing, or if the victim faints, bring the victim to the nearest emergency room, or call 911.
- People who are prone to hyperventilation may want to learn deep-breathing exercises, such as those taught in yoga.

Insect Bites

Most bug bites are harmless. But some insect bites can be very dangerous, even fatal. Here's how to tell the difference between a bite that's a bother and one that's a serious medical problem. The reaction to minor bites is local, that is, confined to the area around the bite itself. Dangerous, life-threatening reactions to insect bites occur throughout the body within minutes of the sting. Reactions include the following:

- dizziness
- nausea
- difficulty breathing
- a rapid or irregular heartbeat
- confusion
- swelling or redness of the body
- swelling of the tongue, lips, or face

If a person has any of these symptoms after an insect bite, take him or her to a hospital or other health care provider, or call 911.

Seek medical help if you receive multiple stings from bees, wasps, hornets, yellow jackets, or fire ants and experience vomiting, diarrhea, headache, fever, muscle spasms, and/or light-headedness.

Call your health care provider if you're bitten by a tick or a spider. He or she can tell you if you need to seek medical care.

(For tick bites, see *Lyme Disease/Deer Ticks*, page 218.)

Allergic to Stings?

If you have ever had an allergic reaction to a bee sting, you should follow these suggestions:

- Carry a bee sting kit at all times. A health care provider can prescribe one and show you how to use it. These kits contain injectable adrenaline, also called epinephrine, which can save your life.
- Carry a card or wear a bracelet that alerts others to the condition.
- Ask your health care provider if venom desensitization injections will help. (Desensitization means a process of making you less sensitive to venom.) This series of injections can make the reaction to bee, wasp, hornet, or yellow jacket stings less serious for some allergic people.
- Call for emergency help if your condition doesn't improve in 10 minutes.

Preventing Insect Bites

- Avoid perfumes, aftershave, scented hair sprays, and scented deodorants.
- Wear insect repellent, light-colored clothing, long-sleeved tops, long pants, socks, and shoes.
- Floral patterns attract bees; so do food, beverages, and garbage cans.
- If a bee comes near you, avoid sudden movements. Stay still or move away slowly.

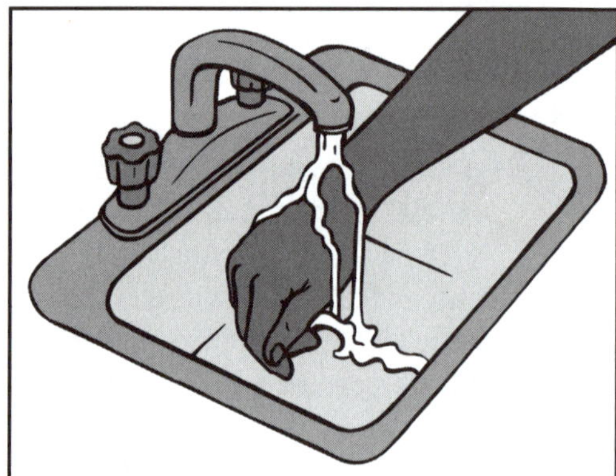

Wash bite in cool running water.

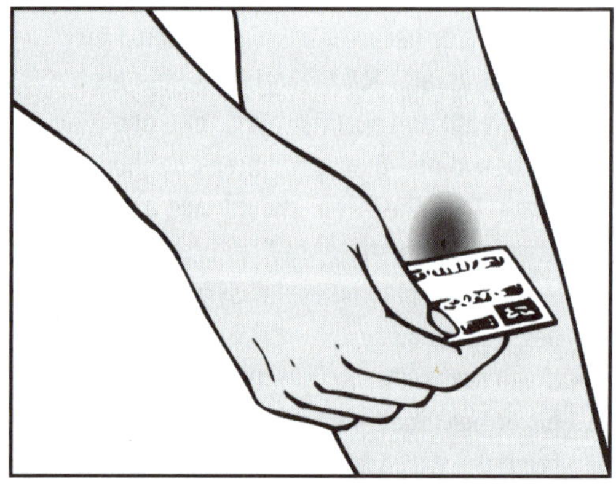

To remove a stinger, scrape it gently with a credit card, fingernail, knife blade, or other rigid object. Do not squeeze with your fingers or tweezers because this can inject more venom into the skin.

Self-Care Steps for Insect Bites

For all insect bites and stings:

- Wash the area with soap and water.
- Apply an antiseptic to prevent infection.
- Wrap a piece of ice in cloth and apply it to the area for 20 to 30 minutes.
- For pain, take acetaminophen, aspirin, or ibuprofen. (Do not give aspirin to children or teenagers. Aspirin has been linked to a severe illness called Reye's syndrome in young people.)
- For itching, use a nonprescription hydrocortisone cream, calamine lotion, soothing oatmeal baths, and/or cool compresses.

For bee, wasp, hornet, or yellow jacket stings:

- Remove the stinger by scraping it with a fingernail or the edge of a credit card. Do not squeeze or pinch; this can release more venom under the skin.

For mosquito bites:

- Apply a paste of 1 teaspoon baking soda mixed with 1 teaspoon water.

For spider bites:

- Apply ice for 20 to 30 minutes.
- Elevate the affected area.
- Seek medical care.

Decision Guide for Insect Bites

Symptoms/Signs	Action
Throbbing pain	Use self-care
Burning, redness	Use self-care
Pain that doesn't subside within 48 hours	Call provider's office
An unusual rash	Call provider's office
Signs of infection (see page 71) or fever of more than 101 degrees	Call provider's office
Bite by a brown house spider or black widow spider (most common in the South)	See provider
Nausea, vomiting, loss of bowel control and bladder control	 Seek help now
Dizziness or fainting, shortness of breath, swelling of throat, difficulty swallowing	 Emergency: call 911
Hives or swelling all over the body	 Emergency: call 911

For more about the symbols, see page 60.

Marine-Life Stings

Stings from some types of marine life are poisonous. Jellyfish and Portuguese man-of-war stings are the most common marine-life stings encountered by swimmers, divers, and beachgoers.

Symptoms of marine-life stings may include:

- skin rash
- muscle cramps
- severe burning pain
- nausea and/or vomiting
- difficulty breathing
- shock due to severe allergic reaction

Jellyfish deliver their venom through cells on their tentacles. These stings produce a mild burning and stinging sensation and produce long, whiplike marks on the skin. In most cases, you can treat these stings at home. However, if the reaction is severe, call your health care provider immediately.

Floating colonies of Portuguese men-of-war are easily spotted, but their transparent tentacles can trail invisibly for up to 60 feet. The pain and burning from these stings can be far more severe than those of jellyfish stings, and may cause breathlessness, stomach cramps, nausea, and shock.

Decision Guide for Marine-Life Stings

Symptoms/Signs	Action
Mild burning and stinging sensation	Use self-care
Severe reaction to sting	See provider
Signs of shock (see page 88)	Emergency: call 911

For more about the symbols, see page 60.

Self-Care Steps for Marine-Life Stings

- Do not raise a venomous bite above the level of the victim's heart. Do not give the victim aspirin, stimulants such as caffeine, or pain medication unless a health care provider tells you to do so.
- To slow the rate at which the venom spreads in the victim's body, do not allow the sting victim to move. If necessary, carry him or her to safety. Remove any rings or other constricting items as a precaution, in case the injured area swells. If pain persists, call the person's health care provider.
- Be careful around pieces of tentacles. They can sting even after the tentacle is removed from the body of the jellyfish. Carefully remove any embedded tentacles from the skin, using tweezers, pliers, or forceps (or with cloth wrapped around your hands). Never rub tentacles off! This will activate more stinging cells.
- If the sting is not bleeding severely, clean the wound and rinse with sea water or salt water. Marine-life stings need to be thoroughly cleaned to remove contaminants such as sand, spines, bristles, shell fragments, and coral. If the sting is bleeding heavily, cover it with a towel and apply direct pressure.
- Apply vinegar to the affected area and place ice wrapped in cloth or a cold compress on it. Be careful not to touch the area with an unprotected hand.
- After washing, apply a thick paste (heavy enough that it sticks to skin) of baking soda or a vinegar solution (1/3 cup vinegar to 2/3 cup water). Scrape off the paste after 30 minutes and reapply the solution. Do not rub the wound or rinse it with fresh water, since this may discharge inactivated cells. If a significant reaction or signs of shock occur, call 911.

Poisoning

Poison can enter the body in many ways—by swallowing, breathing, injection, or contact with skin. Poisons can include household chemicals and cleaners, drugs (both prescription and nonprescription), and any other substance that can be toxic. Some poisons interfere with the blood's ability to carry oxygen, while others burn and irritate the digestive tract and respiratory system. Suspect poisoning and act immediately if you see any of these signs:

- poisonous product in person's possession
- missing pills or poisonous product
- chemical smell on person's breath, clothing, or skin
- sudden vomiting or diarrhea without other illness
- burns around mouth
- sleepiness, lethargy, delirium, or excitable, irritable, or irrational behavior
- pale, rashy, or sweaty skin, or flushing
- gagging, choking, or coughing
- convulsions, shock, or collapse

Poison Fumes

Many substances or combinations of substances may produce fumes that can be toxic in a closed area (see *Carbon Monoxide Poisoning*, page 66).

To help a person who has succumbed to breathing poison gas, you must first remove him or her from the area. Take a few deep breaths of fresh air, then hold your breath before entering the area. If possible, quickly shut off any open source of fumes. Do not flip a switch or light a match; either action could produce a spark or a flame and cause an explosion. Drag or pull the victim to fresh air.

Self-Care Steps for Poisoning

Poisoning is life-threatening. If you suspect poisoning, even if there are no symptoms, immediately call 911, your local poison control center, the hospital emergency room, or your health care provider. Be prepared to provide the following details:

- information from the label of the substance container (keep the original container)
- the victim's age
- the name of the poison and how much was swallowed
- the time poison was swallowed
- whether the victim has vomited
- how long it will take to get the victim to a hospital

If the victim is unconscious, keep the airway open. Be prepared to begin artificial respiration if necessary (see *CPR for Adults and Children Ages 8 and Older,* page 56, or *CPR for Children Under 8 Years Old,* page 59). Do not induce vomiting unless a medical professional tells you to do so.

If you have been told to induce vomiting, use syrup of ipecac, if available. Do not attempt to give ipecac to a victim who is not alert enough to swallow it. Follow the directions on the label. Save a sample of vomit and the poison container for analysis at the hospital if necessary.

For poison fumes:
Check breathing and pulse (see *CPR for Adults and Children Ages 8 and Older,* page 56, or *CPR for Children Under 8 Years Old,* page 59). If the victim is not breathing, have someone call 911, and begin CPR. Continue until medical help arrives. If the victim is conscious and breathing, cover him or her with a blanket and check on breathing until help arrives.

Shock

Shock is a life-threatening condition that requires immediate medical treatment. Shock occurs when the heart and blood vessels can't send enough oxygen to every part of the body. Without oxygen, the brain, heart, kidneys, and other organs will slow down and may ultimately stop working.

Any serious injury or illness such as blood loss, heart failure, severe infection, burns, or breathing trouble can result in shock. Shock does not improve on its own, but typically goes from bad to worse. Without treatment, a shock victim will die.

A person in shock may experience the following symptoms:

- shallow breathing
- rapid and weak pulse
- nausea and vomiting
- pale, clammy skin
- shivering and coldness in limbs
- confusion
- bluish tint to skin

Self-Care Steps for Shock

- Call 911 and say that you have a medical emergency. People in shock need to go to an emergency room as soon as possible. The following suggestions for action are things you can do until the ambulance arrives.
- If you suspect that the victim has neck or back injuries, see steps at right. Try to find the cause of shock and check for a medical alert tag or card. Make sure the victim has an open airway and is breathing. If necessary, begin rescue breathing or CPR (see *CPR for Adults and Children Ages 8 and Older,* page 56, or *CPR for Children Under 8 Years Old,* page 59).
- Stop any bleeding. Lay the victim flat and raise his or her feet 8 to 12 inches, using any available materials for support. Do not raise the person's feet if you suspect any head, neck, back, or leg injuries or if he or she is having trouble breathing. Do not place pillows under the victim's head.

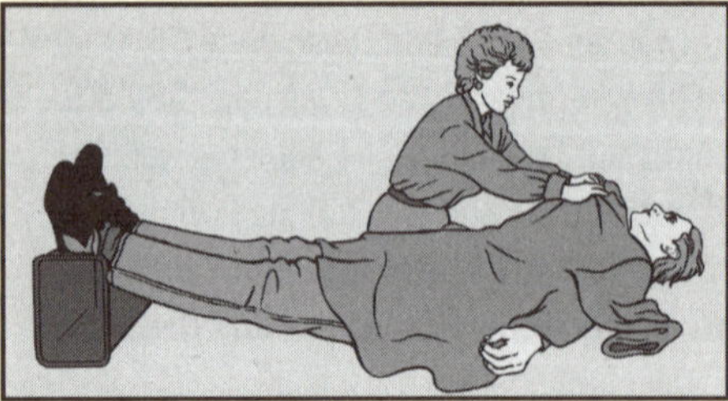

- Give first aid for the underlying illness or injury, if possible. Cover the victim with a blanket or coat for warmth. Do not apply direct heat. If the victim drools or vomits, turn the head to one side so fluids can drain. Check the victim's breathing and pulse until medical help arrives.

For a shock victim with possible spinal injury:

- Do not move a shock victim who may have a neck or back injury. Keep the victim in the same position unless he or she is in immediate danger. Cover the victim with a coat or blanket for warmth. Do not apply direct heat.
- Try to find the cause of shock and see if the person has a medical alert tag or card. Make sure the victim has an open airway and is breathing. If necessary, begin rescue breathing or CPR (see *CPR for Adults and Children Ages 8 and Older,* page 56, or *CPR for Children Under 8 Years Old,* page 59).
- If the victim vomits or drools, protect the airway by rolling the victim onto one side while carefully supporting head and neck. Get others to help gently roll the victim. Begin CPR if needed. Continue to check the victim's breathing and pulse until medical help arrives.

Smashed Finger

Smashing a finger in a car door or with a hammer is a common and extremely painful injury. However, if only the end of the finger has been hurt, it may be possible to treat the finger at home.

The nail may be partially pulled off during the accident. Do not remove the nail, but see your health care provider, who may be able to fix it. Blood may pool under the nail of the smashed finger, causing severe throbbing pain. Your provider can relieve this pressure by draining the blue-black blood that is visible through the nail. If the blood is under more than one third of the nail, see your provider.

Self-Care Steps for Smashed Finger

- If the victim can move the smashed finger easily and the injury does not involve the nailbed (the portion of the finger covered by the nail), apply an ice pack to reduce swelling, and use acetaminophen or a similar nonprescription pain reliever.
- If the finger is bleeding, apply pressure on the wound and elevate it above the heart until bleeding stops. Wash the wound with soap and water, and watch for signs of infection (see *Decision Guide for Signs of Infection,* page 71). If you suspect a bone fracture or if the smashed finger involves a deep or serious cut, seek medical attention immediately.

Decision Guide for Smashed Finger

Symptoms/Signs	Action
Minor discomfort	 Use self-care
Suspected bone fracture (see *Fractures,* page 76)	 Call provider's office
Numbness in the finger	 See provider
Nail completely pulled off (bring nail to health care provider)	 See provider
Finger badly cut (see *Cuts, Scrapes, and Wounds,* page 69)	 Seek help now
Unable to move finger normally	 Seek help now

For more about the symbols, see page 60.

Snakebites

Bites from poisonous snakes are rarely fatal when medical assistance is provided quickly. If you are bitten by a snake, try to kill it without deforming its head and bring it with you when you seek medical attention. If you are unable to kill the snake, remember what it looked like.

Preventing Snakebites

- Your best defense is to leave snakes alone.
- Learn to identify snakes in your area, and find out if any are poisonous.
- When hiking, wear boots and long pants to protect your feet and ankles.
- Walk on cleared paths and carry a walking stick.
- Never reach into a hole or cave without looking into it first. Be cautious when looking.
- Stop walking if you see a snake. Quickly move away at least 20 feet back along the path you just walked. Watch for other snakes in the area.

Self-Care Steps for Nonpoisonous Snakebites

- Keep the bite below the level of the heart.
- Clean the area thoroughly with soap and water, and place a bandage over the wound.
- Seek medical help promptly.

Self-Care Steps for Poisonous Snakebites

- Don't panic! Venom will spread more rapidly through the body if the victim runs or becomes excited. Before giving first aid, identify the snake. Do not use ice on the snakebite; this may result in extensive tissue damage.
- If the bite involves a coral snake, elevate and immobilize the bitten area and go to the nearest emergency facility.
- If the bite involves a poisonous snake that is not a coral snake, within 30 minutes tie a light tourniquet (a constricting band of any sort) 3 to 4 inches above the bite, between the bite and the torso. Do not cut off circulation. You should be able to slip a finger beneath the band.
- Avoid manipulation of the bitten area and do not consume alcohol or stimulants. Do not use a snakebite kit to suction venom unless medical treatment is more than an hour away. If you need to use the kit, make an incision over the bite, 1/4 inch long by 1/8 inch deep, being careful not to cut deeper than the skin. Place suction cups over the wound and draw out body fluids containing venom. Do not suction by mouth.

Section Four

Self-Care for Common Problems

Even if you have the best health care provider in the world, you probably don't love to visit him or her. It's no fun being sick, and it's inconvenient and often uncomfortable to go to a provider's office for treatment. That's why it is important to know when you or a family member has symptoms that can be cared for at home and when symptoms are serious enough to go see your health care provider.

Just knowing how to care for yourself will help you make better choices about when you need to see your provider. For serious problems, you will be more likely to get care when you need it. For problems that do not require a visit to see your provider, educated patients are more likely to use the right home remedies.

To help you make decisions about how to relieve symptoms, we offer self-care tips whenever possible. For some health problems, only a few self-care remedies are suggested. This is because we try to recommend only remedies that have been proven effective.

For a quick review of symptoms, check the Decision Guide at the end of each medical topic. You will see that for many symptoms, we recommend that you call your health care provider's office. In many cases, your provider needs to consider your medical history along with your current health risks and health status to decide whether your symptoms warrant a visit. A lot of this can be done over the phone, saving you the time of a trip to the office.

Remember, these self-care guidelines are not intended as a substitute for your health care provider's advice. If you are not sure whether these guidelines apply to you, or if your symptoms do not seem to improve with self-care, call your provider's office. You also need to consider your medical history and health to decide whether self-care is a good idea given your symptoms.

Equipping Your Home for Self-Care

Also see *Stocking Your Own First-Aid Kit*, page 55.

Stocking your home with some special tools and equipment is the first step in handling health problems successfully. Some of these tools prepare you for treating minor health problems at home. Others give you the information you'll need to decide whether you need to see your health care provider. Here are some basic home medical supplies to keep on hand.

- other medical and self-care reference books, including ones on specific topics such as asthma, diabetes, women, or children
- thermometer
- a heating pad for treating sore or tense muscles
- an assortment of adhesive bandages, including butterfly-shaped bandages for closing cuts
- sterile gauze pads for cleaning cuts and scrapes and covering larger wounds
- paper tape (which pulls off painlessly) for holding gauze pads in place
- an elastic bandage for wrapping sprained ankles or wrists or for supporting and putting pressure on injured, swollen, or sore knees
- a cold-mist vaporizer for relieving congestion of colds and coughs (when using a vaporizer, clean it daily to avoid spreading germs)
- a penlight for examining sore throats
- two pairs of tweezers: a blunt-tipped pair for tasks such as removing an object from a child's nose, and a pair with pointed ends for removing splinters
- an ice pack, either the type that holds ice cubes or the newer cold/hot packs that you can keep in the freezer

Stomach, Digestive, and Urinary Health

This section describes common problems related to your vital digestive and urinary organs and suggests how to take care of nonurgent health problems at home.

Abdominal Pain

We all know the kind of abdominal pain caused by an occasional attack of vomiting, diarrhea, or "stomach flu." Abdominal pain can also point to indigestion, gallbladder disease, appendicitis, ulcers, inflammatory bowel disease, irritable bowel syndrome, colon cancer, and many other problems. Minor stomach pain in adults is usually from common disturbances like emotional distress, overeating, or the flu (for stomach pain in children, see the box on page 94).

The type and location of pain often gives a clue to its cause. Sharp pain (like heartburn) in the upper middle part of your stomach could be an ulcer. Sharp pain under the right rib cage that's worse after eating points to gallbladder disease. Diverticulitis,

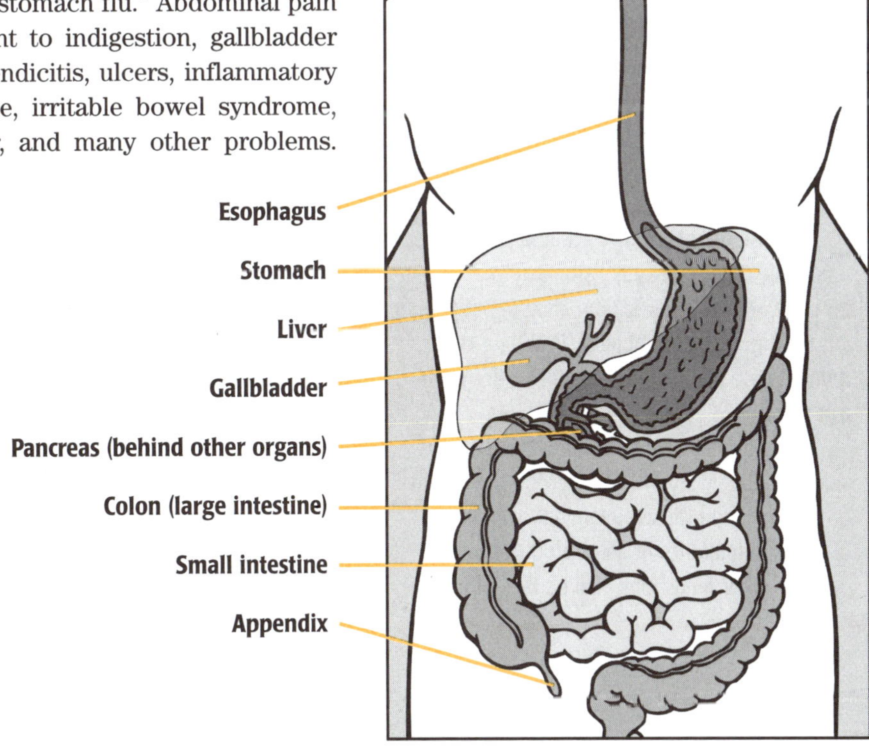

Abdominal Pain

Self-Care Steps for Mild Abdominal Pain

- Eat bland foods, and not spicy ones.
- Use acetaminophen for pain relief. Children and teenagers should not be given aspirin because of the risk of Reye's syndrome, a rare but potentially fatal disease.
- Avoid irritants such as alcohol, nicotine, caffeine, aspirin, and ibuprofen.
- Take warm baths, or apply a warm water bottle to the abdominal area for comfort.
- If you experience the following symptoms, call your health care provider. You could have appendicitis.
  - Pain that starts at the navel and moves to the lower right side of the abdomen
  - Nausea, vomiting, or loss of appetite
  - Tenderness in the lower right side of abdomen
  - Inability to walk upright
  - Fever ranging from 100 to 102 degrees

Special Concerns for Children

Most stomach upsets in children are caused by overeating or constipation. Children will often complain of a stomachache right before getting a cold, sore throat, or the flu.

Because the digestive tract is sensitive to emotions, children may get stomachaches when they are anxious. Talk to your child about the worries he or she might have. Putting a child's mind at ease may help relieve his or her stomach pains.

When a child's stomach hurts, always consider diet. Some studies say that too much fruit or fruit juice can cause abdominal cramps and diarrhea. Intolerance of dairy products, wheat, eggs, or other foods may also be the culprit.

Decision Guide for Abdominal Pain

Symptoms/Signs	Action
Mild pain that comes and goes for less than 4 weeks	 Use self-care
Pain that comes and goes for more than 4 weeks	  Call provider's office
Sudden abdominal pain, constipation, loss of appetite, or loss of energy	 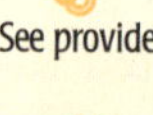 See provider
Sudden, severe pain that worsens over a few hours	 See provider
Abdominal pain and fever; jaundice; pale, pasty stools; or dark urine	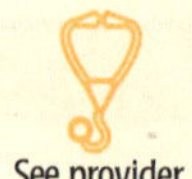 See provider
Very bad, constant abdominal pain after an injury or sudden black, tarry stools (see page 95)	 Seek help now
Symptoms of appendicitis (see above)	 Seek help now
Symptoms of ectopic pregnancy	 Seek help now
Abdominal pain and sudden, bright red rectal bleeding or vomiting of blood or a substance that looks like coffee grounds	 Seek help now

For more about the symbols, see page 60.

a disorder of the intestine, often causes pain in the lower left-hand side of the abdomen. Pain from bleeding or infection is often felt throughout the abdomen.

What to do. In most cases, staying away from certain foods is enough to take care of mild stomachaches. However, if you have symptoms that last more than four weeks, severe stomach pains with chills and cold, clammy skin, a sudden change in bowel habits, diarrhea that wakes you up at night, or other symptoms that may indicate a more serious condition (see *Decision Guide for Abdominal Pain*, page 94), call your health care provider.

Black or Bloody Stools

Stools that look tarry, black, or bloody can be caused by drugs, hemorrhoids, bleeding ulcers, colon cancer, or other significant bowel disorders. Black or tarry stools may mean bleeding in the upper gastrointestinal tract. Large amounts of iron or iron-rich foods in your diet such as spinach, and stomach medications containing bismuth compounds can also cause stools to temporarily turn black.

Hemorrhoids. These are swollen blood vessels in the anal canal and lower rectum, and are a common cause of pain, itching, and rectal bleeding, especially during bowel movements. People with hemorrhoids may notice bright red blood on the toilet tissue or on the stool itself. Hemorrhoids can usually be treated with self-care at home.

Ulcerative colitis. Frequent, mucus-covered, bloody diarrhea accompanied by fever and weight loss can be caused by an intestinal disorder called ulcerative colitis. This serious condition must be treated by a physician.

Colon cancer. Blood in the stool can be a symptom of colon cancer. This form of cancer may also cause changes in bowel movements, lower abdominal pain, and thin, pencillike stools. When diagnosed and treated early, colon cancer is often curable (see *Colon Cancer*, page 51).

Self-Care Steps for Hemorrhoids

To relieve hemorrhoid symptoms:

- Sit in warm water for 15 minutes a few times daily to ease swelling.
- Apply a cold pack to ease swelling.
- Wipe area with soft, moistened toilet paper to prevent irritation.
- Ease soreness by applying petroleum jelly or zinc oxide ointment to the affected area.

To avoid constipation that can irritate hemorrhoids:

- Go to the bathroom when nature calls, to avoid straining later.
- Don't strain. Straining will only create more pressure.
- Avoid prolonged sitting, especially on the commode.
- Gradually increase the amount of fiber you eat (see page 97).
- Use a bulk-forming stool softener containing methylcellulose psyllium. Avoid other types of laxatives, which can cause diarrhea.
- Talk with your doctor about any medications you take regularly; some may cause constipation.
- Drink plenty of fluids.
- Get regular exercise.

Decision Guide for Black or Bloody Stools

Symptoms/Signs	Action
Symptoms of hemorrhoids (see page 95)	Use self-care
Symptoms that last more than 24 hours	Call provider's office
Hemorrhoids suspected but not diagnosed	See provider
Black, tarry stools unrelated to food or medicine	Seek help now
Bright red rectal bleeding and abdominal pain (see page 95), fever, changes in bowel habits, recent weight loss, bleeding problems or gastrointestinal bleeding, history of colon problems such as Crohn's disease, irritable bowel syndrome, or colitis	Seek help now
Blood in the stool of a person taking a blood thinner	Seek help now
Current bleeding ulcer or prior ulcer, or person is taking aspirin or NSAIDs	Seek help now
Sudden onset of heavy, continuous, bright red rectal bleeding or black, tarry stools and dizziness; lightheadedness; rapid pulse; cool, clammy skin	Emergency: call 911

For more about the symbols, see page 60.

What to do. The first thing to do is to figure out what's making you have black or bloody stools. If you've ruled out causes such as hemorrhoids or overeating certain foods, call your health care provider. If your problem is hemorrhoids, you can often take care of this condition by yourself at home with a few simple self-care steps. Avoid nonsteroidal anti-inflammatory drugs (NSAIDS) and pain relievers, including ibuprofen, naproxen sodium, and aspirin. They may cause intestinal irritation and bleeding.

Constipation

Constipation—the passage of hard, dry, or infrequent stools—is usually easy to cure naturally. Constipation is often the result of ignoring your body's signals to move your bowels. The large intestine draws water from stools, so the longer stools are present, the more water the large intestine will absorb, making the stools harder and more difficult to pass.

The myth that one should have a bowel movement every day is just that: a myth. Each person has a schedule. How often doesn't matter (unless the frequency has changed a lot); it is the consistency of the stool, or the discomfort that tells you when you're constipated.

Children sometimes become constipated, although their parents are usually more worried about it than the children. Stress triggered by toilet training can lead to constipation. Older adults, who may become less active as they age, may also complain of constipation.

Constipation sometimes signals a more serious underlying problem. Alternating

Self-Care Steps for Constipation

- If you have no other symptoms, relax and wait it out. It's not unusual for bowel movement frequencies and consistencies to vary from time to time.
- Learn to heed the call. Your body will signal you when it's ready for a bowel movement. When you discover the natural time during the day for you to have a bowel movement, try to set aside that time each day. Relax while sitting on the toilet.
- Change your diet. Increase your liquid intake; plain water and fruit juices are best. Prune juice is especially good for relieving constipation. Add fresh fruits and vegetables and whole-grain breads to your diet.
- Exercise more. Exercise not only helps your bowels move more freely, it helps reduce the stress that may make you temporarily constipated.
- Use a bulk-forming stool softener containing methylcellulose psyllium. Avoid other types of laxatives, which can cause diarrhea.
- Once your bowel movements have returned to normal, adjust your diet and exercise, and use stress reduction techniques to stay regular.

Decision Guide for Constipation

Symptoms/Signs	Action
Constipation without other symptoms	Use self-care
Constipation and abdominal pain (see page 93); cramps, gas, or vomiting (see page 113); fever, or loss of appetite	Call provider's office
Pencil-thin stools, which may suggest a bowel tumor	Call provider's office
Suspicion that a drug is causing constipation (antacids, antidepressants, antihistamines, antihypertensives, diuretics, and narcotics can cause constipation)	Call provider's office
No relief, or discomfort increases after a week of self-care	Call provider's office
Bowel movement that becomes impacted in the rectum; only mucus and fluids will pass	See provider

For more about the symbols, see page 60.

diarrhea and constipation may be due to an irritable colon. Diverticulitis, an inflammation of small pockets in the colon wall, causes alternating diarrhea and constipation, fever, and pain in the lower left abdomen.

What to do. A change in diet can help get your bowels back on course. Fresh fruits and vegetables have a natural laxative action and also provide fiber, which draws water to the stool. Foods such as bran, celery, and whole-wheat breads also add fiber. Extra fluids are also a good idea, particularly plain water and fruit juices. Replace carbonated beverages and coffee with plain water. Exercise can also help stimulate the bowel. Walking is an excellent choice.

You can use mild laxatives (such as milk of magnesia) or enemas to relieve temporary symptoms of constipation, but do not use them often as an aid to regular bowel movements. Fiber supplements may also help ease symptoms.

Diarrhea

Diarrhea is frequent, loose or watery stools, often with abdominal cramps, vomiting, or fever. Stools move so quickly through the intestines that the body is unable to absorb the water in them. Because of this loss of fluid, diarrhea can lead to dehydration.

Diarrhea is always unpleasant, but it's usually not a major health concern for healthy adults. It can seriously weaken young children and older people, however, and may even require hospitalization.

Diarrhea can be caused by bacteria, viruses, emotional upset, stress, certain drugs, and some chronic bowel diseases. With bacterial infections of the colon, however, diarrhea is usually more severe, lasting longer than usual. Prolonged diarrhea may also be a symptom of conditions such as giardiasis (if you have been traveling), amebic dysentery, Crohn's disease, ulcerative colitis, or food intolerances.

What to do. Most diarrhea goes away on its own or with home care within two days. When a diet of clear liquids doesn't help, contact your health care provider. He or she may prescribe a prescription drug that will slow down bowel activity. These drugs are not recommended for children. Your provider will also be able to determine whether your diarrhea is caused by a serious underlying condition.

Diarrhea in Children

Diarrhea is common in infants and young children because their digestive systems are still developing. Diarrhea in children most often goes away on its own. A parent's

Preventive Steps

- Wash your hands after you use the toilet or diaper a baby and before eating or preparing food. This is an important way to prevent the spread of organisms that can cause diarrhea.
- Unpasteurized dairy products and undercooked fish, poultry, eggs, and meat—especially hamburger—can also have bacteria that can cause diarrhea and other gastrointestinal problems. Always cook foods thoroughly. Wash cutting boards, utensils, and hands that have touched uncooked meat products in warm, soapy water. Eat only pasteurized dairy products. Be sure to keep hot foods hot and cold foods cold. Harmful bacteria can grow in foods left at room temperature for too long.
- If you have diarrhea, don't prepare food for others at home unless you wash your hands thoroughly. Do not work as a waiter, waitress, cook, or in any food-handling position until your diarrhea and upset stomach are gone and you know you are not contagious.
- Travelers often get diarrhea. About half the North Americans and Northern Europeans who travel to less developed areas of the world will have some type of diarrhea during their trip, or just after.
- Travelers to foreign countries should avoid drinking or cooking with unpurified water. You can purify water by boiling it for 15 to 20 minutes or by adding iodine or chlorine drops or tablets. It's very important to follow product directions exactly when using water-purifying products. Travelers should also avoid fresh fruits and vegetables unless the foods have been thoroughly washed in purified water or can be peeled. Be wary of foods such as melons, which are often injected with water (most likely contaminated) to increase their weight.

job is to closely watch the child with diarrhea and to see that the child gets enough liquids, the right diet, and lots of tender loving care.

As with adults, the major concern for children with diarrhea is dehydration. Because of their smaller body size, children can become dehydrated more rapidly than adults. Be alert to the following signs of dehydration:

- no urination (more than 8 hours without urinating for children under 1 year old; more than 12 hours without urinating for children 1 year and older)

Decision Guide for Diarrhea in Children

Symptoms/Signs	Action
3 or more stools per day for more than 1 week, with no other symptoms	 Call provider's office
Diarrhea with fever over 100.4 degrees for more than 48 hours	 See provider
8 or more stools per day over 48 hours, with no improvement after dietary changes	 See provider
Intermittent abdominal pain and cramps for more than 24 hours	 See provider
Signs of dehydration (see above and page 101)	 Seek help now
Diarrhea and breathing difficulty; severe and constant abdominal pain or cramps; blood in stools; more than 1 stool per hour; child acting very sick	 Seek help now

For more about the symbols, see page 60.

Decision Guide for Diarrhea in Adults

Symptoms/Signs	Action
Diarrhea that lasts less than 48 hours, with mild cramping that's relieved by bowel movements	 Use self-care
Diarrhea associated with international travel; ingestion of water from lakes, streams, or wells; or blood streaking on toilet paper and no history of hemorrhoids	 Call provider's office
Diarrhea for more than 1 week	 Call provider's office
Diarrhea in a person who is elderly or has a chronic illness, such as diabetes	 See provider
Persistent mucus or blood in stool	 Seek help now
Intermittent abdominal pain or cramps that last 24 hours or more	 Seek help now
Temperature over 101 degrees 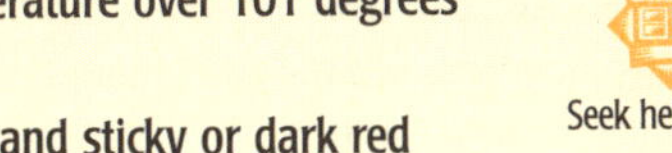	 Seek help now
Black and sticky or dark red stools (see page 95), brief loss of consciousness, dizziness, sweatiness, fast heart rate	 Seek help now
Diarrhea associated with severe, constant abdominal pain (see page 93) for more than 2 hours	 Seek help now
Diarrhea associated with signs of dehydration (see above and page 101)	 Seek help now
Diarrhea associated with breathing difficulty	 Seek help now

Self-Care Steps for Diarrhea in Adults

- Drink room-temperature liquids.
- Avoid alcohol, smoking, caffeine, milk, and fruit juice.
- Don't eat if your stomach feels very upset or crampy.
- Drink only clear liquids such as water, flat soda (such as ginger ale—but not diet soda), clear chicken or beef broth, or an oral rehydration solution. Sip a few ounces a bit at a time throughout the day.
- Suck ice chips if you cannot keep down other liquids.
- When your appetite returns but diarrhea continues, eat ripe bananas, rice, applesauce, white toast, cooked cereal, potatoes, chicken, turkey, and cooked carrots.
- Avoid fresh fruits, green vegetables, alcohol, greasy or fatty foods (cheeseburgers, bacon), and highly seasoned and spicy foods until diarrhea is gone.
- Take over-the-counter antidiarrheal medications, following the product instructions. Note that products containing bismuth salicylate may temporarily darken the stools or tongue.
- Call your health care provider if you believe the diarrhea could be caused by a drug. Diarrhea is a common side effect of the following drugs: nonsteroidal anti-inflammatory drugs, antibiotics, gold compounds, and some antidepressants (Prozac, Zoloft, and Paxil).

Self-Care Steps for Diarrhea in Children

- Make sure children get lots of fluids. Avoid fruit juices and highly colored drinks (food dyes may make the problem worse). Infants may have breast milk or soy formula. Also offer water and electrolyte solutions sold over the counter at your pharmacy. Older children can have flat, clear carbonated beverages, such as ginger ale. Give small amounts of fluids every 30 minutes or so.
- If your child doesn't have an appetite, don't encourage him or her to eat solid foods. When your child's appetite returns, offer small amounts of starchy, easily digested foods such as white rice, bread, and crackers; potatoes; ripe bananas; cooked carrots, squash, or sweet potatoes; noodles; bland soups such as chicken rice or chicken noodle; or turkey or chicken, cooked without the skin.
- Don't give products containing bismuth salicylate to children or teenagers. It contains an ingredient that has been linked to a serious condition in children called Reye's syndrome.
- Diarrhea can be very hard on the tender skin of young children, especially those still in diapers. To protect the skin, change diapers soon after each stool. Wash the bottom with plain water or sit the child in a tub with a few inches of warm water (a sitz bath). You don't need to use soap, but if you do, use mild soap in small amounts and rinse it off well.
  - To clean the skin, use a soft washcloth and plain water or a commercial diaper wipe that has been rinsed out well with water. Dry the area completely by patting with a soft cloth or towel or using a blow dryer on the low/cool setting.
  - A generous layer of petroleum jelly or other ointment will help protect the skin. Since cloth diapers are more gentle on the skin than disposables, consider switching to cloth diapers or lining disposable diapers with cloth ones during prolonged bouts with diarrhea.

- dry mouth
- absence of tears/dry eyes
- dizziness or disorientation
- dry skin that doesn't spring back after being touched
- dark circles around eyes
- fever

Gallstones

The gallbladder is a small organ under the liver that stores bile, the substance the liver secretes to help digest fats in the small intestine. Occasionally, lumps of solid material can form in the gallbladder or the ducts connecting the gallbladder with the liver. These lumps are called gallstones, and are often largely made up of cholesterol.

Gallstones are more prevalent in women, particularly those who are overweight or have had several children. Some birth control pills may also increase the risk of gallbladder disease in women younger than 29 who have taken the pill for less than 5 years. About 4 out of 5 people with gallstones have no symptoms. However, gallstones can cause a great deal of pain if they become lodged in the duct between the gallbladder and liver. Symptoms include biliary colic (severe, steady pain in the upper right abdomen or between the shoulder blades that is not relieved by changing position or passing gas). Rarely, gallstones can lead to inflammation of the gallbladder (cholecystitis) and obstruction of the bile duct, which can cause jaundice.

What to do. There are three treatment methods for gallstones: watchful waiting, nonsurgical treatment, and surgery. In watchful waiting, the health care provider will not take steps to treat the gallstones but instead will carefully monitor your health to see if more severe complications develop. Nonsurgical treatment involves dissolving the gallstones with medications (either taken by mouth or injected into the gallbladder) or even using sound waves to break the gallstones down and allow them to pass into the small intestine. With surgery, or cholecystectomy, the gallbladder is removed.

Call your health care provider if you experience biliary colic. He or she can determine whether you have gallstones by using ultrasound scanning, a diagnostic method that creates an image of the inside of the body by using sound waves.

Heartburn

Heartburn has nothing to do with your heart. When you eat, the sphincter muscle at the lower end of your esophagus relaxes and opens to admit food to your stomach.

Decision Guide for Heartburn

Symptoms/Signs	Action
No relief after 2 weeks of self-care	Call provider's office
Heartburn that may be caused by a drug you are taking	Call provider's office
Heartburn with symptoms of heart attack (see page 136); if you are under 35 with a low risk of having a heart attack, call your health care provider first. You could be having a panic attack.	Call provider's office

For more about the symbols, see page 60.

The sphincter then closes to prevent stomach acid from washing back up the esophagus. Heartburn occurs when this sphincter doesn't close completely. Acid and bile from the stomach come back up the esophagus, causing a burning sensation. Nearly everyone has heartburn once in a while.

What to do. There are many things you can do to reduce or relieve the symptoms of heartburn. The self-care steps below will help cut down acid levels in your stomach, reduce pressure on your stomach or esophagus, and neutralize the effects of acid. Although heartburn can be treated easily with changes in diet and over-the-counter drugs, it may also be a symptom of more serious problems. Heartburn that won't go away needs medical attention because it may be a sign of ulcers or other gastrointestinal problems.

Self-Care Steps for Heartburn

- Don't smoke.
- Don't overeat. Try eating smaller meals, more often. Don't eat within a few hours of going to bed.
- Make mealtimes relaxed. Eat slowly and chew thoroughly.
- Lose weight if you're overweight. That will reduce the pressure on the esophagus.
- Loosen or remove tight-fitting clothes when you eat.
- Don't lie down immediately after eating.
- Sleep with the head of your bed elevated.
- Avoid alcohol, caffeine, decaffeinated coffee, and any other drinks or foods that regularly give you heartburn.
- Avoid aspirin, ibuprofen, naproxen sodium, and other pain-relieving medications other than acetaminophen.
- If needed, use over-the-counter antacids to relieve heartburn symptoms.
- Several prescription heartburn medications that work by reducing the amount of acid in the stomach have been approved for over-the-counter sales. Talk to your doctor before trying any of these drugs if you are currently taking theophylline (for asthma), warfarin (for blood-thinning) or phenytoin (for seizures).

Hepatitis

Hepatitis, or inflammation of the liver, is most often caused by one of several viruses. This disease often first shows itself with flulike symptoms: fatigue, headache, loss of appetite, nausea, or vomiting, and a low-grade fever (below 101 degrees). As symptoms get worse, jaundice (a yellow color to the skin and the whites of the eyes), brown urine and pale stools, and pain or pressure on the right side below the ribs may be present. In some cases, however, people with hepatitis have no symptoms at all. There are three main types of hepatitis.

Hepatitis A

The hepatitis A virus is spread through food, water, eating utensils, toys, and other objects that have been contaminated by feces, usually due to dirty hands. Prevention of hepatitis A is the main reason restaurant employees and child care workers are required to wash their hands after using the washroom or changing babies' diapers.

After exposure to the virus, symptoms do not usually appear for two to six weeks. During this time, the exposed person is contagious. Most symptoms usually go away within several days or a few weeks, but tiredness can continue for a few months as the liver continues to heal. Complete recovery takes a few months. Hepatitis A does not usually damage the liver permanently. However, serious and sometimes fatal complications can occur.

All people who have had close contact with someone who has hepatitis A should get a shot of gamma globulin to prevent or reduce the symptoms of hepatitis A. Your health care provider may also give you a gamma globulin shot if you are going abroad. A vaccine to protect against hepatitis A is now used in some parts of Europe and is expected to be approved soon in the United States.

Hepatitis B

Hepatitis B is a more serious form of viral hepatitis. About 10 percent of people with hepatitis B will develop chronic hepatitis, a long-term inflammation of the liver that in some cases causes more extensive liver damage and even cirrhosis. Hepatitis B can be prevented with a vaccine (see *Preventive Care Recommendations*, on page 104).

Hepatitis B spreads mainly through blood and body fluids, sexual contact, and contaminated needles used with intravenous drugs. It can also be spread by contaminated needles used for tattooing, acupuncture, or ear piercing. In years past, transfusions of contaminated blood frequently transmitted the hepatitis B virus. But since 1972, screening of donated blood has almost wiped out the risk of getting the virus from transfusions or receiving blood or blood products.

Symptoms of hepatitis B are basically the same as those of other forms of hepatitis, but they appear later, may last longer, and may be worse. Symptoms can take up to two to three months to develop. During this time, hepatitis B is most contagious. A hepatitis B vaccination series before exposure can prevent the illness. Hepatitis B immunizations given shortly after exposure may prevent the disease from developing.

Hepatitis C

Hepatitis C, a third form of viral hepatitis, spreads mainly through blood transfusions and through contaminated needles used

Decision Guide for Hepatitis

Symptoms/Signs	Action
Headache, low-grade fever, loss of appetite, nausea or vomiting, fatigue for more than 3 to 5 days	Use self-care
Suspected exposure to hepatitis	Call provider's office
Symptoms persist despite rest and self-care	Call provider's office
Jaundice (see page 102)	See provider
Dark urine and light stools	See provider
Severe symptoms, especially if the person is unable to eat or drink*	See provider

*A brief hospitalization of a few days may be needed if the person is unable to get adequate nutrition or hydration because of nausea and vomiting, but a person with viral hepatitis can usually be cared for at home.

For more about the symbols, see page 60.

with intravenous drugs. It can also spread through sexual contact or by contaminated needles used for tattooing, acupuncture, or ear piercing. Symptoms usually appear 1 to 10 weeks after exposure. Symptoms are often less severe than they are for hepatitis A and B, and jaundice may not develop. Like hepatitis B, hepatitis C can lead to chronic hepatitis.

Until recently, about 2 percent of those who received blood transfusions got hepatitis C. However, a screening test is now available for detecting hepatitis C in donated blood.

What to do. There is no specific treatment for hepatitis, aside from resting and eating well while waiting for your symptoms to go away. However, you can do several things to get well and avoid spreading the disease to others.

See your health care provider if you think you may have hepatitis. He or she will give you a blood test to determine whether you have hepatitis, and which type of hepatitis you might have. Then as you recover, your provider can monitor the course of the disease. Unless hepatitis is ruled out, assume that your body fluids and stools are contagious. Drinking too much alcohol habitually may predispose you to, or worsen, any form of hepatitis. It can also slow the recovery process.

Preventive Steps for Hepatitis

Preventing Hepatitis A:

- Wash your hands after using the bathroom.
- If you travel to an area where hepatitis A is widespread or sanitation is questionable, boil water before drinking it and peel fruits and vegetables before eating them.

Preventing Hepatitis B and Hepatitis C:

- Practice safe sex.
- Do not share razors, needles, toothbrushes, and nail clippers.
- Get a hepatitis B vaccination if you are at risk.

Self-Care Steps for Hepatitis

- Get plenty of rest.
- Eat well. Hepatitis interferes with the liver's ability to help break down food. Therefore, it is very important to eat enough easily digestible food to get enough calories. Fatty food is often poorly tolerated. Try eating mostly carbohydrates (such as grains and fruits).
- Check in with your health care provider regularly. He or she may run blood tests for several months to see if your liver is recovering and whether the inflammation is continuing.
- Avoid alcohol and drugs that irritate the liver. While you are ill and recovering, alcohol, birth control pills, tranquilizers, some antibiotics, antidepressants, and even acetaminophen can also irritate the liver. Until you are fully recovered, check with your health care provider or pharmacist before taking any drugs.
- Wash your hands after using the bathroom and before handling food.
- Talk with your health care provider about having a hepatitis B vaccination. Many providers believe that everyone should have a vaccination for hepatitis B. Current recommendations are for all children to have this vaccine routinely. Risk factors for hepatitis B include being sexually active outside of a mutually monogamous relationship, having the human immunodeficiency virus (HIV), being an intravenous drug user, being a sexually active gay male, needing dialysis, or being a health care or dental professional.

Hernias

A hernia occurs when part of an internal organ protrudes through the muscle that usually surrounds it. The most common types of hernias are hiatal and inguinal.

Hiatal hernias. These hernias occur when the stomach bulges back through the diaphragm (the muscle that separates the chest cavity from the abdominal cavity) into the esophagus. These hernias are usually not painful by themselves. However, food or acid may pass back into the esophagus, causing heartburn, indigestion, chest pains, hiccuping, and belching after meals. Hiatal hernias are more common in overweight people and in people who smoke.

Inguinal, or groin hernias. These hernias are caused by a part of the intestine ballooning into the muscles of the groin. These hernias are common in older adults as a result of strained or weak abdominal muscles. Inguinal hernias are more common in men than in women. Hernia symptoms and pain may start slowly, or one day you may feel that something isn't quite right. Symptoms include:

- a gurgling feeling
- aches and pain in the abdomen that start and stop
- a feeling of pressure or weakness in the groin
- visible bulges slightly above or within the scrotum
- pain and tenderness in the lower abdomen and scrotum

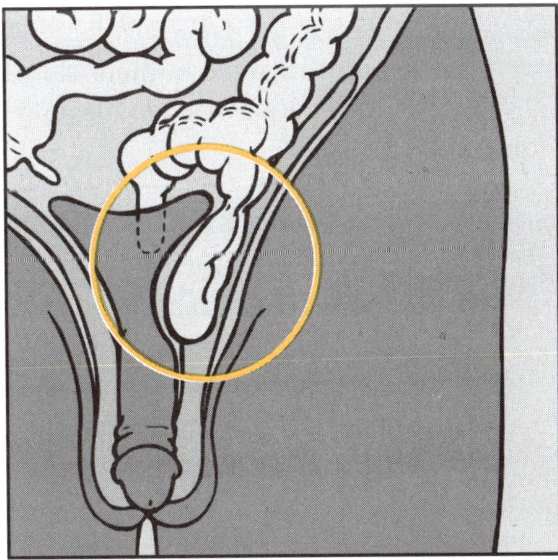

In the above inguinal hernia, the intestine has bulged through the passage where the testicle descends into the scrotum.

Self-Care Steps for Hiatal Hernias

- Treatments for hiatal hernias include taking antacids, avoiding irritating foods, and raising the head of the bed several inches to help prevent stomach contents from flowing back into the esophagus.
- Other treatments that can offer relief include making sure you don't go to sleep or lie down shortly after eating, and eating small, frequent meals. Surgery to tighten the hiatal opening is a last resort if other measures fail to provide relief. See your health care provider if you suspect that you have a hernia.

Self-Care Steps for Inguinal Hernias

- Avoid activities such as heavy lifting that can cause straining and more abdominal pressure.
- Use correct lifting techniques.
- Don't strain during bowel movements.

The chief cause of inguinal hernias is too much abdominal pressure caused by heavy lifting or straining during bowel movements. Correct lifting (using your legs and keeping the back straight) can reduce your risk of hernia.

Strangulated hernias. These hernias occur when hernias are so pinched by the abdominal wall that the blood supply is cut off and the tissue dies and swells. Rapidly increasing pain in the groin is a signal that the hernia is strangulated. The dead tissue quickly becomes infected and can lead to a life-or-death situation within hours.

What to do. If you have these symptoms or suspect that you have a hernia, call your health care provider for a full diagnosis.

In most cases, eating small meals, never lying down after meals, and sleeping with the head of your bed elevated will help alleviate the symptoms of a hiatal hernia. In severe cases, a health care provider may recommend surgery to repair the hernia.

Treatment for inguinal hernias includes surgery to repair the abdominal wall or, if there is no discomfort, simply living with the hernia and watching that it doesn't get worse.

Kidney Stones

You may have kidney stones without ever knowing it. However, if symptoms do appear, they can be extremely painful.

Kidney stones can form in the kidneys, bladder, or urethra (the tube leading from the bladder to the outside of the body). These small, solid lumps are composed of minerals that naturally occur in urine, but are in high concentration due to an infection, dietary imbalance, metabolic problems, or some other cause. This condition affects more men than women.

If a stone moves into the ureter (the tube leading from the kidney to the bladder), you may experience an intense pain in your side and groin. This pain is called renal colic. Stones can also block the flow of urine at various points in the urinary tract. When urine is blocked, a serious kidney infection can result.

What to do. Kidney stones are usually treated with bed rest, pain relievers, and by drinking large amounts of fluid to help the stone pass. If stones are especially large, it may be necessary to remove them surgically. X-rays are generally used to diagnose kidney stones.

Self-Care Steps for Kidney Stones

- Drink 2 to 3 quarts of water a day while you wait for the stone to pass.
- Take an over-the-counter pain medication, or your health care provider may prescribe a pain reliever.

Preventive Steps

Drinking lots of liquids—especially water—is one of the best ways to prevent kidney stones.

Once you have a kidney stone, it's important to figure out what caused it in order to prevent it from happening again. Your health care provider may ask you to save the stone once you have passed it and to collect your urine for 24 hours after the stone has been removed or passed.

An analysis of the stone and urine can determine what caused the stone. Your provider may then prescribe medication or recommend changes in your diet to prevent future formation of stones.

Decision Guide for Kidney Stones

Symptoms/Signs	Action
Intense spasms of pain on one side of the back or in the side, lower abdomen, or groin	 Call provider's office
Blood in the urine	Call provider's office
Any of these symptoms with fever and chills	 Seek help now

For more about the symbols, see page 60.

Rectal Pain

Hemorrhoids (very swollen veins in the rectal area) or fissures (cracks in the skin around the rectum) are the most common causes of rectal pain (see *Hemorrhoids*, page 95). Rectal pain may also accompany intense itching, fever, and bleeding with bowel movements. Obesity, pregnancy, chronic diarrhea or constipation, and some infections—especially of the bowel—may contribute to the problem.

Rectal itching is usually not a medical emergency. You can usually treat it at home and, in many cases, prevent it. Wearing cotton underwear and loose clothing will help. Drinking plenty of water and eating fresh fruit and high-fiber foods will soften stools and help you avoid constipation. Try avoiding foods that may contribute to irritation, such as highly spiced or acidic foods, coffee, alcohol, and chocolate.

Decision Guide for Rectal Pain

Symptoms/Signs	Action
Pain that lasts less than 1 week	Use self-care
Pain that lasts more than 2 weeks with self-care, or itching that occurs with bleeding or pain	 Call provider's office
Pain that is severe or lasts longer than 1 week	 See provider
Bleeding that is heavy or dark in color	See provider
Heavy bleeding with signs of impending shock (see page 88)	Seek help now

For more about the symbols, see page 60.

Self-Care Steps for Rectal Pain

- Avoid straining during bowel movements.
- Clean rectal area well after each bowel movement. Try moistened wipes instead of or after using toilet paper. Or use a soothing, unscented lotion on the toilet paper.
- Use a soft, white, unscented toilet tissue to reduce irritation.
- Try dusting the area with cornstarch.
- Use zinc oxide ointment to decrease chafing and absorb excess moisture.
- Avoid prolonged sitting.
- Raise legs when sitting, especially if obese or pregnant.
- Apply cold compresses (ice packs, moistened wipes, or witch hazel) 4 times a day for pain.
- Follow a cold compress with a warm bath to soothe and cleanse.
- If needed, take aspirin or use medicated suppositories to relieve discomfort.

NOTE: Anal ointments with a local anesthetic may cause an allergic reaction. These medicines will have the suffix "-caine" in the name or listed among their ingredients.

Special Concerns for Children

Sometimes a child will awake suddenly with rectal pain and itching. This often means pinworms. Seldom visible–but quite common and harmless–these small worms are contagious and can be picked up from contaminated food. (Adults may also get pinworm, but less frequently.) Call your health care provider's office to get a prescription for medication that will get rid of the worm infestation. Wash hands thoroughly after using the bathroom and before preparing food.

Urinary Incontinence

Urinary incontinence—the inability to control the leakage of urine—can strike people at any age, for a variety of reasons. Childbirth, being overweight, and aging can all weaken the muscles of the pelvic floor, causing incontinence in women. As men age, the prostate gland often enlarges and blocks the flow of urine, which can build up in the bladder until it overflows (see *Prostate Health*, page 228). Incontinence may also accompany aging.

In almost all of these cases, urinary incontinence is treatable. Treatment will vary, depending on the cause of incontinence. The following are some of the most common types and their symptoms.

Stress incontinence. This is caused when activities place pressure on the bladder, and the muscles designed to prevent leaks are weak. People who suffer from stress incontinence leak small amounts of urine when they cough, sneeze, laugh, lift heavy objects, exercise, or even get up from a chair.

Urgency incontinence. This affects people who suddenly feel the need to urinate so badly that they can't hold back. A bladder infection may be the cause, especially if symptoms of pain and burning accompany urination.

Overflow incontinence. This occurs when the bladder never completely empties. People with overflow incontinence tend to leak small amounts of urine throughout the day. They often feel the need to go to the bathroom—especially at night—but can only produce small amounts of urine. They don't feel completely "empty" after they urinate.

What to do. Talk to your health care provider about the type of incontinence you are experiencing, and he or she will be able to recommend treatment. Exercises can tone and strengthen sphincter muscles. Bladder training techniques help patients empty their bladders as completely as possible and help lengthen the time between trips to the bathroom. Medications can also help correct some types of incontinence. In postmenopausal women, for example, estrogen may help eliminate stress incontinence. Surgery may also be an option, but it is usually a last resort. The following self-care steps include special exercises and techniques that may help control incontinence.

Self-Care Steps for Urinary Incontinence

- Practice starting and stopping the flow of urine several times. Tighten the muscles around the anus and urinary sphincter, hold for a few seconds, then relax the muscles. Repeat 20 times. Perform exercises during a daily routine activity—while brushing your teeth, doing dishes, or reading the paper. Doing a set of 20 exercises several times during the day should improve symptoms of incontinence within a few months.
- Set a specific schedule for going to the bathroom—every 3 hours, for example—even if you have no urge to go. Use an alarm or timer to help stay on schedule.
- After urinating, wait a minute, then try to empty the bladder again. People often find they are able to release additional urine this way.
- Try to resist the urge to urinate more often. If this isn't possible without risking an accident, reduce the timing to every 2 hours, and then try to increase to every 4 hours.
- Extend the time between bathroom trips in the following way: When you feel the urge to go to the bathroom, contract the muscles of the pelvic floor until the urge goes away. Try to hold off going to the bathroom a little longer each time. Keep track of how long you can wait between urinating. Within 2 to 3 weeks, you should see an improvement.
- If your problem occurs mainly at night, avoid drinking any fluids after the evening meal.
- Avoid stimulants such as coffee, especially after dinner.
- Don't stop drinking water—especially when it's hot or when you are working or playing in a hot climate. It is important to drink fluids regardless of the weather.
- If getting to the toilet in time is a problem, keep a portable urinal nearby (you can buy one at a drugstore or medical supply store). Drugstores also carry a variety of absorbent undergarments.
- Keep a record of your symptoms. Your record keeping can help your health care provider understand the specific problem and recommend the right treatment. For several days, keep a record of each time you drink fluids, each time you urinate, and each time you leak urine—even during the night. Use "D" for drink, "U" for urinate, and "L" for leak. Note the time next to each letter. For every "L," also note the circumstances, for example, "while coughing," or "couldn't get to the bathroom in time."
- See your health care provider if incontinence interferes with your life. Some people prefer to try self-care techniques before consulting their provider. Whatever approach you choose, know that incontinence usually isn't something you just have to live with. Together, you and your provider can do something about it.

URINARY TRACT

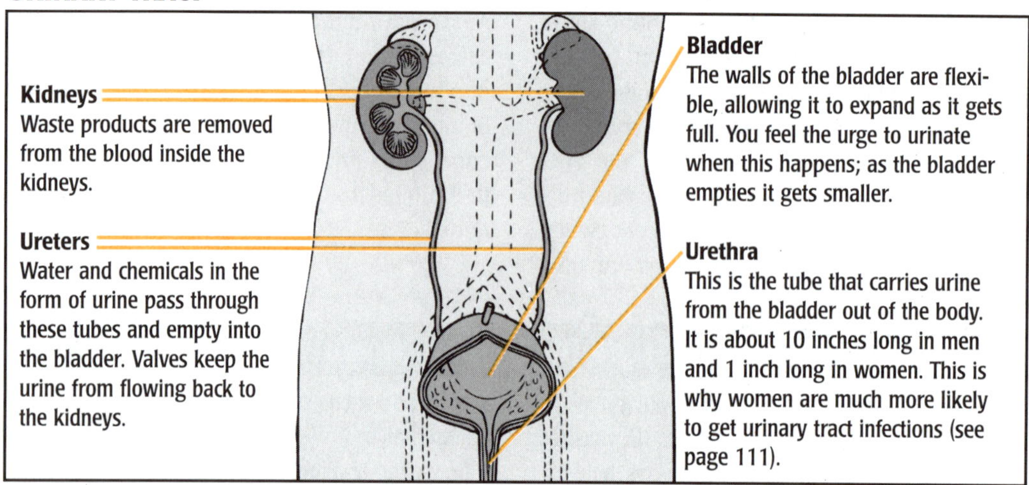

FEMALE URINARY TRACT

MALE URINARY TRACT

Sometimes surgery helps incontinence. One operation for women moves the bladder, allowing the bladder neck to return to its normal, closed position. For men, surgery can be performed to remove the part of the prostate gland that blocks urination.

Decision Guide for Urinary Incontinence

Symptoms/Signs	Action
Symptoms are occasional and manageable	Use self-care
Problem doesn't improve with self-care	Call provider's office
Symptoms are frequent, troublesome, and interfere with your lifestyle	See provider

For more about the symbols, see page 60.

Urinary Tract Infections

Urinary tract infections can be bothersome and painful. Occasionally, they indicate a serious health problem. Urinary tract infections are more common in women because the urethra is shorter and the anus and urethra are closer together than they are in men. But most cases can be cleared up quickly, often with just several days of treatment.

However, some urinary tract infections have few symptoms, making them hard to detect. Because urinary tract infections can be particularly troublesome for pregnant women, watch carefully for any symptoms during pregnancy.

The symptoms of urinary tract infections are as follows:

- frequent and/or urgent urination, especially at night
- a burning feeling during urination
- blood in the urine
- pressure in the lower abdomen
- urine that looks cloudy and/or smells very bad

A urinary tract infection that involves the bladder, the sac where urine is stored before it leaves the body, is called cystitis. Cystitis is often caused by *E. coli* bacteria, which are common in the bowel. *E. coli* can infect the urinary tract if the bacteria come into contact with the urethra, the tube through which urine passes. Bacteria may also enter the urinary tract during sexual intercourse or when a woman uses a diaphragm. Perfumed soaps, powders, and bubble bath products can cause irritation that may lead to infection.

Urinary tract infections can be a problem for men as well as women, especially those over 50. An enlarged prostate gland, common in older men, can restrict the flow of urine and lead to bacterial growth and infection (see *Prostate Health*, page 228).

If the infection reaches the kidneys, it's called pyelonephritis and can sometimes cause permanent kidney damage.

What to do. If you have an uncomplicated urinary tract infection, a short course of antibiotics will usually cure it. Call your health care provider if you experience any of the symptoms listed above. In some cases, a provider will ask questions about your symptoms and past problems, and may prescribe antibiotics without a urine test. More complicated cases may require an appointment with your provider.

Women who have frequent urinary tract infections and have been evaluated by their provider can often keep antibiotics at home and begin taking them at the first sign of a bladder infection.

See your health care provider if your symptoms persist, or if you are thirstier than usual, have blurred vision, feel tired, or have lost weight (see *Diabetes*, page 280).

Decision Guide for Urinary Tract Infections

Symptoms/Signs	Action
Suspected urinary tract infection	 Use self-care
Symptoms that last more than 48 hours	 Call provider's office
Blood in urine	 Call provider's office
Men: Frequent, burning, urgent urination, regardless of fever	 Call provider's office
Women: Frequent, burning, urgent urination, with fever above 101 degrees	 See provider
Nausea and vomiting	 See provider
Shaking chills	 See provider
4 or more urinary tract infections in the past 12 months	 See provider
Symptoms in person who has diabetes or symptoms of diabetes (see page 280)	 See provider
Symptoms of urinary tract infection while pregnant	 See provider
Symptoms in person who has compromised immune system (is HIV-positive or taking radiation or chemotherapy treatments)	 See provider
Symptoms in person who has kidney disease or kidney stones	 See provider

For more about the symbols, see page 60.

Self-Care Steps for Urinary Tract Infections

- Avoid caffeine, alcohol, and spicy foods, all of which can make the symptoms worse.
- Drink 8 glasses of fluid per day. Water is best.
- Take tepid or cool sitz baths to relieve the discomfort (fill the tub with enough water to immerse the hips and buttocks).
- Call your health care provider. He or she may tell you to have a urine test, may suggest prompt treatment treated with antibiotics, or may have you schedule an appointment. Your provider may tell you to go to an urgent care center or emergency room if your symptoms include fever and chills.

Preventive Steps

- Drink a lot of water.
- Avoid caffeine and alcohol, which can irritate the bladder.
- Wear clean cotton underwear.

For women:

- Urinate often, especially before and after you have intercourse.
- Wipe from front to back after using the toilet, to avoid spreading bacteria from the rectal area to the urinary tract.
- Avoid bubble bath, perfumed soaps, douches, and deodorant tampons.
- If urinary tract infections are a problem and you use a diaphragm, switch to another type of birth control.

Special Concerns for Children

- Children can suffer urinary tract infections. Their symptoms are the same as those of an adult. Urinary tract infections in children may be more serious and should be checked by their health care provider.
- Children may urinate frequently for other reasons, too. Some children have small bladders and need to go to the bathroom quite often. Stress at school or at home can also cause a child to urinate more often. If this is the case for your child, tactfully explain the situation to teachers or other caregivers. If you have any concerns, speak with your child's health care provider.

Vomiting

In most cases, vomiting is caused by an infection (located anywhere from the stomach to the colon) that will disappear by itself in a few days. Vomiting can also be the body's reaction to eating spoiled food, or it can be the side effect of a drug or drinking too much alcohol. Nervousness, emotional stress, or tension can also cause an upset stomach. Upsets can be brought on by motion sickness, too much excitement, or too much exposure to sun, particularly in children.

What to do. While you're recovering from vomiting, it's very important that you drink enough liquids to avoid dehydration (a serious condition that occurs when the body loses too much water). Fortunately, sensible and safe home remedies can satisfy your body's need for fluids and provide relief. Over-the-counter drugs are rarely necessary. Although they may make you more comfortable, you will get better without them.

You should call your health care provider if you have a temperature that is 101 degrees or higher for two days or more, if you are in severe pain, if you are vomiting blood, or if you have symptoms of hepatitis (see *Hepatitis*, page 102). Also, be sure to watch for signs of dehydration (see box on page 114), particularly in children and older people.

Self-Care Steps for Vomiting

- Let your stomach rest. Adults should eat nothing for several hours and gradually add liquids as the nausea stops.
- Stay on clear liquids for the first full day after you stop vomiting. Try water, cracked ice, broth, gelatin, chicken soup, or flat carbonated beverages (not diet soda). Sip a little at a time throughout the day.
- Add bland foods on the second day. Choose foods such as bananas, rice, applesauce, dry toast, soup, plain crackers, or dry cereals without milk. Eat small amounts as you can tolerate them comfortably.
- Avoid milk and other dairy products. You should also avoid cigarettes, caffeine, and alcohol.
- Get plenty of rest.

Decision Guide for Vomiting

Symptoms/Signs	Action
Possible motion sickness	Use self-care
Vomiting after eating too much	Use self-care
Vomiting after drinking too much alcohol	Use self-care
Vomiting that may be related to stress or tension	Use self-care
Oral temperature higher than 101 degrees for more than 48 hours	Call provider's office
Possibility of pregnancy	Call provider's office
Listless, less-than-normal activity level	Call provider's office
Severe, constant pain	Call provider's office
Yellowish whites of the eyes or skin (see *Hepatitis,* page 102), and vomiting or diarrhea, dark brown urine, and light-colored stools	Call provider's office
Person who is vomiting has diabetes	Call provider's office
Early signs of dehydration (see box at right)	Call provider's office
Signs of dehydration that have progressed (see page 99)	See provider
Vomiting blood or a substance that looks like coffee grounds	Seek help now

For more about the symbols, see page 60.

Dehydration in Children and Seniors

- Because dehydration is especially serious for young children and seniors, limit fluids for the first 2 hours only. Then begin offering fluids by the teaspoon, gradually increasing the amount. For some children, fruit juices can make diarrhea worse; limit juices if symptoms persist.
- When a child younger than 2 years of age keeps vomiting for more than 8 hours or has diarrhea (more than 5 runny stools a day) for more than 2 days, call your child's health care provider.

For the young and old, medical attention is also important for these early signs of dehydration:

- dark circles around the eyes
- less than normal urination (for infants, fewer than 5 soaked diapers per day)
- dry skin that does not spring back into place normally when picked up between thumb and index finger

Eye, Ear, Nose, and Throat Problems

This chapter describes common problems related to your eyes, ears, nose, and throat and suggests ways to take care of non-urgent conditions at home.

Bad Breath

Although there are dozens of possible causes of bad breath (also referred to as halitosis), it is often a result of poor dental hygiene. Without proper brushing and flossing, food particles and plaque build up on the teeth, gums, and tongue. Bacteria begin to grow and produce bad mouth odors.

Conditions such as tonsillitis, pneumonia, mouth sores, sore throats, sinus infections, and even the common cold can also cause bad breath. Stomach problems such as heartburn can produce bad breath. Smoking is another leading cause of foul-smelling breath.

Breathing through the mouth, talking for long periods, or sleeping with the mouth open can dry out the mouth and turn breath sour. And, of course, eating garlic, onions, cabbage, or hot and spicy foods can leave breath smelling ripe for a day or so after the meal. Foods high in milk and butterfat are also culprits. And some medications, such as antidepressants, may make your mouth dry, resulting in the growth of bacteria.

What to do. In many cases, caring for your teeth, gums, and tongue will eliminate halitosis. See the self-care steps on page 116 for tips.

Decision Guide for Bad Breath

Symptoms/Signs	Action
Most instances of bad breath	Use self-care
Constant or recurring bad breath that doesn't respond to home care	Call provider's office
Bad breath from decayed teeth or gum disease	See dentist

For more about the symbols, see page 60.

Self-Care Steps for Bad Breath

- The best way to fix a problem with bad breath is to brush up on the care of your teeth. Brush your teeth after every meal and floss at least twice a day. See your dentist for a checkup and cleaning twice a year.
- If your gums bleed when you floss or brush, you may have gum disease (gingivitis), which can cause bad breath. If the condition doesn't improve after 3 weeks of careful dental hygiene, see your dentist.
- Brush the top of your tongue with a soft toothbrush. The tongue, especially far in the back near your throat, can have bacteria that cause bad breath. Studies have shown that people who brush the surface of the tongue as well as the teeth have better breath than people who brush only their teeth.
- If you smoke, stop now. It takes 2 weeks after you stop smoking before the effects of tobacco on your breath are gone.
- Drink plenty of fluids to avoid having a dry mouth. Eat apples, citrus fruits, lettuce, and other raw vegetables, which cleanse the teeth. Avoid strong-smelling foods such as onions, garlic, cabbage, and hot and spicy foods.
- Parsley freshens the breath naturally. Mouthwashes, breath mints, and sprays may mask the odor of bad breath temporarily, but they don't get at the source of the problem. Avoid sugary breath mints. They can make bad breath worse because bacteria thrive on sugar.

Burning Eyes

Your eyes can burn and itch for many different reasons. The cause can be an irritant, infection, or problems with your eyes' own protective mechanisms.

Irritation. Smoke, pollen, or cosmetics can cause eyes to itch, burn, water, and redden. Burning and itching usually go away when the irritant is removed.

Dryness. Age, some medications, and disease can cause chronic dryness in the eyes, which sometimes leads to a burning feeling. Over-the-counter wetting drops (artificial tears) can relieve this type of burning.

Infection. Itchy, burning eyelids can also result from infection. Over-the-counter lid scrubs are available to treat this problem at home. See your health care provider if these treatments don't clear up your condition (see *Eye Discharge/Pinkeye*, page 122).

Chemical burns. Caustic substances such as paint thinner, dish washing detergent, lye, toilet cleaner, drain cleaner, and gasoline can burn the eyes. Chemical burns are painful medical emergencies that can result in impaired vision and increased sensitivity to light. Always wear protective eyeglasses or goggles when working with caustic chemicals.

Ultraviolet rays. Unprotected eyes can also be burned by ultraviolet (UV) rays from the sun, tanning lamps, or arc welding equipment. As with sunburned skin, the pain isn't felt until hours later. UV rays can damage the retina, the light-sensitive surface at the back of the eye that conveys visual impulses to the optic nerve. The risk of sunburning the eyes is very high when sunlight is reflected off water, sand, or snow. Wear sunglasses with UV protection when in the sun.

Self-Care Steps for Burning Eyes

- If your eyes burn and water, try to trace the source of irritation and then avoid it. Smoke, cosmetics, chemical fumes, and pollen are some possibilities.
- To treat chemical burns to the eye, see *Chemical Burns*, page 65.
- Apply a cool compress (a cloth pad soaked in cold water) to sunburned eyes. Stay out of the sun until swelling is gone.

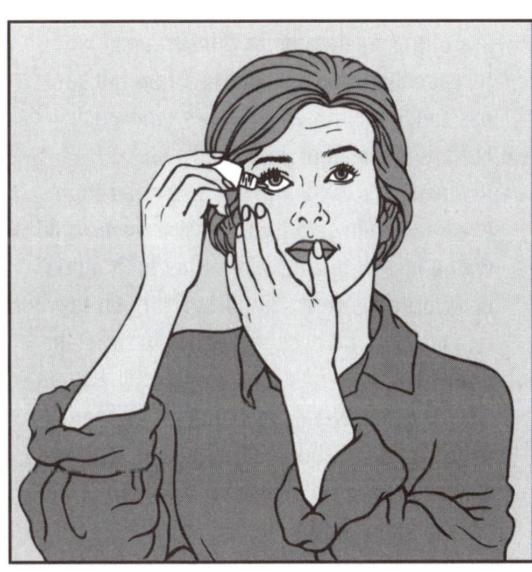

To put eyedrops into the eye, pull down the lower lid and look up.

Decision Guide for Burning Eyes

Symptoms/Signs	Action
Irritated eyes	 Use self-care
Sunburned eyes	 Call provider's office;  Use self-care
Irritated eyes that don't respond to self-care	 Call provider's office
Pain and swelling from sunburned eyes that last longer than 24 hours	 See provider
Any chemically burned eyes (see *Chemical Burns*, page 65)	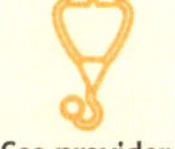 See provider
Blurred vision	 See provider
Iris (colored part of eyes) appears whitish or cloudy	 See provider
A substance oozing from the eye (see page 122)	 See provider

For more about the symbols, see page 60.

Special Concerns for Children

- Make sure that children wear sunglasses with UV protection. The label on the glasses should state whether they provide this feature. Be sure to shade your baby's eyes from the sun with a hat that has a wide brim or an umbrella. Face infants away from the sun when outside and keep them shaded.
- Store cleaning products and other caustic substances out of children's reach.

Croup

Croup is a viral infection that causes narrowing and swelling of the air passages below the vocal cords in children up to about age 6. This condition is marked by a distinctive seallike barking cough, hoarseness, and difficult breathing. A croupy cough and tight breathing may start slowly or suddenly at any time of the day or night. Symptoms last three to five days and may be accompanied by a cold or fever. Some children develop croup every time they get a cold. Episodes of croup are outgrown as the airway passages grow larger. After the age of 7, croup is uncommon.

Croup without fever, the most common and mildest type, comes on during the night. The child may have seemed perfectly healthy during the day but wakes up at night with a violent coughing fit.

Croup with fever is more serious. It is usually accompanied by a cold. The child's temperature remains below 102 degrees.

Epiglottitis is a bacterial infection of the airway that sometimes seems like severe croup with a fever, but the temperature is usually higher than 102 degrees. Epiglottitis usually starts very quickly. The child will drool and gasp for air, will not respond to the simple measures that bring relief of croup, and must receive immediate medical attention.

What to do. Most children with croup can be cared for at home (see self-care steps at right). If your child does not respond to simple home measures within 10 to 15 minutes, call his or her health care provider.

Self-Care Steps for Croup

- Cough medicines and antibiotics are not effective in treating croup.
- Adding moisture to the air makes it easier for a child with croup to breathe. One way to do this is to take the child into the bathroom, close the door, turn on the hot water faucet of the shower, and sit with the child upright on your lap on the bathroom floor for 15 to 20 minutes, inhaling steam. Do not leave the child unattended. Other options are a brief walk outdoors or a cold-mist humidifier in the child's bedroom.
- Once breathing difficulty is relieved, give the child plenty of clear fluids to drink. This will prevent dehydration and help thin the mucus in the child's airways.
- Use acetaminophen to reduce fever and discomfort. Do not give a child aspirin, because use of this medication in children and teenagers has been linked to a rare but serious condition known as Reye's syndrome.
- Elevate the head of your child's bed.
- Remember, a child with croup is often frightened and crying, so try to reassure your child with a hug or distract him or her with a book or favorite game. It's important for you to remain calm, because this will help the child relax, too.
- For the next several days after an episode of croup, a parent should sleep within hearing distance of the child and check on him or her several times during the night.

Decision Guide for Croup

Symptoms/Signs	Action
Child wakes with a croupy cough but no fever; may make high-pitched noises when inhaling	 Use self-care
Child cannot relax enough to sleep after 20 minutes of steam inhalation	 Call provider's office
Child has had croup symptoms for more than 3 nights	 Call provider's office
Child is coughing and breathing with increasing difficulty	 Call provider's office
Child drools and has great difficulty swallowing	 Seek help now
Child cannot bend his or her neck forward	 Seek help now
Child has blue or dusky lips or skin	 Seek help now
Child has symptoms of epiglottitis, such as drooling, gasping, and a fever of 102 degrees or higher (see page 118)	 Seek help now

For more about the symbols, see page 60.

Earaches

The most frequent cause of earache is an infection of the middle ear. Although uncommon in adults, young children have middle ear infections frequently. If you are a parent, it is important to be well-informed about the care and treatment of children's ears, particularly if your child often has ear pain. The symptoms, causes, and treatment of various types of earaches are described on the following pages.

THE EAR

Eustachian tube—Plugging of the eustachian tube leads to fluid buildup in the middle ear. Fluid can build up in this tube from congestion caused by colds or allergies. This fluid can become infected with bacteria, resulting in a middle ear infection. Middle ear infections require medical attention.

Middle Ear Infections

Inflammation of the middle ear (otitis media) results from a buildup of fluid in the middle ear, which becomes infected. This occurs when the eustachian tube, which allows air and fluid to pass in and out of the middle ear, becomes blocked. These tubes are not fully developed in children, so fluid often does not drain as effectively. The fluid collects between the inner and outer ear and then becomes infected with bacteria.

Colds or allergies are almost always to blame for congestion and fluid buildup. Children who live with smokers, have allergies, or have a history of ear infections in their family tend to get ear infections more frequently.

Self-Care Steps for Middle Ear Infections

- If your health care provider has prescribed an antibiotic, take it as directed to reduce the risk of recurring problems. That means you should measure doses carefully, and take all of the prescribed amount even if the symptoms have gone away. Do not skip doses. Store the antibiotic as directed; some may require refrigeration.
- Follow your provider's recommendations for follow-up exams or other measures to prevent ear problems.
- For relief from pain, take acetaminophen instead of aspirin.
- Since colds are a common cause of ear infections, teach your children to prevent colds by avoiding contact with people who have a cold. Remind children to wash their hands after they have contact with someone who has a cold. (For more on preventing colds, see page 138.)

When an infant tugs at his or her ears, acts very irritable, or has a fever after a cold, suspect an ear infection and seek medical attention. If ear infections are left untreated, they can cause hearing loss.

Decision Guide for Earaches

Symptoms/Signs	Action
Swimmer's ear (see page 121)	Use self-care
Ear stuffiness (see page 121)	Use self-care
Mild wax buildup (see page 121)	Use self-care
Discharge of fluids from the ear or any type of severe, constant ear pain	See provider
Symptoms of a middle ear infection (see above)	See provider
Ear stuffiness or blocked ear passages that do not respond to self-care steps within 3 days	See provider
Temperature over 101 degrees	See provider
Child who has ear pain	See provider
Painful, itchy outer ear	See provider
Earwax that is not easily removed (see page 121)	See provider
Hearing loss	See provider

For more about the symbols, see page 60.

What to do. This condition requires medical attention and treatment with an antibiotic. For children with chronic ear infections, regular treatment with low doses of antibiotics is sometimes recommended. Your child's health care provider may recommend ear tubes to properly drain fluid from the ears if your child has recurring problems.

Swimmer's Ear/Earwax Buildup

Inflammation caused by an infection of the outer part of the ear canal (otitis external), known as swimmer's ear, usually results from water or other substances entering the ear and irritating it. The symptoms are itching, redness of the outer ear, and pain from simply wiggling the ear. Pus discharge and temporary hearing loss may also occur.

What to do. Call your health care provider within a day if you suspect that you or your child has swimmer's ear. Your provider may prescribe antibiotic ear drops to treat the infection. Even if your child begins to feel better, be sure to give the drops for the length of time prescribed. He or she will probably have to stay out of the water until the infection clears up. If your child has frequent cases of swimmer's ear, you may want to ask your child's health care provider about ear drops to prevent infections.

You can keep your child's ear dry during baths or showers by placing a cotton ball over the ear opening and coating it with petroleum jelly.

Self-Care Steps for Swimmer's Ear/Earwax Buildup

- To prevent swimmer's ear, use a clean towel or a hair dryer set on low to dry your ears after a swim. You may also want to use drying ear drops (sold over the counter) if your health care provider recommends them.
- If earwax has built up, do not probe in your ear with cotton swabs—they often jam earwax deeper into your ear, causing more problems. Instead, direct a warm (never hot) shower at your ear to loosen the wax, and then wipe it out with a clean towel. It may help to gently squeeze warm water into the ear using a soft rubber-nose syringe. Don't try to wash your ear if you think you have ruptured your eardrum (symptoms include partial hearing loss and bleeding from the ear) or if you have ear drainage. You can also buy an over-the-counter earwax remover.
- A heating pad or a warm cloth on the ear may also provide relief.

Stuffiness/Airplane Ears

Airline passengers may experience barotitis, commonly called airplane ears. As the plane goes down, the air pressure inside the ears is lower than the air pressure outside. This pushes your eardrums inward and makes your ears feel full or stuffed up. If you have allergies or a cold when traveling by plane, descent can cause real pain. Your health care provider may advise that you or your child should delay airplane travel when one of you has an upper respiratory or ear infection.

What to do. There are several simple ways to equalize the pressure between you and your environment. See the self-care steps on the following page.

Self-Care Steps for Ear Stuffiness/ Airplane Ears

- Clear your ears by swallowing, yawning, or chewing gum.
- Try the ear-clearing technique pilots use: Squeeze your nostrils shut, take a big gulp of air, and clamp your mouth shut; then try to blow the air out against your closed mouth and nose. If you're successful, you will feel your ears pop.
- Don't sleep during landings. You don't swallow as often when you're asleep.
- If children are too young to chew gum, give them something to drink. That will make them swallow.
- If you must fly when you have an upper respiratory tract infection such as a cold, take an oral decongestant about 2 hours before you expect to land.
- Use a nasal decongestant spray 1 hour before landing and then again 5 to 10 minutes later. (Decongestant sprays should not be used for more than 3 days.) Do not use nasal decongestant sprays if you have high blood pressure. Nonprescription saline nose sprays may also help.

Eye Discharge/Pinkeye

Conjunctivitis, also known as pinkeye, is an infection of the membrane that lines the inside of the eyelids and covers the surface of the eye. Along with discharge, conjunctivitis can cause red, swollen, itchy, watery eyes. Eyes may burn or feel like they have sand in them. People with conjunctivitis may find their eyes stuck together when they wake up.

Conjunctivitis caused by allergies, pollution, or irritants is not contagious, but the viral forms of pinkeye are contagious. The most common form of conjunctivitis is caused by a virus similar to the type that causes a cold.

What to do. Doctors treat conjunctivitis with antibiotic ointments or eyedrops (antibiotics have no effect on viruses), but the infection will often clear up on its own within five days. If left untreated for long, some forms of conjunctivitis can seriously damage the eyes.

Self-Care Steps for Eye Discharge

- Apply warm compresses to the eyes to help relieve irritation and buildup of the discharge.
- Apply a cold compress to help relieve itching. Gently wipe away the discharge or crust with warm water and a washcloth or cotton ball.
- Don't rub your eyes. It can spread the infection from one eye to the other.
- Don't share towels, washcloths, or anything else that touches the eyes. Wash these items separately in hot water.
- Wash your hands frequently and thoroughly if you have conjunctivitis, if you are caring for someone who does, or even if you are around someone who has the infection.

Special Concerns for Children

Keep your child home when you notice symptoms of conjunctivitis, and keep the child away from other people as much as possible. Follow your school or day care policy on when the child can return to class. Avoid contact between an infected child and infants, other children, elderly people, and those with chronic illnesses or weakened immune systems.

Decision Guide for Eye Discharge

Symptoms/Signs	Action
Mild infection that lasts less than 5 days	Use self-care
Eyes that are sensitive to light	Call provider's office
Pinkeye	Call provider's office
Thick and yellow or greenish discharge	See provider
History of recent eye injury or foreign object in eye	See provider
Infection that doesn't get better after 3 days	See provider
Blurry vision	See provider
Infection that recurs	See provider
True pain, rather than irritation, in the eye	See provider
Pupils that are different sizes	See provider

For more about the symbols, see page 60.

Foreign Objects in the Eye

Pain is the body's way of getting our attention, and nothing grabs attention quite like an object that becomes trapped in the eye. It simply cannot be ignored.

What to do. If you feel something in your eye, don't rub it. Rubbing can damage the cornea, the clear tissue covering the eye.

Decision Guide for Foreign Object in the Eye

Symptoms/Signs	Action
Object is on the white part of the eye	Use self-care
Home care methods fail to remove the object	Call provider's office
Pain continues after the object has been removed	Call provider's office
Eye becomes red, warm, swollen; is increasingly painful; and discharges a yellow-green pus	See provider
Object is on the colored part of the eye	See provider
Eye is bleeding	See provider
Object in eye is a piece of metal or glass	Seek help now
Vision is impaired	Seek help now

For more about the symbols, see page 60.

Wash your hands and take a look in the eye. Put a patch over your eye (without putting pressure on the eyeball) and see your health care provider right away if you find any of the following:

- a piece of glass or metal
- an object that has penetrated the eyeball or is stuck on or embedded in the eye
- an object floating or stuck on the colored part of the eye (the iris or pupil)

If the object is on the cornea (the clear layer covering the iris and pupil), you need to see a health care provider at once. If the object is on the white part of the eye, follow the self-care steps below.

Self-Care Steps for a Foreign Object in the White Part of the Eye

- Wash the eye with water dropped from an eyedropper or squeeze bottle. The object may loosen and flow out of the eye with the water.
- Fill the sink or other large open container with lukewarm water. Hold your breath and plunge your face into the water with eyes open. Roll your eye and move your head around until the object floats away. (Don't try this with young children who don't know how to hold their breath.)
- Roll the corner of a clean handkerchief, tissue, paper towel, or other clean cloth to a point and gently slide the object out of the eye with the cloth.

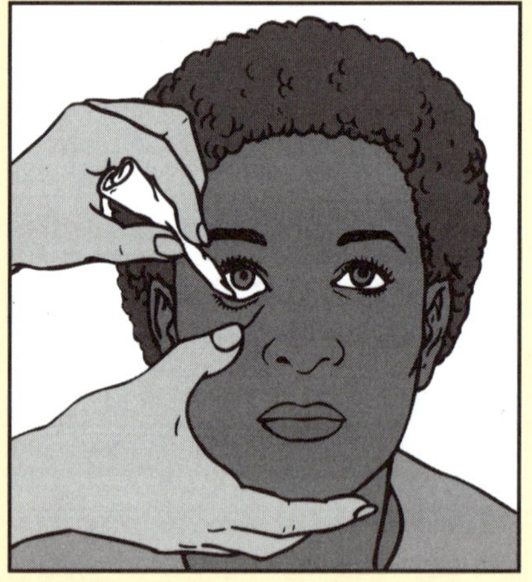

- If the object feels as though it is stuck on the inside of the upper lid, pull the lid out and down over the lower lashes and hold for a few seconds. This may help dislodge the object.
- The following technique works best when someone else helps you. Look up and pull the lower lid down while your helper looks under the lower lid. Then look down at your shoes and pull the upper lid up by the lashes while your helper looks under the upper lid. A cotton swab can help you grasp the upper lid (see illustration). Never insert a toothpick, matchstick, tweezers, or other hard instrument into the eye itself to remove an object.
- You can remove something stuck on the under surface of your upper eyelid with a moistened cotton swab if you take care to avoid brushing the cornea (the clear layer over the colored part of the eye).

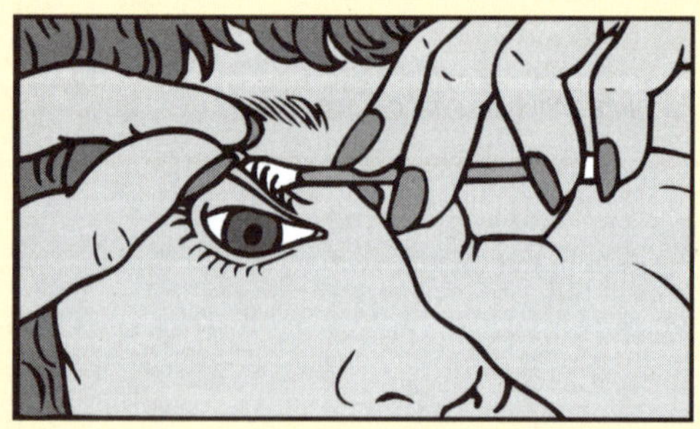

Special Concerns for Children

Try to help the child understand that rubbing the eye will make the problem worse. Give the child something to squeeze or hold to keep his or her hands occupied while you examine the eye. It's also important for the child to stay calm so that he or she can follow your directions. Speak soothingly and stay calm yourself.

Always wear eye protection when working around flying objects or caustic chemicals.

Hoarseness/Laryngitis

Laryngitis is a swelling of the vocal cords that keeps them from vibrating normally. Your voice may sound hoarse or husky or disappear altogether. Smoking, alcohol, and air pollution can dry the vocal cords and cause hoarseness. Cheering at a sporting event, shouting, singing, and speaking for long periods can all cause temporary hoarseness or loss of voice. A cold, sore throat, or other upper respiratory infection can also rob you of your voice if the infection spreads to the voice box.

What to do. Hoarseness caused by overuse or by a cold or other infection will usually go away on its own within two weeks. Constant or repeated hoarseness not linked to overuse or an infection may be something more serious, such as cancer of the larynx. See your doctor if hoarseness does not go away within a month.

Decision Guide for Hoarseness/Laryngitis

Symptoms/Signs	Action
Hoarseness or loss of voice caused by overuse or infection associated with cold symptoms	 Use self-care
Repeated bouts of hoarseness not caused by overuse or infection associated with cold symptoms	 Call provider's office
Hoarseness that lasts longer than 1 month, particularly if you are over the age of 40 and smoke	 See provider

For more about the symbols, see page 60.

Self-Care Steps for Hoarseness/Laryngitis

- Give it a rest. Avoid talking and whispering as much as possible. (Whispering strains vocal cords as much as talking.) Use hand gestures and a pencil and paper to communicate.
- Drink plenty of fluids. Water is best to keep your vocal cords moist.
- Don't smoke or drink alcohol. Both can dry out and irritate vocal cords.
- Humidify your home with a cool-mist vaporizer.
- If you must go out in extremely cold weather, wear a scarf or mask over your mouth.

Mouth Sores

Canker sores and fever blisters (also known as cold sores) are the most common type of mouth sores. Both are irritating and painful, but will eventually go away on their own. Mouth sores that don't heal within three to four weeks may indicate a more serious problem. See your health care provider if you have mouth sores that won't heal.

Canker Sores

Canker sores appear inside the mouth, and affect about 20 percent of the population. These sores begin as red swellings and then rupture, leaving a sore covered with a white or yellow membrane and surrounded by a red halo. Canker sores usually go away within two weeks. Their exact cause is unknown, but outbreaks of the sores appear to be linked to stress, mouth injury, and certain phases of the menstrual cycle. Canker sores are not contagious.

What to do. If you get canker sores frequently, your health care provider may want to test you for certain nutritional deficiencies or food allergies. You can ease the pain of canker sores by using over-the-counter mouthwashes and ointments. Avoid spicy or salty foods.

Self-Care Steps for Mouth Sores

- For canker sores, apply over-the-counter products that contain benzocaine, and try a medicated lip balm for cold sores. These won't make the sores heal any faster, but they may reduce the pain.
- Avoid eating acidic foods such as citrus fruits or tomatoes. Salty, spicy, or vinegary foods may irritate mouth sores, too. Also avoid foods with sharp edges, like potato chips.
- Cold sores are contagious. If you have one or feel one coming on, avoid skin-to-skin contact with anyone else until the sore has healed.

Special Concerns for Children

The virus that causes cold sores can be dangerous to newborn babies. Keep newborns away from anyone who has a cold sore or the itching, burning symptoms that precede a cold sore.

Children may also develop hand-foot-and-mouth disease (unrelated to foot and mouth disease in cattle), which can produce blisters on the inside of the mouth, soles of the feet, and palms of the hands. Symptoms may also include slight fever. This illness usually lasts only a few days. The only treatment is to take acetaminophen to relieve the pain and discomfort caused by the blisters.

Fever Blisters

Also called cold sores, fever blisters are usually caused by the virus herpes simplex type 1, and appear on the lips, the edge of the nostril or, less often, on the face or inside of the mouth. Once a person is infected with this virus, it remains in the body, even though it may not be active. Sunlight, stress, hormonal changes, and injury may trigger outbreaks of fever blisters. The blisters usually collapse to form sores with a yellowish crust over them. The sores usually heal within two weeks. Fever blisters are highly contagious.

What to do. There is no cure for fever blisters. Ointments can ease the pain and antibiotics can treat bacterial infection of

Decision Guide for Mouth Sores

Symptoms/Signs	Action
For canker sores: one or more red, craterlike sores inside the mouth, on gums, or inside lips or cheeks	Use self-care
For cold sores: one or more blisters on the outside of the mouth area	Use self-care
Recurring mouth sores	Call provider's office
Mouth sores caused by poorly fitting dentures or rough or broken teeth	See dentist
Mouth sores that don't heal within 3 weeks	See provider
Small, whitish, lacy sores	See provider
Creamy yellow patches on inside of mouth that may be sore or painful	See provider
Large, bleeding, and painful ulcers on gums	See provider

For more about the symbols, see page 60.

the blisters. If you have fever blisters, eat bland food to avoid irritating them and don't touch them, because it's easy to spread the virus to other parts of your body or to other people.

Sore Throats

Low humidity in your home, failing to drink enough fluids, winter dryness, or smoke can all cause a sore throat, but sore throats are often a sign of infection.

During an infection, your throat fights back by increasing the blood flow to your neck. This is what causes the swelling, soreness, and cough that often accompany a sore throat.

Two types of infections cause sore throats: viral infections, and streptococcus, a rarer and more serious bacterial infection, that causes strep throat. Here are the usual differences between the two:

Viral Sore Throat. The following are symptoms of a viral sore throat:

- usually causes a dry cough and a lighter colored mucus
- less likely to be accompanied by a fever
- often associated with cold or the flu

Strep Throat. The following are symptoms of strep throat:

- very red throat with white patches or pus; swollen tonsils and neck glands
- often produces a temperature over 101 degrees
- requires treatment with antibiotics

What to do. Viral sore throats will go away in a few days, but a sore throat lasting for up to 7 to 10 days is not uncommon. Sore throat pain can usually be eased with a few simple self-care steps. Strep throat can lead to more serious problems. Call your health care provider when you have symptoms of strep throat.

Decision Guide for Sore Throats

Symptoms/Signs	Action	
Temperature below 101 degrees		Use self-care
Cough that comes and goes		Use self-care
Dry, sore, itchy throat		Use self-care
Coldlike symptoms		Use self-care
Cough that gets worse	Call provider's office	Use self-care
Swollen glands	Call provider's office	Use self-care
Very red throat with white patches or pus; swollen glands		Call provider's office
Temperature over 101 degrees that lasts longer than 48 hours		Call provider's office
Sore throat that develops into chest symptoms with cough getting worse		Call provider's office
Difficulty breathing		Seek help now
Unable to swallow saliva		Seek help now

NOTE: To determine whether you have strep throat, your health care provider may recommend that you have a throat culture. Be sure to tell your provider if you have recently been exposed to someone with strep or if you are allergic to any antibiotics.

For more about the symbols, see page 60.

Self-Care Steps for Sore Throats

- Raise the humidity at home. You can sit in the bathroom with a hot shower running or use a humidifier or vaporizer (a cool mist is preferred). Do not leave a child unattended in the bathroom with a hot shower running. If using a humidifier, empty and clean it daily, following the manufacturer's instructions.
- Drink extra fluids. Warm fluids are especially soothing for irritated throats.
- Gargle with salt water. Dissolve 1/2 teaspoon salt in 8 ounces of warm water to help relieve a sore throat. Throat lozenges or even hard candy may also help soothe a sore throat.

Special Concerns for Children

- Fluids are very important for children. Be sure to give them plenty of soups, juice, or water.
- Fever doesn't necessarily mean serious illness in children. Be more concerned about changes in eating or sleeping habits or an unhealthy appearance. Acetaminophen can be used for fever. Do not give aspirin to children or teenagers because of the risk of Reye's syndrome.
- If a child doesn't feel too tired, staying active is fine.
- Teach your children to prevent sore throats and other infections by washing their hands often and keeping their hands away from the face. If your children have been with friends who are infected, these preventive steps may keep them from getting the illness or spreading it to themselves and others.

Sties

A sty is a red, tender bump on the eyelid that swells and feels itchy. A sty is normally smaller than a pebble.

A sty appears when an oil gland at the base of an eyelash becomes clogged. Over a few days, a sty usually comes to a head —like a pimple—and drains on its own. Good hygiene can help hair follicles from becoming clogged and forming sties. Sometimes a sty will persist for weeks without coming to a head. In these cases, a health care provider may decide to open and drain the sty. Growths on the eyelid that are not red and painful are usually cysts, rather than sties.

What to do. Although any unusual lump or growth should be checked by a health care provider, most eyelid cysts are harmless and do not need to be removed.

Self-Care Steps for Sties

- Hot compresses will help a sty come to a head and drain. Place a clean washcloth in water as hot as you can stand it without burning yourself. Wring out the cloth and place it on your eye for 5 to 10 minutes. Repeat 3 or 4 times a day.
- If pus discharges on its own or during the self-care process, carefully clean the entire area with water. If you apply antibiotic eye ointment to the area, it may help prevent sties from coming back.

Decision Guide for Sties

Symptoms/Signs	Action
Red, swollen, itchy lump on eyelid	Use self-care
Lump on eyelid that isn't painful	Call provider's office
Sty that persists and remains painful for a week or more	See provider
Sty that returns	See provider

For more about the symbols, see page 60.

Special Concerns for Children

A child's skin is much more sensitive to heat than is an adult's. Use lukewarm compresses instead of hot ones to treat a child's sty. Have the child test the temperature of the compress before you apply it.

Swollen Glands

The lymphatic system is made up of vessels and nodes that help fight infection and also drain fluid from tissue back into the blood. The system is filled with lymph, a fluid made up of white blood cells, proteins, and fats. Some white blood cells fight infection by engulfing foreign cells, while others produce infection-fighting chemicals.

Lymph nodes, sometimes referred to as lymph glands, cluster at the neck, armpit, and groin. Occasionally these glands will become swollen. This is almost always a sign that the body is fighting an infection. Swollen glands may be painful and tender. The area where the swelling occurs can indicate where the infection is located. For example, swollen glands on the sides and back of the neck can be caused by German measles, mononucleosis, or an infection in the scalp. A swollen gland in the armpit might be from an infected cut on the arm or finger.

A bacterial infection will sometimes lodge in the gland, making it hot and sore and causing the skin over the area to redden. In rare cases, swollen glands may indicate cancer of the lymph system.

What to do. Swollen glands usually require no treatment, but will go away on their own. They are most often caused by viral infections and the only treatment is acetaminophen to relieve pain. Bacterial infections often require antibiotics.

Decision Guide for Swollen Glands

Symptoms/Signs	Action
Swollen glands without more serious symptoms, such as redness and extreme tenderness	Use self-care
Swollen glands with a sore throat and/or temperature higher than 100 degrees	Call provider's office
Swollen glands that are very tender and red	See provider
Swelling that lasts for more than 2 weeks	See provider
Difficulty opening the mouth or moving the neck	Seek help now
Difficulty breathing and swallowing	Emergency: call 911

For more about the symbols, see page 60.

Vision Problems

Blurry or fuzzy sight or other vision problems can be caused by a number of conditions. Most can be corrected. If your vision suddenly blurs, see your health care provider right away. The following conditions can cause blurry vision to develop slowly.

Nearsightedness. Also called myopia, nearsightedness is difficulty in seeing objects that are far away. Objects close up are seen clearly. Depending on how bad their vision is, nearsighted people may hold reading material just a few inches from their noses.

Farsightedness. Also called hyperopia, farsightedness causes objects to appear fuzzy when close up. Objects at a distance are seen clearly. Farsighted people often hold their reading material at arm's length.

Astigmatism. This can cause areas of blurry vision because the lens in your eye is not smooth. People with astigmatism may find it hard to see vertical, horizontal, or diagonal lines clearly.

Presbyopia. This is a problem of aging. As we get older, the eye lens hardens and loses its flexibility, making it difficult to focus on nearby objects. Eyeglasses that have bifocal lenses can correct most cases of presbyopia.

Cataracts. Cataracts cloud the lens of the eye and impair sight. Cataracts usually grow very slowly over several years. Most cataracts are a result of aging but they can also be caused by injuries, birth defects, too much heat or ultraviolet (UV) light, drugs, or diabetes. Lenses affected by cataracts can be replaced by surgery if necessary.

Diabetic retinopathy. This condition affects people who have diabetes. With diabetic retinopathy, damage to the blood vessels that nourish the retina—the part of your eye that is sensitive to light—can damage the retina and may ultimately cause blindness. The early stages of this condition often produce no symptoms. However, if caught early enough, blindness due to diabetic retinopathy can usually be prevented. The American Academy of Ophthalmology recommends that people with diabetes have their eyes examined annually by an eye care provider. However, a recent study found that less than half of people with diabetes have an eye exam every year.

Self-Care Steps for Vision Problems

- Have regular eye exams—every 3 to 5 years if you don't have vision problems, every 2 years if you wear glasses, contact lenses, or have other vision problems. Your health care provider or eye specialist may recommend more frequent exams. People with severe nearsightedness are prone to getting a detached retina, and may need to see a retina specialist.
- Wear safety glasses or goggles whenever you use power tools, lawnmowers, and other devices that could cause objects to fly toward the eye.
- Wear sunglasses with ultraviolet (UV) light protection when you are out in the sun. Be sure to wear sunglasses when near water or snow, which increases sunlight's glare. Too much UV light has been linked to cataracts.

Glaucoma. A major cause of blindness, glaucoma is an increased pressure within the eyeball due to injury, structural abnormality in the eye, or other causes. This pressure can damage the optic nerve, which controls sight. Symptoms of glaucoma include loss of vision to each side (peripheral vision), halos around lights, pain in the eye, blurred vision, and gradual loss of sight. African-Americans and people with diabetes are more likely to develop glaucoma.

Glaucoma often causes a gradual loss of peripheral vision that may be imperceptible to the person, so the condition may go undetected until a good deal of vision is lost. Early diagnosis through routine glaucoma checks after age 40 is the key to treating this problem. Glaucoma can be treated with prescription eyedrops or other medication that reduces pressure in the eye. Laser surgery may also be used.

Macular degeneration. This is the leading cause of blindness in the United States. The macula, a part of the retina, is responsible for seeing detail at the center of the field of vision. When the macula deteriorates, vision begins to blur or may darken in the center. This condition most often strikes elderly people. If diagnosed early, laser treatment can sometimes keep it from getting worse.

Special Concerns for Children

Children should have their first eye exam at age 3 or 4, unless you suspect a vision problem earlier. If a school-age child starts having headaches or is having trouble concentrating or learning at school, he or she may have a vision problem.

Decision Guide for Vision Problems

Symptoms/Signs	Action
Decreased vision while taking medication	Call provider's office
Decreased vision in person over age 50 (possible cataracts)	Call provider's office
Tunnel vision or loss of peripheral vision	See provider
Eyes that protrude or bulge out of sockets	See provider
Sudden loss or blurring of vision	See provider
Loss of vision associated with injury to head or eyes	Seek help now
Seeing flashing lights or black spots	Seek help now

For more about the symbols, see page 60.

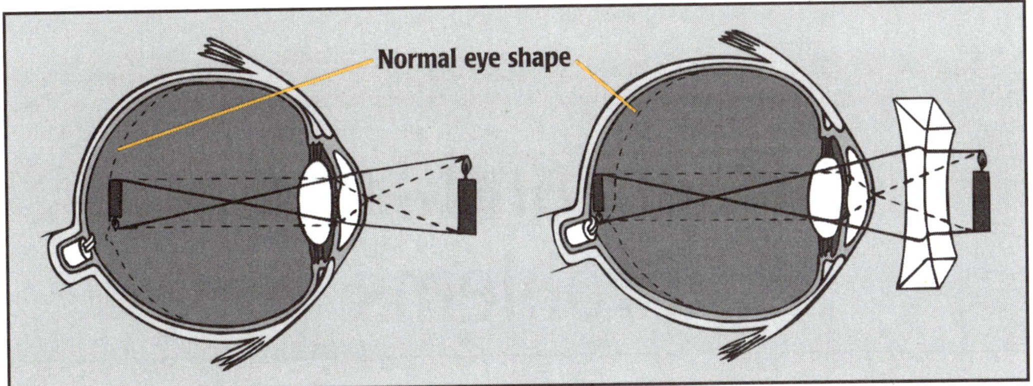

Nearsightedness (myopia) is difficulty seeing objects that are far away. It happens when the eyeball is longer than normal. The focal point falls short of the retina, causing objects at a distance to appear blurry. Eyeglasses with lenses that curve in (concave) bend the light rays so that they fall on the retina.

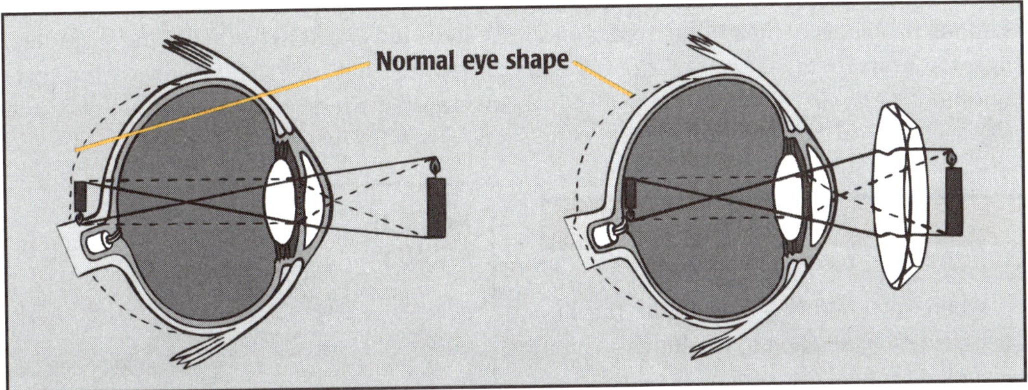

Farsightedness (hyperopia) is difficulty seeing objects up close. It happens when the eyeball is shorter than normal. The focal point falls beyond the retina, causing objects up close to appear blurry. Eyeglasses with lenses that curve out (convex) bend the light rays so that light falls on the retina.

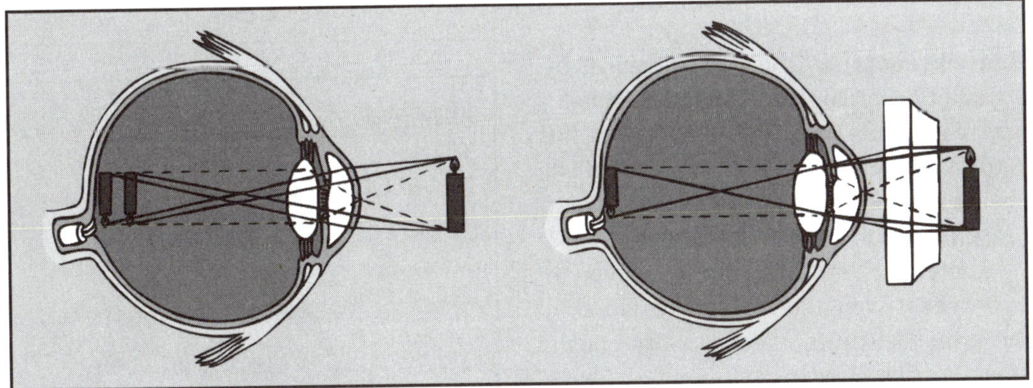

Astigmatism, an irregular curve of the cornea and/or lens, can cause two focal points to fall in different locations. This makes objects up close and at a distance look blurry. A person can have astigmatism combined with nearsightedness or farsightedness.

Heart and Lung Problems

Your heart and lungs are the organs that offer the most dramatic evidence of your body's well-being. This section describes common problems of these vital organs and suggests how to take care of nonurgent conditions at home.

Bronchitis

When someone has bronchitis, the lining of the tubes leading to the lungs (which are called bronchi) swells and produces too much mucus. Symptoms include coughing up gray or yellow mucus (also called phlegm), wheezing, difficulty breathing, chest pain, and fever.

Acute bronchitis. This is often caused by a viral or bacterial infection of the bronchi, and tends to strike after a cold or the flu. Airborne irritants such as smoke, dust, chemical fumes or even cold weather may also cause bronchitis.

Acute bronchitis usually lasts one to two weeks. Even after the inflammation in the bronchial tubes is gone, a dry cough, sometimes with wheezing, remains for as long as four to six weeks. During this time, exposure to cold weather, dry air, smoke, or dust can irritate the bronchial tubes and bring on coughing.

Chronic bronchitis. This is bronchial swelling that doesn't go away but gets worse. Smokers, people with asthma, and people who live or work in polluted areas

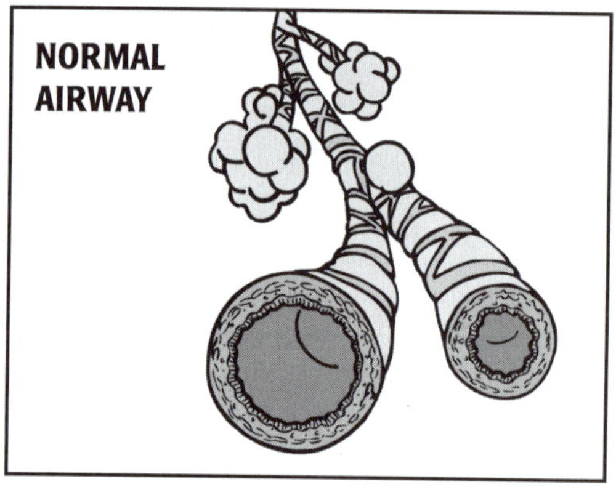

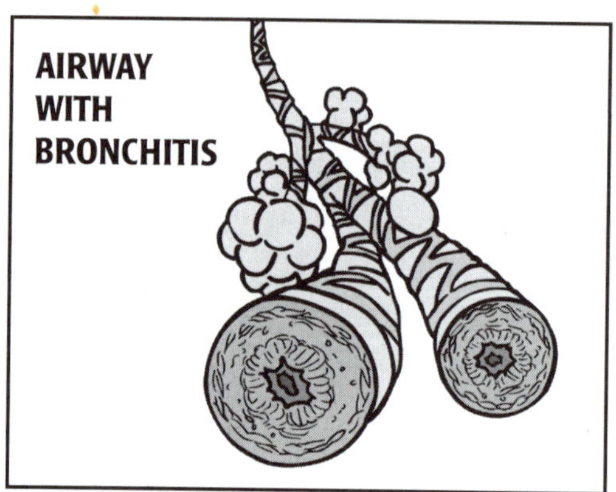

Self-Care Steps for Bronchitis

The best treatment for bronchitis is to drink plenty of fluids. By drinking 6 to 8 glasses of clear liquids (not milk) a day, you will help keep the mucus from gumming up your bronchial tubes. When the mucus is thin and fluid, it is easier to clear away by coughing. And when the bronchial passages are clear and the inflammation has gone away, so will the cough.

Here are some other things you can do to treat bronchitis on your own.

- Get plenty of rest. Listen to your body. You can continue your daily routine while you have bronchitis, but don't overdo it. If you feel tired, rest.
- Avoid alcohol and caffeine. Either can make you lose body fluid, which you need to keep mucus thin.
- If you think you need medicine, choose a cough suppressant with dextromethorphan. Some cough medicines contain antihistamines or other preparations you probably don't need or want when you have bronchitis. If you are coughing up mucus, you might also try a cough suppressant that contains the expectorant guaifenesin. (An expectorant is a substance that helps expel mucus from the respiratory tract.)
- Watch for signs of pneumonia. These include the following:
  - coughing
  - shaking and chills
  - temperature (sometimes as high as 104 or 105 degrees)
  - white, yellow, green, blood-streaked, or rust-colored mucus
  - shortness of breath; chest pain
  - fatigue
- Because pneumonia left untreated can be life-threatening, see your health care provider if your bronchitis becomes worse or you start to have the symptoms above. Severe cases of pneumonia require hospitalization.

are at greatest risk of developing chronic bronchitis. Symptoms include a morning cough that produces mucus. In the later stages of chronic bronchitis, periods of wheezing and breathlessness may occur frequently. This condition can lead to more serious lung damage, pneumonia, emphysema, and even heart failure (see *Bronchitis* and *Emphysema*, page 279).

What to do. Because bronchitis is closely related to pneumonia (see *Pneumonia*, page 143), it is important to see your health care provider to rule out pneumonia if symptoms get worse or if they last longer than a week. A chest examination is often the only thing needed, but your provider may also order chest X-rays or a mucus culture, in which he or she takes a sample of mucus to send for testing. If your provider prescribes an antibiotic, take it for the length of time prescribed, even if you start feeling better.

Over-the-counter cough suppressants and decongestants may help relieve your cough, or your health care provider may prescribe other drugs. If your cough lasts longer than four to six weeks, your provider should check it.

If you have chronic bronchitis, your health care provider may prescribe an aerosol inhaler that will help you breathe easier by relaxing your bronchial muscles. He or she may also prescribe antibiotics to protect you from developing a more serious

Decision Guide for Bronchitis

Symptoms/Signs	Action
Productive or dry cough after a cold or the flu; tiredness; no fever	Use self-care
Cough that worsens or lasts longer than 1 week	Call provider's office; Use self-care
Temperature of 101 degrees or higher, or any fever that lasts longer than 3 days	Call provider's office
Blood in phlegm or mucus	Call provider's office
Cough that lasts longer than 4 to 6 weeks	See provider
Shortness of breath and heavy coughing	See provider
Person has asthma (see page 274) and gets symptoms of bronchitis	See provider
Person has chronic obstructive pulmonary disease (see page 279) and gets symptoms of bronchitis	See provider

For more about the symbols, see page 60.

infection. If you smoke, quit. Talk with your provider about groups and other strategies that can help you quit. If your everyday environment is the cause of your chronic bronchitis, your provider may recommend that you move or change jobs.

Chest Pain

Feelings of pain or pressure in the chest area could signal a problem as simple as heartburn (see *Heartburn*, page 101) or as serious as a heart attack. Pay attention to those signals, and call your health care provider's office if you aren't sure what your symptoms mean.

Heart Pains

A myocardial infarction—commonly known as a heart attack—occurs when part of the heart muscle dies because it is not getting enough blood and oxygen. The symptoms that heart attack victims may experience include:

- feeling of pressure in the chest
- pain that spreads to the jaw, arms, neck, or back
- no relief from pain after rest or taking prescribed drug
- pain that lasts longer than 15 minutes
- nausea; vomiting
- shortness of breath
- sweating
- pain that occurs at rest or awakens you from sleep

The risk factors for a heart attack include high blood pressure (hypertension), diabetes, or a family history of early heart disease (see *Heart Disease*, page 283).

What to do. If you think you could be having a heart attack, call 911 or your local emergency response team and get to the hospital as quickly as possible. Every minute counts. If you are unsure, call a health care provider or go to the emergency room anyhow. Do not drive yourself! Be pre-

Self-Care Steps for Chest Pain

- If you think your chest pain is related to muscle strain from exercise or a fall or other accident, and the pain is worse when you press on the affected area, take an anti-inflammatory pain reliever such as ibuprofen or acetaminophen. Heat and rest can also help this kind of chest pain.
- If you think you have angina, call your health care provider (see page 273).
- If you think you have gallbladder pain, see *Gallstones,* page 101.
- If you think you are having a heart attack or pulmonary embolism, call 911. Seek medical help immediately.
- If you think you have heartburn (indigestion), see page 101.

Decision Guide for Chest Pain

Symptoms/Signs	Action
Heartburn and indigestion	Use self-care
Angina episode	Use self-care
Undiagnosed chest pain	Call provider's office
Gallbladder pain	Call provider's office
Heart attack	Emergency: call 911
Pulmonary embolism	Emergency: call 911

For more about the symbols, see page 60.

pared. If someone in your family suffers from heart disease, learn cardiopulmonary resuscitation, or CPR, and be prepared to use it in an emergency. It could save a life. (See *CPR for Adults and Children Ages 8 and Older*, page 56, or *CPR for Children Under 8 Years Old*, page 59.)

Other Chest Pains

Angina. This is a pressure or pain in the heart that feels similar to a heart attack but comes and goes (see *Angina*, page 273). Rest or prescribed medications usually ease the pain of angina.

Panic disorder. This is characterized by sudden chest pains that last half an hour or less in people under 35 years of age. Panic disorder can include chest pain symptoms such as heart palpitations (a fast, strong, or uneven heartbeat) and shortness of breath. Other symptoms are anxiety and fear of suffocation or dying. Most people with panic disorder can be helped with therapy (in which patients learn to reduce anxiety, view panic-causing situations differently, and may be exposed to situations they fear), medication, or both (see *Anxiety*, page 258).

Chest wall pain. This occurs when muscles, ligaments, cartilage, and other tissues in the chest wall become quite painful from strains caused by exercise, a fall, or even coughing. This type of chest pain usually feels worse when you press down on the sore area.

Heartburn. This is also called indigestion, and often occurs after eating a heavy or spicy meal. Heartburn can cause chest pains that seem similar to those of a heart attack (see *Heartburn*, page 101).

Ulcers and gallbladder problems. These problems may also cause spreading pains in the chest. Ulcer pains are worse if the stomach is empty. Gallbladder pains are usually worse after a meal high in fat and often occur in the upper right side of the body. A brief, sharp pain that lasts only a few seconds or a pain at the end of a deep breath is fairly common. Although they are unexplained, these pains are usually harmless (see *Gallstones*, page 101).

Pulmonary embolism. This is a blood clot blocking one of the arteries that leads from the heart to the lungs. A pulmonary embolism is a medical emergency. This condition is rare and mainly occurs in bedridden patients. Risk factors for a pulmonary embolism are surgery within the past six weeks, a cast, or some other condition that confines a person to bed.

You should know the signs of a pulmonary embolism (a blood clot in your lung), but be aware that these symptoms also apply to other conditions:

- sudden shortness of breath, often associated with chest pains, which are worse when you breathe deeply
- a bloody cough
- pain and swelling of the calf
- anxiety, sweating, and rapid heartbeat (see *Hyperventilation*, page 83).

If you think you may have a pulmonary embolism, call 911 or your local emergency response team; you should get to a hospital immediately.

Colds (Viral Upper Respiratory Infections)

Although myths abound about this common annoyance, the fact is you can't catch a cold by walking in the rain, failing to bundle up in the cold, or sitting by a draft. A cold is a viral infection.

Cold symptoms start quickly. They worsen during the first three to five days and then slowly improve. Sinus congestion, discolored nasal discharge, and headaches frequently accompany the common cold and do not always mean a serious infection. Temperatures during a cold are usually lower than 101 degrees and last less than three days. Some loss of appetite or difficulty sleeping is normal with colds, especially for children.

Decision Guide for Colds

Symptoms/Signs	Action
Sore throat (see page 127), cough	Use self-care
Congestion, general achiness	Use self-care
Scratchy throat, runny/stuffy nose	Use self-care
Symptoms that worsen after 3 to 5 days	Call provider's office
Symptoms that don't improve and still bother you after 7 days	Call provider's office
Symptoms that don't resolve after 14 days	Call provider's office

For more about the symbols, see page 60.

Decision Guide for Colds in Children

Symptoms/Signs	Action
Bothersome cold symptoms and a fever (see page 74) lasting longer than 48 hours or associated with symptoms of ear infection	 Call provider's office
Wheezing or difficulty breathing or swallowing	 Seek help now
Less responsive, poor eye contact (for infants/young children)	 Seek help now

For more about the symbols, see page 60.

Special Concerns for Children

- Children have colds more frequently than adults; 5 to 8 colds each year is not unusual. They are exposed to a wider variety of illnesses while at school or in day care.
- Over-the-counter medicine is not recommended for children without a health care provider's advice.
- Encourage children to drink a lot of fluids and stay active if they do not feel too tired.
- If your child has a fever, call his or her provider for advice about how to treat it and when to check in again. A fever is defined for children as a rectal temperature over 100.4 degrees or an oral temperature over 99.5 degrees.
- For an infant younger than 3 months of age, call his or her provider when the child's rectal temperature is over 100.4 degrees, if the infant is feeding poorly, can't be comforted, can't stay awake, or has a weak cry.

Self-Care Steps for a Cold

- Raise the humidity at home. You can sit in the bathroom with a hot shower running or use a humidifier/vaporizer (a cool mist is preferred). If using a humidifier, empty and clean it daily following the manufacturer's instructions. Remember, you should never leave a young child alone in the bathroom while the shower is running.
- Drink extra fluids. Warm fluids are especially soothing for irritated throats.
- To relieve nasal congestion, sleep with your head raised on pillows.
- Gargle with salt water or suck hard candy. Dissolve 1/4 teaspoon salt in 8 ounces warm water to help relieve a sore throat. Hard candy is as effective for sore throats as cough drops.
- Try over-the-counter saline nose drops or sprays.
- Remain up and about. You will benefit from extra rest, but you'll usually feel better if you stay moderately active.
- Over-the-counter nasal sprays or decongestants may provide temporary relief. Because of potential side effects, be sure to follow the recommended dosage and precautions. If you have high blood pressure, diabetes, thyroid disease, or asthma, check with your health care provider before using decongestants. Also be aware that using nasal sprays and decongestants too can often worsen symptoms even after they have been alleviated for awhile. This is called rebound congestion.
- Use medicine for discomfort as recommended by your provider. It may be better to use medication for specific symptoms than to take cold medicines, which may be formulated to treat an array of symptoms you don't actually have.

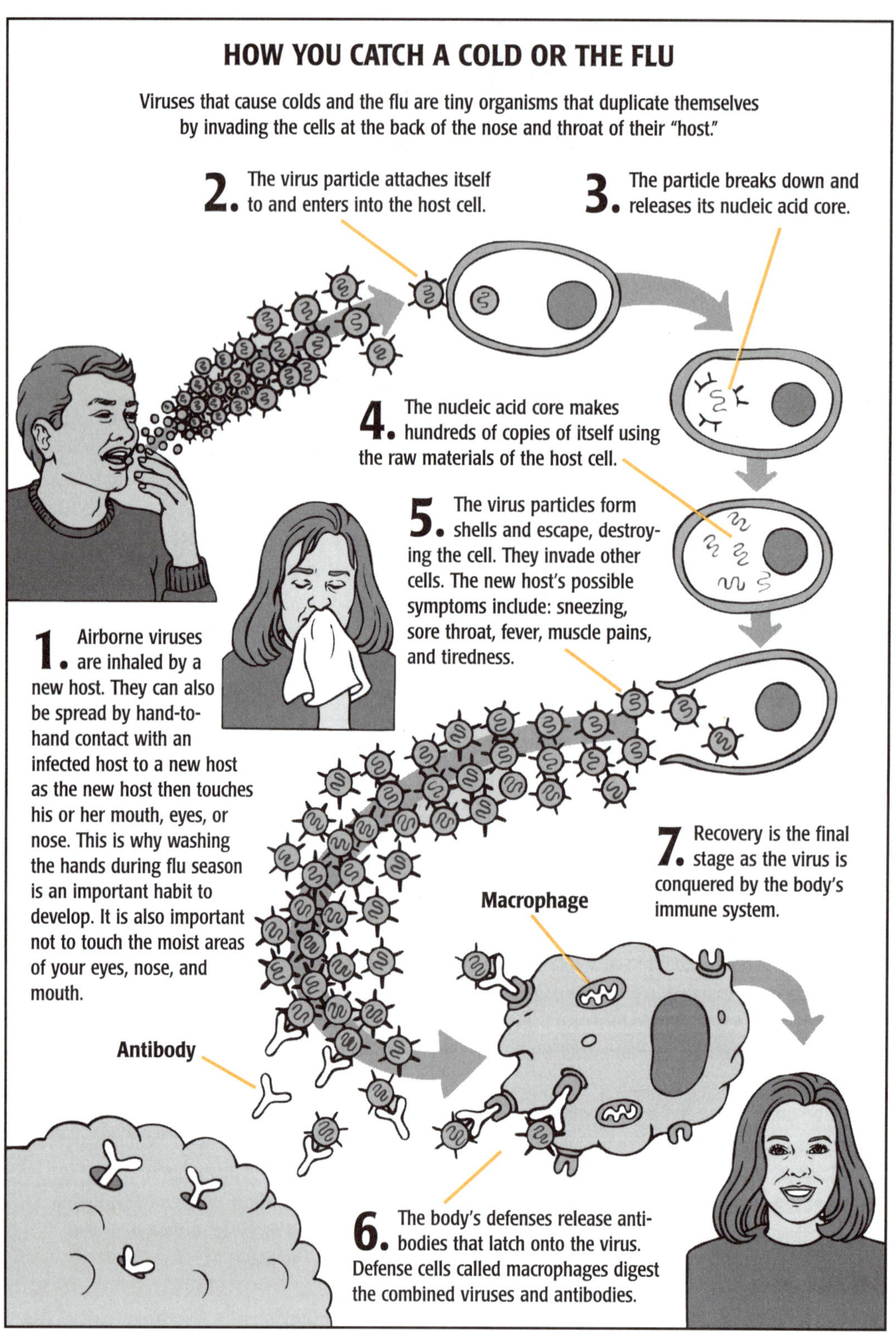
HOW YOU CATCH A COLD OR THE FLU
Viruses that cause colds and the flu are tiny organisms that duplicate themselves by invading the cells at the back of the nose and throat of their "host."
2. The virus particle attaches itself to and enters into the host cell.
3. The particle breaks down and releases its nucleic acid core.
4. The nucleic acid core makes hundreds of copies of itself using the raw materials of the host cell.
5. The virus particles form shells and escape, destroying the cell. They invade other cells. The new host's possible symptoms include: sneezing, sore throat, fever, muscle pains, and tiredness.
1. Airborne viruses are inhaled by a new host. They can also be spread by hand-to-hand contact with an infected host to a new host as the new host then touches his or her mouth, eyes, or nose. This is why washing the hands during flu season is an important habit to develop. It is also important not to touch the moist areas of your eyes, nose, and mouth.
7. Recovery is the final stage as the virus is conquered by the body's immune system.
Macrophage
Antibody
6. The body's defenses release antibodies that latch onto the virus. Defense cells called macrophages digest the combined viruses and antibodies.

Because the common cold is a viral infection, there are no medicines that will cure it or shorten its length. A cold will usually go away on its own in 7 to 14 days, regardless of what you do. Cold medications only ease symptoms temporarily.

The easiest way to catch these viruses is from other people—by shaking their hands, being within sneezing distance, or touching things they have handled. The best way to prevent the spread of the common cold is to avoid people who have colds. Wash your hands if you have physical contact with someone who has a cold.

What to do. A cold is uncomfortable, but it is usually just an inconvenience. Commonly used cold remedies do not cure or shorten the length of a cold, but the self-care steps on page 139 list a variety of ways to help relieve your symptoms while you wait for a cold to pass.

Flu (Influenza)

Influenza, or the flu, is a general name for several related viruses that infect the respiratory tract. This disease is highly contagious and usually occurs in epidemics during the fall and winter months. Symptoms can include fever, sore throat, cough, headache, fatigue, and aches and pains in the muscles. The flu can last from three days to a week, but full recovery may take longer.

The flu can also attack the digestive system of children under 5, who may experience vomiting and diarrhea along with other flu symptoms. Children this age generally have a fever of 102 to 105 degrees that comes on suddenly. They also may develop croup (see *Croup*, page 118). Older children and teens tend to have a fever of 101 to 103 degrees.

The flu is much more dangerous when it affects older people, people with weakened immune systems, or people with lung or heart disease, which is why these people should get flu vaccines (see a full list of high-risk groups on page 142).

Complications from the flu can include pneumonia (see page 143), bronchitis (see page 134), and, rarely, encephalitis in children (see page 209).

What to do. You can treat most cases of influenza at home. By resting and returning to activity gradually you can usually ensure that a relapse will not occur. It's also important to drink plenty of fluids and eat nutritious foods. Acetaminophen can ease aches and pains and reduce fever. Do not give

Self-Care Steps for Influenza

- Rest in a room with good ventilation.
- Drink plenty of liquids.
- Eat a nutritious, balanced diet.
- Take acetaminophen for aches, pain, and fever.
- Return to normal activities gradually.

Decision Guide for Influenza

Symptoms/Signs	Action
An otherwise healthy individual develops flu symptoms	Use self-care
Person with the flu is elderly, has heart or lung disease, or a weakened immune system	Call provider's office

For more about the symbols, see page 60.

Influenza

aspirin to children or teenagers, because it has been associated with the development of a serious condition called Reye's syndrome, especially in children who have influenza.

Some people should get a flu vaccine because the flu can be life-threatening to them. Flu vaccines are recommended for the following high-risk groups:

- people over the age of 65
- nursing home residents
- people with heart or lung disease, diabetes, chronic anemia, or weakened immune systems
- children who have asthma
- health care providers
- household members of anyone in these groups

Palpitations

When the heart beats normally, the two smaller chambers contract together and then the two larger chambers contract together. This produces the familiar two-thump heartbeat sound. Heart palpitations, known in medical terms as arrhythmias, occur when the beating heart gets out of step. Arrhythmias vary, from the feeling that the heart has skipped a beat to feeling that the heart is racing or fluttering. Heart palpitations are not usually dangerous. Everyone has them from time to time. Many arrhythmias are caused by caffeine, nicotine, alcohol, stress, or worry, and relieving or ridding yourself of any or all of these can correct your heartbeat.

However, you should discuss a rapid heart rate or persistent palpitations with your health care provider. If you have palpitations that may be caused by panic disorder (see *Panic disorder*, page 137)—a common cause of chest pain in people under 35—tell your provider.

Keep in mind that serious heart conditions are usually marked by other symptoms too.

Self-Care Steps for Palpitations

- Stop smoking. Get help to stop (see page 4).
- Avoid caffeine and alcohol.
- Practice stress-reducing techniques such as meditation, biofeedback, or yoga.

Decision Guide for Palpitations

Symptoms/Signs	Action
Persistent heart palpitations or a rapid heart rate; before you call, write down exactly what happened.	Call provider's office
Palpitations and dizziness, shortness of breath, or sweating	Emergency: call 911
Palpitations and chest pain (see page 136)	Emergency: call 911

For more about the symbols, see page 60.

Pneumonia

Pneumonia is an inflammation of the lungs usually caused by a bacterium or virus. This condition can be a complication of many other serious illnesses. Symptoms include a cough that produces blood or a yellow-green substance, fever, chills, and difficulty breathing.

What to do. If the case is very mild, you may be able to treat pneumonia at home—but talk with your provider first. However, if pneumonia accompanies another illness or the person has a weakened immune system, hospitalization may be necessary. A person with severe pneumonia may require artificial ventilation and oxygen therapy. Several drugs may be used to treat pneumonia, depending on the type of infection that caused the condition.

Decision Guide for Pneumonia

Symptoms/Signs	Action
Respiratory illness with cough, fever, and shortness of breath	See provider
Chills, fever	See provider
Bloody phlegm or mucus	See provider
A bluish tint to the skin under the nails and the lips	Seek help now
Confusion	Emergency: call 911

For more about the symbols, see page 60.

You should consult your health care provider immediately if you think you might have pneumonia.

Stroke

Strokes are the third leading cause of death for adults in the United States. Strokes are also known as brain attacks because of their similarity to a heart attack. In a stroke, the arteries leading to the brain are blocked or rupture, and oxygen-starved brain cells begin to die. The same thing happens to the heart in a heart attack.

Effects of stroke can include paralysis, difficulty speaking or understanding speech, memory lapses, problems performing tasks, and death.

Risk factors for stroke are similar to those for a heart attack: smoking, having high blood pressure, being overweight, and having high cholesterol. African-Americans have about twice the risk of having a stroke that Caucasians do. But you can control most risk factors and reduce your chance of having a stroke.

What to do. If you are having a stroke, get immediate medical attention. Do not delay! The sooner you are treated, the less likely you are to have extensive brain damage, paralysis, and other types of impaired function. Warning signs of stroke include the following:

- sudden weakness or numbness of the face, arm, or leg on one side of the body
- sudden dimness or loss of vision, particularly in one eye
- loss of speech, trouble talking, or trouble understanding speech

- sudden, severe headaches with no apparent cause
- unexplained dizziness, unsteadiness, or sudden falls, especially when combined with any of the above symptoms

Treatment for stroke can involve giving the victim drugs to prevent or reduce blood clotting or lower blood pressure, which will allow blood to reach the brain and reduce the chance of a ruptured blood vessel. If the stroke causes a person to lose movement or speech abilities, rehabilitative therapy can help him or her to relearn lost skills.

Wheezing

If you hear a whistling sound that feels as if it's coming from your chest when you breathe out, you are wheezing. Wheezing occurs when airways in the lungs constrict. A common symptom of asthma (see *Asthma*, page 274), wheezing can also be caused by bronchitis, smoking, allergies, pneumonia, sensitivities to chemicals or pollution, emphysema, lung cancer, heart failure, or even an object that is trapped in the airways.

The conditions that cause most cases of wheezing require medical attention. If you are under a health care provider's care for asthma and have developed an action plan with your provider, you don't have to run to his or her office or the emergency room when you start to wheeze. Just follow your provider's recommendations. If you do not have asthma and develop wheezing, call your provider.

Decision Guide for Wheezing

Symptoms/Signs	Action
Mild bouts of wheezing associated with known asthma	Use self-care
Person who has asthma with wheezing that lasts or worsens despite care	Call provider's office
Any new wheezing	Call provider's office
Wheezing and shortness of breath	Seek help now
Wheezing caused by an object lodged in the throat; if the person is completely unable to breathe, try the Heimlich maneuver, page 67	Emergency: call 911

For more about the symbols, see page 60.

Muscle and Joint Problems

From everyday tasks like typing to dramatic athletic feats like windsurfing and gymnastics, your muscles and bones perform day after day and year after year. Aches and pains are signals from your musculoskeletal system that you have pushed too hard. This chapter describes common problems of your muscles and joints, and suggests ways to take care of nonurgent conditions at home.

Aches and Pains in Muscles and Joints

Whether it's your shoulder, ankle, or some other joint, pain in or around joints has similar origins and treatments no matter what part of the body it affects. Joint pain and limited mobility are usually caused by an injury to muscles, ligaments, or connective tissue. Knowing what happened before the pain started gives you an important clue to the problem. The following are common sources of muscle and joint pain.

Accidents. A fall, bump, blow, or sudden twist can cause bruising of soft tissues; bone fractures; joint dislocations; or torn muscles, tendons (fibers connecting muscle to bone), or ligaments (bands that hold joints together and connect bone to bone).

Repetitive motions or prolonged overuse. All good things require moderation, including work and play. Even an athlete in top shape can strain a muscle while training. Too much of any activity—such as pitching too many games of softball or working long hours at a computer—can cause inflammation and pain in the joint and surrounding tissues.

Overdoing it. If you've been indoors and inactive for months, a 10-mile bike ride or a day digging in the garden can cause some muscle soreness. Injuries from overdoing it occur most often when people are out of shape and do moderate or strenuous activities. You need to slowly build the strength and endurance needed for any demanding physical activity.

Muscle imbalance. When muscles on one side of the body are much stronger than those on the other side, they put added stress on weaker muscles, often causing injury. For example, a weight lifter who overdevelops the arm and chest muscles but neglects the muscles that support the upper back and shoulder blades may wind

Self-Care Steps for Aches and Pains in Muscles and Joints

THE RICE METHOD

With a few exceptions, the RICE (Rest, Ice, Compress, Elevate) method explained below will reduce pain and help speed recovery of joint and muscle injuries.

R est. For most injuries, rest the area until the pain stops. For simple sore muscles, however, gentle stretching will reduce stiffness sooner. Hold the stretch for 30 to 60 seconds, then rest and repeat 5 to 10 times. Do not bounce. Do this several times a day.

I ce. Ice is the most effective way to reduce inflammation, pain, and swelling of injured muscles, joints, and connective tissues (such as tendons, ligaments, and bursas). The cold helps keep blood and fluid from building up in the injured area, reducing pain and swelling. Apply ice as soon as possible after injury, even if you are going straight to your health care provider.

To speed recovery and ease pain, raise the injured area and apply ice for 20 minutes (10 to 15 minutes for children) every 2 to 3 hours while awake. For best results, use crushed ice in a moist towel as an ice pack. Use an elastic bandage to hold the ice pack in place. During the first 48 to 72 hours, or as long as there is any swelling, do not apply heat to an injury. Heat increases blood flow to the affected area, which makes swelling and pain worse.

C ompress. Between icings, wrap the injured area with an elastic bandage to help control swelling and provide support. Begin wrapping at the point farthest from the body and wrap toward the heart. For example, to wrap an ankle you would begin at the toes and wrap to the mid-calf. Don't sleep with the wrap on, unless your health care provider tells you to do so. And don't wrap too tightly! If the wrap begins to cause pain or numbness, or if toes are cool or white, remove the elastic bandage and wrap it more loosely.

E levate. Raising the injured area above your heart will allow gravity to help reduce swelling by draining excess fluid. At night, place a pillow under the area to support and raise it.

In addition to RICE, there are several other things you can do to promote healing and relieve pain of most muscle and joint injuries. These are the basics to remember, but see the topic later in this chapter that addresses the joint where you are having pain.

PAIN RELIEVERS

If you need to, take acetaminophen or non-steroidal anti-inflammatory drugs (NSAIDs) such as ibuprofen, naproxen sodium, and aspirin. Acetaminophen, aspirin, and NSAIDs often treat muscle and joint injuries effectively. Sometimes aspirin and NSAIDs work best because they reduce inflammation. Acetaminophen does not reduce inflammation.

Aspirin and other NSAIDs are often more irritating to the stomach and bowel. Acetaminophen is better for patients with ulcers or other digestive problems or for those who suffer stomach problems when they take NSAIDs. When using aspirin, choose buffered aspirin or enteric-coated aspirin, which is easier on the stomach. All aspirin and NSAIDs should be taken with food. If NSAIDs cause minor stomach upset after 7 to 10 days of use, stop medication, take antacids, and call your health care provider.

Again, children and teenagers with muscle or joint injuries should be given acetaminophen only, unless your child's health care provider says otherwise.

(continued)

Self-Care Steps for Aches and Pains in Muscles and Joints (continued)

Slowly strengthen the injured area. Slow strengthening of the injured area after it has healed is advisable for keeping most injuries from occurring again. Your health care provider or a physical therapist can recommend specific exercises, including range-of-motion exercises, muscle stretches, and specific weight training.

Warm up before you exercise. You are less likely to injure muscles that have been gradually eased into activity. Before you launch into any strenuous activity, try jogging in place, quick walking, or other activities that will get you moving and eliminate stiffness.

Heat before, ice after. Once the swelling has subsided—which often takes weeks—and you are working to strengthen the recovering area, you may apply heat before exercise to prepare the muscles, joint, and connective tissues for the workout. Apply ice soon after your workout to prevent inflammation and swelling.

Fractures, Sprains, and Strains

FRACTURES

Fractures are breaks in bone, most often caused by a blow or a fall. Fractures can range in seriousness from a hairline fracture (a thin fracture that may not run through the whole bone or in which both ends of the bone remain aligned), to a compound fracture, in which the broken bone protrudes through the skin.

Symptoms can include tenderness over the bone, shooting pain, visible deformity of the limb, and increased pain with movement.

What to do. If a fracture is suspected, call your health care provider. If a spinal injury is suspected or the person cannot walk, call 911. Do not move the person. Until help arrives, apply ice to the area. If there is bleeding, apply pressure to stop the bleeding (see *Fractures,* page 76).

SPRAINS

Sprains are stretched or torn ligaments. Ligaments connect bone to bone and bone to cartilage, and help hold joints together. Any joint can be sprained, but sprains occur most commonly at the ankle, knee, finger, or wrist. Symptoms include swelling, pain, and bruising.

What to do. Treat with the RICE method (see page 146) for at least 72 hours, or until swelling begins to decrease. Self-care is usually sufficient to treat a mild sprain. However, more severe sprains may require that a health care provider apply a cast or splint to the joint.

STRAINS

A strain is also known as a pulled muscle or muscle tear, and is caused by forcing a muscle past its normal range of motion. Strains most often occur in the middle of the muscle. Symptoms include pain, swelling, muscle spasm, and limited movement.

What to do. In most cases, you can successfully treat a strained muscle by icing and massaging it and gently stretching it 3 to 5 times a day. However, if a muscle is severely torn, it may need to be repaired surgically.

up with a back or neck injury. The reason: The chest muscles overpower the back, causing constant tightness and muscle or joint pain.

Referred pain. Sometimes pain felt in one area of the body originates in a different area. For example, pain in the left shoulder or arm may be a sign of a heart attack. Likewise, knee pain may be caused by a hip or foot problem. Whenever pain appears suddenly without an apparent cause such as accident or injury, call your health care provider. If you feel sudden left-arm pain, chest tightness, shortness of breath, or pain in the jaw with no apparent cause, call 911 immediately.

Special Concerns for Children

- Muscle and joint pains in children are treated much the same way as they are in adults. Children and teenagers, however, should be given acetaminophen to relieve pain. Do not give them aspirin, due to the risk of Reye's syndrome. If the child cannot move the joint or if pain increases with movement, call your child's health care provider. Inability to bend a joint can be a sign of a fractured bone or infection in the joint—both serious conditions.
- Before a child reaches maturity, the long bones in the body (arms and legs) have growth plates, called epiphyses. The epiphysis allows the bone to grow or lengthen. A fracture or dislocation can damage the epiphysis. This may slow or stop bone growth or make a bone grow crooked. Although common sense tells you that any suspected broken bone should be seen by your child's health care provider, this is particularly important if the child complains of pain around a joint. A fracture to the epiphysis can occur without trauma, often through overuse (pitching too many fastballs or lifting heavy weights).
- Broken bones and other injuries aside, it is common for children having growth spurts to have vague aches and pains for no apparent reason (see *Lower-Leg Pain, Special Concerns for Children,* page 182).

Ankle Pain

The ankle is one of the most frequently injured joints of the body. Strains and sprains are the most common ankle injuries, but many people experience problems with tendinitis, bursitis, and fractures. Because of the ankle's crucial role in walking and standing, ankle injuries should be taken seriously and treated properly.

Strains, Sprains, and Fractures

Twisting your ankle may cause stretching or tearing of the ligaments and tendons. (Definitions of strains, sprains, and fractures are on page 147.) This most often occurs on the outside of the ankle.

Mild strains or sprains may cause mild to moderate pain and little or no swelling. The ankle can support weight, but a limp is usually apparent. Moderate sprains hurt more when you move, and swelling and tenderness increase. Walking is hard and crutches are often needed for a few days.

A sprain is considered severe when the ligament and tendons are stretched or completely torn (ruptured). Severe sprains are accompanied by acute pain, swelling, tenderness, and bruising. The joint is hard to move, and you can't walk or bear weight on

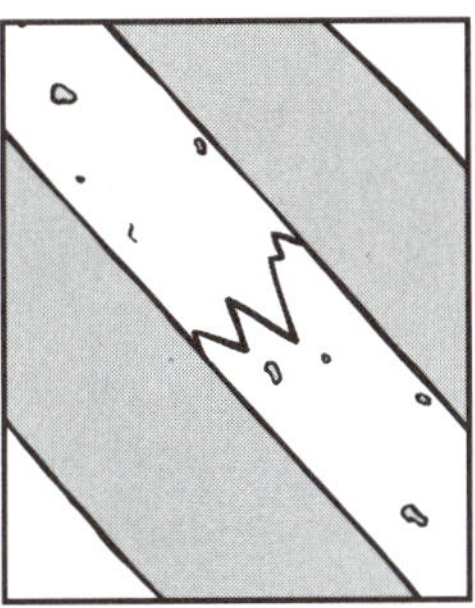

Simple Fracture
Bone breaks but does not puncture the skin.

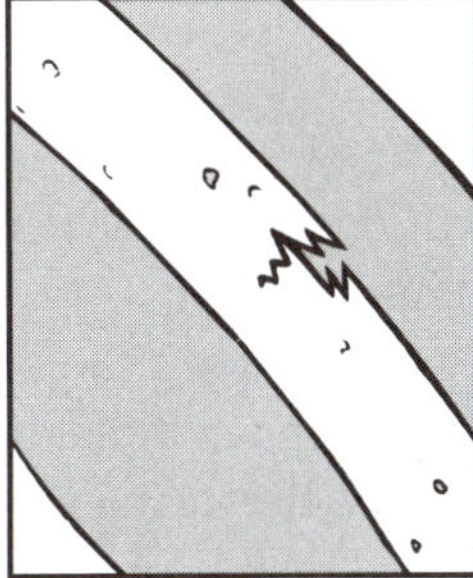

Greenstick Fracture
One side of a bent bone breaks; this usually occurs in children.

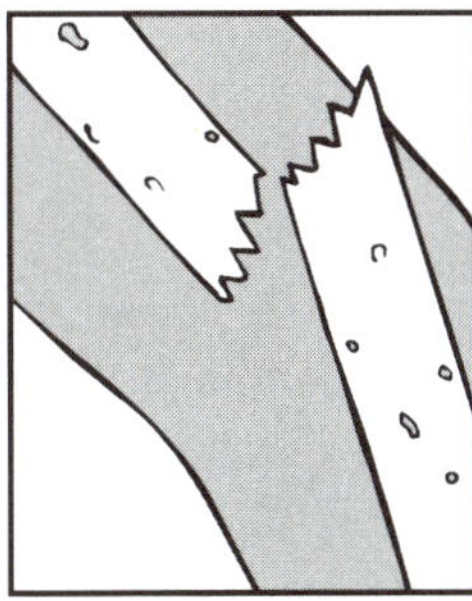

Compound Fracture
Bone breaks and punctures the flesh and skin.

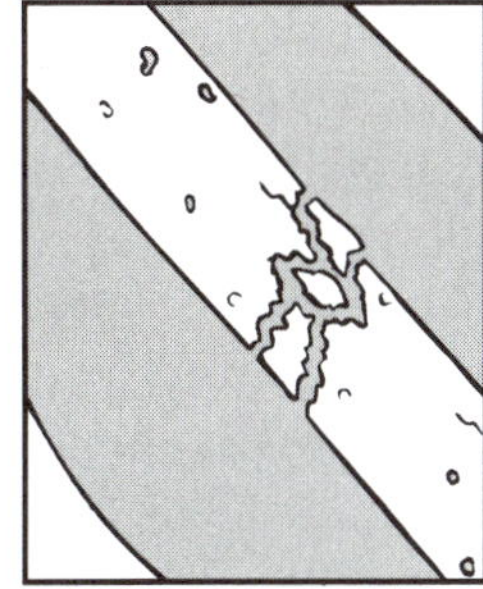

Comminuted Fracture
Bone shatters into more than two pieces; this is most often caused by a heavy blow.

THE DIFFERENCE BETWEEN A SPRAIN AND A STRAIN

A strain is the stretching or tearing of muscles or tendons.

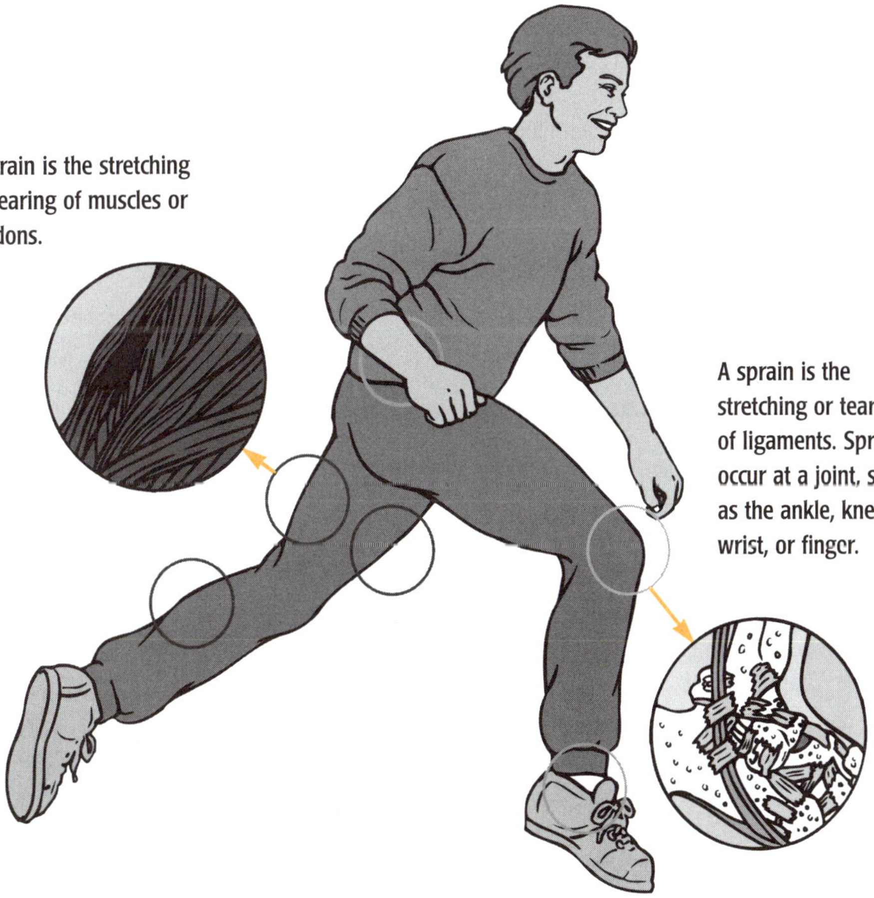

A sprain is the stretching or tearing of ligaments. Sprains occur at a joint, such as the ankle, knee, wrist, or finger.

the ankle. Moderate and severe sprains may also cause bruising in the foot and toes and up the side of the leg.

What to do. Unless the ankle is obviously deformed, very painful, or unable to bear any weight, a sprained ankle can be treated safely at home for the first 24 hours by using the RICE method (see *The RICE Method*, page 146). and making sure you don't put weight on the sprain. With a mild or moderate sprain, swelling should stop within 24 hours and the ankle should begin to improve (although it won't be healed) within 48 hours. If it doesn't, see a health care provider.

Because of the strength of the ligament on the inner ankle, bone will often give way before the ligament does. Pain on the inner ankle may be a fracture and in most cases should be X-rayed.

Self-Care Steps for Ankle Pain

- As with other joint injuries, the first step in treatment for most ankle injuries—including sprains, strains, and Achilles tendinitis and bursitis—is the RICE method and anti-inflammatory drugs (see *The RICE Method,* page 146). But there are a number of things you can do to treat sprains and other injuries.

SPRAINS

- Stay off the ankle as much as possible until the swelling stops, usually about 24 to 48 hours.
- Use the RICE method (see page 146).
- Use crutches if bearing weight on your ankle is painful.
- If swelling lasts longer than 3 days, alternately soak the ankle in cold water (45 to 60 degrees) for 1 minute and then in warm water (100 to 105 degrees) for 2 to 3 minutes. Do this for 15 to 20 minutes total, and stop if swelling increases. Print the alphabet in the air with your big toe to help increase range of motion.
- As the swelling and pain decrease, begin gentle stretching and strengthening exercises to regain range of motion.

STRAINS

- Follow the RICE method (see page 146) and avoid bearing weight on the ankle for 24 to 48 hours.
- If pain and swelling are worse after 24 hours, call your health care provider.
- If you still can't bear weight on the ankle after 48 hours, see your health care provider.
- As the swelling and pain decrease, begin gentle stretching and strengthening exercises to regain range of motion (see illustration below).

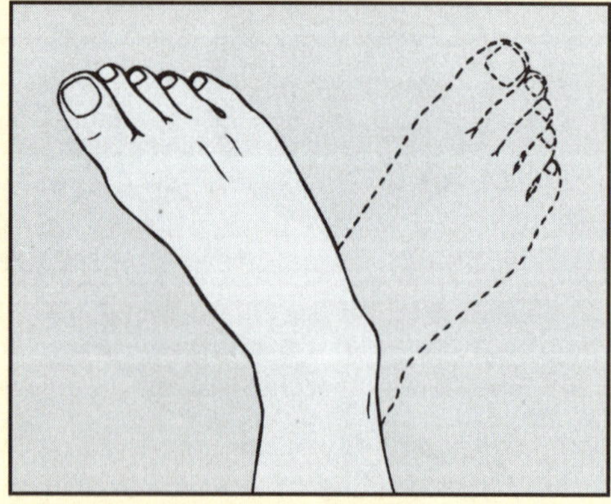

Range of Motion Exercise
Keeping your leg still, bend your ankle back and forth from left to right 10 times. Repeat this exercise several times a day.

Achilles Tendinitis and Bursitis

The treatment, causes, and symptoms of tendinitis and bursitis at the back of the ankle are very similar. The Achilles tendon is a large, strong band that attaches the calf muscle to the heel. Symptoms of Achilles tendinitis include pain in the calf and ankle that is worse when you wake up in the morning and gets better as the ankle is warmed up with use. Due to an improper warm-up or sudden movement, the Achilles tendon can occasionally tear or even rupture.

Underneath the Achilles tendon are bursas (small, fluid-filled sacs that cushion and lubricate joints) that may also become inflamed. Bursitis is inflammation of a bursa, and causes a soft, fluid-filled lump at the back of the ankle, along with pain similar to that of tendinitis.

Common causes of tendinitis and bursitis in the ankle include tight calf muscles, overuse, sudden stress from a quick movement, and repeated motion such as running. But you don't have to be athletic to have either problem. Shoes are often the culprit. Switching from high heels or cowboy boots to flat shoes, or wearing shoes that fit poorly or provide inadequate support and cushioning can also inflame tendons and bursas in the ankle.

What to do. If you have bursitis or tendinitis, treat the area with RICE (see *The RICE Method*, page 146) and take nonsteroidal anti-inflammatory drugs to relieve inflammation and pain (see *Pain Relievers*, page 146). With tendinitis, decrease activity for one to two weeks or until you are fairly pain-free. Apply heat to the area before stretching, and ice when you have finished. If there is no improvement in your tendinitis in 10 to 14 days or in your bursitis in 7 days, call your health care provider.

Gout

Gout is a metabolic disorder that causes arthritis (see *Arthritis*, page 152). Sudden pain, swelling, redness, and extreme tenderness in a joint are usually the signs of an acute attack of gout. An attack usually affects a single joint, most commonly the big toe. Other joints frequently affected include the foot joints, the ankle, knee, or wrist. Pain worsens within the first 24 to 36 hours and may be so severe that even the touch of a bedsheet is too much.

What to do. Raise your legs and apply ice, if you can stand it, and call your health care provider. Gout can be treated effectively with prescription drugs.

Swelling Without Injury

Sitting or standing for long periods without moving may cause the ankles and feet to swell. This type of swelling usually goes away overnight or lasts only a few days. But swollen ankles can also be a sign of something more serious, such as phlebitis (see *Phlebitis*, page 180) or congestive heart failure (see *Congestive Heart Failure*, page 180).

What to do. If your ankles swell after you've been sitting or standing for a long time, raise your legs. Increase activity and movement to prevent swelling. If swelling continues longer than three days or if you have pain without having had an injury, see your health care provider immediately.

Decision Guide for Ankle Pain

Symptoms/Signs	Action
Swelling, pain, and possible bruising from sudden twist or force	 Use self-care
Pain at back of ankle; begins slowly and may be worse when you wake up (Achilles tendinitis)	 Use self-care
No improvement of tendinitis symptoms after 10 to 14 days	 Call provider's office
Unable to bear any weight after hearing or feeling a pop, snap, or crack	 Call provider's office
Pain and swelling that increases 24 hours after injury	 See provider
Red, warm, swollen ankles; fever; feeling ill or having recently been ill with a sore throat or skin infection	 See provider
Chronic swelling in ankles, feet, or lower legs; difficulty breathing (see *Heart Disease,* page 283)	 See provider
Swelling in only one ankle or leg with pain; no injury (see *Phlebitis,* page 180)	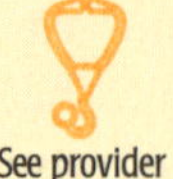 See provider
Pain on inner side of ankle; ankle twisted inward when injury occurred (see *Fractures,* page 76)	 See provider

For more about the symbols, see page 60.

Arthritis

Arthritis is one name for a number of diseases that produce inflammation, swelling, pain, and stiffness in the joints. Joint pain due to arthritis usually features fluid buildup and swelling around the joint, as well as a change in the joint's appearance. Joint pain that is not due to arthritis (often caused by muscle strains) usually has the following features:

- no swelling or joint damage
- joint that can be moved without a lot of difficulty
- often follows a recent bout of activity

Types of Arthritis

There are two main types of arthritis: inflammatory and noninflammatory. Each has features that set it apart from other types of joint pain.

Inflammatory arthritis. There are three main types of inflammatory arthritis: rheumatoid arthritis, gout, and arthritis caused by infection. Signs of inflammatory arthritis include:

- swelling
- redness, warmth, and tenderness
- loss of motion or function of the joint
- joint damage

For some people, the start of inflammatory arthritis pain is sudden and intense. For others, the pain begins gradually.

Noninflammatory arthritis. The most common type of noninflammatory arthritis is osteoarthritis. Osteoarthritis starts slowly, usually over many months to years. Signs of osteoarthritis include minor to nonexistent swelling and changes in the joint cartilage, which can lead to joint damage, pain, and loss of function.

See your health care provider. Your provider is qualified to evaluate and treat less complicated joint problems. If he or she thinks you need to see a specialist, you will get a referral to a rheumatologist or an orthopedic surgeon. A rheumatologist specializes in diagnosing and treating diseases of joints and muscles. Orthopedic surgeons also treat diseases of bone and joints, but they focus mostly on surgical treatment of these conditions.

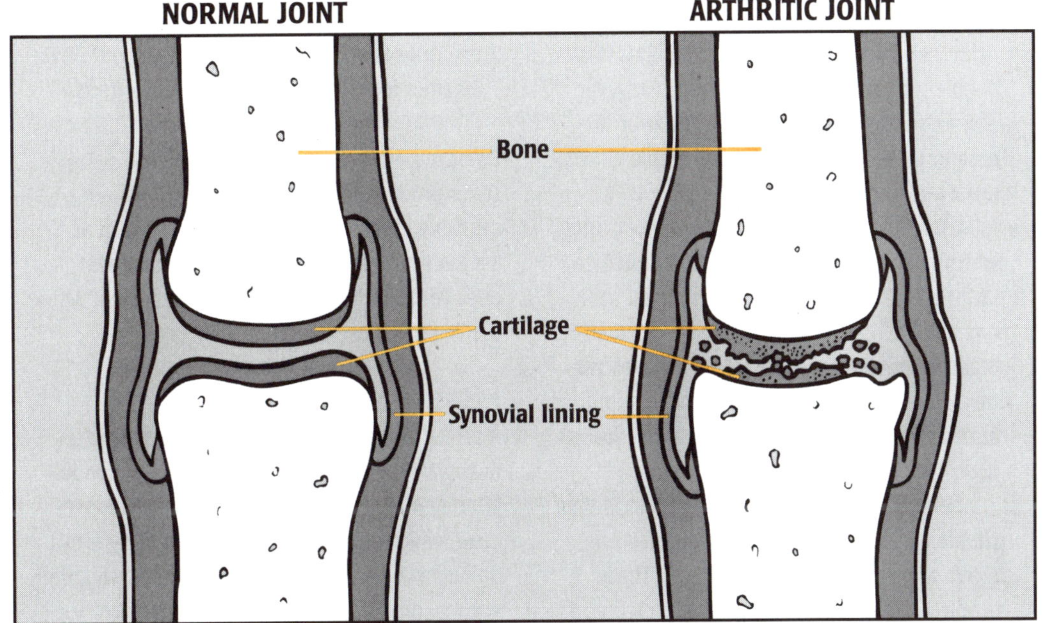

Arthritis, the inflammation of a joint, can cause pain, swelling, stiffness, and redness. There are many kinds of arthritis. The illustration on the right is typical of osteoarthritis, in which the protective cartilage cushion on the bone breaks down and bones of the joint rub against one another.

Arthritis

Self-Care Steps for Arthritis

OVER-THE-COUNTER MEDICINES

Over-the-counter medicines are often the first thing to try for arthritic pain. Two main types of medicines are used to treat arthritis: simple pain relievers and NSAIDs. Neither type is perfect for every situation.

- **Simple pain relievers.** Medicine such as acetaminophen can control arthritis pain effectively. Acetaminophen, like any medicine, must be taken over time to determine its effectiveness. Therapeutic doses may be as high as 2 extra-strength tablets 3 to 4 times daily. Most people can tolerate acetaminophen. However, acetaminophen can worsen existing liver disease or cause liver problems for people who drink alcohol heavily.
- **NSAIDs.** Nonsteroidal anti-inflammatory drugs, which relieve pain and decrease inflammation, include aspirin, ibuprofen and naproxen sodium, all of which are available over the counter. Many other NSAIDs are available by prescription. NSAIDs are effective pain relievers and also reduce inflammation, which usually helps decrease pain.

  NSAIDs have more serious side effects than simple pain relievers. The biggest concern is ulcers or bleeding from the stomach. These problems occur more frequently in patients with a history of ulcers, elderly patients, those with other illnesses, or those who are also taking other medicines. NSAIDs may also cause stomach upset. Fortunately, these side effects are relatively uncommon.

  Another concern about NSAIDs is the possibility that they will harm kidney function. This is a rare but potentially serious problem. The most important risk factor is kidney disease. Other factors that pose a smaller risk include having liver disease, being elderly, and taking other types of medicine, particularly diuretics.

  If you have any of these risk factors, you should talk with your health care provider about using these medicines before taking them.

  As with acetaminophen, the effectiveness of NSAIDs may not be evident right away. You may need to take them for a week or more before you feel better.

  It is impossible to predict which NSAID will work best for an individual. Therefore, people are often directed to choose one, use it regularly, and, if it doesn't work, choose another. Use only one drug at a time, since using multiple NSAIDs together increases the chance of side effects.

OTHER PRODUCTS

Other products useful in treating arthritis are available in most drugstores. Products such as aspirin in cream form and capsaicin ointment offer limited relief. Products that create heat where applied may ease pain on a short-term basis.

ASSISTIVE DEVICES

A broad range of assistive devices is available to support painful areas or improve function in affected joints. Wrist splints restrict wrist movement, which often relieves pain caused by arthritis. Tennis elbow straps ease pain by altering the stresses on the injured tendon. Padded arch supports and heel pads decrease various kinds of foot pain. Other devices include doorknob extenders, enlarged handle grips for silverware, adjustable canes, and special pillows to support the neck while you sleep.

NUTRITION

Eating a well-balanced diet will make you less likely to develop other problems that could complicate your arthritis. Good diets to follow include those supported by the American Heart Association, the American Diabetes Association, and the American Cancer Society.

(continued)

Self-Care Steps for Arthritis (continued)

Maintaining your ideal body weight is another key to better health. Carrying extra pounds increases wear and strain on arthritic joints (see *Losing Weight,* page 42). Fish oils can ease inflammation that often comes with rheumatoid arthritis. Studies suggest that fairly high doses are needed to achieve this effect, and inflammation is only modestly reduced; however, the effects are real. As a practical matter, substituting fish for meat is sensible. Fish oil pills are also available. If you choose to supplement your diet with fish oil pills, it's best to discuss this with your health care provider.

People with inflammatory arthritis may find that a specific food makes them feel worse. This is uncommon, but some studies indicate that 1 patient in 100 may have a food-related flare-up. Food-related arthritic flare-ups usually occur within 12 to 48 hours after eating the problem food. Food reactions, as well as the offending food, vary from person to person. If you recognize a pattern, it might help to discuss it with your health care provider.

OTHER APPROACHES

- **Exercise.** Exercise helps preserve joint health and function, even in damaged joints. By improving the function of structures that surround the joint—such as the tendons and the muscles—exercise decreases the amount of work the joint has to do.

  There is no preferred exercise for arthritis. Choose an exercise you like and begin adding it to your regular activities. Work out for a short time at first, and increase the length of your sessions gradually. Aerobic exercises are ideal, and low-impact activities such as walking, biking, and water exercises are usually the most comfortable. As long as the activity doesn't increase pain or swelling, it is probably not causing any more joint damage. If pain or swelling occurs and lasts for more than 30 minutes after the activity, it is probably the wrong type of exercise, or you may have been exercising too intensely.
- **Schedule changes.** People with arthritis are often less mobile and suffer more pain in the morning. Shifting activities until later in the day may help you take advantage of your greatest mobility and make it easier to deal with the pain. This strategy is particularly helpful for people who have inflammatory arthritis.
- **Reducing stress.** Finding better ways to deal with stress may help decrease pain from arthritis and other joint conditions. Some stress reduction options include meditation, biofeedback, and professional counseling. Exercise is also an excellent stress reliever.

COMMUNITY RESOURCES

Most communities have organizations and programs to serve people with arthritis or other disabilities. The Arthritis Foundation has chapters in every state. The organization provides educational materials and cosponsors support groups, self-help programs, educational seminars, and exercise classes. It also supports research on the causes and cures of arthritis.

- **Transportation services.** In larger communities, transportation services are usually available for people unable to drive or travel by public transportation. Social service agencies may also offer help in finding child care services, homemaking help, and meals-on-wheels programs. Additional assistance may be available to help explore financial and health care options. Many health care organizations offer specific programs designed to help people cope with arthritis. (For addresses and phone numbers of organizations, see *Resources,* page 292.)

Back Pain

Backaches are one of the most common reasons that people visit a health care provider. Studies show that 4 out of 5 people in the United States will suffer a serious bout of back pain at some time in their lives. Back pain is rarely the result of one incident. Rather, most back problems result from a lifetime of stress or strain to the back, a little at a time.

Poor posture, improper lifting habits, prolonged standing, a stressful job, or declining physical fitness can contribute to a bad back. One episode of disabling back pain may simply be a cue that you have put more stress on your back than it can handle.

Muscles weakened or strained over time are responsible for most back pain. Only about 10 percent of back complaints are linked to pressure on the nerves in your back. This type of pain tends to spread more into your buttocks or legs.

Acute low back pain is also called lumbar muscle strain or backache. It is described as low back pain that you've had for six weeks or less that does not go past the knees. Although quite painful, this condition usually improves after a few days of simple treatment.

Acute sciatica. Also known as disk pain or radiating leg pain, acute sciatica usually goes away more slowly than acute low back pain. Acute sciatica is low back pain that you've had for six weeks or less with pain that extends below the knee. Sciatica pain is often caused by nerve irritation from disks in the lower back.

Chronic back pain and sciatica. If your back pain and sciatica persist longer than six weeks, your condition is considered chronic and other evaluation is needed. You may need to go to the doctor for X-rays or other tests. If you have chronic back pain and sciatica, consider some type of back education class or instruction to help you learn to handle these problems.

If there has been no significant improvement, your health care provider may refer you to a specialist who diagnoses and treats the problems that can cause chronic back pain. Most often, these specialists work in departments of rehabilitation medicine, orthopedics, or neurosurgery. In certain cases, your provider may refer you to a specialist in neurology, occupational medicine, rheumatology, or another field.

Although treatment may vary for each individual, the procedures described follow a typical pattern of care for back pain. Your provider may follow procedures similar to these or make other arrangements for your treatment. Either way, it is important to understand how back problems get better and what to expect if they don't.

Warning symptoms. Tell your health care provider right away if you have any of the following symptoms or conditions:

- unexplained weight loss
- constant night pain
- fever
- trouble urinating
- leg weakness

Tests. X-rays are usually considered unnecessary in the early stages of treatment because they do not show inflamed muscles and disks. X-rays are rarely needed except for severe trauma (like a fall or motor vehicle accident), for older patients who may have bone fractures, or for people who have other medical problems.

If you have low back pain that does not improve after six weeks, X-rays will probably be ordered if they have not already been done. If you have sciatica pain longer than six weeks and surgery is being considered, then other procedures may be done. One is a CT scan, which stands for computerized tomography. This is a type of X-ray that produces a detailed image of tissues inside the body.

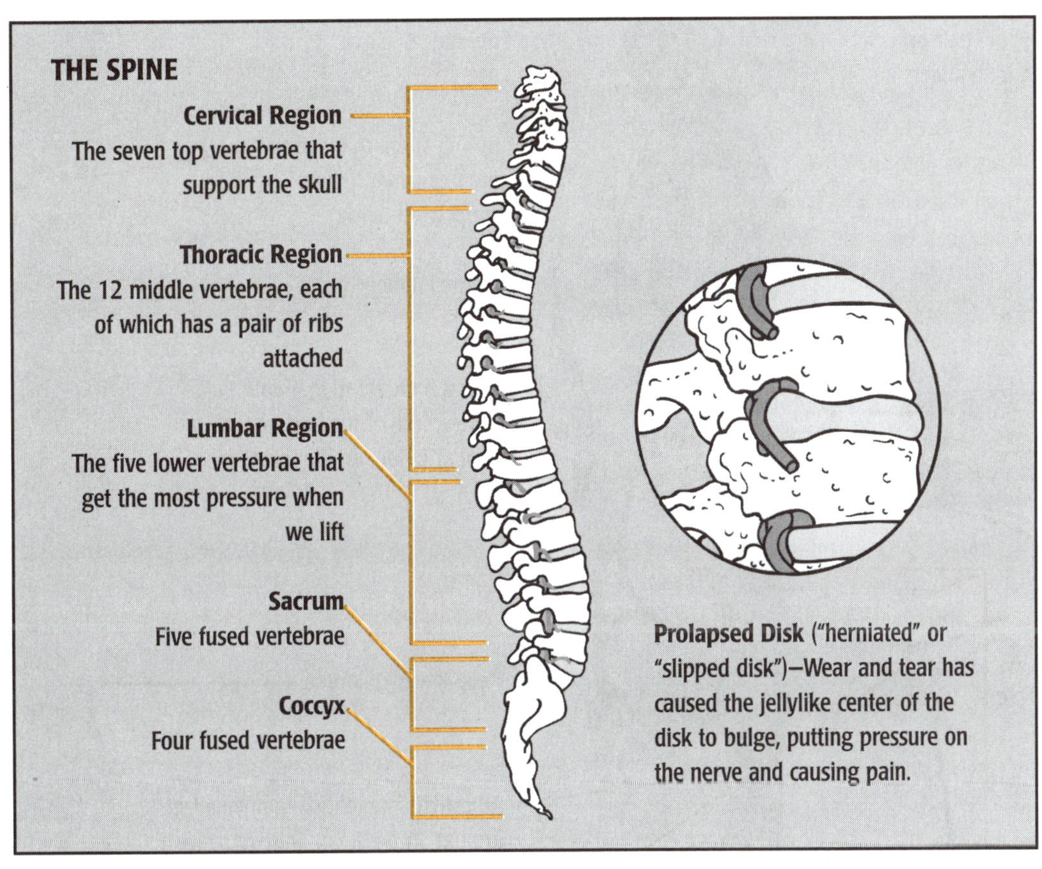

Back Pain

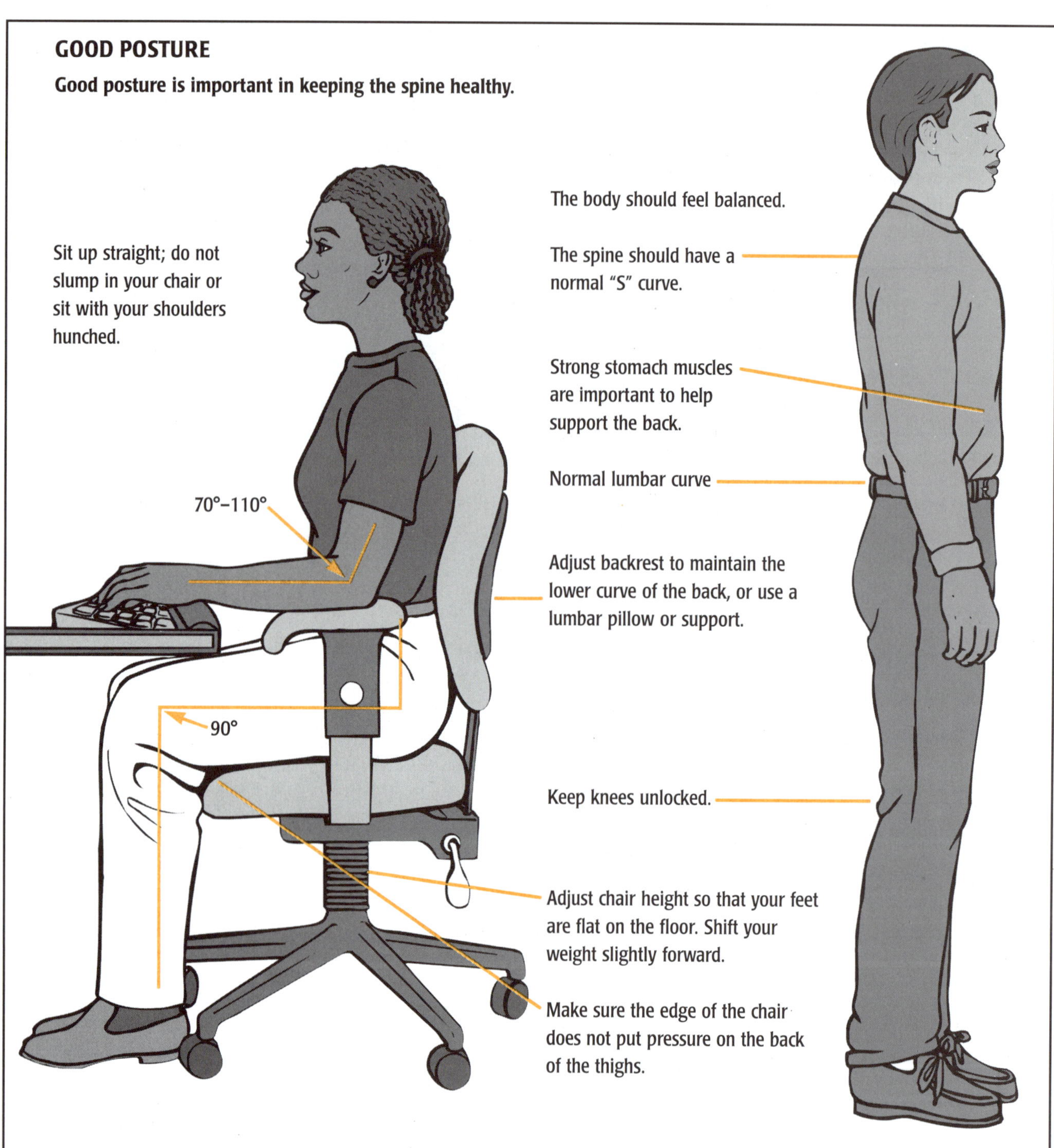
GOOD POSTURE
Good posture is important in keeping the spine healthy.
Sit up straight; do not slump in your chair or sit with your shoulders hunched.
70°–110°
90°
The body should feel balanced.
The spine should have a normal "S" curve.
Strong stomach muscles are important to help support the back.
Normal lumbar curve
Adjust backrest to maintain the lower curve of the back, or use a lumbar pillow or support.
Keep knees unlocked.
Adjust chair height so that your feet are flat on the floor. Shift your weight slightly forward.
Make sure the edge of the chair does not put pressure on the back of the thighs.

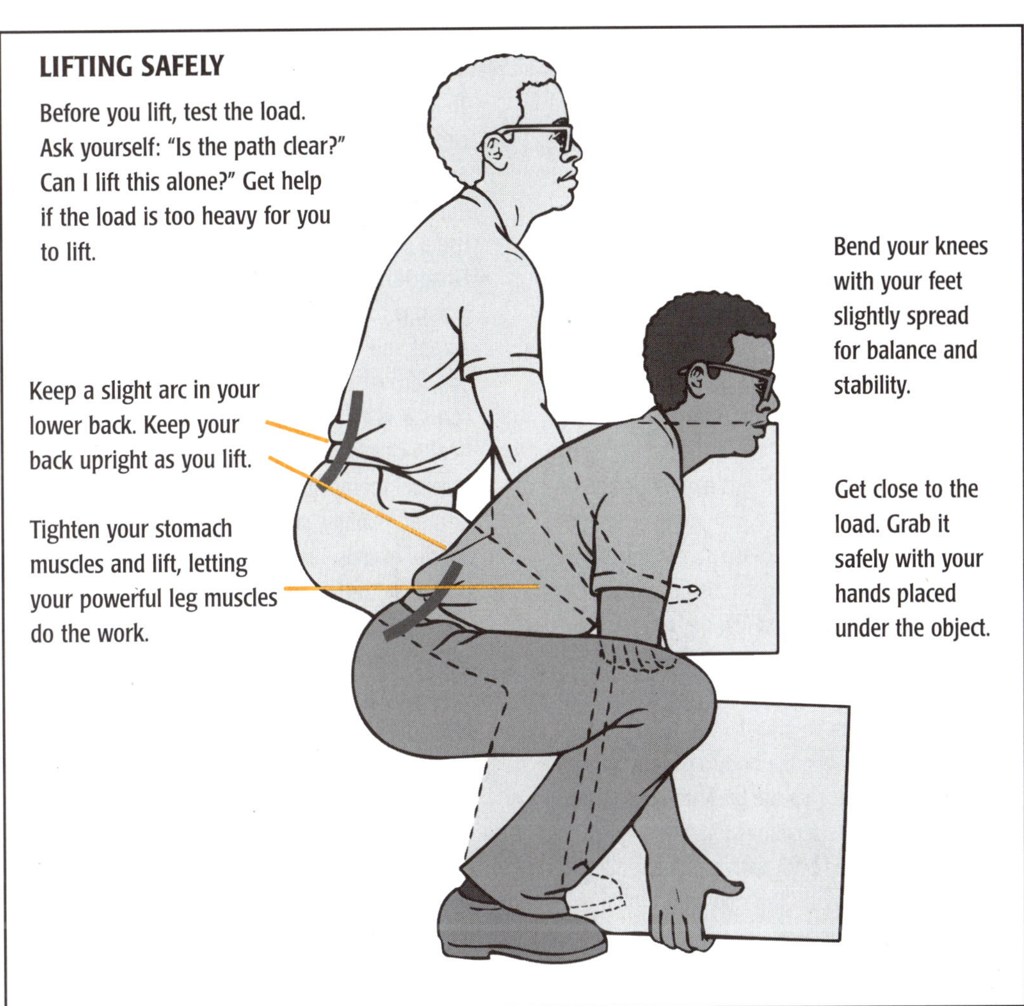
LIFTING SAFELY
Before you lift, test the load. Ask yourself: "Is the path clear?" Can I lift this alone?" Get help if the load is too heavy for you to lift.
Bend your knees with your feet slightly spread for balance and stability.
Keep a slight arc in your lower back. Keep your back upright as you lift.
Get close to the load. Grab it safely with your hands placed under the object.
Tighten your stomach muscles and lift, letting your powerful leg muscles do the work.

Back Pain

Self-Care Steps for Low Back Pain

- Medical studies show that prolonged bed rest is not necessary for most back problems. In fact, staying in bed for more than 2 days may increase your pain and stiffness. Moderate activity is more helpful.
- Cold packs or ice can reduce the pain and swelling of a muscle strain or spasm. Use them for 20 minutes 3 or 4 times a day during the first few days. After that, a hot bath or heating pad may be used to reduce pain and stiffness, but ice may still help.
- Anti-inflammatory medicines like ibuprofen or aspirin can help ease the pain and swelling in the lower back. If they cause stomach upset, try acetaminophen. You can also use muscle relaxants during the first few days to ease muscle spasms, but they often cause drowsiness. Narcotic painkillers are rarely prescribed because they can be addictive.
- Good posture keeps the body's weight aligned and reduces stress on the back muscles. The most comfortable positions for sleeping are often lying on the back with a pillow under the knees or lying on the side with a pillow between the lower legs.
- Being overweight increases stress on the lower back, and weight loss is important to prevent future problems.
- An important part of the recovery process is returning to work or usual daily activity in a few days or less—either with lighter duties or limited hours. Some discomfort will occur, but this prevents the back from becoming weak and stiff.
- To manage lower back problems, back pain experts suggest avoiding lifting heavy objects, and repeated bending and twisting. It is also important to change positions frequently and use a chair with good lower back support.
- Financial worries, family problems, or work pressures can affect back pain. Learning to accept and deal with everyday stress can help you recover from back pain. If you have concerns about stress, discuss them with your health care provider.
- Physical therapists will show you how to regain normal mobility, strength, and function through special exercise, manual therapy technique, pain relief techniques (like ultrasound, heat, and cold), and patient education. Your provider will consider physical therapy if you have severe incapacitating pain for more than 1 week, no improvement after 2 weeks of home therapy, or you are unable to return to work (limited activity) within 1 week.
- Fortunately, surgery is rarely needed for either back pain or sciatica. Many studies show that nonsurgical treatments and exercise are often as effective at relieving pain and preventing relapse. Surgery is usually considered only after months of nonsurgical treatment have failed to ease the pain or improve the function of the back. In these cases, an orthopedic surgeon or neurosurgeon can help decide. Only 5 to 10 percent of patients with sciatica ever need surgery.

Decision Guide for Back Pain

Symptoms/Signs	Action
Pain from tension, posture pain, soreness from exercise	Use self-care
Usual back or neck soreness	Use self-care
Pain that lasts for days	 See provider
Back pain and temperature over 100 degrees that lasts longer than 48 hours	 See provider
Back pain and nausea, vomiting, or diarrhea	 See provider
Back pain and painful or frequent urination, menstrual bleeding, or stomachache	 Call provider's office
Pain traveling down leg or arm; paralysis or numbness of a lower limb	 See provider
Paralysis, confusion, or shock (see *Shock*, page 88)	 Seek help now

NOTE: Workers' compensation regulations require that any injury occurring at work be reported.

For more about the symbols, see page 60.

Exercises to Keep Your Back Fit

It is important to keep your back flexible and strong even if you don't have back problems. Back exercises can help prevent back problems, improve posture, and fight off future trouble with back pain if you've had it in the past. Aerobic exercise is also very effective for people who have lower back pain. You should plan regular daily walks as soon as you can, along with other exercise as soon as you can tolerate it. Swimming or biking are also good activities for the lower back.

You can start the back exercises described below at home or with the help of a physical therapist. You should start the exercises as soon as the pain improves, but don't do any that worsen pain or stiffness.

THE PELVIC TILT

Lie flat on your back (or stand with your back to a wall), knees bent, feet flat on floor, body relaxed. Tighten abdominal muscles and tilt pelvis so that the curve of the small of your back is flat on the floor (or wall). Tighten the buttocks. Hold 10 seconds and then relax.

KNEE RAISE

Lie flat on your back, knees bent, feet flat on floor. Do a pelvic tilt and raise your knee slowly to your chest one at a time. Hug your knee gently, let go, then lower your bent leg slowly. Do not straighten your knees.

PARTIAL PRESS-UP

Lie face down on a soft, firm surface. Rest for a few minutes, relaxing completely. Staying in the same basic position, raise your upper body enough to lean on your elbows. Let your lower back and your legs relax as much as you can. Hold this position for 30 seconds at first. Slowly work up to 2 minutes.

Cramps and Spasms

Cramps occur when a muscle suddenly contracts painfully. Both activity and inactivity can lead to cramps and spasms. Muscles that have been overused, such as in exercise, may cramp. Similarly, muscles that have been underused, such as by sitting in the same position too long, may also cramp.

What to do. To relieve cramps, try stretching gently and massaging the muscles involved. Do not bounce. Cramps will usually go away on their own after a few minutes. Cramps lasting longer than an hour may indicate a serious problem.

Decision Guide for Cramps and Spasms

Symptoms/Signs	Action
Occasional cramps that come and go	 Use self-care
Episodes of muscle cramps or spasms that are not relieved after several weeks of prevention steps	 Call provider's office
Heaviness and pain deep in the leg or calf muscle (also see *Lower Leg Pain,* page 180), or swelling, redness, or unusual warmth	 Call provider's office
Neck or back spasm with numbness, tingling, or weakness	 Call provider's office

For more about the symbols, see page 60.

Self-Care Steps for Cramps and Spasms

- Stretch out the cramped muscle. For a leg cramp, sit with your leg flat on the floor and pull your toes toward you. For a foot cramp, walk on it.
- Gently but firmly massage the cramped muscle.
- Another pain management technique that works for some people is pinching the upper lip. Tightly squeeze the skin of your upper lip, just below the nose, between your thumb and index finger.
- Take acetaminophen or ibuprofen for pain that continues after the cramp.

Preventive Steps

- Drink plenty of liquids before, during, and after exercise. Although water is best, any other drinks (except caffeinated ones, which cause dehydration) are fine. Drink an hour before exercising, and then every 12 to 15 minutes during exercise.
- Be sure to warm up and cool down before and after exercising.
- Changes in diet are sometimes recommended for controlling cramps. Try to add foods high in calcium and potassium to your diet. Eat low-fat dairy products to increase calcium. Foods such as dried apricots, whole-grain cereal, dried lentils, dried peaches, bananas, citrus fruits, and fresh vegetables are good sources of potassium. Even if these changes do not help your cramps, it won't hurt to get more variety into your diet.

Elbow Pain

Pain in the elbow can occur from overuse, a fall or blow to the joint, or a force that causes the elbow to bend backward. Some common elbow injuries are described below.

Tendinitis. Elbow tendinitis has many names—tennis elbow, golfer's elbow, pitcher's elbow—and is caused by any number of repeated motions. The action isn't as important as the repetition.

Tendinitis pain is usually concentrated at the inside or outside of the elbow and may spread up or down the arm, depending on which tendon is inflamed. The pain may occur only with certain movements, such as lifting objects in certain ways, rotating your hand, or clenching or squeezing something in your fist.

Self-Care Steps for Elbow Pain

- Tendinitis, bursitis, and hyperextended elbow in adults can usually be treated effectively using the RICE method and anti-inflammatory drugs (see *Self-Care Steps for Aches and Pains in Muscles and Joints,* page 146) until the pain and swelling decrease. It is rarely necessary to see a health care provider for these conditions.
- It is very important to rest from the activity that caused the pain in the first place. But this might not be possible if the injury is due to a task that is a normal part of a job (for example, hammering for carpenters). If this is the case, consult your health care provider.
- Gentle stretching and strengthening exercises are also an important part of recovery and preventing future injury. Stretches, flexing the arm while using light weights, and squeezing a rubber ball in the palm of your hand are all exercises you can do to regain strength and range of motion after the pain is better. Ask your health care provider to recommend specific exercises for you.

Decision Guide for Elbow Pain

Symptoms/Signs	Action
Pain in elbow, limited to only certain movements of elbow and hand, especially after overuse	Use self-care
Swelling on inner side of elbow	Use self-care; Call provider's office
Pain, swelling, or soft lump on tip of elbow without fever, redness, or pain	Use self-care; Call provider's office
Bruise from a fall or blow	Use self-care; Call provider's office
Numbness or tingling in fourth and fifth fingers	See provider
Loss of strength in hand or arm	See provider
Elbow that cannot be bent or straightened	See provider
Joint or bursa red, swollen, or hot; fever present (possible infection)	See provider
Elbow deformity after fall	Seek help now
Severe pain in upper arm (biceps) after sudden or violent motion	Seek help now

For more about the symbols, see page 60.

What to do. Treatment is the same, no matter which tendon is involved (see *Self-Care Steps for Elbow Pain*, page 163).

Bursitis. Inflammation of a bursa causes a soft, fluid-filled lump at the point of the elbow. Bursitis can be quite painful, especially at the tip of the elbow. If not adequately treated, acute bursitis can lead to chronic bursitis and small, painful lumps at the point of the elbow can form.

What to do. With self-care, acute cases will usually heal within 7 to 10 days. See your health care provider if the bursa is red or hot, the elbow looks infected, or pain and swelling do not improve by this time.

Cubital tunnel syndrome. A blow to the "funny bone" isn't really funny. In fact, it can be very painful. But more than that, if repeated, blows to the back of the elbow (for example, in contact sports) may cause scar tissue to form over the ulnar nerve, which runs along the "tunnel" or groove between the inner side of the elbow and the point of the elbow (the ulna). Cubital tunnel syndrome causes loss of strength in the hand and numbness and tingling that spread from the elbow down to the ring and little fingers.

What to do. Because the pressure on the nerve is usually caused by scar tissue, surgery may be needed to free the nerve (see *Self-Care Steps for Elbow Pain*, page 163).

Hyperextended Elbow. This occurs when the elbow is bent backward by force, such as from a fall or a backhand tennis swing that goes awry. The result is pain and swelling in the joint and soft tissues at the front of the elbow.

What to do. A splint or sling may be needed to support the elbow until the pain stops. With self-care, recovery can be expected within three to six weeks.

Special Concerns for Children

- Elbow injuries aren't common in children, but when they occur they can be serious. If left untreated, a fractured elbow from a fall or blow or elbow overuse injuries—often from baseball pitching and weight training—can interfere with bone growth.
- The term "Little League Elbow" refers to a variety of overuse injuries in the elbows of young baseball players—especially pitchers—and sometimes in gymnasts. On the milder end is tendinitis at the inner side of the elbow. Pain and stiffness usually build gradually over several days. Until the pain and tenderness disappear entirely, the child should not throw a ball or exercise the elbow. This may take as long as 6 weeks to 6 months. Continued throwing may cause the growth center in the bone to separate from the main bone. If the separation becomes too great, the bone may begin to grow crooked or stop growing entirely.
- In severe cases, overuse injuries of the elbow can cause fragments of bone and cartilage to break off into the elbow joint, causing pain, stiffness, and even occasional grinding or clicking sounds. Left untreated, this can cause permanent damage to the joint.
- Because of its potential seriousness, elbow pain in children and adolescents should always be evaluated by a health care provider. To prevent injury, young baseball players should follow league rules limiting the number of practices and games they can pitch.

Foot Pain

The foot is one of the most complex parts of the body; so complex, in fact, that a medical and surgical specialty—podiatry—is devoted solely to treating and studying foot problems. The main source of most foot pain involves improper foot function or biomechanics. Shoes can worsen and, in some cases, even produce foot deformities. A properly fitting shoe, with good arch support, cushioning, and a "toe box" (the area surrounding the toes and the ball of the foot) that does not pinch and squeeze the toes or ball of the foot can help prevent irritation to bony joints and the skin that covers them.

Flat feet or high arches can contribute to painful problems in the feet, knees, and even hips. When the arch is too high or low, other structures in the foot and leg have to work longer and harder than intended. The added stress, weight, and poor motion can cause fatigue, pain, and inflammation. Arch supports (orthotics) and exercises to stretch and strengthen the arch and lower leg help relieve many problems related to weak arches. Fortunately, many people who have flat feet or high arches never have any problems with them.

Heel Pain

Two closely related conditions—heel spurs and plantar fasciitis—are common sources of pain in the heel and arch of the foot. They involve the heel bone and the plantar fascia, a strong band of connective tissue at the bottom of the foot that runs from the heel to the base of the toes. This band helps maintain or hold the arch together and serves as a shock absorber during activity. Overstretching of this band of tissue can result in strain and later inflammation where it's attached to the heel bone.

Plantar fasciitis. This condition is marked by a dull ache in the arch or pain in the heel. The pain is worst when you wake or after resting. Walking may hurt at first, but once the plantar fascia is warmed up, the pain may decrease.

Plantar fasciitis most often occurs when activity suddenly increases, or is due to shoes with poor support. Switching from high heels to flat shoes can irritate the fascia, causing pain. Gaining 10 to 20 pounds can have the same effect. Working out or standing and walking on hard surfaces, such as concrete, or wearing shoes that do not have good arch support can also lead to the problem.

Heel spurs. A heel spur is bone growth on the heel bone where it connects to the plantar fascia. If the plantar fascia is pulled and overstretched, it pulls the lining of the heel bone away from the main bone, causing a bony growth, or spur, to develop. The pain stems from the irritation of the plantar fascia pulling on the bone. The spur does not necessarily require removal to relieve heel pain.

Heel pain and plantar fasciitis often have similar symptoms and are sometimes considered together as heel spur syndrome. However, heel spurs may cause a deep tenderness in the bottom of the heel when weight is placed on the foot.

What to do. Self-care (see *Self-Care Steps for Foot Pain*, page 168) and rest will sometimes relieve heel spurs and plantar fasciitis. If symptoms continue despite these measures or if pain is severe, see your health care provider. Steroid injections may help relieve inflammation. Surgery is a last resort and is needed only in worst and prolonged cases.

Stress Fractures

Sometimes it's not the connective tissues in the foot that give way or get inflamed, but the bones themselves. Stress fractures occur most often in the second metatarsal, one of the long bones that connect to the toes.

High-impact activities such as running, basketball, or high-impact aerobics pose particular risk for stress fractures of the foot. People experiencing bone loss may be more likely to have stress fractures. This includes postmenopausal women with lower bone density, women with absent or infrequent periods, or anyone on long-term steroid or hormone therapy.

Stress fractures most often appear several weeks into a new or more intense training schedule or from landing wrong after jumping. At first, pain may be mild enough that it can be ignored. After time, however, the mild pain gives way to sudden, intense pain. Both the top and bottom of the foot may be tender to the touch.

What to do. Treating stress fractures in the foot mostly involves time—usually at least one month—to allow the bone to heal. With the exception of fractures in the fifth metatarsal, a cast is usually not needed. A wooden shoe or postoperative shoe is usually worn to allow the fracture to heal. A stress fracture in the fifth metatarsal (one of the long bones of the foot) can be serious because it often resists healing. Fractures may need a cast, and crutches may have to be used for six weeks to several months. In some cases, surgery may be needed.

Morton's Neuroma

Morton's neuroma is a noncancerous enlargement of one of the nerves running between the metatarsal bones (long bones of the foot). The enlargement occurs when the nerve is squeezed between the bones, sometimes from narrow, tight shoes or stress from repeated motions. Most often, neuromas develop between the metatarsal bones leading to the third and fourth toes. Occasionally, they may develop between the second and third metatarsals.

Morton's neuroma causes local swelling and tenderness. A person with this condition may feel as though he or she is walking on a lump, especially when barefoot. Pain may spread to the toes or toward the heel. Pressure makes the pain worse, and if constant, may cause numbness, burning, and tingling in the toes, between the toes, or at the ball of the foot.

What to do. Rest and a change in footwear should be enough to clear up this problem (see *Self-Care Steps for Foot Pain*, page 168).

Corns

These yellowish calluslike growths develop on tops of the toes in spots where shoes rub. If the rubbing continues, corns can become red, inflamed, and painful. The best way to prevent corns is to wear shoes with a toe box—the area surrounding the toes and ball of the foot—large enough to comfortably fit your foot without rubbing.

What to do. You can usually treat corns at home (see *Self-Care Steps for Foot Pain*, page 168). However, if you have diabetes, see your health care provider for treatment.

Bunions

A bunion is a swelling on the side of the foot. Usually, bunions show that the foot isn't working properly, perhaps because of flat-footedness. Instability and muscle imbalance can also cause the big toe to slant in toward the other toes. The joint where the big toe connects to the foot (the end of the first metatarsal, which is one of the long bones leading from the heel to the toe) then pokes out on the inner side of the foot. This is caused by poor alignment and is not a growth of bone. The bunion may also become inflamed and sore, especially if rubbed by a shoe. A similar problem, called a tailor's bunion, may develop on the opposite side of the foot, where the little toe meets the fifth metatarsal.

What to do. For bunions that cause persistent pain despite self-care (see *Self-Care Steps for Foot Pain*, page 168), steroid injections or surgery may provide relief.

Hammertoe

Hammertoe is a deformity in which the toe buckles, causing the middle joint of the affected toe to poke above the other toes. The deformity may also cause the toe to become bent at the middle joint so that it turns in toward the toe next to it. Tight shoes can rub and put pressure on the raised portion of the hammertoe, often causing a corn to form. Hammertoes may cause no problems at all, or they can be a source of pain, especially if the person wears tight or ill-fitting shoes.

What to do. If self-care (see *Self-Care Steps for Foot Pain*, page 168) fails to relieve the symptoms, surgery may be needed to straighten the toe or remove the bony protrusion.

Decision Guide for Foot Pain

Symptoms/Signs	Action
Foot pain from overuse or injury; can bear weight	Use self-care
Inability to move foot or bear weight after a trauma, such as a blow or fall	Call provider's office
Pain in heel or arch, especially upon awakening; tender points on bottom of foot between heel and ball (see *Heel spurs* or *Plantar fasciitis,* page 165)	Call provider's office
Corns, plantar warts, bunions, or hammertoes	Call provider's office
Pain, burning, tingling, or numbness in the toes, between the toes and at the ball of the foot; swelling at the top of the foot; symptoms worse with pressure (see *Morton's Neuroma,* page 166)	Call provider's office
Heel spurs or plantar fasciitis not relieved with self-care within 3 to 6 weeks	See provider
Suspected stress fracture	See provider

For more about the symbols, see page 60.

Self-Care Steps for Foot Pain

With the exception of plantar warts or trauma to the foot, the first step in caring for most kinds of foot pain is checking the shoes you've been wearing. Good shoes can be important in preventing and relieving foot pain.

Shoes should support the arch and cushion the heel, ball, and outside of the foot. For shoes that don't already offer enough arch support or cushioning, consider buying commercial arch-support and cushion inserts.

Shoes shouldn't pinch the foot or toes or be so loose that your feet slide around in them.

A good heel height is generally between 1/2 and 1 1/2 inches.

Anti-inflammatory drugs (aspirin, ibuprofen, or naproxen sodium) will help relieve pain and inflammation. Other treatments for specific conditions are discussed below.

For heel spurs and plantar fasciitis:

- Rest the foot, avoiding high-impact activities such as running for 3 to 6 weeks. Switch to low-impact activities, such as walking, biking, or swimming. Walking is particularly good.
- Apply ice to the heel 2 to 3 times daily.
- Support the arches of your feet to protect them from further stretching and tearing. Place arch supports even in your slippers and put them on first thing when getting out of bed.

For stress fractures:

- See your health care provider if pain continues or worsens after 1 to 2 weeks of nonimpact activity and anti-inflammatory drugs.
- Avoid high-impact activities such as running or playing basketball. Switch to weight-bearing, low-impact or nonimpact activities, such as walking or low-impact aerobics. Weight-bearing exercises—in which the legs support the body (such as running and walking) or in which weights are lifted—strengthen bones and prevent bone loss. Resume your regular workout or other activities slowly after pain eases and the fracture heals.

For Morton's neuroma:

- Avoid the original activity that caused the pain, and other high-impact activities such as running, for 3 to 6 weeks. Resume the original activity only after pain is gone.
- Try wearing shoes with a wider toe box to prevent pressure on the nerve. (The toe box is the part of the shoe that surrounds the toes and ball of the foot.)

For corns:

- Soak feet in a solution of Epsom salts and water for 15 minutes. Dry carefully and apply a moisturizer. Rub the corn with a clean nail file or pumice stone, using a side-to-side motion. Repeat daily until the corn is gone. People with diabetes should not use this method for corn removal, because they are at risk for developing sores on their feet that can lead to dangerous infections.
- Use a nonmedicated corn pad to relieve pressure on the area.

For hammertoes:

- Wear shoes with a toe box (the part of the shoe that surrounds the toes and the ball of the foot) large enough to accommodate the hammertoe.
- Treat accompanying corns as described above.

For bunions:

- Choose shoes with a larger, squared or rounded toe box (the part of the shoe that surrounds the toes and the ball of the foot).
- Put a piece of foam or cotton between the affected toes to ease the pressure.

(continued)

Self-Care Steps for Foot Pain (continued)

- Place padding around the bunion to relieve pressure and rubbing from shoes. Moleskin and bunion pads are available at most drugstores.
- Try using an arch support to stop the jamming of the long bone and the big toe.
- See your health care provider if pain lasts, interferes with walking, or is not relieved with self-care.

For plantar warts:

- Soak foot for 10 minutes in a solution of 2 tablespoons mild household detergent (such as dish soap) and 1/2 gallon warm water. Cut a piece of 40 percent salicylic-acid plaster (available at drugstores) the size of the wart and apply it to the wart. Cover with tape or a bandage. Remove the plaster in 2 days. Brush the wart with a toothbrush soaked in soap and water. Repeat this procedure for 2 weeks until the wart is gone.
- If warts remain despite self-care, or if they interfere with walking, see your health care provider.
- Do not try to cut warts out!

Plantar Warts

Plantar warts, like warts in other areas of the body, are caused by a virus. The weight of the body on the foot causes plantar warts to grow inward. The result is a painful lump on the bottom of the foot that feels like you are walking on a pebble. Children and teens are more likely than adults to get plantar warts.

What to do. Plantar warts are often difficult to treat, but a slow approach is best (see *Self-Care Steps for Foot Pain*, above). If plantar warts interfere with walking, you should see your health care provider or a podiatrist to have them removed.

Hip and Thigh Pain

Because of its stability, few problems occur with the hip joint. Most often, pain in the hip and thigh involves injury to muscles, tendons, or bursas (the small, fluid-filled sacs that cushion and lubricate joints), usually from a fall, a blow, or overuse of some kind. Some common hip injuries are discussed below.

Hip pointer. A hip pointer is a bruise or tear in the muscle that connects to the top of the ilium, the crest of the pelvis just below the waist. Symptoms may include local pain, tenderness, and swelling. Climbing stairs may be difficult, and it may hurt to walk. A hip pointer can be caused by a blow, a fall, or a quick twist or turn of the body. Often the pain increases several hours after the injury. This injury can take a long time to heal.

Groin pull. This is a pull of the adductor muscles, which bring your leg back to the body. Groin pulls are fairly common among those who play sports such as hockey, tennis, or basketball. A groin pull can cause pain, tenderness, and stiffness deep in the groin, making activity difficult.

Pulled hamstring. The hamstring is a group of muscles at the back of the thigh that attach at the pelvis and end just below the knee. Pulls or tears may occur from a sudden forceful move, such as sprinting to steal a base. Hamstring injuries most often occur in the center of the muscle, but the hamstring can also tear from the pelvic bone, just under the buttocks. Hamstring pulls and tears cause pain and sometimes bruising or a lot of swelling.

Avulsion fractures. Avulsion or occult fractures are closely related to hip pointers and groin pulls. Instead of a blow or fall affecting just the muscles, a fragment of bone breaks away from the pelvis or femur (upper leg bone).

What to do. Symptoms are similar to those of a groin pull or hip pointer. For this reason, whenever hip pointer or groin pull symptoms do not improve within 7 to 10 days, you should see a health care provider to check for an avulsion fracture. This is especially important for children and teenagers.

Bursitis. The hip contains 13 bursas, which are small fluid-filled sacs that cushion movement in the joint. Most often, bursitis in the hip involves the hip socket. It causes tenderness, pain, and swelling on the outer part of the hip where some of the large buttock muscles attach. Bursitis in the hip can cause pain that spreads to the buttocks and down as far as the ankle. It can be caused by activities (such as speed walking, aerobic dance, or carrying a baby on your hip) or conditions (such as one leg being shorter than the other) that alter the normal tilt of the pelvis.

What to do. To keep it from happening again, you must correct the problem causing the abnormal tilt, for example, by wearing a shoe lift insert if one leg is a bit longer than the other.

Charley horse. A charley horse is a painful muscle cramp caused by bruising of the thigh. In addition to cramping, charley horses are often accompanied by swelling, pain, stiffness, and skin discoloration (from the bruising).

What to do. Apply the RICE method (see *The RICE Method*, page 146) as soon as possible after any significant blow to the thigh.

Myositis ossificans. A serious muscle bruise or repeated bruising in the same area can cause bone growth within the muscle tissue. This condition, called myositis ossificans (which means "bone forming in muscle") causes pain, swelling, and limited range of motion of the thigh muscles.

What to do. This condition needs to be evaluated and treated by a health care provider to prevent further bone growth. Aggressive physical therapy is recommended, and the area should be protected from further injury. Once again, apply the RICE method (see *The RICE Method*, page 146) right after any significant blow to the thigh.

Muscle tightness. Anytime you tighten a muscle repeatedly, as when running or hammering, or hold it in one position for a long time, as when squatting or working at a computer, it may become stiff. You may not feel stiffness and pain until the next day. The tensor fasciae latae muscle, which runs along the outside of the upper leg and allows the leg to move outward to the side, is a common site for muscle tightness. But other muscles, including those in the buttocks and in the inside, front, and back of the thigh, can also become tight.

Special Concerns for Children

Children can have most of the same hip and thigh problems as adults—most of which involve the muscles and connective tissues of the hip, thigh, and buttocks. But several problems unique to children may affect the bones directly. And because children are still growing, these problems require medical attention to prevent long-term problems. Whenever a child or teenager has a limp that lasts more than a few days, he or she should see a health care provider. For any child or teenager involved in athletics, proper stretching (smooth, slow stretches—not bouncing) and slow strengthening of muscles are important to prevent injuries in the hips and legs, as well as other parts of the body. Conditions of the hip that affect children are described below.

LEGG-CALVÉ-PERTHES DISEASE

Named for the doctors who first described it, Legg-Calvé-Perthes disease is a breakdown of the ball (femoral head) of the femur, the long thighbone with a ball on top that fits in the hip joint. Loss of blood supply to the hip causes part of the femoral head to die and deteriorate, but no one knows exactly what interrupts the blood supply.

Symptoms may include limping, pain in the groin area or inner thigh, and knee pain. Rest usually relieves the pain, while activity makes it worse. The hip may also be stiff and the thigh may be weak.

Old bone is absorbed by the body, and new bone grows in its place naturally. But if the femoral head is not held in proper position, the new bone may grow in too large, too flat, or in the wrong shape. The hip socket provides a natural mold for the new bone to grow.

Unless the hip is inflamed or the health care provider recommends traction, a child with Legg-Calvé-Perthes disease may play as usual. The deterioration caused by Legg-Calvé-Perthes disease usually heals completely, and the disease does not recur once healed.

What to do. In some cases, a child with Legg-Calvé-Perthes disease may need to wear a cast or brace, or require rest, traction, or even surgery to make sure the new bone on the femoral head grows properly. But in other cases, especially when only a small area is affected or in children age 4 or younger, monitoring by a health care provider is all that's needed.

SLIPPED CAPITAL FEMORAL EPIPHYSIS

In this condition, the femoral head actually slips out of place, along the growth plate of the upper thighbone (femur). This condition usually occurs in children at about the time puberty begins (between the ages of 9 and 12). The slip may be slow over several months or occur suddenly following a fall or other significant injury to the hip. Symptoms are similar to those of Legg-Calvé-Perthes disease (see above).

What to do. Your child's health care provider may recommend bed rest or traction (holding a limb under tension with weights and pulleys) to help reduce inflammation. Surgery is usually needed to stabilize the slip. Treatment for slipped capital femoral epiphysis is usually very effective. Left untreated, however, the condition can lead to arthritis in early adulthood.

SYNOVITIS

Synovitis is an inflammation of any joint. In children, synovitis of the hip occurs most commonly between the ages of 6 and 10.

What to do. Care by both a pediatrician and an orthopedist or by an orthopedist specializing in children is often required. Your child's health care provider will make a referral to an orthopedist if needed.

Self-Care Steps for Hip and Thigh Pain

Simple muscle tightness is probably the most common injury in the hips and thighs. The RICE method (see *The RICE Method,* page 146), anti-inflammatory drugs (see *Pain Relievers,* page 146), and gentle stretching of the tight and painful muscles will help speed recovery.

Stretching before and after an activity and slowly strengthening muscles before demanding major efforts from them are effective ways to prevent muscle tightness and most other hip and thigh injuries. The following excercises can help. You can do the following things to speed recovery of other hip and thigh injuries.

For a hip pointer and groin or hamstring pulls or tears:
The RICE method (see *The RICE Method,* page 146) and anti-inflammatory drugs (see *Pain Relievers,* page 146) usually reduce pain. Depending on the damage to the muscle tissue, you may need crutches for a few days.

Hamstring stretch—Lie on the floor on your back with your left leg bent. Grab the back of your right knee. Slowly straighten your leg. Feel the stretch on the back of your thigh. Hold for a count of 5. Switch to your left leg and repeat.

For bursitis:
Use the RICE method (see *The RICE Method,* page 146) and anti-inflammatory drugs (see *Pain Relievers,* page 146). Avoid the activity that started the inflammation.

For a charley horse or myositis ossificans:
Apply ice to the entire muscle (or as much of it as you can) right after the injury to slow blood flow and swelling. Rest the area; don't work through the pain. Use the RICE method and anti-inflammatory drugs (see *The RICE Method,* page 146). If the injury isn't better in 7 to 10 days, see your health care provider.

Iliotibial band stretch—Stand and cross your right leg in front of left leg; shift weight onto your left leg. Push left hip out to the side, leaning torso to the right, for a slow, controlled stretch. Hold for 5 counts, then switch leg. Do not bounce. Repeat 3 to 5 times.

For piriformis syndrome:
Stretching and strengthening muscles in the buttocks and leg will help relieve this condition. While lying on your stomach, raise one leg from the floor, toes pointed. Repeat as many times as you can, and then do the same with the other leg. Gradually work on raising your leg higher and increasing the number of repetitions.

(continued)

Self-Care Steps for Hip and Thigh Pain (continued)

For chronic hip pain:

Because excess body weight can stress the hip joint, losing weight (see page 42) can often help relieve hip and thigh pain from chronic conditions. Walking is a good way to shed pounds and strengthen hip and thigh muscles. But any time hip or thigh pain lasts more than 7 to 10 days, you should see your health care provider.

Quadriceps stretch—Stand leaning against a wall.

Grab your left foot with your left hand. Gently pull backward, feeling a stretch in the front of your thigh. Hold for a count of 5. Be sure your other leg is bent slightly at the knee. Switch to your right leg and hand.

What to do. Muscle tightness usually lessens by taking a warm bath, stretching, and drinking plenty of water.

Piriformis syndrome. The piriformis muscle is one of several smaller muscles lying underneath the larger muscles of the buttocks. Overuse—such as from sitting or standing for long periods, or repeated motions over time—can irritate the smaller underlying muscles of the buttocks, causing the piriformis muscle in particular to tighten and spasm. When this happens, pressure may be placed on the sciatic nerve, a large nerve serving the lower body. The irritation, called piriformis syndrome, can cause pain, numbness, and tingling from the buttocks down the back of the leg to the foot.

The symptoms of this condition are often confused with those of disk disease in the spine. One way to tell if the problem is piriformis syndrome is to lie on your stomach with your knees together and bent, so your feet are in the air. Gently allow your feet to spread apart, toward the floor. If you feel a pain in your buttocks as your feet move apart, your problem may be piriformis syndrome.

What to do. Muscle strengthening and stretching can help treat this condition. See the exercise described for piriformis syndrome (see *Self-Care Steps for Hip and Thigh Pain*, page 172).

Chronic hip pain. Many other conditions can cause hip and thigh pain. Some, like arthritis or chronic bursitis, involve the hip directly. But low back problems, hernias (see *Hernias*, page 105), and inflammation of the urinary tract, reproductive system, or intestine can also cause hip pain—sometimes with few or no symptoms in the area of the body that has the real problem.

What to do. Whenever hip or thigh pain lasts more than 7 to 10 days, call your health care provider.

Decision Guide for Hip and Thigh Pain

Symptoms/Signs	Action
Overuse or injury pain that lasts less than 7 days	 Use self-care
Pulled or torn muscle causing tenderness to touch, stiffness, pain, difficulty walking, running, or climbing stairs	 Call provider's office
Pain on outside of hip, possibly down to the knee	 Call provider's office
Swelling, pain, or stiffness after a blow to the thigh	 See provider
Any of the above symptoms that do not improve within 7 to 10 days	 See provider
Dull pain in hip and groin while walking or climbing stairs	 See provider
Severe pain in buttocks with exercise; pain that stops when activity stops	 See provider
Pain that interrupts sleep	 See provider
Severe pain after a fall or blow	 Seek help now

For more about the symbols, see page 60.

Knee Pain

Knees bear a great deal of the stress from high-impact activities, such as running, aerobic dance, and skiing. Even everyday activities such as squatting, stooping, kneeling, lifting, and climbing stairs can take their toll. In addition to wear, tear, and sudden twists, the knees are open targets for blows, especially during contact sports.

Most knee injuries involve a blow, sudden twist, or a hard landing after a jump. Complex injuries are not unusual. A single strong blow in just the right place may tear cartilage and sprain several ligaments. Except for overuse injuries such as runner's knee and mild sprains, you should see your health care provider to find out how bad the knee injury is and exactly what structures are affected. Common injuries are described below. (For any of these injuries, see *Self-Care Steps for Knee Pain*, page 177.)

Sprains. A blow or sudden twist of the knee can sprain ligaments on either side of the knee, causing swelling (usually within an hour), pain, and difficulty walking. The sprained side may be tender to the touch. Even mild knee sprains often take two to three weeks to fully heal.

A strong blow to the inner or outer side of the knee will sprain the ligament on the opposite side as the knee is forced to bend sideways. If you feel pain on the side where the blow occurred, it's probably a bruise and not a sprain.

Anterior cruciate ligament (ACL) injuries. ACL injuries are the second most common sports injury, after ankle sprains. If the force from a blow, twist, or hard landing is strong enough, the anterior cruciate ligament (which runs diagonally within the knee and helps hold the ends of the femur and tibia bones together) can be stretched or torn. ACL injuries are common in contact sports, skiing, or basketball, or as a result of a trip or fall. You may hear or feel a loud pop when the injury occurs. ACL injuries often bring sudden pain, knee instability, rapid swelling, and limited movement. But in some cases, symptoms may take as long as 6 to 12 hours to appear.

What to do. See your health care provider within 24 hours of an ACL injury to find out how bad the ligament damage is. Surgery may be needed to reconstruct the ligament. (Also see the self-care steps on page 177.)

Torn cartilage. The same traumas that can result in sprains can also tear the menisci, two disks of cartilage that attach to the cartilage of the knee and fit into the joint to form shock-absorbing cushions. Cartilage tears often occur with sprains. This is especially true of anterior cruciate ligament injuries. Repeated squatting or kneeling can also weaken cartilage, increasing the risk of injury. Swelling may happen immediately or appear within 24 hours of injury. Continuing pain and a clicking or locking with knee movement are other symptoms of torn cartilage.

Once the cartilage is torn, the knee may buckle or lock without warning, putting surrounding ligaments and tendons at risk of injury. Wearing a brace during activity can help protect the knee from further injury, but surgery may be needed to remove pieces of torn cartilage. Unlike bone, tendons, and ligaments, cartilage does not knit back together once it is torn.

Terrible triad. The "terrible triad" is a combination of torn cartilage, anterior cruciate ligament injury, and a sprained ligament at the inner side of the knee—all from a single blow. Damage this bad usually requires surgery.

Joint mice. Joint mice are loose bodies (often pieces of torn cartilage or bone chips) floating within the knee. A strong blow to the knee may cause a small portion of bone surface to die. Pieces of dead bone then fall away from the main bone to become joint mice. Symptoms often take as long as a year after a trauma to appear. When joint mice get trapped between moving bone, they cause sudden pain and can make the knee lock or buckle.

Dislocations. The kneecap normally rides in a groove at the end of the femur (thighbone), where it is held in place with tendons attached to the quadriceps muscle in the front of the thigh and lower leg. A blow, quick pivot, or twist can knock the kneecap out of its groove, usually to the outer side of the knee. The femur and tibia may also be dislocated.

Dislocations of the knee or kneecap cause visible deformity and extreme pain. A dislocated knee (the femur and tibia out of alignment) is particularly serious because it can prevent blood from flowing to the lower leg. Immediate surgery is required to realign the bones and ensure that blood vessels are not damaged or pinched.

What to do. Both conditions are serious and require prompt medical attention. Call your health care provider, who will advise you as to whether you need to go to the emergency room. A dislocated kneecap may pop back into place on its own, but you should still see your provider to check for fractures. If the kneecap is broken, surgery may be needed to wire the bone together so it can heal.

Runner's knee (chondromalacia patella). The most frequent cause of knee pain and the most common overuse injury in the knee is runner's knee. Runner's knee develops because the kneecap fits incorrectly in its groove at the end of the femur. The crooked fit is often caused by the foot rolling too far inward. If not properly centered, the kneecap rubs against the femur, causing wear and tear on the cartilage behind the kneecap. Aching and swelling may be present around the kneecap or at the back of the knee, especially during and after activity. Squatting or sitting with the knees bent for a long time can also be painful. Grinding or popping may be felt as the knee bends and straightens. This condition can be brought on by any number of activities that place stress on the knee. Wearing shoes that provide poor support may contribute to it.

Jumper's knee (patellar tendinitis). This condition is an inflammation of the quadriceps tendon at the top of the kneecap or the patellar tendon, attached at the bottom. Jumping is a common cause of inflammation and tearing.

Housemaid's knee (prepatellar bursitis). Carpet layers, roofers, and people who install flooring are candidates for prepatellar bursitis, which is also called housemaid's or milkmaid's knee. Symptoms include a squishy, swollen area in front of the kneecap, pain, and stiffness. In more severe cases, swelling may extend above and to the sides of the kneecap. An inflamed bursa (one of the sacs of fluid that cushions movement within a joint) may break internally. If this happens, the body absorbs the excess fluid and the swelling and inflammation usually stop. The best prevention for housemaid's knee is wearing knee pads whenever you have to work on your knees for any length of time.

Iliotibial band syndrome. The iliotibial band consists of a muscle that begins at the top rim of the pelvis (the portion of the hip felt just below the waist) and a tendon that fits into the outside of the knee. Exercise can cause the band to tighten, irritating the knee and sometimes the point of the hip. The pain usually begins 10 to 20 minutes into a run or other exercise routine and stops when the activity stops. Iliotibial band syndrome often grows worse, with pain increasing and starting sooner in a workout.

What to do. Stretching and applying ice are the keys to relieving the syndrome (see the self-care steps on page 177).

Self-Care Steps for Knee Pain

Overuse injuries, such as runner's knee, tendinitis, and bursitis, can usually be treated safely at home with the RICE method (see *The RICE Method,* page 146), anti-inflammatory drugs (see *Pain Relievers,* page 146), and exercise to strengthen the area after the pain is gone (see illustrations in this section). Make sure your shoes provide proper support, and avoid wearing high heels.

With the exception of mild sprains, knee injuries from trauma should be seen by a health care provider to find out how bad the damage is. Injuries that should be seen immediately include dislocations of the knee or kneecap and "terrible triad" injuries, in which the knee swells severely and cannot be moved. Most knee injuries, however, do not require a trip to the emergency room. Here are guidelines for how to treat common knee injuries on your own and when to see your health care provider.

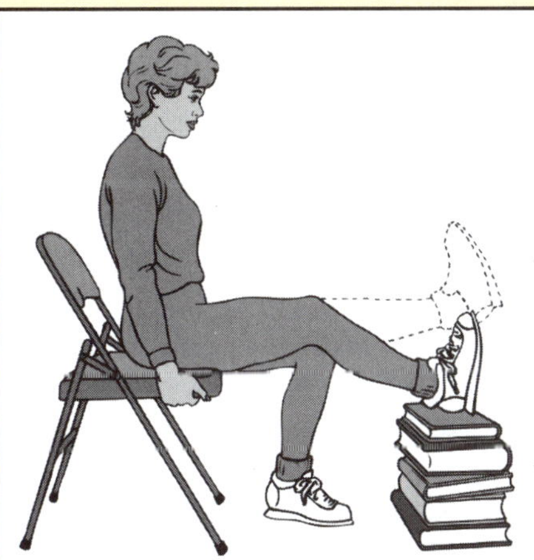

Leg extension—Sit with knees bent at a 60-degree angle; straigten leg; hold for count of 5, then slowly bend leg to rest on stool or pile of books. Switch legs. You can add leg weights for more resistance.

For mild sprains:

- Follow the RICE method (see *The RICE Method,* page 146). Rest the knee as long as it aches. After the first 72 hours, soak your knee in a warm whirlpool or bath. Use crutches if needed.
- After the pain is better, work to strengthen the muscles around your knee. Leg curls (see page 179), leg extensions (see this page), and riding a stationary bike are good strengthening exercises. If you choose a stationary bike, set the seat high enough so that your knee doesn't bend much and set the controls to make pedaling easy.
- See your health care provider if symptoms do not improve within 3 to 4 days.

For severe sprains, ACL injuries, and cartilage tears:

- Follow the RICE method (see *The RICE Method,* page 146) and take anti-inflammatory drugs (see *Pain Relievers,* page 146) for pain and swelling. Use crutches if needed. See your health care provider within 24 hours of injury.

For runner's knee, tendinitis, bursitis, and joint mice:

- Follow the RICE method (see *The RICE Method,* page 146) and use anti-inflammatory drugs (see *Pain Relievers,* page 146). Check your shoes to make sure they provide proper support (see *Self-Care Steps for Foot Pain,* page 168). If self-care fails to do the trick, your health care provider may prescribe custom-made inserts.
- After the pain is better, exercise to strengthen the area. Recommended exercises are illustrated on page 179 and at left.

(continued)

Self-Care Steps for Knee Pain (continued)

- If swelling from bursitis lasts or is very bad, a health care provider may drain the fluid with a needle and then inject the bursa with cortisone. After this procedure, watch for signs of infection, such as redness, swelling, and local heat. Surgery may be required if bursitis lasts despite other treatment.

For iliotibial band syndrome

- Stretching is the key to relieving this problem. Stretch the iliotibial band (see illustration, page 172), holding the stretch for 20 to 30 seconds and repeating 3 to 6 times. Do this 3 to 5 times a day until you no longer feel pain when you run. To prevent it from happening again, do this stretch before and after each run. Do not bounce as you stretch.
- If symptoms are not better within 10 to 14 days with the stretching routine, see your health care provider.

Decision Guide for Knee Pain

Symptoms/Signs	Action
Pain after sudden twist or blow to side of knee; swelling; can bear weight, but may limp	 Use self-care
Tendon below kneecap inflamed; pain going up stairs or jumping	 Call provider's office
Soft, squishy swelling beginning in front of knee; pain; stiffness (see *Housemaid's knee*, page 176)	 Call provider's office
Pain around or under kneecap; pain that increases when you are climbing stairs or sitting for long periods	 See provider
Bursitis symptoms that do not improve within 7 to 10 days, or signs of infection (local heat, redness, increased swelling, pain and tenderness)	 See provider
Pain after sudden twist or blow to side of knee; swelling; cannot bear weight	 Seek help now
Pain after sudden twist or blow to side of knee; rapid swelling; limited movement	 Seek help now
Severe blow or injury to knee; severe swelling; unable to move knee; visible deformity of knee	 Seek help now

For more about the symbols, see page 60.

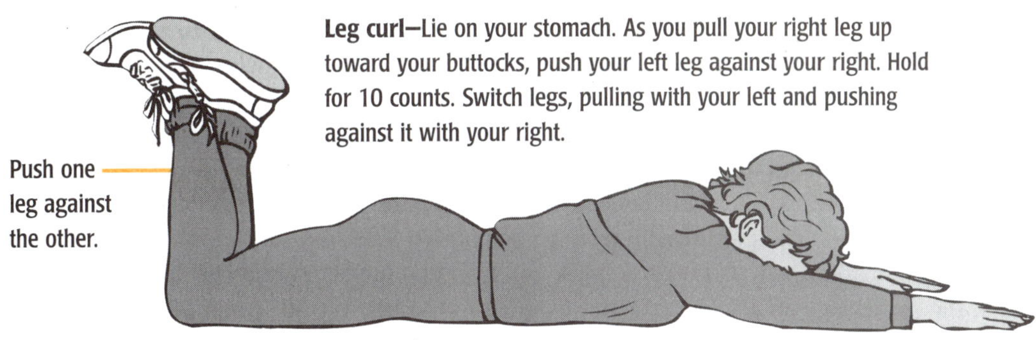

Leg curl—Lie on your stomach. As you pull your right leg up toward your buttocks, push your left leg against your right. Hold for 10 counts. Switch legs, pulling with your left and pushing against it with your right.

Special Concerns for Children

OSGOOD-SCHLATTER DISEASE

Osgood-Schlatter disease occurs during adolescence. It causes pain for the growing teenager, but generally no long-term problems. It is marked by a dull ache that comes and goes with changes in activity level and by swelling and tenderness on the bony spot just below the knee (tibial tubercle), where the kneecap (patellar) ligament connects.

In normal teenagers, growth spurts cause the tibial tubercle to grow. At the same time, the ligament is growing and trying to attach new tissue to the tubercle. Running, jumping, and other high-impact activities stress the ligament and frustrate its efforts to connect to the growing bone. Muscle imbalance and immature cartilage and bone also contribute to the syndrome. The ligament becomes inflamed, which increases blood flow to the area. This stimulates bone growth at the tibial tubercle, forming an enlarged bump just below the knee, which is permanent. But the on-and-off pain and inflammation of Osgood-Schlatter disease stops by about the age of 16 or 17.

What to do. Because the syndrome causes no permanent harm, a young person with Osgood-Schlatter disease can be as active as he or she likes, using pain as a guide. If it hurts too much, stop. Icing the area after activity will help prevent swelling and pain. Acetaminophen or ibuprofen may also help relieve pain (children and teenagers should not be given aspirin, due to the risk of Reye's syndrome). If the condition flares up, resting for a few days is advised. Exercises to strengthen the leg, such as straight leg lifts, can help prevent inflammation.

OTHER KNEE INJURIES

As with adults, knee injuries are common in young athletes. Wearing knee pads and supportive shoes can help prevent such injuries. But when they do occur, the young person should not be allowed to continue playing until the injury is examined by a health care provider to rule out a growth plate fracture (see page 148).

Lower Leg Pain

The lower leg is made up of two bones, the tibia and the fibula. As with other parts of the leg, pain in the lower leg can be caused by overuse, overexertion, or trauma from a fall or blow. In addition to orthopedic problems, the lower leg can also be affected by heart and circulatory diseases, such as congestive heart failure, or blood clots and inflammation in the veins of the legs. The main symptom of such diseases is swelling in the legs and feet from extra fluid (edema).

Swelling (edema) in the lower leg. Occasional swelling in the leg is common. It can occur from sitting or standing for long periods, water retention related to a woman's period or during pregnancy, allergies, varicose veins, or even sitting in the sun too long. In most cases, it goes away on its own overnight. Chronic swelling, however, can be a sign of the following serious conditions that require medical care.

What to do. See the self-care steps on page 181.

Phlebitis. Phlebitis is an inflammation of a vein, sometimes accompanied by a blood clot. The inflammation can cause aching, swelling, and redness in the lower portion of one leg. A blood clot in one of the veins of the leg can further increase swelling by blocking the flow of blood back to the heart. With nowhere else to go, the blood seeps out of the vein into the surrounding tissues, causing swelling.

What to do. Phlebitis requires immediate medical attention to keep a potential clot from moving into the heart or lungs.

Congestive heart failure. Congestive heart failure occurs when the heart muscle is weakened (for example, by a heart attack) and is no longer able to pump blood well. When the heart is pumping inefficiently, the result is a backup of blood that leads to a buildup of fluids in the legs. The liver and lungs may also be affected, enlarging the liver and causing shortness of breath because fluid collects in the lungs. Unlike phlebitis, congestive heart failure brings swelling in both legs at the same time and does not cause pain.

What to do. Raising the legs may relieve swelling, but if you have these symptoms, you should see your health care provider.

Drugs. Drugs such as testosterone, estrogen, blood pressure drugs, birth control pills, and long-term corticosteroid use may also cause swelling in the legs.

What to do. If you are taking any of these drugs and have swelling, call your health care provider.

Intermittent claudication. Intermittent claudication is pain caused by narrowing of the arteries (atherosclerosis) that creates a buildup of fluid in the leg and keeps the lower leg muscles from getting enough oxygen. The condition usually occurs in older adults and heavy smokers. Activity may cause pain, as the working muscles fail to get the oxygen they need. The pain is relieved shortly after exercise or activity is stopped.

What to do. If you have these symptoms, see your health care provider.

Of course, overuse and trauma can also cause pain in the lower leg. The following conditions are among the most common.

Shin splints. A shin splint is an overuse injury that causes inflammation of the shin muscles and sometimes results in the pulling away of muscle from the bone. Tiny tears in the muscle may also contribute to the pain. Symptoms include aching at the front or inner side of the lower leg. Generally there is no swelling, redness, or bruising. The pain may begin suddenly or build slowly.

The most common causes of shin splints include the following:

- muscle imbalance (calf muscle is much stronger than the shin muscle)
- not enough shock absorption during high-impact exercise (from wearing worn-out shoes or shoes without enough padding)
- running on the balls of the feet, without allowing the heel to touch the ground
- flat feet
- doing too much activity too fast (starting out jogging five miles instead of two, or hiking in boots you're not used to)
- a tight Achilles tendon (the tendon at the back of the heel and ankle)

Shin splints are a common injury among runners and other athletes, store clerks, warehouse and factory workers, and others who are on their feet all day on hard concrete floors in shoes (especially high heels or cowboy boots) that don't provide good support.

Contusion and anterior compartment syndrome. A strong blow to the shin, or contusion, can cause a painful bruise. After the skin color returns to normal, a bump as hard as bone may remain for as long as several months, but it usually goes away on its own with time.

But a blow to the front of the leg on the outside can cause more serious problems than bruising. Internal bleeding may cause

Self-Care Steps for Lower Leg Pain

- As with most other injuries in the extremities, the RICE method and anti-inflammatory medications (see *Self-Care Steps for Aches and Pains in Muscles and Joints,* page 146) provide the core of treatment for shin splints, stress fractures, and contusions. For chronic swelling in both legs without pain, try raising your legs and call your health care provider to see if he or she wants to see you.
- For shin splints, rest the leg for 1 to 2 weeks, then do only low-impact activities (bicycling, walking, swimming) to keep up strength and prevent shin splints from occurring again. After aching has eased, return slowly to your usual activities.
- Wrap the ankle and shin for added support.
- Doing Achilles tendon stretches and exercises to strengthen the front of the leg may help.
- An ice massage 4 times a day will help: freeze water in a paper cup; tear away the cup to expose the ice, and massage the ice over the painful area for 10 or 15 minutes.
- Wear shoes with good support and cushioning. Even if the outside of an athletic shoe looks fine, the cushioning in the sole may have lost its bounce with wear and you may need a new pair. Also check to see if the heel counter (the part that supports your heel) is broken down and the bottoms are worn evenly.
- See your health care provider if a shin splint does not get better after 2 to 3 weeks or if you feel numbness or tingling in your foot after a blow to the shin.

Special Concerns for Children

Growing pains are not a myth, but a real problem in children between the ages of 6 and 12. The pains usually occur in the evening, often in the calves and thighs. Acetaminophen or ibuprofen, along with a heating pad set on "low" (for short periods; watch the child) or soaking in a warm bath, will provide relief. (Do not give aspirin to children or teenagers due to the risk of Reye's syndrome.) Call your child's health care provider if the pain is always in the same spot; if there is swelling, redness, tenderness to the touch, or fever; or if your child is limping.

swelling, which puts pressure on the nerves and blood vessels—a condition called anterior compartment syndrome. If not treated immediately with surgery to relieve pressure, the swelling may permanently damage the main nerve connected to the foot. When this happens, the injured person loses the ability to lift his or her foot, which will seriously affect walking. This condition is known as "drop foot."

Symptoms of anterior compartment syndrome may begin with mild pain and swelling that builds to loss of color, feeling, and pulse; severe pain; paralysis; and swelling so bad that the skin turns shiny. If the latter symptoms appear, prompt treatment is crucial to prevent or lessen permanent nerve damage.

What to do. If you have these symptoms after a blow to the shin, apply ice and seek medical help immediately.

Stress fractures. Stress fractures can result from overuse, a blow, or twisting the lower leg. Stress fractures are common as a

Decision Guide for Lower Leg Pain

Symptoms/Signs	Action
Pain from overuse or blow; can bear weight	Use self-care
Chronic swelling without pain	Use self-care
Blow to shin area; bruising; no swelling	Use self-care
Pain along the front or inner edge of the shinbone	Call provider's office
Shin splint that does not get better within 2 to 3 weeks	Call provider's office
Gradual increase in shin or ankle pain; pain that increases during or after activity	Call provider's office
For children: pain in legs, calves, or thighs at the end of the day or at night (see box)	See provider
Painful and sudden swelling and redness in only one leg (see *Phlebitis*, page 180)	See provider
Swelling and pain after a blow to the front of the leg (see *Contusion and anterior compartment syndrome*, page 181)	Seek help now
Numbness or tingling in foot after a blow to the shin	Seek help now

For more about the symbols, see page 60.

result of high-impact activities such as running and basketball. Stress fractures are hard to detect on X-rays until about 10 to 14 days after the fracture begins. You may notice a sudden spreading pain in your shin during or after exercise. In most cases, people with stress fractures can pinpoint exactly where the pain is coming from by pressing on the spot.

What to do. Rest is the best way to treat stress fractures. Avoid high-impact activities for about six weeks. Although a cast is not needed, stress fractures should be checked with X-rays until fully healed. Low-impact activities, such as walking, bicycling, or swimming, are usually safe to do while a stress fracture heals.

Neck Pain

The neck, or cervical spine, is the most flexible part of the spine. But because it is not well protected by muscles, it's also easy to injure. Daily stress, poor posture, trauma, and wear and tear from overuse and aging are the most common sources of neck pain. Neck pain can often be relieved or prevented with a few adjustments to the way we work and rest. Even if the pain is caused by an injury or a worsening condition, self-care may provide relief; talk with your health care provider first.

Severe trauma to the neck can cause a fracture that may lead to permanent paralysis. For possible neck or other spinal injuries from a severe blow or other trauma, keep the injured person still. Do not move the person without a back board or cervical collar and the help and direction of a trained paramedic or other medical professional.

A bad night's rest. How you sleep at night can affect your neck during the day. If you awaken with a crick in the neck, it may be due to a soft mattress, pillows that force your neck into awkward angles, or uncomfortable sleeping positions. But tossing and turning may be less to blame than awakening suddenly from a sound sleep. A sudden jerk of the neck upon awakening can leave neck muscles tight and sore (see *Insomnia*, page 271).

Body mechanics. Poor sitting and standing posture—slumped shoulders, a drooping head, slouching or rounding of the lower back—can cause neck pain. But bad body mechanics are more than poor posture. Repeated tasks, such as holding the phone with your shoulder or always carrying a heavy briefcase or shoulder bag on the same side of the body, can also cause muscle stiffness or imbalance. Workstations may also force your body into a position that is less than optimal.

Stress. The neck and upper back muscles are often among the first to become tense when a person is under emotional stress. Whenever these muscles remain tight for a long time, they may ache, become sore, and even cause headaches.

Neck sprains and strains. The term "whiplash" is often used to refer to neck sprains and strains that result when the neck is forced suddenly forward, backward, or both, such as from a rear-end car collision. But contact sports, a fall, or a sudden twist can cause similar injuries. Pain from neck sprains and strains may spread into the shoulders, upper back, and arms, and sometimes as far as the legs. Pain may remain for six weeks or longer, but usually improves with normal use.

What to do. In some cases, physical therapy or special exercises may be helpful.

Degenerative joint disease (DJD). Degenerative joint disease usually occurs in people over the age of 40. This condition often causes painful muscle spasms in the neck and upper back, a dull aching in one arm, or numbness and tingling in the arm or fingers.

Between each bone (vertebra) of the spine is a cartilage disk filled with a gelatin-like substance that provides cushioning. As we age, these disks thin, losing some of their capacity for absorbing shock. The joints of the neck may also become inflamed due to arthritis or bone spurs, or a disk may herniate (push outward) from its normal space and place pressure on the nerves. A direct blow can also make disks bulge or break, causing similar problems to those of disk degeneration.

What to do. Any pain, numbness, or tingling should be evaluated by a health care provider.

Brachial plexus stretch. A brachial plexus stretch, often called a burner or stinger, occurs when the neck and shoulder are twisted in opposite directions at the same time, stretching the brachial plexus nerves. The result is shooting, burning pain, weakness in the shoulder muscles, and loss of feeling in the shoulders, which require an immediate visit to a health care provider. This type of injury tends to occur most often in contact sports.

Meningitis. Meningitis symptoms include a very stiff neck, fever, and headache.

Decision Guide for Neck Pain

Symptoms/Signs	Action
Stiff, sore neck upon awakening	Use self-care
Muscle tension and pain, especially while working or under stress	Use self-care
Pain after a sudden twist or blow, or after the head was thrown forward or backward	Use self-care; Call provider's office
Pain that is the same or worse after 7 to 10 days of self-care	See provider
Burning, shooting pain; shoulder weakness; or loss of feeling in shoulder after a trauma that caused neck and shoulder to twist in opposite directions at the same time	Seek help now
Stiff, sore neck with fever and headache	Seek help now
Any severe trauma or blow to the head or neck	Emergency: call 911

For more about the symbols, see page 60.

What to do. Because meningitis can be life-threatening if not treated promptly with antibiotics, you should see your health care provider immediately if you have these symptoms.

Self-Care Steps for Neck Pain

- If you wake up often with a sore neck, consider sleeping in a different position, getting a new mattress and box spring, or putting a 3/4-inch plywood board between the mattress and box spring for extra support.
- If you sleep on your side, choose a pillow that allows your head to rest comfortably centered between your shoulders. If you sleep on your back, choose a pillow that doesn't push your chin toward your chest. A cervical support pillow or a rolled towel pinned around your neck can also help you position your spine correctly. Avoid sleeping on your stomach.
- If daily stress makes your neck and upper back muscles tense, take time out to relax (see *Self-Care Steps for Stress,* page 265).
- If your neck or upper back muscles feel tight and sore, especially from stress, ask a friend to massage the area for a few minutes.
- The spine naturally curves in at the neck, out at the upper back, and in again at the lower back. An easy way to improve your posture is to focus on keeping the natural curve at the lower back. When you do this, the rest of the spine tends to pull into place, straightening your shoulders and head as well. Be sure, however, that your effort to straighten up doesn't cause your neck or abdomen to stick out.
- Improve your work area. Use a telephone headset if you spend a lot of time on the phone. Keep your briefcase or purse as light as possible and routinely switch the side you carry it on. When either is packed full, try to distribute the weight evenly on each side of your body by splitting the contents into two bags or briefcases. Hold reading materials and place computer screens at eye level; don't bend over your work. Type with your elbows, hips, and knees at 90-degree angles, and make sure you have good support for your lower back.
- Ice a sore neck for 10 to 15 minutes, several times a day, to relieve pain and inflammation. A bag of frozen peas or corn makes a great cold pack for the neck. Switching between heat and ice may also work.
- A warm shower or moist, warm towel can help loosen sore, tight muscles. Apply heat for 20 minutes, 3 times a day, starting no sooner than 2 days after an injury. But ice may be better for relieving pain even long after an injury, especially if muscle spasms are present. Follow with gentle stretching.
- Take anti-inflammatory drugs (ibuprofen or, for adults, aspirin) for pain. If pain persists, your health care provider may prescribe other medications.
- When pain is at its worst, rest. Lie flat on your back for an hour or so with a fairly flat pillow supporting your head. Extended bed rest, however, can make neck problems worse by allowing muscles to weaken from lack of use.
- Stretch! Reduce stiffness and soreness by gaining motion and strength with the stretches shown below.
- After exercise, cool down in a healthy posture. One of the best and easiest times to assume a healthy posture is when your muscles and joints are loose after exercise.

Shoulder Pain

The shoulder is one of the most vulnerable joints in the body because it is made for movement in all directions. Like other joints in the body, the shoulder can be injured by trauma (such as a fall or a blow) and overuse or repeated motions that add up over time.

Referred pain

Sudden onset of shoulder pain without an injury can be a sign of other problems. When in the left shoulder, it may mean a possible heart attack, angina, or neck, spleen, liver, or lung problems. When in the right shoulder, it may mean gallbladder problems. When pain is referred from somewhere else, moving the arm will not increase the pain.

What to do. Call a physician or 911 immediately if you have these symptoms or the symptoms of heart attack (see *Chest Pain*, page 136).

Overuse Injuries

Three common overuse injuries include tendinitis, bursitis, and rotator cuff injuries.

Bursitis. Bursitis is inflammation of the bursas, the small fluid-filled sacs that cushion and lubricate the joints. This inflammation can be caused by pressure, friction from overuse, or injury.

Tendinitis. This is painful inflammation of the tendons, usually caused by overuse or an injury. Symptoms include pain, swelling, muscle spasm, and limited movement.

Decision Guide for Shoulder Pain

Symptoms/Signs	Action
Shoulder pain after activity, limited to only certain movements	Use self-care
Overuse injury that is still present or worse after 7 to 8 days, despite self-care	Call provider's office
Inability to raise arm	Call provider's office
Trauma with sudden pain; a pop, snap, or cracking sound or feeling; inability to move shoulder; a deformity or lump	Seek help now
Sudden pain in right or left shoulder without injury, and ability to move arm without increasing pain	Emergency: call 911

For more about the symbols, see page 60.

What to do. If you have bursitis or tendinitis, treat the area with RICE (see *The RICE Method*, page 146) and take aspirin or other non-steroidal anti-inflammatory drugs such as ibuprofen to relieve inflammation and pain (see *Pain Relievers*, page 146). With tendinitis, decrease activity for one to two weeks or until you are fairly pain-free. Apply heat to the area before stretching, and ice when you have finished. If there is no improvement in your tendinitis in 10 to 14 days or in your bursitis in 7 days, call your health care provider.

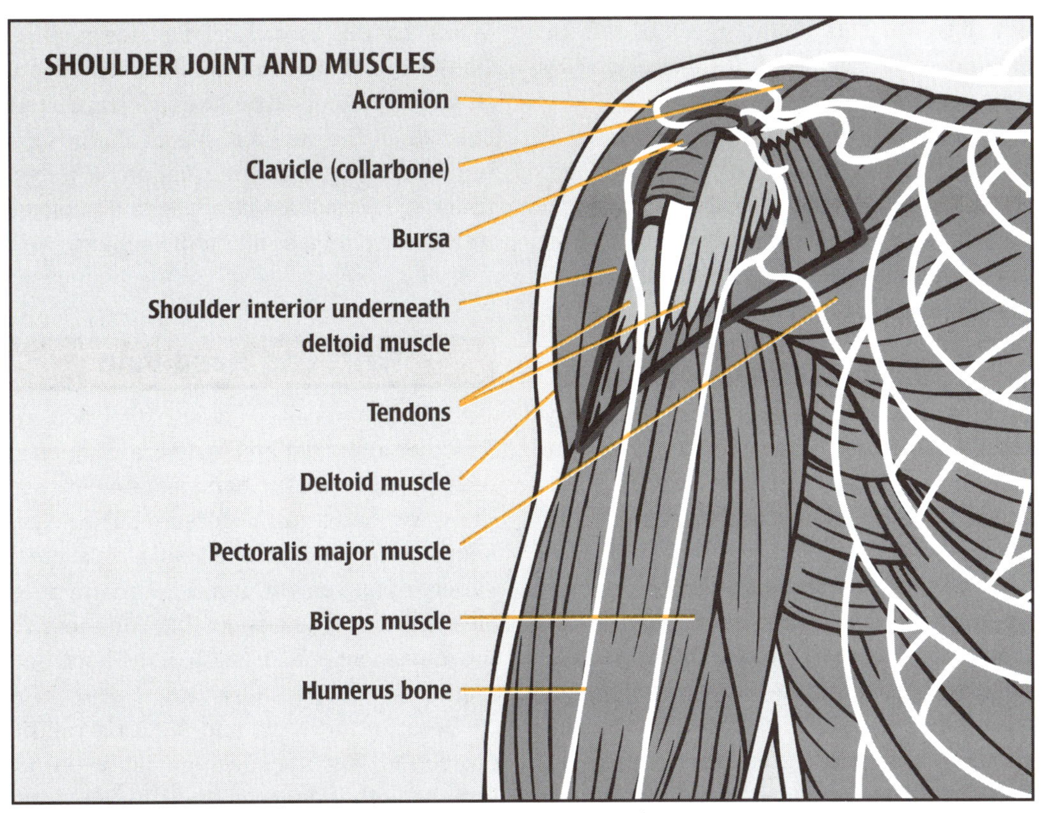

Rotator cuff injuries. This is a catch-all term often used to describe more than one problem, including tiny tears of the tendons supporting the shoulder (the rotator cuff) and impingement syndrome (compressing the tendons between bones, resulting in painful inflammation). The cause, result, and treatment, however, are similar.

Repetitive overhead motions, such as throwing a softball, painting a ceiling, or swimming, often cause rotator cuff injuries. Symptoms include shoulder pain at night and pain when raising or lowering the arm between waist and shoulder height. If the tendons are compressed between the bones, pain may be worst when the arm is raised with the palm turned down—as when emptying a can of soda. You may also feel tingling or numbness in your arm or fingers.

Self-Care Steps for Shoulder Pain

Although injuries should be seen by a health care provider as soon as possible, overuse and muscle imbalance injuries can usually be treated with self-care. The RICE method (see *The RICE Method,* page 146) and anti-inflammatory drugs (see *Pain Relievers,* page 146) are the basics of self-care for shoulder injuries. Also, to keep it from happening again, you should work to strengthen the muscles around the joint. Your health care provider, the staff at his or her office, or a physical therapist can suggest appropriate exercises.

What to do. This condition can usually be treated at home (see *Self-Care Steps for Shoulder Pain*, page 187).

Trauma

A sudden twist, fall, or blow can lead to a sprain, shoulder dislocation (the upper arm bone comes "out of its socket"), a partial dislocation, or broken bone. With any of these conditions, you may hear or feel popping, snapping, or tearing when the injury occurs. You may be unable to move your shoulder and, except in the case of a sprain, there may be visible deformity of the shoulder.

Another possible injury caused by falls or blows to the shoulder is an acromioclavicular (AC) joint separation. The AC joint is held together by ligaments, which connect the collarbone to a narrow part of the shoulder blade that extends to the front of the shoulder. AC separations can range from bruising the joint to stretching or completely tearing the ligaments. With AC separations, a painful lump may form at the end of the collarbone, near the shoulder.

What to do. Although a sprain can be treated safely at home using the RICE method (see *The RICE Method*, page 146), see your health care provider to make sure the shoulder isn't dislocated or fractured.

Muscle Imbalance

General muscle aches and tightness around the shoulder, upper back, or neck are often caused by muscle imbalance, which occurs when one side of the body is much stronger than the other side.

What to do. Stretching and ice applications can help relieve the pain. To keep it from happening again, weight training to strengthen the weaker side of the body is important. For more information on weight training, take a class, work with a personal trainer, or read a book on the subject.

Wrist and Hand Pain

Together, the wrist and hand are composed of 29 bones: 19 in the hand and fingers, 8 in the wrist, and 2 in the forearm. The wrist, hand, and fingers are capable of a great variety of movement. But the forearm muscles are actually responsible for most of the movement and strength of the hand and fingers.

Because the wrist and hand have little protection, they may be more likely to fracture than other bones in the body. Falls and blows are common causes of wrist and hand injuries. But, as with other joints, overuse and repeated motions can take their toll on the hand and wrist, causing a variety of conditions, such as tendinitis and carpal tunnel syndrome. The injuries listed below are by no means the only conditions that can cause pain or limit the function of the hand and wrist, but they are some of the most common ones.

Fractures and sprains. Fractures and sprains of the wrist, hand, and fingers can be hard to pinpoint without an X-ray.

When a wrist is fractured, the break often occurs at the end of the radius, one of the long bones of the forearm. These fractures require careful attention. Another fracture near the wrist—a navicular (a small wrist bone located at the base of the thumb) fracture—can cause long-term problems, is difficult to diagnose, and takes a long time to heal. Because the bone is so small and almost all of its surface touches other bones, an improperly healed fracture can cause the navicular to rub and scrape in places it shouldn't. The result is pain and loss of range of motion in the wrist.

What to do. Unless deformity, a change in feeling, or lack of motion is noticeable, you may start with self-care. However, you may want to call your health care provider's office to ask if your injury needs medical attention. If pain or stiffness lasts more than 24 hours after injury, see your provider. Children who suffer obvious discomfort during the night should be seen right away.

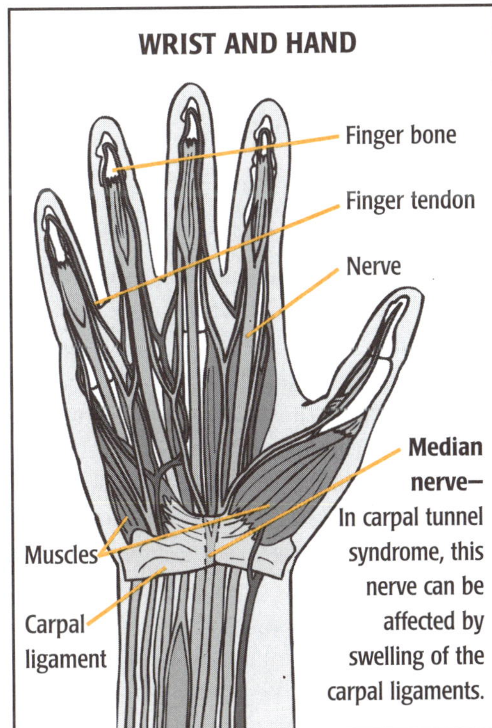

If you fall on your outstretched hand, bending your wrist back, and the pain does not get better within a day, you should see your provider and have an X-ray. If your X-ray shows no sign of fracture but the pain is still present one week later, you will need another X-ray. Sometimes small fractures are easier to see by X-ray 7 to 10 days later.

Tendinitis. It is common for tendons in the wrist, hand, and fingers to become irritated from overuse or repeated motions, causing pain, swelling, and stiffness. Tendinitis pain in the wrist may spread down to the fingers or up to the elbow. Tendinitis in the fingers may affect one or more fingers at the same time. You may feel pain constantly or only with certain movements. The area around the tendon may be tender. You may even notice a cracking sound or odd feeling when you bend or flex the finger or wrist.

What to do. If you have tendinitis, treat the area with RICE (see *The RICE Method*, page 146) and take aspirin or another non-steroidal inflammatory drug to relieve inflammation and pain (see *Pain Relievers*, page 146). Decrease activity for one to two weeks or until you are fairly pain-free.

Self-Care Steps for Wrist and Hand Pain

There are some general self-care guidelines for handling wrist and hand pain. However, for specific injuries, treatment is needed.

- Apply ice immediately.
- Always remove rings before exercising or doing manual labor. If you are wearing rings and hurt your hand, remove them immediately before swelling has a chance to begin.

Apply heat to the area before stretching, and ice when you have finished. If there is no improvement in your tendinitis in 10 to 14 days, call your health care provider.

Ganglia. A ganglion (swelling on a tendon, especially on the wrist, fingers and foot) is harmless, may or may not cause pain or discomfort, and may go away eventually on its own.

What to do. If you find a ganglion bothersome, your health care provider may drain it with a needle or remove it surgically. In most cases, the risks of surgery outweigh the benefits of removing the ganglion, so just watching for changes is preferred.

Carpal tunnel syndrome. A condition caused by pressure on a large nerve in the wrist as it passes through a "tunnel" formed by tendons, carpal tunnel syndrome causes pain that may spread into the hand and forearm. You may feel numbness and tingling in the fingers (especially your thumb, index finger, and middle finger), and lose strength in the hand. You may find yourself dropping things often or even being awakened at night by tingling and numbness in your hand.

What to do. This condition should be seen by a health care provider.

Mallet finger. You reach to catch a ball and instead of landing in your palm, it smacks right into the end of your finger. The result: a mallet finger. Inside the finger, a tendon is partly torn. From the outside, you may see very little, but you cannot fully straighten the finger.

Decision Guide for Hand Pain

Symptoms/Signs	Action
Injury that does not affect movement	Use self-care
Symptoms that are not relieved after 4 to 8 hours of self-care	Call provider's office
Mallet finger (see below)	Seek help now
Tender spot on shaft of finger bones (not at joint)	Seek help now
Pain, swelling, and bruising after thumb is accidentally bent backward	Seek help now

For more about the symbols, see page 60.

What to do. An X-ray is recommended. With time, mallet fingers usually heal on their own.

Skier's thumb. Any forceful motion that pulls the thumb in the wrong direction can cause skier's thumb, a tear in the ligament connecting the thumb to the metacarpal bone (the five thin bones that form the palm of the hand and connect to the fingers) of the hand. The name comes from the fact that the injury often occurs after skiing falls. In bad cases, the ligament severs completely.

What to do. This injury should be seen by a health care provider.

Decision Guide for Wrist Pain

Symptoms/Signs	Action
Tendinitis symptoms (see page 189)	Call provider's office
Numbness or tingling in fingers during day or awakened by these symptoms at night	Call provider's office
Pain after falling on outstretched hand	See provider
Fever or rapid swelling in joint, accompanied by pain	See provider
Shooting pains	See provider
Pain spreads up from wrist to elbow, shoulder, or neck	See provider
Pain and neck stiffness	See provider
Dropping objects or difficulty holding objects	See provider
Clicking, popping, grinding	See provider
Visible deformity after a fall	Seek help now

For more about the symbols, see page 60.

Sexual Health

Your sexuality is an important part of who you are and of your overall well-being. And, of course, sex is how we reproduce. Being sexually active also brings with it a set of responsibilities, and being well-informed about sexual issues is just one of them.

You should also be aware of the signs of sexual problems—sexually transmitted diseases (STDs), infertility, and impotence, for example—and understand what causes these conditions and how to deal with them. Not only can health problems related to sexuality have a devastating affect on you as an individual; such problems almost always affect other people as well. If you're ready to have sex, you should be ready to take responsibility for your sexuality by protecting yourself—and your partner—against sexually transmitted diseases (STDs) and unwanted pregnancy.

Almost everyone experiences problems such as impotence or lack of interest in sex at least once in their lives. These problems may have something to do with the relationship or the psychological or physical issues affecting one or both partners. There are many ways you and your partner can ease yourselves through these bumpy spots. Being able to talk freely about your sex life is the first step. If problems with sex persist, you may want to call your health care provider for advice.

AIDS and Other Sexually Transmitted Diseases

Millions of Americans are affected by sexually transmitted diseases (STDs) of all kinds. Yet since we first began hearing about the AIDS epidemic in the early 1980s, many people seem to have forgotten that the other STDs are still out there. Although AIDS is the most deadly STD, syphilis, gonorrhea, genital herpes, hepatitis B, and chlamydia also pose serious health risks. Many STDs also pose special dangers for pregnant women, but knowing about these risks and taking the proper steps can protect the fetus (see *Special Risks During Pregnancy*, page 195).

Acquired Immunodeficiency Syndrome (AIDS)

An estimated 1 million to 1.5 million Americans have human immunodeficiency virus (HIV)—the virus that causes AIDS. The virus is spread through unprotected vaginal or anal intercourse (and less frequently oral sex), shared intravenous (IV) needles, and transfusion of infected blood. However, blood products are now carefully screened so that your chance of contracting HIV through a transfusion is very small. One sexual contact with an infected partner can be enough to infect you.

Risk factors for HIV infection include the following:

- sharing IV needles with an HIV-infected person
- having unprotected vaginal or anal intercourse or oral sex
- having unprotected sex with an HIV-infected person
- having unprotected sex with a person who uses IV drugs
- having multiple partners
- having unprotected sex with a man who has had sex with other men
- for men: having unprotected sex with another man

Once a person is infected with HIV, it can take years before AIDS actually develops. There may be no symptoms, and only a blood test can show at this point whether a person is infected with HIV. AIDS is usually fatal. Although drugs like zidovudine (formerly called AZT) can help the body fight HIV infection, there is no cure. HIV can damage the immune system, putting a person at greater risk for certain infections and cancers.

A person who is infected with HIV can spread it to other people, even if he or she is otherwise healthy and has not yet developed AIDS.

Chlamydia

About three million to four million people in the United States have this bacterial infection. Those at high risk for chlamydia infections include those whose sexual partner has chlamydia, sexually active young adults (under age 25, especially teenagers), those who have had several sexual partners, and those who have had other sexually transmitted diseases.

In women, chlamydia can cause inflammation of the cervix as well as pelvic inflammatory disease (PID), a leading cause of ectopic pregnancies, and infertility in American women. (An ectopic pregnancy occurs when the fetus attaches and grows in the fallopian tubes instead of in the uterus.) In men, it can cause inflammation of the urethra, the organ through which urine passes, and the epididymis, where sperm are stored. Fortunately, chlamydia is easily cured by taking antibiotics for a week. Detecting this condition and treating it early can head off the development of more serious health problems.

Genital Herpes (Herpes Simplex Virus Type 2)

An estimated 20 million people in the United States have genital herpes. Herpes simplex virus type 2 causes painful sores on the genitals and around the mouth. Even after the initial outbreak of sores heals, an infected person may carry the virus for years, with new sores erupting from time to time. The herpes virus can be spread to other people through sexual contact whether sores are present or not. Although there is no cure for herpes, there are drugs that can reduce the length and pain of herpes outbreaks.

Gonorrhea

About two million Americans get gonorrhea each year. In men, the infection can cause inflammation of the genitals and rectum. In women, it can cause pelvic inflammatory disease (PID) and complications during pregnancy. People who have had several partners are at high risk for gonorrhea, but anyone who is sexually active can get infected. Fortunately, gonorrhea is easily treated with antibiotics.

Hepatitis B Virus (HBV)

The hepatitis B virus spreads through sex and causes inflammation of the liver, which can lead to cirrhosis and cancer of the liver. Risk factors for getting HBV include using intravenous drugs, having several sexual partners, or having a partner who is currently infected or is a chronic carrier. If you think you have been exposed to HBV, your health care provider may be able to give you hepatitis B immune globulin to prevent hepatitis from developing (see *Hepatitis*, page 102).

Human Papilloma Virus (HPV)

The human papilloma virus causes genital warts, a common STD. The virus is transmitted through sexual contact.

Genital warts are more common among people who have had multiple sexual partners. In women, they appear on the external genitals, in the vagina, and on the cervix. In men, they appear on the penis. Although the warts are not dangerous themselves, HPV infection can increase a woman's risk of developing cervical cancer.

Men or women who have genital warts should have them removed to lessen the chance that the virus will spread. Regular Pap tests can detect HPV infection in women when no warts are visible. Warts can be treated with acid, with cryotherapy (destroying the warts by freezing), laser treatment, electrosurgery (using an electric current to remove the warts) or excisional biopsy (cutting away the warts surgically). These treatments can usually be done in an office visit to your gynecologist or primary health care provider.

Even after the warts are gone, the virus may remain in the body and be passed along to your partner through sexual contact. A woman who has had genital warts—or whose partner has had them—should make sure to have annual Pap smears.

Nongonococcal Urethritis (NGU)

NGU is an infection of the urethra (the tube carrying urine from the bladder) in both men and women. It can be caused by several organisms, but most commonly—and most seriously—is a result of chlamydia infection. NGU is the most common STD in the United States, where more than four million new cases are reported each year.

Men with NGU may have discharge from the penis, experience burning while urinating, and itch or burn around the opening of the penis. These symptoms are felt most often in the morning. Women may have vaginal discharge, burning urination,

Signs of STDs

See your health care provider if you have any of the following symptoms:

- irritation, discomfort, itching, swelling, soreness, or pain in or around the vagina, penis, or rectum
- genital or anal sores, blisters, rashes, or growths
- painful urination or bowel movements
- abdominal pain
- fevers, chills, and aches
- swelling, soreness, or redness in the throat
- sores or white patches inside the mouth
- unusual discharge from the penis or vagina

abdominal pain, and bleeding between periods. In later stages of NGU, women may have low-grade fevers. Because symptoms for women are internal, women may have NGU for a longer time without it being detected.

NGU can lead to serious problems if left untreated, including permanent damage to both male and female reproductive systems. The infection can ultimately cause infertility in women. If a pregnant woman has NGU, this condition can cause spontaneous abortion, and can also cause her baby to develop eye, ear, or lung infections. NGU is treated with antibiotics.

Syphilis

In early stages, this bacterial infection causes painful sores on the genitals and rectum, and in the throat. If left untreated, syphilis can produce warts in the genital area, contagious sores on other parts of the body, disease of the lymph nodes, problems with the nervous system and heart, and mental illness. Unfortunately, the number of syphilis cases in America is now at its highest point since 1950. Syphilis, however, is easily treated with antibiotics.

Special Risks During Pregnancy

All the STDs discussed above can be passed from mother to child during pregnancy, at birth, or shortly after. That's why it's important to see your health care provider for a prepregnancy exam if you are planning to conceive, or a prenatal visit as soon as you know you are pregnant. Your health care provider can check for STDs at those visits.

Preventive Steps

- The best ways to prevent sexually transmitted diseases are to abstain from sex or to have a mutually monogamous sexual relationship (that is, you have sex with only one person who has sex only with you) with someone who is uninfected. If neither option works for you, or if you or your partner is at risk for STDs or already has an STD, here are some things you can do:
- Always use a latex condom and spermicidal gel. Choose latex condoms with receptacle tips rather than natural-membrane condoms, which may be more likely to break or allow viruses and bacteria to pass through. The spermicide nonoxynol-9 has been shown to provide added protection against HIV, HBV, and the herpes simplex virus. It also reduces the risk of chlamydia and gonorrhea in women. Keep in mind that neither condoms nor spermicides offer foolproof protection. In fact, condoms fail at a rate of 10 to 15 percent as a result of flaws or improper use. Learn to use them correctly.
- Limit the number of sexual partners you have. Remember that when it comes to STDs, having sex outside of a mutually monogamous relationship puts you at the same risk as if you had had sex with all your partner's partners. So the more sexual partners you have, the greater your risk for STDs may be.
- If you think you may have an STD, see your health care provider. He or she can advise you on whether you should be tested, and treat you properly if you test positive.
- Avoid alcohol and other drugs, which can impair your judgment when making decisions about having sex or using condoms.

STDs can often lead to health problems for newborns. For example, chlamydia can cause pneumonia, gonorrhea causes blindness, and AIDS can kill. Many children who get hepatitis at or before birth carry the virus for life.

Women who have syphilis, gonorrhea, or chlamydia can be treated with antibiotics during pregnancy to prevent complications for themselves and their babies. Women with active genital herpes sores may need to deliver by cesarean section to keep their babies from getting the virus. Women who are HIV-positive can take the drug zidovudine (AZT) during pregnancy to greatly reduce the risk of passing the virus to the baby. If you are HIV-positive and pregnant, talk with your health care provider about taking AZT.

What to do. If you have any of the signs of STDs listed on page 194, see your health care provider. He or she can determine whether you have an STD, and if so, how to treat it. Before you conceive, see your health care provider for a prepregnancy exam (see *Pregnancy*, page 247). You should also ask your health care provider about the risks of passing on an STD to your child during childbirth or by breast-feeding.

If You or Your Partner Has an STD

When you are diagnosed with an STD, it will probably be necessary for you to abstain from sex until the disease is completely cured. Your partner should also be checked for the disease and treated. In cases when the STD cannot be treated, you should be sure to use "safe sex" methods to protect yourself and your partner (see *Preventive Steps*, page 195).

Contraception

The decision to have or not have children is a personal one for individuals and couples. For married couples and those in other long-term relationships, the decision of whether or when to use birth control and the choice of method is best made together.

Birth control options range from natural methods, such as the rhythm method, to surgical sterilization (vasectomy for men, tubal ligation for women). In between are many other choices, some of which are more effective than others, and most effective when used properly.

The effectiveness of a contraceptive method is measured in terms of the number of pregnancies that can be expected if 100 couples used the method for one year. Thus, a 2 percent failure rate means that of those 100 couples, two women could expect to become pregnant during the year while using that method. Without any method of birth control, 85 of the 100 couples would conceive within the year. Failure rates include improper use. So if you always use a birth control method correctly, you are more likely to prevent a pregnancy.

When choosing a birth control method, you and your partner may wish to talk with your health care provider to discuss the options and decide which is most suited to your needs. Your provider can help you weigh the risks and benefits of the options you are considering and tell you how to properly use the method you choose.

Below are descriptions of various birth control methods and their effectiveness rates.

Natural Methods

(20 percent failure rate)

These methods are called natural because they do not rely on devices, pills, or other products. The rhythm method involves abstaining from intercourse during the time each month when a woman is fertile. The woman calculates her fertile period by one of four methods: by calendar, basal body temperature, ovulation (monitoring changes in vaginal mucus to identify when ovulation occurs), or symptothermal (a combination of basal body temperature and ovulation methods). The calendar method, which relies simply on predicting ovulation mathematically based on the average number of days between periods, has a very high failure rate. When used diligently and correctly, the latter three rhythm methods can have failure rates as low as 5 percent. On average, however, they fail about 20 percent of the time.

The other natural method is withdrawal. Using this method, the man withdraws his penis from the woman's vagina before ejaculation. Withdrawal requires a great degree of control and flawless timing on the man's part. The failure rate of this method is quite high. And, like the rhythm method, withdrawal does not provide protection against sexually transmitted diseases.

Spermicides

(18 percent failure rate)

Spermicides kill sperm before they can enter the uterus. They come in foams, jellies, suppositories, creams, and foaming tablets, which are inserted into the vagina before intercourse, providing protection for up to two hours. Spermicides must be applied for every act of intercourse. When used with condoms or diaphragms, spermicides provide added protection against pregnancy and even some STDs. Occasionally, a man or a woman may be allergic to spermicides.

Barrier Methods

(12 to 18 percent failure rate)

Condoms, diaphragms, and cervical caps fall into this category. Condoms can be bought over the counter and do not cost much. Worn over an erect penis, condoms can fail if they break or if the penis remains in the vagina after it is no longer erect and the condom slips off (see *How to Use a Condom*, page 200). Condoms used without spermicide fail to prevent pregnancy 12 percent of the time. Condoms with reservoir tips, spermicide, or both are safer in preventing pregnancy.

A diaphragm is a saucer-shaped piece of rubber that surrounds a flexible metal rim. Diaphragms must be fitted by a doctor or nurse practitioner. The diaphragm is inserted into the vagina where it sits snugly against the cervix, or entrance to the uterus. Although the diaphragm is a partial physical barrier against sperm, the real protective agent is the tablespoon of spermicidal cream or jelly it holds against the cervix. Diaphragms must be kept in place for six hours after sex. If intercourse is repeated within this time, spermicide should be reapplied. When used with spermicide, diaphragms fail to prevent pregnancy 18 percent of the time.

A cervical cap is shaped like a cup and made of flexible, natural rubber. It is about an inch and a half in diameter and must be fitted by a health care provider. The cervi-

Methods of Contraception

Spermicides are inserted into the vagina before intercourse. They come in foams, jellies, suppositories, creams, and foaming tablets. They provide protection for up to 2 hours. They have an 18 percent failure rate.

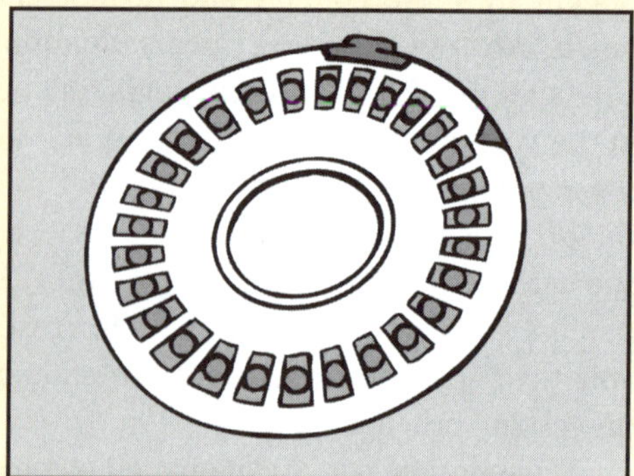

Birth control pills work by preventing ovulation. They come in various formulations of the female hormones estrogen and progesterone, as well as a progesterone-only formulation. They have a 1 to 3 percent failure rate.

Implants are placed surgically under the skin on the arm. They provide up to 5 years of protection. They have a less than 1 percent failure rate.

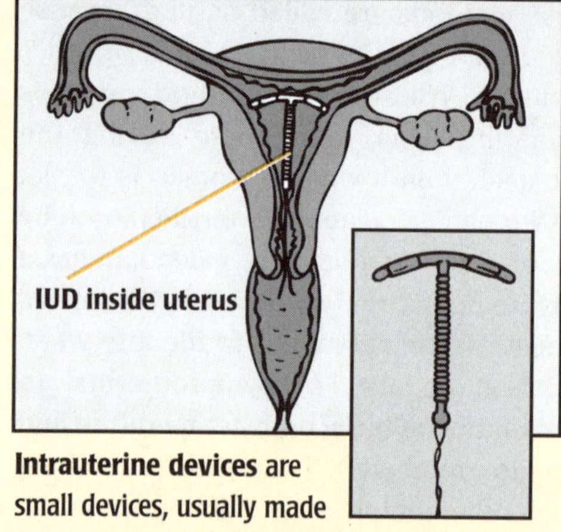

Intrauterine devices are small devices, usually made of plastic, that are placed inside the uterus. They can be worn for up to 10 years, and have a 2 percent failure rate.

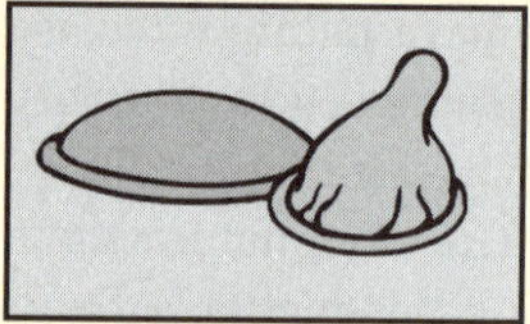

Barrier methods include condoms, diaphragms, and cervical caps. Condoms are worn over the penis and prevent semen from entering the vagina. Diaphragms are inserted into the vagina where they fit snugly against the cervix, or entrance to the uterus. Cervical caps work in a similar way. Spermicide should be used with diaphragms and cervical caps. Diaphragms have an 18 percent failure rate when used with spermicide. The cervical cap has a failure rate of approximately 15 percent.

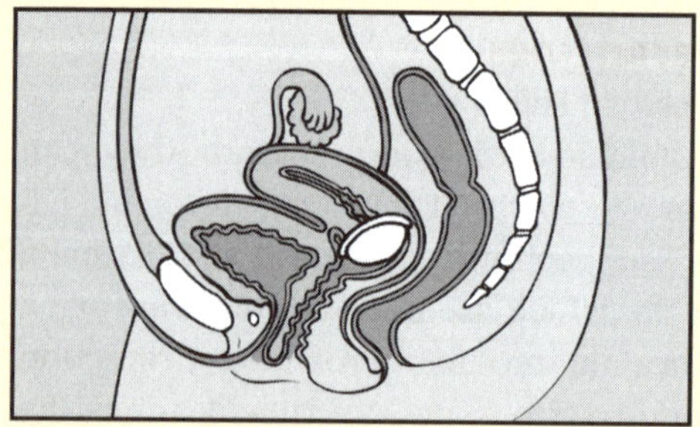

Diaphragm in place

Decision Guide for Contraception

Symptoms/Signs	Action
You need more information about a contraceptive	Use self-care
You want to use a birth-control method requiring a prescription or would like surgical sterilization	See provider
A woman suspects that she is pregnant	See provider

For more about the symbols, see page 60.

cal cap sits at the base of the cervix, the entrance to the uterus. You must use the cap with spermicidal cream or jelly, but if you have intercourse more than once in a 48-hour period, you do not need to reapply spermicide. When used with spermicide, cervical caps fail to prevent pregnancy about 15 percent of the time.

Intrauterine Devices

(2 percent failure rate)

Intrauterine devices (IUDs) are small devices placed inside the uterus. They may be made of plastic and may contain copper or hormones. No one knows exactly how they work. They are thought to keep the fertilized eggs from implanting in the uterine lining, possibly by causing changes in the lining itself. The copper IUD also kills sperm as they approach the IUD, thereby preventing fertilization.

Depending on the device and the woman, an IUD can be worn for up to 10 years. Fertility returns as soon as the device is removed. IUDs must be put in and removed by a doctor or nurse practitioner. They are best for women who have had children and want time between pregnancies but are not ready for permanent sterilization.

Birth Control Pills

(1 to 3 percent failure rate)

Birth control pills, or "the pill," work mainly by preventing ovulation and changing cervical mucus and the lining of the uterus. Birth control pills are available only by prescription. They contain synthetic versions of the female hormones estrogen and progesterone, or just progesterone. Side effects include breast tenderness, bleeding between periods, and nausea, all of which often go away if the woman switches to another type of pill. The pill is convenient and highly effective if taken at the same time each day. If you are taking antibiotics for an infection, use another form of birth control. Antibiotics make the pill less effective. Women who have heart disease, take certain other medications, smoke, or have high blood pressure or problems with blood clots may not be able to take the pill.

Implants

(less than 1 percent failure rate)

Norplant is the only birth control implant now available in the United States. Like the pill, it contains hormones. A local anesthetic is used to surgically place the implants under the skin on the inner side of the upper arm. Implants can provide contraceptive protection for five years. Irregular bleeding and weight gain are common side effects of contraceptive implants. Implants can be removed by a health care provider at any time.

How to Use a Condom

1. Make sure the condom has a reservoir, or leave at least 1/2 inch of extra space at the top for semen.
2. Put on the condom when the penis is fully erect. Squeeze the reservoir end free of air and roll the condom down to the base of the penis.
3. Withdraw the penis soon after ejaculation while the penis is still erect. Hold on to the base of the condom while withdrawing, to avoid spilling the semen.

Use a lubricant to help keep the condom from tearing. Be sure to use only water-based lubricants. Oil-based lubricants like petroleum jelly or baby oil can damage condoms and can cause them to break.

Use only latex condoms and follow instructions. Condoms made of other materials have tiny holes that can let sexually transmitted diseases through. If a man is allergic to latex, he can wear a natural condom with a latex on top. If a woman is allergic to latex, the man should wear a natural condom over a latex condom.

Check the expiration date on the condom package. Do not use the condom if the expiration date has passed. Store condoms in a cool, dark, dry place. Heat can harm them.

Progesterone Injections

(less than 1 percent failure rate)

Depo-Provera is an injection of progesterone given once every three months that prevents ovulation. It also prevents implantation, if an egg is fertilized, by keeping the lining of the uterus from building up. Proper timing of the injections is important for maintaining contraceptive protection. When the first injection is given within the first five days of a normal menstrual cycle, protection from pregnancy is immediate. Infrequent or irregular periods are a common side effect of Depo-Provera. Weight gain can also be a side effect.

Infertility

Infertility—the inability of a couple to conceive a child—affects more than five million people of childbearing age in the United States. It can be caused by a woman's failure to ovulate or blocked fallopian tubes (the passages leading from the ovary to the uterus) or a man's low sperm count or impotence, among many other factors. In cases of infertility, about one third are due to factors affecting the man, while another third are due to factors affecting the woman. The remaining percentage is caused by factors affecting both partners.

About 85 to 90 percent of women will get pregnant during a year of unprotected sex. If you and your partner do not conceive after a year of trying, call your health care provider. He or she can determine whether one of you is infertile, and may recommend that you see an infertility specialist for treatment.

Infertility is diagnosed by first analyzing the man's semen to determine his sperm count. Discovering whether a woman is fertile is somewhat more complex, and may include studying the woman's menstrual patterns by following her body temperature throughout the cycle and testing blood and urine for the presence of certain hormones.

Treatment of infertility is successful about half of the time. Sometimes it can be as simple as having the man stop smoking or drinking alcohol, both of which can reduce his sperm count. When the male sperm count is low for reasons that cannot be corrected, a couple may try artificial insemination with the man's sperm, artificial insemination with a donor's sperm, or administering hormonal drugs to stimulate sperm production.

If a woman's fallopian tubes have been damaged, surgical treatment to correct the damage may be successful. Women who are having trouble producing eggs may be given drugs to stimulate egg production. If a woman's internal reproductive structures cannot support fertilization but can support pregnancy, the couple may opt for in-vitro fertilization, in which the egg and sperm are united outside the body. The fertilized egg is then implanted in the woman's uterus.

Sexual Problems

There is no "right way" or "right" frequency to have sex. Every couple has different preferences and finds different things satisfying. However, anxiety and physical, emotional, or relationship issues can sometimes interfere with a person's or couple's ability to enjoy or participate fully in sex.

Simply growing older brings changes in sexual function for both men and women. Most people don't have the same level of sexual desire at age 55 that they had when they were 20. Interest in sex usually declines slowly with age, though it seldom disappears totally. Similarly, as people grow older, they usually need more time and more direct genital stimulation to reach orgasm. Unfortunately, without knowing that such changes are a normal part of aging, many people worry that something is wrong with them sexually or with their relationships.

Common sexual problems that can occur at any age include differing sexual desires or a decrease in sexual desire, erection problems, rapid ejaculation, and problems with orgasm. These problems are often caused by a combination of physical and psychological or relationship issues.

Problems affecting men. At some time in life, most men will have temporary erection problems, during which they are unable to achieve or keep enough of an erection for intercourse. This condition is known as impotence. In older men, erections are usually not as firm as they once were and more time (days, as opposed to hours) may be needed after ejaculation before they are able to have another. About 30 million American men, however, have a long-term problem that could benefit from medical treatment, counseling, or both. One half to three quarters of cases of impotence have a physical cause, such as diabetes, vascular problems, or drug side effects.

Early or premature ejaculation (when semen is released before the man's partner has time to achieve climax) and delayed ejaculation often can be relieved by making a few simple adjustments (see *Self-Care Steps for Sexual Problems*, page 202).

Problems affecting women. Some women experience vaginismus, in which the muscles around the vagina contract involuntarily, making intercourse impossible. This may be caused by certain conditions that make intercourse painful, such as infection, and it can also be related to anxiety about intercourse. Treatment of vaginismus involves curing the underlying condition. Then the woman inserts dilators of various sizes into the vagina (beginning with the smallest) so she can gradually become accustomed to penetration.

In postmenopausal women, vaginal dryness may cause discomfort during intercourse. Water-soluble lubricants are available to help you with this problem (see *Menopause*, page 252, and *Vaginal Discharge and Irritation*, page 242).

Problems affecting both sexes. Differing sexual desire is problematic only if a couple cannot find a mutually satisfying compromise. Sexual desire naturally varies from person to person. Some may want to have sex three times a day; others, three times a year. There is no "right" or "normal" level of desire.

Diminished desire is common among both men and women in times of stress, when ill or recovering from an illness, or when tension exists in a relationship. Alcohol and some other drugs—birth control pills, antihistamines, some antidepressants, and blood pressure medications, among others—can also cause a loss of desire. These same factors can cause temporary erection problems (impotence) and inhibit orgasm in both men and women.

Self-Care Steps for Sexual Problems

- **Talk.** Good communication is the key to good sex and a good relationship. Tell and show your partner how you like to be touched. Talk through other problems and tensions in your relationship as they arise. If you aren't getting along well the rest of the day, you'll be less likely to get along in bed.
- **Focus on your senses.** This can help reduce sexual anxiety and heighten responsiveness for men and women. Agree not to have intercourse for at least a month. During that time, set aside an hour or more each day to massage each other. While naked, explore and massage all parts of each other's body, except the genitals and breasts. Once you are fully comfortable with this, begin to include the breasts and the genitals, but do not have intercourse. Finally, when you are both more relaxed, start having intercourse. Continue to use whole-body sensuality in your foreplay.
- **Pause, change positions, or think about something else.** If fast ejaculation is a problem, doing any of these things at the first sensation of ejaculation can allow a man to hold an erection longer.
- **Remember, good sex is possible even without intercourse.** Try doing other things, too.
- **Avoid alcohol, as well as drugs that warn that drowsiness may be a side effect.** If you are having sexual problems, ask your health care provider whether any drugs you are taking could be a cause.

For both men and women, there's more to sex than intercourse. Touching, kissing, caressing, giving massages, and even holding hands and talking are all as important to intimacy and sexual pleasure as intercourse. In women, orgasm is achieved by stimulating the clitoris. Many women do not have orgasms during intercourse. Some women find that orgasm from oral or manual stimulation of the clitoris, however, is just as satisfying or more satisfying than intercourse. In men, stimulating the head of the penis brings orgasm. As men age, they often need more direct stimulation of the penis to achieve an erection or orgasm. But foreplay that focuses only on the genitals doesn't always give either partner time to become mentally and emotionally aroused for sex—an important step to orgasm. Whole-body massage and caresses can help arouse and prepare a man or woman for more direct genital stimulation.

Couples and individuals can often deal with sexual problems on their own, but sometimes need medical help or counseling. Your health care provider can recommend a qualified counselor or a doctor specializing in sexual health, and the self-care steps on page 202 list some things you can try on your own.

Decision Guide for Sexual Problems

Symptoms/Signs	Action
Loss of sexual desire or erection; ejaculation or orgasm problems	 Use self-care
Sexual problems that continue or worsen despite self-care	 Call provider's office
Sexual problems that may be caused by a physical problem or medical condition (such as diabetes or heart disease)	 See provider

For more about the symbols, see page 60.

Skin and Hair Problems

Problems affecting skin and hair can be annoying, but you can treat many of them easily at home. You can prevent many of these problems by taking precautions such as avoiding too much sun and staying out of poison ivy patches. Your health care provider can also offer advice and treatment for many skin and hair problems. If your condition is especially difficult to handle, he or she may refer to you a specialist, such as a dermatologist or allergist.

Acne

When hair follicles in the skin become plugged with a combination of sebum (fat) and dead skin, a pimple results. Despite what you may have heard, this problem isn't caused by eating chocolate or greasy food or not washing your face often enough. Acne is mainly due to hormonal activity.

About 3 out of 4 teenagers have some acne, and many adults continue to have acne in their 20s, 30s, and 40s. In teens, pimples appear on the face, back, chest, and upper arms. Adult acne shows up mainly on the face.

The good news is that acne eventually goes away. The bad news: It doesn't go away overnight. A health care provider may recommend an acne ointment or cream, oral antibiotics, or both. Prescription lotions, creams, or gels containing vitamin A acid (tretinoin, commonly called Retin-A) help stop pimples from forming by preventing dead skin cells from sticking to the wall of the hair follicle. Antibiotics kill bacteria, which contribute to inflammation. Severe cases of acne can be treated with a pill containing a chemical relative of vitamin A called isotretinoin (Accutane). Accutane does have side effects, however, and pregnant women cannot take it.

Self-Care Steps for Acne

- Gently wash the affected areas once or twice daily with the cleanser of your choice.
- Use an acne cream or lotion. Start with over-the-counter lotions that contain benzoyl peroxide, sulfur, resorcinol, or salicylic acid as the main ingredient.
- If you use moisturizer, choose one that is labeled noncomedogenic (this has been tested and found not to cause pimples).
- Don't squeeze your pimples. Your health care provider can show you how to lance them.
- Practice stress management techniques (see page 265). Stress can worsen acne or help bring on outbreaks.

How Acne Develops

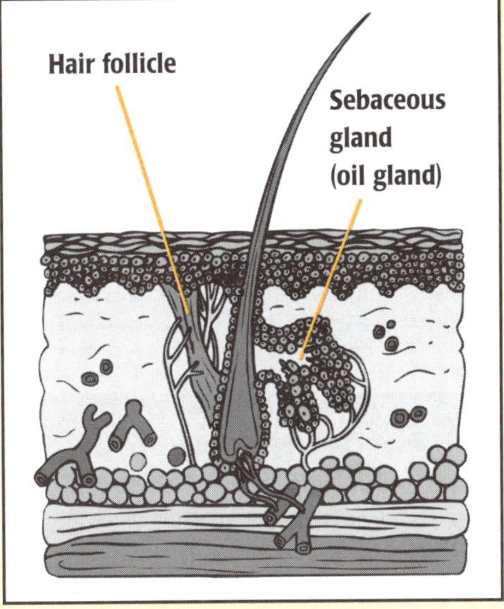

Normal hair follicle and skin structure

Blackheads form when the clogged pore is invaded by bacteria and pus. Blackheads should not be squeezed because this can cause further spreading of the bacteria.

Whiteheads form when pores become clogged with oily secretions and hair follicles break down.

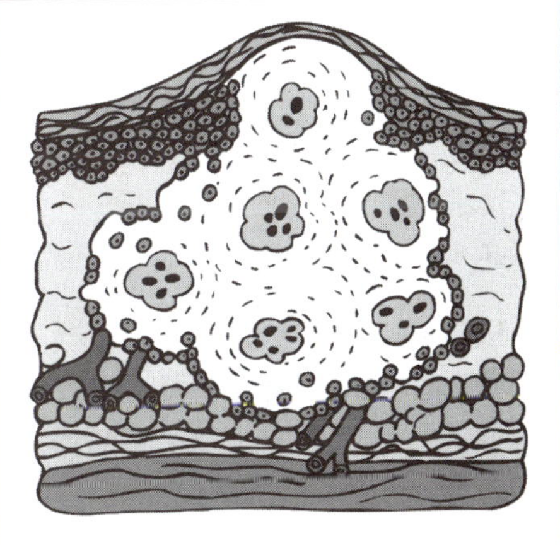

Acne or pimples form when the hair follicle walls rupture. Acne can then spread. Squeezing the pimple can cause the infection to spread further.

A regular skin care regimen, perhaps combined with medicine prescribed by a health care provider, can help prevent outbreaks and potential scarring. Rosacea usually responds well to medical treatment.

Blisters

Blisters are usually caused by repeated rubbing or friction against tender skin until fluid collects under the outer layer of skin. Blisters often form on hands unaccustomed to physical labor and on feet squeezed into ill-fitting shoes. Blisters can also be caused by burns, allergic reactions, and chemical irritation.

Blisters can also signal other health problems. Blisters that appear on the genitals may be herpes simplex virus type 2 (see *Genital Herpes*, page 193). Blisters that form a ring on the scalp or body might be ringworm (see *Ringworm*, page 213). These blisters and others that form suddenly should be examined by your health care provider.

Decision Guide for Acne

Symptoms/Signs	Action
Mild acne	Use self-care
No improvement or acne that worsens after 6 to 8 weeks of self-care	Call provider's office
Large, red bumps that are sore and last longer than 3 days	Call provider's office
Lowered self-esteem because of appearance	See provider
Tendency to scar	See provider

For more about the symbols, see page 60.

To keep common blisters from developing, wear work gloves when doing physical labor. Extra socks, a bandage, or petroleum jelly on a foot likely to blister can reduce friction and prevent a blister. Hikers, runners, and walkers should wear good shoes and thin inner socks, and change their socks at least once a day. Use moleskin for any areas of skin that feel hot, one of the first signs of a blister. You can buy moleskin in the foot care section of most drugstores.

Self-Care Steps for Blisters

- Don't break a blister, since the skin that covers it protects you from infection.
- If the blister breaks, treat it like an open wound. Wash it with soap and warm water. Apply an antibacterial ointment and cover with a clean bandage. Watch for signs of infection—redness, pain, swelling, or red streaks leading toward the body. Call your health care provider if the wound becomes infected.

Decision Guide for Blisters

Symptoms/Signs	Action
Minor blister	Use self-care
Common blister infection	Call provider's office
Unusual blister that appears without warning	See provider

For more about the symbols, see page 60.

Boils

When skin bacteria—usually a type called staphylococci—infect a hair follicle (a pit in the skin that contains the root of each hair), a boil results. Skin tissue swells, and a tender and red, pus-filled lump emerges. The pus contains white blood cells that fight the infection. Until the boil opens and the pus is released, the boil is painful and tender to the touch.

Although boils may appear anywhere on the body, they most commonly occur in areas where there is hair and chafing, such as the neck, armpits, genitals, breasts, face, and buttocks. They can range in size from a pea to a walnut.

Boils can be contagious. Scratching can spread the infection to other areas of the body. Your health care provider may lance the boil by making a small cut with a surgical blade so that the pus can drain. Never attempt to lance a boil yourself without approval from your provider.

Carbuncles are extremely large boils or a series of boils usually deeper and more painful than regular boils. Always check with your health care provider if you suspect that you have a carbuncle. There is a danger that the infection from the skin can enter the bloodstream. If it does, you will have to take antibiotics to get rid of the infection.

Self-Care Steps for Boils

- Do not squeeze the boil or attempt to drain it before it clearly comes to a head. Squeezing it before this happens may drive the infection deeper into the skin.
- Apply warm compresses to relieve pain and bring the boil to a head.
- Keep the area clean to prevent the spread of bacteria. Always wash your hands after touching the boil.
- Take a pain reliever to reduce pain and Inflammation.
- When the boil opens, carefully wipe away the pus. Wash gently and cover with thick, absorbent gauze.

Decision Guide for Boils

Symptoms/Signs	Action
Boil that responds well to self-care	Use self-care
Boil that does not come to a head or improve after 3 days of self-care	Call provider's office
Temperature of 101 degrees or higher	See provider
Boil above the lips, on the nose, or in the ear	See provider
Red streaks leading away from the boil	See provider
Boil that appears on person who also has diabetes	See provider

For more about the symbols, see page 60.

Bruises

Bruises, also referred to as black-and-blue marks, are usually caused by a hard knock on the skin. The impact causes tissue and blood vessels to be compressed between skin and bone. When this happens, blood cells seep from veins into the skin surrounding the injured area. New bruises are dark. As they heal, they turn green and yellow. Some drugs such as anticoagulants and aspirin can cause people to bruise more easily.

Decision Guide for Bruises

Symptoms/Signs	Action
Taking medication that makes you more likely to bruise	Call provider's office
Pain from a bruise that becomes worse	See provider
Temperature of 101 degrees or higher	See provider

For more about the symbols, see page 60.

Self-Care Steps for Bruises

- Apply ice as soon as possible. This helps veins constrict (narrow), reducing the flow of blood into the skin tissue and helping to minimize the bruise.
- Raise and rest the bruised area.

Chicken Pox

Chicken pox is normally a mild childhood disease that affects four million American children each year. A highly contagious disease, chicken pox is caused by the varicella-zoster virus. Only 4 percent of people reach adulthood without having a bout with chicken pox. These people run the risk of getting it as adults, when symptoms tend to be worse and the risk of complications is higher.

Chicken pox is usually spread by inhaling droplets that are coughed, sneezed, or exhaled by an infected person. After exposure to the disease, it can take 10 to 21 days before symptoms appear. A person usually develops the symptoms 14 to 16 days after exposure.

A person can spread the disease to others before he or she has any symptoms of chicken pox. Early signs of chicken pox are coldlike symptoms, fever, abdominal pain, headache, and a general feeling of illness. These can come with the rash or precede the rash by a day or two. The fever may be higher the first few days after the rash appears. The contagious period begins about two days before the rash appears and continues until new sores stop appearing. Once all the sores have turned to scabs, the contagious period is over.

The rash appears as small, itchy, red bumps and spots on the face, scalp, shoulders, chest, and back. Bumps may also appear inside the mouth, on the eyelids, and in the genital area. Some people may have just a few bumps, while others may be covered with them.

The early bumps are usually flat, red marks with a central clear blister. The blisters break open quickly and become dry crusts or scabs, which fall off within two weeks. New sores continue to appear for the first four to five days, so all stages of the rash may occur at the same time. Chicken pox may leave permanent scars, especially in teenagers and young adults. Temporary marks may remain for six months to a year before fading away.

If you've been exposed to chicken pox, there is nothing you can do to prevent the disease if you aren't already immune to it. Chicken pox is a serious health concern in people with weak immune systems, such as people with AIDS, people undergoing radiation therapy or chemotherapy, and people who have had organ transplants. These high-risk people may be candidates for a chicken pox vaccination to prevent them from getting this disease.

Encephalitis, a viral infection of the brain, is a rare complication of chicken pox. But you should watch for its symptoms: fever, mental confusion, forgetfulness, tiredness, and a stiff neck. If you see these symptoms, take the person at once to his or her health care provider's office or an emergency room. A vaccine for chicken pox has been approved for general use in the United States. It is recommended for children over 12 months of age who have not had chicken pox (see *Chicken Pox Vaccine*, page 30). The vaccine may be given to children with weakened immune systems who have been exposed to chicken pox. Although having had a case of chicken pox usually makes you immune to getting the disease again, the virus may lay quiet and then later become active in some

Special Concerns During Pregnancy

- Call your health care provider if you get chicken pox while pregnant. Pregnant women are more at risk for pneumonia.
- There is a slightly higher risk of birth defects among children born to women who had chicken pox in their first or second trimesters of pregnancy. You will not give chicken pox to your unborn baby if you are exposed to the virus but have already had chicken pox.

Decision Guide for Chicken Pox

Symptoms/Signs	Action
Normal chicken pox symptoms, including rash, fever, and itching	Use self-care
Temperature is higher than 101 degrees for more than 4 days	Call provider's office
Lymph nodes become larger or more painful to the touch	Call provider's office
Itching lasts more than 2 weeks and does not respond to treatment	Call provider's office
Pain with urination	Call provider's office
Suspicion that several sores are infected (pus drains from sore)	Call provider's office
Sore in or near the eye, causing redness, drainage, pain, or changes in eyesight	Call provider's office
Blistery, red rash and confusion, delirium, forgetfulness, or other mental changes	See provider
Hard to awaken, very tired	Seek help now
Stiff neck and very bad headache; difficulty breathing	Seek help now

For more about the symbols, see page 60.

adults. This rash, called shingles (or herpes zoster), is more common among people over the age of 60 and people with weakened immune systems. Shingles rarely result from direct exposure to a person with chicken pox.

Self-Care Steps for Chicken Pox

To relieve the itching:

Scratching the scabs off chicken pox sores can lead to more itching and/or infection. These steps will help reduce the urge to scratch:

- Take cool baths every 3 to 4 hours.
- Bathe in warm water using an oatmeal bath product (follow directions) or baking soda (about half a cup).
- Take acetaminophen up to 4 times a day to relieve fever, headache, and other symptoms.
- Keep fingernails trimmed short and wash hands often to prevent infection.
- Wear clean, cotton gloves to bed to reduce the danger of scratching with your nails while asleep.
- Apply calamine lotion to itchy areas; it is sold over the counter. Ask your health care provider or pharmacist about other products that relieve itching.
- For painful or itchy chicken pox in the genital area, apply a petroleum-based ointment or an over-the-counter local anesthetic that is safe for use in that area.

To manage other symptoms:

- Drink plenty of cold fluids.
- To reduce fever, take acetaminophen. Do not use aspirin.
- For mouth ulcers, eat a soft, bland diet. Avoid salty foods and citrus fruits and juices, which may irritate mouth sores.
- Gargle with a mouthwash of cold tea after meals and before bed.
- If a sore seems to be infected, wash with antibacterial soap and apply antibacterial ointment.

Preventive Steps

- Avoid contact with others during the contagious period—until all sores have turned to scabs. That means anyone with chicken pox should not be at work, school, or day care while contagious. If other people may have been exposed to the disease, be sure to call and tell them to watch out for spots about 2 weeks from the date of exposure.
- It is nearly impossible to prevent the spread of chicken pox within a household. Some studies find that 9 times out of 10, siblings of a child who has chicken pox will get the disease.
- If you need to take someone to his or her provider's office, call ahead and tell the staff that you suspect chicken pox. The staff may want to make arrangements to avoid spreading the disease to other patients. In most cases, people who have chicken pox don't need to see a health care provider. The condition can be successfully handled at home, with calls to the provider's office for advice.

Special Concerns for Children

- Children and teenagers with chicken pox should not take aspirin because it may be linked to Reye's syndrome, a dangerous condition of the liver and brain that sometimes develops as a complication of viral illnesses such as influenza and chicken pox.
- Children don't have to stay in bed, but should be kept cool and quiet.
- Children may return to school or day care when they have no fever and all sores are crusted over.

Cradle Cap

Cradle cap is oily, yellowish scales or crusts that appear on babies' heads—behind the ears, on eyebrows, and along the lash line—and occasionally, in the groin area. Common in children less than 1 year old, cradle cap could/ be a mild form of dermatitis (skin inflammation). Cradle cap doesn't cause the baby any discomfort, but new parents may be unhappy about the baby's appearance. This condition is easily treated at home.

Self-Care Steps for Cradle Cap

- Soften the crusty scales with baby oil or mineral oil and leave on the baby's head for about 15 minutes.
- Use a soft brush to loosen the scales after soaking in oil.
- To remove scales, dip a washcloth or gauze in oil and gently rub difficult areas.
- Shampoo the baby's head.
- Don't use dandruff shampoos on your infant without checking with your doctor.

Decision Guide for Cradle Cap

Symptoms/Signs	Action
Prompt response to self-care	Use self-care
No signs of improvement after 2 weeks of self-care	Call provider's office
Cradle cap that spreads beyond the scalp	Call provider's office

For more about the symbols, see page 60.

Dandruff

Dandruff is a common problem affecting about 1 in 5 American adults. It is not contagious. Normally, the skin all over your body—including your scalp—sheds dead cells all the time. Dandruff occurs when dead skin cells on the scalp stick together and become visible white flakes.

Self-Care Steps for Dandruff

- Gently brush hair before each washing.
- Wash hair every day, which may be enough to keep mild dandruff under control.
- Use antidandruff shampoos if the scalp is red and scales are obvious.
- Follow antidandruff shampoo directions: most say to lather and let it sit for at least 5 minutes before rinsing.
- If a dandruff shampoo seems to lose its effectiveness after several weeks, try another brand.
- Try not to scratch or brush the scalp hard. Too much scratching may cause more dandruff.

Decision Guide for Dandruff

Symptoms/Signs	Action
Prompt response to self-care	Use self-care
No improvement after several weeks of self-care	Call provider's office
Constant irritation or itchiness	Call provider's office
Thick scales, yellowish crusts, or red patches	Call provider's office

For more about the symbols, see page 60.

Although there is no cure for dandruff, it's fairly easy to control with medicated shampoos, which are sold over the counter. If these self-care measures don't help, call your health care provider to see if your dandruff might be related to a more serious skin problem.

Eczema and Other Types of Dermatitis

There are several different types of eczema or dermatitis. Both of these are inflammations of the skin and are marked by patches of itchy, reddened skin that look flaky or scaly.

Eczema/atopic dermatitis. This condition develops in childhood and may last into adulthood, although an adult can develop eczema without having a history of it. Atopic dermatitis is a type of eczema. With eczema, the skin is extremely itchy and usually dry. This condition has no known cause. People who have atopic dermatitis have a greater chance of developing allergies such as hay fever or asthma. In babies, eczema takes the form of a rash around the mouth and cheeks. When older children have eczema, rashes may appear behind the knees, in the creases of the elbows, and on the neck.

Contact dermatitis. This condition results from an allergy or other reaction to an irritant that touches the skin. Symptoms include red swollen patches, raised red dots, itching, burning, and blisters that may weep or ooze. Poison ivy (see *Poison Ivy*, page 220), cosmetics, deodorants, soaps, metals, and dozens of other natural and artificial substances can cause contact dermatitis. Diaper rash is a common type of contact dermatitis. Allergic reactions can be caused by hair dyes, jewelry containing nickel, and some rubber compounds. Irritant contact dermatitis may be caused by repeated use of soaps, solvents, and detergents.

Decision Guide for Eczema and Dermatitis

Symptoms/Signs	Action
Prompt response to self-care	Use self-care
No relief after 2 weeks of self-care	Call provider's office
Crusting or weeping sore or very bad itching	Call provider's office

For more about the symbols, see page 60.

Self-Care Steps for Eczema and Dermatitis

- Wash the skin gently in cool or warm water. Don't bathe too often or for too long if you tend to have dry skin.
- Use mild soaps or cleansers and moisturize skin with bath oil after each bath or shower.
- Keep nails short to reduce damage to the skin from scratching.
- Dress lightly and wear soft clothes that are not scratchy.
- For temporary relief of itching, apply a cold compress to affected areas.
- Apply over-the-counter hydrocortisone creams to relieve itching.
- Protect the skin from contact with harsh chemicals and substances to which you are allergic; use rubber gloves and wear protective clothing if possible.

Itch-scratch-itch cycle dermatitis. This develops when an itchy area is scratched or rubbed repeatedly. The skin becomes harder and annoyingly itchy. Scratching makes this worse. It may be hard to break the itch-scratch-itch cycle.

Seborrheic dermatitis. This is red, flaky, slightly itchy skin on an adult's scalp and face (for infants, see *Cradle Cap*, page 211). The area from the side of the nose to the corner of the mouth may be affected, as well as the scalp and eyebrows. The person often has dandruff, too (see *Dandruff*, page 211).

Fungal Infections

Ringworm, jock itch, and athlete's foot are all caused by the same thing: infection by a microscopic fungus. This organism thrives in hot, moist conditions. All of these infections are contagious and should be treated quickly before they spread to other parts of your body—or to other people.

Athlete's foot. This infection usually shows up between the toes. You don't have to be an athlete to get it. Symptoms include red scales and peeling or dead skin. The affected area may itch and develop a musty odor. Athlete's foot usually responds to prompt treatment at home. Left unchecked, however, it can spread to the toenails, causing nails to thicken and discolor.

Jock itch. This infection is marked by red, raised, itchy areas in the groin and mainly affects men. In most cases, self-care will clear up jock itch in one to two weeks.

Ringworm. Ringworm is an outdated term that comes from the idea that the skin infection was caused by a worm that buried itself in the skin. This fungal infection starts as a small spot, then spreads or radiates out in a ringlike pattern. Ringworm can infect most surfaces of the body, including the nails. On the scalp, it may show up as areas of hair loss. Ringworm is contagious, and some kinds can be spread to humans by cats and dogs.

Self-Care Steps for Athlete's Foot

- Wash feet often and dry thoroughly, especially between toes.
- Use a hair dryer, set on the coolest setting, to dry skin fast and well.
- After drying, apply an antifungal product such as clotrimazole or tolnaftate. These over-the-counter medications come in powders, lotions, and creams. Powders help keep the area dry, which adds to comfort and may prevent spread of infection. Lotions and creams can attack the infection more directly.

Hair Loss

About 90 percent of the hairs on your head are growing. The other 10 percent are resting, a stage that lasts for two to six months, after which hair falls out. The average life span of a hair is three to four years, and everyone loses between 50 and 100 hairs per day.

Hereditary balding is the most common cause of excessive hair loss, and can be inherited from either the mother's or father's side. Hereditary balding affects both men and women, although in different ways. Men's hairlines recede and eventually meet up with bald spots on the top and back of the head. Women with hereditary balding will notice a gradual thinning of the hair on the front of the head.

Several things can cause you to lose hair temporarily. Some blood pressure medicines, anticoagulants, antidepressants, antiarthritic drugs, and antigout drugs can cause reversible hair loss. Radiation and chemotherapy used to treat cancer can cause people to lose up to 90 percent of their hair. Birth control pills can cause increased hair loss while women are taking them or for two to three months thereafter, because of the drug's effect on hormone levels. Naturally rising and dipping hormone levels can also cause hair loss in women. Many women may lose hair after childbirth, and a few have hair loss during menopause (see *Menopause*, page 252). or during postmenopausal hormone therapy.

Crash diets have also been implicated in hair loss, and ringworm (see *Ringworm*, page 213), a fungal infection, can cause scaly bald spots. Alopecia areata is a disease that causes hair to fall out in smooth, round patches. Thyroid disease and lupus can cause thinning hair. Major surgery, infection, or high fever can make hair shed for up to three months afterward. Hairstyle traction baldness can occur in those who wear tight braids or ponytails.

Self-Care Steps for Hair Loss

Although there is no cure for hereditary baldness, the following remedies may help if your appearance bothers you:

- Use toupees, wigs, or hairpieces to cover thinning or bald areas.
- Some tips from hairstylists: Perm your hair; use a blow-dryer and lightweight products like mousse or spray for more volume; wash daily with a gentle shampoo; avoid overcoloring which will weaken and break hair.
- If you suspect that your hairstyle is causing your hair to fall out, avoid curlers, braiding, ponytails, or anything that pulls on your hair.

Medical Help

- Balding people may opt for hair transplants, which move hair from other parts of your body to your scalp, sometimes a hair at a time. The total cost can be several thousand dollars, which is rarely covered by health insurance.
- Alopecia areata often heals on its own if left untreated. If the condition does not improve, however, your health care provider may prescribe treatment with a potent steroid lotion.
- Minoxidil, a hair restorer, is successful in producing fine, downy hair in about one third of the people who try it. The newly grown hair falls out, however, if you stop taking the drug. This medication is now available without a prescription.

Hives and Rashes

Though the causes may differ, hives and rashes are rarely serious and can usually be treated at home.

Hives. Why does a person taking penicillin suddenly break out in itchy pink lumps? The person is having an allergic reaction called hives. Hives occur when a substance prompts the body's cells to release histamines. Histamines, which are chemicals found in the skin, are produced by the body to attack foreign substances. Fluid leaks out and collects under the skin in a raised, flushed, itchy bump called a hive. Some hives look like mosquito bites. They often come in groups and may be as small as pencil erasers or as large as two to three inches across.

Some people know that certain foods or drugs give them hives. For most others, the causes may not be obvious. Acute hives that are caused by something avoidable, such as a drug or a certain type of food, can last for hours or days. Chronic hives (often of unknown cause) can last for weeks or months.

Some foods that occasionally cause hives are peanuts and other nuts, eggs, beans, chocolate, strawberries and other berries, tomatoes, seasonings, fresh fruits, corn, fish and shellfish, milk, wheat, and cheese. Drugs that have been known to cause hives include penicillin, sulfa and other antibiotics, and codeine.

Some extensive hive outbreaks are very serious, especially when hives form on the lips and in the throat, interfering with breathing and swallowing. Shock—in which severe swelling, dizziness, and even loss of consciousness occur—can accompany widespread hives (see *Shock*, page 88). These are medical emergencies. In either case, medical treatment should be sought as quickly as possible.

Self-Care Steps for Hives

- Take an oral antihistamine, many of which you can buy without a prescription. Be aware that these medications can make you drowsy. Read directions and warnings thoroughly before taking them. People who are taking certain other medications should not take antihistamines.
- Topical anti-itch treatments seldom help but are an option.
- Rub ice directly over hives or take a cool shower for temporary relief from itching.
- Bathe in warm water, using an oatmeal bath product (follow directions) or baking soda (about a half cup).
- If hives develop after a bee sting or other insect bite, see your health care provider. You may need to carry a prescription kit that contains an injectable dose of epinephrine.

Self-Care Steps for Rashes

For a rash:

First find out what may have caused it. Ask yourself these questions:

- Have I started taking a new drug?
- Have I changed soaps, shampoos, deodorants, cosmetics, or hair dyes lately?
- Does the rash appear on a part of the body covered by clothes?
- Have I worn any new jewelry or used a different lotion or nail polish?
- Have I been near plants such as poison oak, poison ivy, or poison sumac?

If you suspect that any of these substances may have caused the rash, try to avoid them.

Follow these steps to treat the rash:

- Gently wash the affected area with mild soap and water.
- Relieve itching by using calamine lotion or over-the-counter hydrocortisone cream.
- Watch the rash for 24 hours to see if it spreads or changes.

For prickly heat rash:

- Take cold showers or sponge the affected area with cool water.
- Don't use soap on affected areas.
- Apply calamine lotion or cornstarch.
- Wear loose, clean clothes that allow sweat to evaporate.

Rashes. Most of us have had skin rashes at one time or another. One form of skin rash is called contact dermatitis (see *Contact dermatitis*, page 212). The rash develops when the skin comes in contact with an irritating chemical or other substances. Rashes can also be caused by infections such as chicken pox, measles, strep, insect bites (see *Insect Bites*, page 83; also see *Lyme Disease*, page 288), and fungal infections (see *Athlete's Foot*, page 213; *Jock Itch*, page 213; *Ringworm*, page 213).

Decision Guide for Hives

Symptoms/Signs	Action
Hives that respond well to self-care	Use self-care
Cause of hives unknown	Call provider's office
No improvement after a few weeks of self-care	Call provider's office
Hives that develop shortly after you begin taking a new drug; if this occurs, stop taking the drug right away	Call provider's office
Very bad discomfort from hives	Call provider's office
Big hive that develops at bite site after bee sting or other insect bite (see page 83)	See provider
Hives all over body	Seek help now
Difficulty breathing	Seek help now
Extensive hives with swelling around the face and in the throat and mouth	Emergency: call 911

For more about the symbols, see page 60.

Decision Guide for Rashes

Symptoms/Signs	Action
Tolerable pain or itching	Use self-care
Temperature of 101 degrees or higher	Call provider's office
Rash that lasts longer than 2 weeks	Call provider's office
Rash in diaper area that is bright red, raw, or sore-looking; with blisters or crusty patches	Call provider's office
Red streaks that lead away from the rash	See provider
Reddened, sunburned-looking skin that feels like sandpaper	See provider
Swollen joints, chills, dizziness, nausea	See provider
Burning eyes and nose; weeping blisters	See provider
Swollen glands in groin	See provider
Expanding circular rash	See provider

For more about the symbols, see page 60.

Prickly heat rash. When a person perspires and the sweat doesn't evaporate properly, prickly heat rash can result. This rash is very common among infants, appearing as small red dots on an infant's head, neck, and shoulders.

To check for overheating, feel an infant's skin between the shoulder blades to see if it is hot or moist. Once the skin cools and dries, the rash will probably go away, but the itching may last awhile longer.

Impetigo

Impetigo is a contagious bacterial infection most often seen at the site of broken skin. Red sores start to ooze a straw- or honey-colored liquid, which, when partially dried, becomes a crust or scab. Touching or picking the sores can spread bacteria to other parts of the body—or other people.

With early and careful home treatment, impetigo can be brought under control in several days. However, a rare kidney problem called glomerulonephritis can be a complication of impetigo. Its symptoms are red or cola-colored urine, headache, and raised blood pressure. See a health care provider immediately if these symptoms appear.

Self-Care Steps for Impetigo

- Gently and frequently clean sores with antibacterial soap and water or hydrogen peroxide.
- Using a cotton swab, apply an antibiotic ointment.
- Don't cover the area with an adhesive strip unless the sore is in an area where the scab may rub off. For example, to keep children from scratching, cover with a dry gauze pad and keep the tape as far from the sore as possible. Use paper tape.
- Wash your hands well with antibacterial soap and water after cleaning sores and applying ointment.
- Make sure everyone in the household uses separate towels, washcloths, and bath water.
- For facial sores, men should shave around sores, not over them. Don't use a shaving brush, as it may spread infection. Replace the razor blade every day, and don't share your razor.

Decision Guide for Impetigo

Symptoms/Signs	Action
Mild impetigo	Use self-care
Problem that does not improve or clear up after 3 days of self-care (oral antibiotics may be needed)	Call provider's office
For infants: small, pus-filled blisters that break easily and leave a raw spot behind	Call provider's office
Large blisters	Call provider's office
Blisters that show other signs of infection, such as warmth, redness, or tenderness	Call provider's office
Urine that turns red or cola-colored, accompanied by a headache (signs of glomerulonephritis, a rare kidney problem)	Seek help now

For more about the symbols, see page 60.

Lice

Having lice is no longer believed to be a sign of poor hygiene or dirty living conditions, but it's still a miserable experience. Lice feed on human blood. As they burrow into the skin, their saliva causes intense itching. Adult lice are about the size of a pinhead. Lice eggs, which the tiny insects cement to hair shafts with a gluelike substance, are easier to spot. The eggs, called nits, are white and shaped like tiny footballs or cattails. A female louse can lay up to six eggs a day, and between 50 and 100 in her lifetime. Lice are easily spread through shared bedding, hats, and combs.

Self-Care Steps for Lice

- To kill lice, you must use a shampoo just for that purpose. Several are sold over the counter. Shampoos are also available with a doctor's prescription. Follow the directions on the box; be sure to leave shampoo on the affected area for several minutes. This gives the medicine time to work. Do not use commercial pesticides, gasoline, or kerosene.
- After shampooing, use a rinse made of equal parts white vinegar and water. This will help remove stubborn nits.
- Combing hair with a fine-tooth comb will also help remove nits after shampooing.
- If you have pubic lice, make sure your sexual partner treats himself or herself with these methods.
- Wash everything that has touched the affected area. Wash bedding and clothing in hot water for at least 10 minutes and put them in the dryer for at least 20 minutes at the hottest setting. Vacuum furry toys, carpets, drapes, mattresses, and upholstery, including fabric-covered car seats and headrests. Soak all combs, brushes, and hair accessories in hot water or rubbing alcohol for at least 10 minutes.
- See your health care provider if over-the-counter remedies aren't working or if the lice have infested your eyelashes.

Head lice. A case of head lice is often mistaken for dandruff (see *Dandruff*, page 211). Symptoms include itching, white nits on hair shafts that aren't dislodged with regular shampooing, and red bite marks along the nape of the neck and around the ears.

More than six million cases of head lice are reported among school-age children each year, and lice can easily spread to family members. Head lice should be treated promptly and steps should be taken to prevent their spread to others.

Pubic lice. Pubic lice are also known as crabs. They attach themselves to pubic hair and itch like crazy. Pubic lice are spread through sexual contact or contact with lice-infested bedding or clothing. It's important to tell your sexual partner if you have crabs so that he or she can also be treated. Likewise, it's important to thoroughly wash all household bedding carefully (see the self-care steps on this page).

Lyme Disease/Deer Ticks

Humans usually pick up ticks from woodsy underbrush, tall grass, and the fur of outdoor pets. Once on a host, the tick bites the skin, embeds its head, and taps into a small blood vessel. The real danger of the tick's relatively painless bite are the viruses, bacteria, and other organisms that the insect may be passing along.

The most well-known disease harbored by ticks is Lyme disease, spread by deer ticks, which are smaller and look different from dog or wood ticks. The name comes from the town of Lyme, Connecticut, where the bacteria that causes the disease were first identified in 1975. Left untreated, the disease can cause arthritis, disorders of the heart and nervous system, and several other serious conditions. But Lyme disease is relatively easy to treat if it's caught early. Lyme disease symptoms vary greatly from person to person; however, three phases have been identified.

Phase one. Between 3 and 30 days after being bitten by an infected tick, a small red bump may appear at the site. The bump is surrounded by a bull's-eye rash that grows slowly for several days before fading. Flu-like symptoms—fatigue, headache, chills, joint and muscle aches, and a low fever—may occur during this period. One third of people with Lyme disease never get a rash.

The bacteria that cause Lyme disease are sensitive to antibiotics such as tetracycline, penicillin, and erythromycin. If you see or have had a bull's-eye rash, see your health care provider right away.

Phase two. Weeks or months after the bite, about 20 percent of untreated victims have nerve or heart disorders ranging from poor coordination to an abnormal heartbeat. Skin lesions develop in about half of those who are untreated. These symptoms also disappear, usually within a few weeks.

Phase three. As many as 60 percent of untreated victims may develop recurring or

Preventive Steps

When in woodsy areas, check yourself for ticks twice daily. Wear long pants, long-sleeved shirts, and shoes. Tuck your shirt into your pants and your pants into your shoes or boots to help prevent ticks from attaching themselves to your skin. Apply insect repellent containing no more than 30 percent deet to your pants, socks, and shoes. Higher concentrations of deet are not recommended, especially for young children and people with sensitive skin.

Self-Care Steps for Tick Bites

- If you discover a tick on your skin or clothing, remove it immediately. The sooner you remove it, the lower your chance of picking up infectious organisms. If the head of the tick is attached to your skin, don't try to remove it with your bare fingers. Use a pair of fine-tipped tweezers instead.
- To remove a tick, grip it close to your skin and pull it straight out until it releases its hold. Avoid twisting the head or squeezing the body because this may cause the tick to inject bacteria into your skin.
- Wash hands and affected skin with soap and water.
- Watch for the appearance of a bull's-eye rash at the site up to 30 days after being bitten.

Decision Guide for Lyme Disease/Deer Ticks

Symptoms/Signs	Action
Tick that is not attached	Use self-care
Tick that is attached	Use self-care
Rash or infection	See provider
Arthritis symptoms	See provider

For more about the symbols, see page 60.

chronic arthritis after a period of up to two years. The arthritis mainly affects large joints, most often the knees.

Poison Ivy, Poison Oak, and Poison Sumac

A walk through the woods shouldn't make you miserable. But if you touch poison ivy, poison oak, or poison sumac, you may have an allergic reaction to these plants.

These three plants contain an almost invisible, clear-to-slightly-yellow oil called urushiol, which comes from any cut or crushed part of the leaves, stem, or vine. When the oil touches skin, it penetrates within minutes. In 12 to 48 hours, a red, itchy rash and tiny, weeping blisters may appear. The oil can be carried on paws or fur of cats and dogs, on shoes or clothing, or on garden tools. The substance can stay potent for months if not cleaned from these items. You may also develop a rash, even in winter when these plants are covered with snow. Urushiol can also be carried in smoke when these plants are burned.

Poison ivy. This plant usually grows east of the Rocky Mountains as a vine or shrub. Its leaves are in clusters of three, and it has yellowish-white berries. It grows easily and is widespread.

Poison oak. A shrub, small tree, or, less often, a vine, poison oak grows west of the Rockies. It has greenish-white berries and leaves in clusters of three, similar to those of poison ivy.

Poison sumac. This tall shrub is found in swampy, boggy areas in the South and in northern wetlands. Poison sumac has 7 to 13 pointed, small leaves per branch and cream-colored berries.

Self-Care Steps for Poison Ivy, Poison Oak, or Poison Sumac

- Wash suspected areas of contact with soap and water as soon as you can.
- If water isn't available, wipe affected areas with rubbing alcohol.
- Use water to rinse pets, clothes, shoes, and camping or gardening gear if you or your pets have been in infested areas. Urushiol, the substance in these plants that makes you itch, can stay strong for months, so it's important to wipe out any traces of this oily sap before it finds its way to your skin.
- Calamine lotion may relieve initial itching and help dry the rash.
- Soaking in lukewarm water mixed with an oatmeal bath product or baking soda may soothe irritated skin and help dry oozing blisters.
- Your health care provider may recommend an over-the-counter oral antihistamine or for a more severe case may prescribe corticosteroids. He or she may treat a very bad reaction with cortisone by injection or in pill form.

Preventive Steps

- Wear rubber gloves, long pants and sleeves, and boots when working near infested areas.
- Do not burn poison ivy, poison oak, or poison sumac.

Your best defense against these plants is the following: Learn to identify them by sight, and watch what you are handling when gardening, cleaning up around the yard, or wandering in the woods.

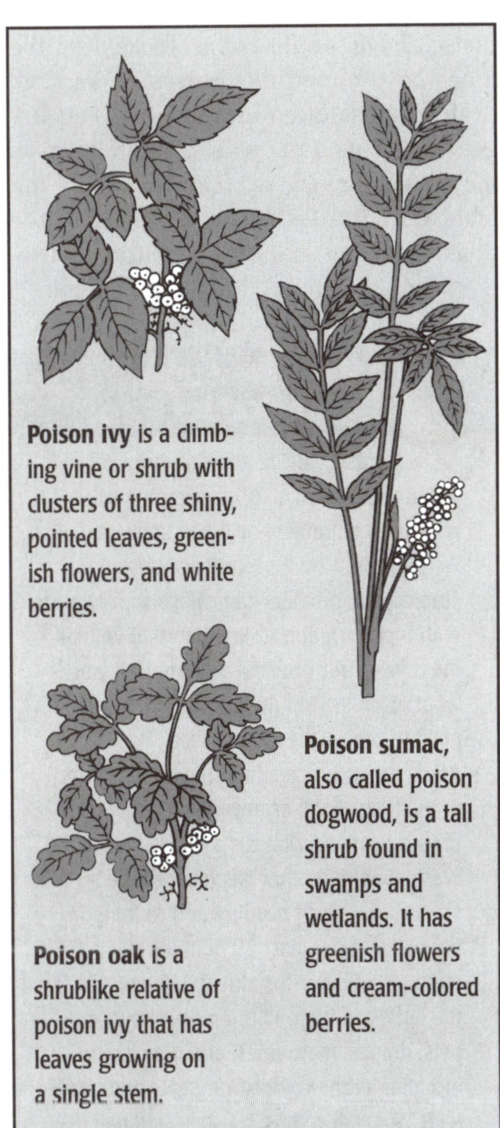

Poison ivy is a climbing vine or shrub with clusters of three shiny, pointed leaves, greenish flowers, and white berries.

Poison sumac, also called poison dogwood, is a tall shrub found in swamps and wetlands. It has greenish flowers and cream-colored berries.

Poison oak is a shrublike relative of poison ivy that has leaves growing on a single stem.

Decision Guide for Poison Ivy, Poison Oak/Poison Sumac

Symptoms/Signs	Action
Mild itching that responds well to self-care	 Use self-care
Rash on a large area or on the face or eyes	 Call provider's office
Very bad swelling from rash	 Call provider's office
Rash may be infected; however, this is rare	 Call provider's office
Temperature of 101 degrees or higher	 See provider

For more about the symbols, see page 60.

Poison Ivy

Scabies

Like head lice, scabies can occur in any family, in any neighborhood. Scabies is no longer believed to be a sign of personal uncleanliness or dirty living conditions.

The tiny mites that cause scabies are passed easily from one person to another. The mites burrow into the skin, where the females lay eggs; these hatch in about five days. The burrowing leaves very tiny grooves and tunnels on the skin that may look somewhat like white splinters.

Scabies causes very tiny bumps that itch a lot, especially at night. The itching doesn't begin until several weeks after the mites have buried themselves in the skin. Scabies most often appears between fingers and around the wrists, but itchy areas may occur anywhere. It often affects the male genital area. When someone in the household has scabies, the entire household should be treated at the same time.

Decision Guide for Scabies

Symptoms/Signs	Action
Very itchy gray lines or red patches on the body	Call provider's office
Criss-crossing, itchy lines or tunnels in the skin	Call provider's office
Rash and itching that you suspect are caused by scabies	Call provider's office
Side effects from insecticide lotion	Call provider's office
Constant itching and rash of an unknown cause	See provider

For more about the symbols, see page 60.

Self-Care Steps for Scabies

- Call your health care provider to discuss the problem. If the symptoms are clearly from scabies—or if you know you were in contact with someone infested by scabies—the provider can call your pharmacy with a prescription for a lotion that will kill the mites. Your provider will also tell you what to do to stop the infestation. You may need to repeat the steps a week later.
- Apply the insecticide lotion to all members of the household, or anyone who had close physical contact with the affected person.
- Wash everything that has touched the affected area. Wash bedding and clothing in hot water for at least 10 minutes and put them in the dryer for at least 20 minutes at the hottest setting. Vacuum furry toys, carpets, drapes, mattresses, and upholstery, including fabric-covered car seats and headrests. Soak all combs, brushes, and hair accessories in hot water or rubbing alcohol for at least 10 minutes.

Skin Cancer

The good news: skin cancer can be cured in 95 percent of cases. The bad news: the number of people diagnosed with skin cancer is increasing, and Americans are getting skin cancer at even younger ages.

Most skin cancer is caused by damage from the sun's ultraviolet (UV) rays. Light-skinned, light-eyed people are at greatest risk for skin cancer, while dark-skinned people have less risk. People who live in areas with higher levels of UV radiation from the sun, such as the southern United States or South Africa, are more likely to develop skin cancer than those from areas where UV radiation is less intense, such as the northern United States or Norway.

Prevention. Your best defense against developing skin cancer is protecting your skin from the sun consistently and at an early age. Avoid getting too much sun, particularly between 10 A.M. and 2 P.M. and in midsummer. The sun's rays are more intense at higher altitudes, nearer the equator, and on the water and in the snow. But your skin can absorb UV rays even on cloudy days.

Sunscreens and sun blocks protect you by filtering out or blocking the UV rays that cause sunburn. Generally, the higher the sun protection factor (SPF), the greater the protection against sunburn. A sunscreen of at least SPF 15 is recommended. Protect yourself with sunscreen whenever you plan to stay outdoors for a long time, no matter what the weather is like.

For the best protection against sunburn, apply sunscreen at least 30 minutes before exposure to sunlight. Reapply sunscreen often during extended exposure. Apply to dry skin after swimming or strenuous activities that cause heavy perspiration. Zinc oxide products block all of the sun's rays and are good for the nose and lips. Most common skin cancers hit the skin right where the sun does—on the back of the hands and neck, the face, the tops of the ears, and the scalps of bald or balding people. Don't forget to apply sunscreen to these areas. Wear loose-fitting, tightly-woven dark clothing, and a hat with a brim.

All forms of UV rays contribute to a person's total lifetime exposure. Using sunscreen reduces the amount of exposure, but does not prevent skin cancer. Tanning beds are deceptive because they don't cause burns, but they provide a large dose of UV radiation, which can contribute to cancer.

Early detection. Skin cancer is most curable if it's caught early, so if you are at risk, you should pay attention to changes in your skin by performing a skin self-examination once a month. After your shower or bath, start by noticing where birthmarks, moles, and blemishes are and what they look like. Be sure to check your entire body, including back, scalp, buttocks, and genitals. Use a mirror to check areas that are hard to see. Giving yourself a thorough exam once a month will help you notice changes that may signal one of the three most common forms of skin cancer.

To identify possibly cancerous moles, follow the ABCDs for detecting skin cancer recommended by the American Academy of Dermatology. You should look for the following changes:

- Asymmetry: One half doesn't match the other half.
- Border irregularity: Edges of mole are ragged, notched, or blurred.
- Color: Pigmentation isn't the same throughout the mole. Shades of tan, brown, and black may be present, and dashes of red, white, and blue may also be noticeable.

- Diameter: The mole is greater than one-quarter inch across (about the size of a pencil eraser). Any growth of a mole may be a cause for concern

Types of skin cancer. The following are the four major conditions related to skin cancer.

Actinic keratosis (precancerous skin changes). This appears as scaly areas on parts of the body exposed to the sun, particularly the ears, face, scalp, and hands. The scaly areas may be easier to feel than to see. They may be premalignant (meaning they could develop into cancer later) and should be treated.

Basal cell cancer. This cancer accounts for more than 90 percent of all skin cancer cases in the United States. It grows slowly and seldom spreads to other parts of the body. Basal cell cancers may look like pearly or waxy bumps and sometimes have depressions in the middle. As the cancer grows, sores can develop in the center that make it look gnawed. Because of the gnawed appearance, basal cell cancers are sometimes called rodent ulcers. They can be removed surgically or treated with radiation therapy.

Decision Guide for Skin Cancer

Symptoms/Signs	Action
Regular exposure to intense sunlight	Use self-care
Any signs of skin cancer, such as skin growths or bumps that grow and/or change shape or color	See provider
Rough, scaly areas on parts of the body exposed to the sun	See provider

For more about the symbols, see page 60.

Squamous cell cancer. This cancer appears as raised or lumpy-looking bumps with rough, scaly surfaces on a reddish base. The border of the bump is often irregular. Squamous cell cancers tend to bleed, but seldom spread to other parts of the body, although this happens more often than with basal cell cancer. Squamous cell cancer may be treated with radiation therapy, surgical removal, or cryotherapy (in which cells are destroyed by being exposed to extreme cold).

Malignant melanoma. This may appear as a mole that changes size, color, surface, shape, or border. The faster these changes occur, the more suspicious the lesion. Look for an irregular border with different colors in the same mole and some black color. Most melanomas are not raised. In the early stage, most resemble a very dark freckle that is larger than normal. Melanomas are most often found on the back in men and on the back, thighs, and calves in women. If not detected early, malignant melanoma can spread to other areas of the body, mainly the lymph nodes, liver, lungs, and central nervous system, and can be lethal. The growths must be removed surgically, and radiation therapy and treatment with anticancer drugs may also be required.

Sunburn

Sunburn results from overexposure to ultraviolet (UV) radiation from the sun. In a first-degree burn, symptoms include redness, sensitivity, and pain. If you have a sunburn, stay out of the sun until the skin recovers. Long exposure can lead to the swelling and blistering of a second-degree burn (see *Burns*, page 62).

Sunburn is uncomfortable, usually for 24 to 48 hours. Frequent overexposure to the sun can cause long-term damage to the skin, resulting in premature aging, wrinkling, and skin cancer (see *Skin Cancer*, page 223). Although most skin cancer is curable, malignant melanomas may be fatal.

Some drugs can make you more sensitive to the sun, causing you to burn with little exposure to sunlight. Before starting a drug, ask your health care provider or pharmacist about the possible reactions to sunlight. Drugs that react to sunlight include tetracycline and sulfa antibiotics.

Sunburn can be prevented by avoiding too much sun, particularly between 10 A.M. and 2 P.M. and in midsummer. Sunscreens and sun blocks protect you by filtering out the UV rays that cause sunburn. For the most protection from sunburn, apply sunscreen at least 30 minutes before exposure to sunlight. Reapply sunscreen frequently if you are outdoors for a long period. Apply to dry skin after swimming or strenuous activities that cause heavy perspiration. Zinc oxide products block all the sun's rays and are good for the nose and lips.

The higher the sun protection factor (SPF), the greater the protection against sunburn. A sunscreen of at least SPF 15 is recommended. Wear sunscreen whenever you plan to stay outdoors for an extended period of time, even on cloudy days. Dress protectively. Most common skin cancers hit the skin right where the sun does—on the back of the hands and neck, the face, the tops of the ears, and the scalps of bald or balding people. Be sure to apply sunscreen to these areas. Wear loose-fitting, tightly-woven dark clothing, and a hat with a brim.

Self-Care Steps for Sunburn

- The best treatment for sunburn is to soak the affected area in cold water (not ice water) or apply cold compresses for 15 minutes. This will reduce swelling and provide quick pain relief. Do not apply greasy lotions such as baby oil or ointment to sunburned areas. They can make the burn worse by sealing in the heat.
- If sunburn affects large areas of your body, soak in a cool bath. A half cup of cornstarch, oatmeal bath product, or baking soda in the bath will help reduce inflammation and soothe sunburned skin.
- Adults who do not have stomach problems or a history of allergy to aspirin products can take aspirin to reduce inflammation.

Decision Guide for Sunburn

Symptoms/Signs	Action
Minor sunburn	Use self-care
Blistering, painful sunburn	Call provider's office
Sunburn and purple blotches, skin discoloration, or blisters	See provider
Fluid-filled blisters	See provider
Chills, nausea, temperature of 102 degrees or higher, faintness, dizziness, or vision problems	Seek help now

For more about the symbols, see page 60.

Men's Health Concerns

Just as women have specific health concerns, men have some unique problems as well. For example, annual death rates for men with prostate cancer are similar to the rates of breast cancer deaths among women. And just as women should have regular screening of their reproductive organs, men should get in the habit of having regular examinations. However, men are much less likely to go to the doctor than women are and are more likely to try to brush off any symptoms or health problems they have. This means that men are less likely to get care early, when diseases are easiest to treat. You can buck this trend by learning more about your well-being and finding out which of your symptoms should be seen by your health care provider.

Your health care provider (family or general practitioner or internist) can offer advice and treatment for most problems you may encounter. If your condition is especially hard to handle, your provider may involve other medical professionals who specialize in diagnosing and treating men's diseases.

Testicular Health

The testes are the pair of male reproductive organs that make and store sperm. These organs also produce the hormone testosterone. The scrotum is the pouch of skin that contains the testes and part of the spermatic cords. Suddenly painful testes can be a very serious medical condition. Because this pain can have several causes, correct diagnosis requires medical expertise. See your health care provider right away if you feel sudden, sharp pain, or swelling in the testes. Prompt medical attention can prevent the unnecessary loss of a testicle.

Lumps within the scrotum are usually benign, and most lumps are cysts or other inflammation. Even if it is not painful, a scrotal lump should always be checked by your health care provider to be sure that it is not a tumor.

Epididymitis. This is the inflammation of the long, coiled tube (epididymis) that runs along the back of each testicle and helps transport sperm. Epididymitis is often caused by a bacterial or chlamydial infection traveling from the urinary duct to the sperm duct.

What to do. Call your health care provider if you suspect that you might have epididymitis. This condition is usually treated with antibiotics.

Orchitis. This is an infection of the testicle that often occurs with epididymitis. Orchitis can also be a viral infection related to the mumps. Although this condition is rare, it can cause infertility and irreversible damage to the testes.

What to do. If you feel sudden pain in your testes or find a scrotal lump, see your health care provider right away.

Testicular cancer. Although cancer of the testes is rare, it is the most common form of cancer in men between the ages of 20 and 35. Only one testicle is usually affected, while the other remains perfectly healthy. Testicular cancer accounts for 12 percent of all cancer deaths in young men, and is four times as common among Caucasian men as it is among African-American men.

Testicular cancer strikes after age 15. Men whose testes have not descended into the scrotum or did not descend until after age 6 have a greater risk for this type of cancer. Testicular cancer usually responds well to treatment, especially if it is detected early.

Performing a testicular self-examination each month can help you become familiar with the size and feel of your testicles and will make it easier for you to notice any changes (see *Testicular Self Examination*, page 228). Your health care provider should also examine your testicles during your routine exams.

What to do. Examine your testicles every month. If symptoms such as pain, swelling, lumps, or heaviness in your testicles last as long as two weeks, you should see your provider as soon as possible. Call him or her if you notice any changes in your testicles. Your provider can then determine whether you have testicular cancer by performing a biopsy (taking a small sample of tissue) of the lump or swelling. If you do have testicular cancer, the cancerous testicle may be surgically removed. This does not cause sterility, because the other testicle is left intact. Chemotherapy and radiation therapy may also be prescribed.

Testicular torsion. This occurs when a testicle gets twisted in the spermatic cord from which it is suspended within the scrotum. Sudden pain, severe enough to cause vomiting and nausea, is the main symptom of testicular torsion. This unusual condition can occur spontaneously—even while the person sleeps—or after strenuous activity at any age. It can strangle the blood supply to the testicle and, without immediate treatment, can cause permanent damage.

What to do. Testicular torsion is a medical emergency. See your health care provider immediately, even if the testicle seems to have returned to its proper place. Although your provider may be able to carefully shift the testicle back into its normal position, surgery is usually performed within several hours to securely anchor it in place.

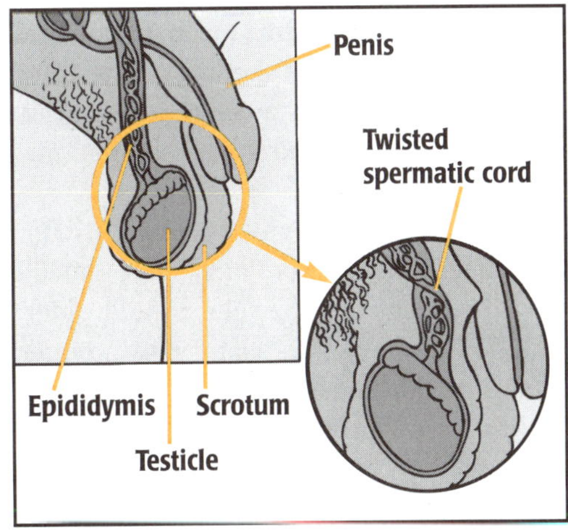

Testicular Self-Examination

While there is no way to prevent testicular cancer, organizations such as the National Cancer Institute and the American Cancer Society recommend that men do a monthly self-examination to check for possible lumps or nodules in the testes.

Testicular self-examination (TSE) is easy and takes only a few minutes. Follow these steps:

- Examine your testicles after a warm bath or shower. The heat relaxes the scrotal skin, which makes it easier for you to feel anything unusual. Perform this exam with each testicle.
- Hold one testicle with both hands. Place your index and middle fingers under the testicle and your thumbs on top. Roll the testicle gently between your thumbs and fingers. It is normal for one testicle to be larger than the other.
- Feel for any abnormal lumps—about the size of a pea—on the front or side of the testicle. These lumps are usually painless.
- Do not confuse the epididymis with a lump. The epididymis, a cordlike structure that runs along the back of each testicle, helps transport sperm.

You should see your health care provider if you notice any of the following symptoms:

- a small painless lump
- slight enlargement of a testicle
- a feeling of heaviness in the scrotum
- aching in the groin or lower stomach
- sudden accumulation of fluid in the scrotum
- any other changes in the way a testicle feels

These symptoms may be signs of other illnesses, such as infections or other nonmalignant disorders, but you should let your provider make the diagnosis. (Also see *Cancer Prevention and Treatment,* page 49.)

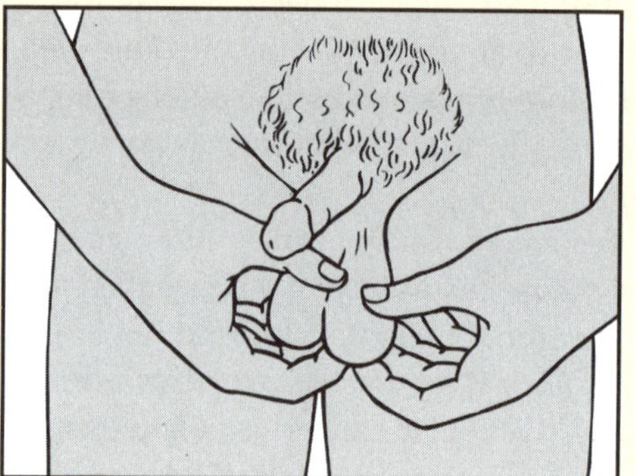

Prostate Health

The prostate is a walnut-sized organ that surrounds the bladder opening and urethra in men. It produces a secretion that is added to the semen during ejaculation.

Benign prostatic hypertrophy (BPH). This affects about half of men older than 60 and 80 percent of men ages 80 and older. With BPH, the prostate gland grows larger than normal. Almost every man older than 45 has some prostate enlargement, but symptoms are rarely felt before age 60. If BPH produces no symptoms, it does not require treatment. BPH does not lead to prostate cancer, but the condition should be monitored.

BPH does cause problems if the enlargement narrows the urethra and makes urination difficult. Symptoms include the following:

- frequent urination
- difficulty urinating
- having a strong urge to urinate but being able to produce only a weak stream of urine
- burning or pain while urinating
- waking up at night to urinate

Difficult urination is annoying but not a significant problem in itself. However, BPH can cause urine backup in the kidneys, bleeding through the urethra, infections, bladder stones, or complete inability to urinate. All of these conditions can lead to serious health problems and must be treated.

What to do. You should see your health care provider if you experience any symptoms of BPH. He or she will feel your prostate through the rectum (an exam also known as a digital rectal exam). Your provider may also check your urine for blood or infection to determine whether the problem is due to prostate cancer. If you have few symptoms, your provider may decide to follow your condition with yearly exams. However, if your condition is complicated, your health care provider may prescribe medication or surgery. Medications can work by relaxing the muscles around the prostate or blocking the action of testosterone, shrinking the prostate. Surgical treatment of BPH often involves removing excess prostate tissue.

Prostate cancer. This is much rarer than BPH, but as common as lung cancer among men. About 8 in 10 cases occur in men older than 65. In its early stages, cancer of the prostate remains in that organ and is not life-threatening. However, if the disease spreads to other parts of the body, it can be fatal. Prostate enlargement—with symptoms similar to those of BPH (see above)—is the only symptom of early-stage prostate cancer. A biopsy (in which a small sample of the enlarged tissue is examined) is the only definitive way to tell the difference between BPH and prostate cancer.

Prostate cancer can be detected and diagnosed with digital rectal exams, blood tests, and ultrasound, in which sound waves are used to create an image of structures within the body. The National Cancer Institute and the American Cancer Society recommend that men over the age of 40 have a digital rectal exam once a year to screen for prostate cancer. Depending on your age and whether you have a relative (father or brother) who has had prostate cancer, your health care provider can tell you whether you should be screened for prostate cancer more frequently.

What to do. Make sure you get screened according to the recommendations above. Detecting disease early is the key to effective treatment. Because prostate cancer chiefly affects older men, and because it often progresses slowly, there are two forms of treatment: relieving the symptoms alone, or attempting to cure the disease.

If you are diagnosed with prostate cancer, you should talk with your health care provider about your lifestyle, general health, age, and the side effects of various treatments, to determine what option is best for you. When the cancer is growing slowly and not producing symptoms, the best option may be "watchful waiting," in which your provider observes your condition carefully to make sure it's not getting worse. Other treatments for prostate cancer are surgical removal of the cancerous part of the prostate, radiation treatment, and hormone therapy.

Women's Health Concerns

Women can care for many of the health problems they experience—such as yeast infections and menstrual discomfort—easily at home. You may find that changing your diet and other behavior is all you need to do. However, you need to consider your own medical history and your current health when deciding whether self-care is right for you. Remember, you can always call your health care provider when you are unsure of what to do. If you have any conditions that do not seem to be healing normally, or if self-care steps do not seem helpful, you should contact your provider.

Staying on Top of Your Health

A woman can maintain her well-being by taking an active role in her health care. Among the things you can do for your health and wellness are exercising, eating right, doing breast self-examinations, and managing your stress. In addition, you need to make an effort to get a well-woman exam every year. This exam gives you and your health care provider an opportunity to assess your health and catch any problems before they become serious.

The Well-Woman Exam

You may choose to have your gynecologist as your primary care physician. Or, you may decide to see a gynecologist for your well-woman examination and see an internist or general or family practitioner for your other health needs.

During your annual well-woman visit, your health care provider will check your health and nutritional status and measure your blood pressure, as well as perform a breast and pelvic exam and do a Pap smear. These screenings can detect early signs of breast or cervical cancer, and may also reveal other problems. To learn more about screenings and immunizations, see page 27. You and your provider can also work out a schedule for screening exams. Depending on your medical history (as well as your family's), your age, and other factors, you may need to have certain screenings more often.

This is also the time to talk with your provider about family planning. Tell him or her whether you're happy with your current birth control method and whether you'd like to learn about others. If you're using the birth control pill or an intrauterine device (IUD), it's especially important for you to get regular checkups (see *Contraception*, page 196).

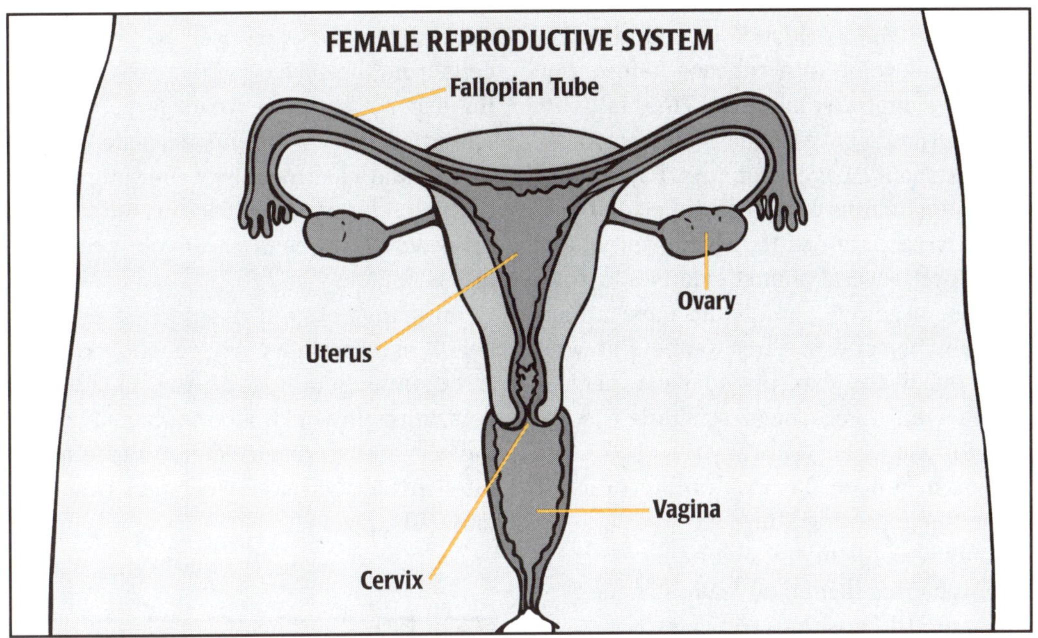

Try to schedule your well-woman visit for when you do not expect to have your period, because Pap smears can't be done then. Avoid using douches, vaginal lubricants, or spermicides one to two days before your exam. (But if you use a spermicide to help prevent pregnancy, don't have sex without using it.) Keep track of the first day of your last period, because your provider will need this information.

Here are descriptions of the screenings you need, along with guidelines for how often to have them.

Pelvic Exam

You should have a pelvic examination at each annual well-woman visit. During a pelvic exam, your health care provider will examine you thoroughly. After checking the external genitalia for any abnormalities, your provider will insert one or two fingers into the vagina while pressing on your abdomen with the other hand. He or she may also use an instrument called a speculum that will allow a closer look at your cervix. The speculum may cause pressure, but it does not usually cause pain. This exam helps your provider detect abnormalities in the shape of the uterus and ovaries, as well as any tenderness that might indicate a problem.

Cervical Cancer and Pap Smears

The cervix is the lower part of the uterus. This organ—made up of muscle and fibrous tissue—separates the vagina from the opening to the uterus. Cancer of the cervix is one of the most common cancers diagnosed in women in the United States. It is also one of the most curable when caught at an early stage. About 13,500 women are diagnosed with cervical cancer each year, and about 4,400 women die each year from the disease. For those women diagnosed early, the survival rate is 89 percent. If the disease hasn't spread, the survival rate is virtually 100 percent. Regular Pap smears can reveal early evidence of cell changes that can develop into cancer—before any visible symptoms appear. This is why women should have regular Pap smears.

You should have your first Pap smear within six months of the first time you have intercourse, or at age 18, whichever comes first. After several annual exams in a row that are negative, you should have a Pap smear every one to three years. But you and your health care provider can decide together on a Pap smear schedule that is best for you.

You may need this exam more often if any of the following things are true:

- You have a history of abnormal cervical cell changes that could lead to cancer.
- You are HIV-positive (you have the virus that causes AIDS).
- You have a suppressed immune system for reasons other than HIV infection.
- You have had any sexually transmitted diseases (STDs).
- You have had several sex partners.
- You had intercourse for the first time before you were 18.
- You smoke.

To perform a Pap smear, your health care provider will insert a speculum into the vagina and scrape a few cells from the cervix with a spatula. This procedure is usually painless and does not pose any risk to your health. Your provider will then send the sample to a laboratory that will review the sample for abnormalities.

If your Pap smear shows early changes in the cells that may lead to cancer, or cervical dysplasia, your provider may want to take a closer look at your cervix through a procedure called colposcopy. He or she will probably recommend that abnormal cells be removed in order to make a definite diagnosis, or as treatment for the condition. Several methods are used to remove the cells from the surface of the cervix, including laser surgery, cryosurgery (freezing abnormal cells with chemicals to destroy them), and electrocautery (burning off abnormal cells with electricity). All of these procedures can be done in your provider's office.

In many cases, if dysplasia is found, a health care provider will recommend hysterectomy (removal of the uterus), or conization, in which a cone-shaped part of the cervix is removed. Radiation therapy is often prescribed when cervical cancer is more advanced.

Breast Health and Breast Cancer Screening

Breast cancer is the most common type of cancer among American women. Each year in the United States, more than 182,000 women are diagnosed with this disease. Although it may not be possible to prevent breast cancer, many women survive it. Early detection increases the rate of survival. Women with small, localized breast cancers (where the cancer has not spread beyond the breast) have a 90 percent chance of living more than 10 years after the cancer is treated.

Risk Factors

It's important for you to know your risk factors for developing breast cancer, and to have regular screenings.

Family history. Your risk doubles if your mother or sister has had breast cancer. It is even higher if they developed breast cancer before menopause.

Precancerous cells on biopsy. Women who have had a previous breast biopsy that was benign but showed certain suspicious cells are at increased risk.

Age. Two thirds of all breast cancers occur in women over the age of 50. As you grow older, your risk increases.

Childbirth and menstruation. Your risk of breast cancer is higher if you have never had children, or if you gave birth to your first child after age 30. If you had your first period before the age of 12 or if you experience menopause after the age of 50 your risk may be higher.

Other factors. Other factors linked to breast cancer include obesity and a history of ovarian or endometrial cancer. Even so, the most important risk factors are growing older and a personal or family history of breast cancer.

You'll want to monitor yourself closely if you have any of the risk factors discussed. Talk with your provider about when you need to begin having mammograms.

Screenings

Appropriate screening for breast cancer should be a part of your well-woman exam. Depending on your age and other risk factors, there are two well-established methods your provider will use: a manual breast exam and a mammogram. You should also examine your breasts each month so you can become familiar with their shape and detect any changes.

Breast exams. Many health care providers perform breast examinations routinely on women of all ages during general office visits or well-woman exams. The provider will check each breast using fingertips to feel for lumps, and look for other suspicious changes, such as dimpled, scaling, or puckered skin, or fluid leaking from the nipple. When combined with a mammogram (depending on your age and risk factors), a breast exam by a health care provider is the best way to detect cancer in its early stages.

Breast self-exams. The American Cancer Society recommends monthly breast self-examination (BSE) for all women age 19 and older. Your provider can show you how to do a BSE. (Also see *How to Do a Breast Self-Exam*, page 234.) It's easy, and it takes only about five minutes a month to do. Many women are afraid to examine their breasts because of what they might find. But most breast lumps are not cancerous. If you do find any lumps, see your provider.

Fibrocystic breast disease is a term often used to describe a number of different conditions causing breast lumpiness or lumps. These conditions are not linked to cancer, and are the most common cause of breast lumps in women. Women who have fibrocystic breast changes usually have a condition in which lumps and cysts in the breast swell and become painful before menstruation. Fibrocystic breast changes affect 1 in 5 women to some degree, and can usually be managed by lifestyle changes such as cutting down on salt and caffeine. In severe cases, your provider may recommend surgery.

Performing a breast self-exam. The best time to do a BSE is one week after your period starts, because any premenstrual swelling or tenderness should be gone by then. If you have already gone through menopause, do a BSE on the first

How to Do a Breast Self-Exam

1. While in the shower, raise your right arm, placing your hand on the back of your head. Starting at the outer edge of the right breast, use the pads of the fingertips of your left hand. Feel for lumps or changes as you move your fingers firmly in small circles, working in a spiral toward the nipple. Check the other side in the same way, then gently squeeze each nipple to check for any discharge.

Pads of fingertips

Small circles about the size of a dime

2. After your shower, clasp your hands together and raise your arms above your head with elbows bent. In a mirror, look for changes in shape or contour, as well as any skin changes, such as dimpling or rashes.

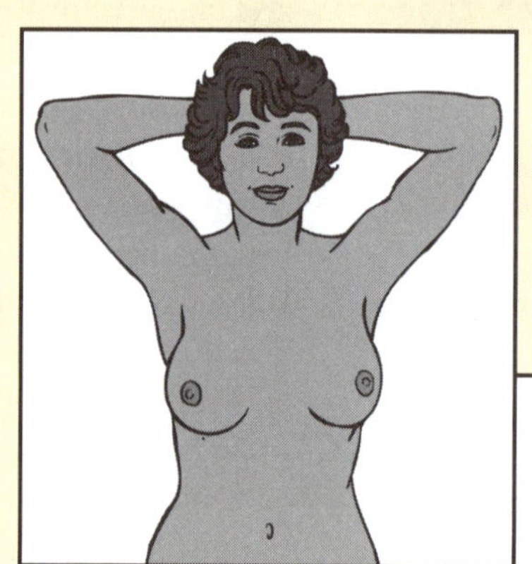

3. Still standing before the mirror, lower your arms. Place your hands on your hips, pull your shoulders and elbows forward, and lean slightly toward the mirror. Look again for any changes in shape or contour, and for skin changes.

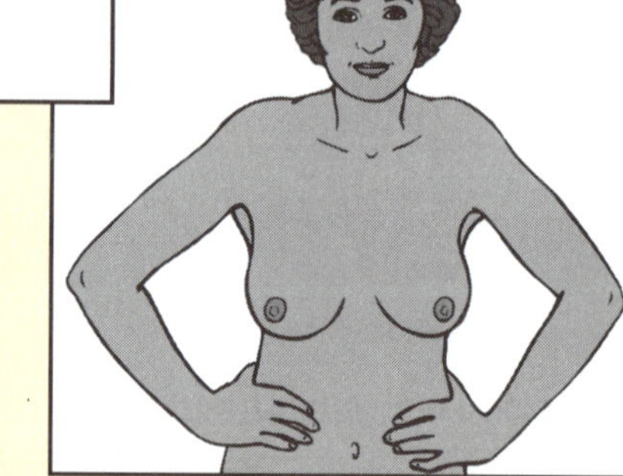

4. Finally, lying down, place a rolled towel or pillow under one shoulder and place the hand on that same side over your head. Examine your breast again as you did in the shower, this time checking your armpit as well. Repeat this on the other breast.

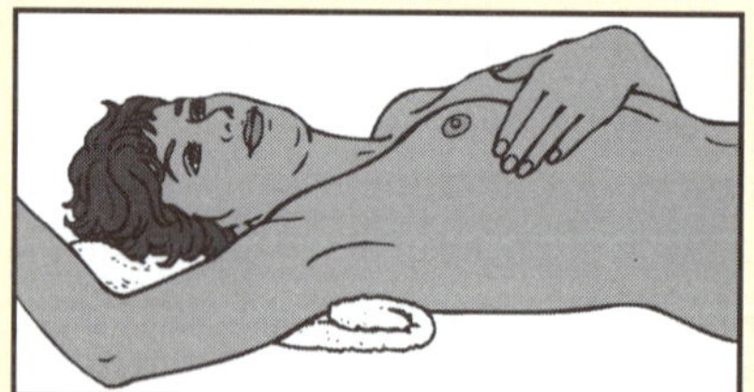

5. Call your health care provider if you find anything that concerns you. After age 50, the American Cancer Society recommends annual mammograms for all women.

day of each month. If you have had a hysterectomy, ask your provider to advise you about the best time of the month for you to perform a BSE.

What to look for. It's normal for your breasts to swell, feel lumpy, or become tender, especially around the time of your period. By performing a BSE each month, you will become familiar with the feel, shape, and size of your breasts, making it easier for you to notice changes, should any occur. Look for the following things while examining your breasts:

- new lumps or changes in the size or shape of existing lumps
- change in the shape or contour of your breasts, or unusual swelling
- changes in skin color or texture
- dimpling, puckering, or crusting of the skin, or rash, especially around the nipple
- any fluid leaking from the nipple

Remember that even if you have some of these signs, it doesn't necessarily mean you have breast cancer. Most breast lumps are not cancerous. You should call your health care provider if you notice any lumps or changes that concern you. He or she can tell you whether you should schedule an appointment.

Mammograms

The most effective way to detect breast cancer early is mammography—a low-dose X-ray of the breast. Mammograms can detect breast cancers while they are very small, sometimes two years earlier than a tumor could be felt by a woman or her health care provider. In the past 25 years, mammography technology has improved considerably. The X-rays are much more sensitive, and far less radiation is used.

But mammography is not perfect. In some cases, a lump you can feel during a breast exam may not appear on a mammogram. Such a lump would still need to be checked, even if the mammogram is normal. Mammography, like most other tests, may also show abnormal results when there is no cancer.

The American Cancer Society (ACS) recommends that women start having mammograms every one to two years at age 40. After age 50, the ACS recommends that women have a mammogram once a year. You may want to discuss your options for breast cancer screening with your health care provider. Regardless of whether you decide to have a mammogram at this time, remember that regular breast self-exams and breast exams by your provider are important practices to follow for early detection of breast cancer.

Treatment of Breast Cancer

Several different types of surgery are used to treat breast cancer, along with chemotherapy and radiation therapy. If the cancer has not spread, only the lump may be removed; this is called a lumpectomy. Other surgeries are variations on mastectomy, or the removal of all or part of the breast. Radical mastectomy involves removing the entire breast as well as the chest muscles. In modified radical mastectomy, the breast, lymph nodes, and a small muscle in the chest are removed. In a partial mastectomy, the lump, some lymph nodes, and the lining of the chest muscle are removed, while the muscles are usually left untouched. Many women choose to have their breasts reconstructed after mastectomy.

Menstrual Problems

Menstruation is the shedding and replenishing of the lining of the uterus. A cycle of changes in levels of the hormones progesterone and estrogen causes you to have a period. On average, the menstrual period—from the first day of bleeding to the day before the next bleeding phase—lasts 28 days. At the beginning of the cycle, estrogen causes the lining of the uterus to thicken so that it can receive a fertilized egg. The ovaries release an egg at about the middle of the cycle. At this time, progesterone levels climb. If the egg is fertilized, it may implant itself in the uterine lining, and pregnancy begins. However, if the egg isn't fertilized, it is shed along with the uterine lining through the vagina, and the cycle begins again.

Young women usually begin menstruating between the ages of 11 and 14. The length of periods varies from woman to woman and from month to month. Bleeding may last only three days or as long as a week. Flow may be light or heavy. Cycles can last anywhere from 21 to 40 days. Over the years, a woman's menstrual pattern is likely to change. In the early years, it may be irregular and heavy. As time goes by, it may arrive like clockwork. The amount of flow may change over time as well. All of these variations are normal. However, if you notice any unusual changes for you (see *Missed Periods*, page 239, and *Bleeding Between Periods*, page 238), you should call your health care provider.

Painful Periods

For most women, menstruation comes and goes each month with ease. But for other women, or at various times in a woman's childbearing years, periods are complicated by pain (dysmenorrhea) or premenstrual symptoms.

Menstrual cramps are most common between the ages of 15 and 24, and among women who have not given birth. Pain can be mild or so bad that it sends you to bed for a few days. Very bad cramps may be accompanied by diarrhea, nausea, and headache.

One type of painful period seems to run in families. Researchers in the 1970s and 1980s discovered higher than average levels of prostaglandins—fatty acids in the body that act a lot like hormones—in the menstrual fluid of women who suffered from cramps. Prostaglandins serve many func-

Decision Guide for Painful Periods and PMS

Symptoms/Signs	Action
Painful periods or cramps that can be relieved	Use self-care
Mild to moderate premenstrual symptoms	Use self-care; Call provider's office
Pain during period that is worse than it used to be	Call provider's office
More than your usual amount of menstrual flow	Call provider's office
Very heavy bleeding (enough to soak a pad or tampon every hour for 2 to 3 hours in a row)	See provider
Severe depression, anxiety, or other premenstrual symptoms that are not relieved with self-care	See provider

For more about the symbols, see page 60.

tions in the body, but when the level is too high it can cause cramplike pain from contractions.

Other types of painful periods may be caused by fibroids (noncancerous growths) in the uterus (see *Fibroid Tumors*, page 244), infection, or endometriosis, which is uterine lining growing outside of the uterus (see *Endometriosis*, page 240). Intrauterine devices (IUDs) can also cause pain during menstruation. Pain in the pelvic area may indicate pelvic inflammatory disease (see *Pelvic Inflammatory Disease*, page 241).

Self-Care Steps for Painful Periods and PMS

For painful periods:

- Use aspirin, ibuprofen, or prescription pain relievers. Aspirin usually relieves mild to moderate menstrual pain. Ibuprofen is often effective when the pain is worse. If you do not get enough relief from these over-the-counter drugs, your health care provider may be able to prescribe a higher dose of ibuprofen or other nonsteroidal anti-inflammatory drug.
- Apply heat. Place a heating pad or hot-water bottle on your lower abdomen to ease the pain.
- Raise your hips. If you find yourself in bed because of cramps, try lying on your back with your hips elevated above the level of your shoulders. Put your feet up on the footboard of the bed or the arm of the couch, and place pillows under your hips. Firm massaging of the lower back may also help.

For premenstrual symptoms or premenstrual syndrome (PMS):

- Avoid salt and caffeine, and drink plenty of fluids to relieve water retention and bloating.
- Exercise regularly and eat a well-balanced diet, low in sugar and high in protein.

If your periods become more painful or begin to last longer than they once did, see your health care provider.

Premenstrual Syndrome (PMS)

If you're like many women, you may dread the days before your period. Premenstrual syndrome (PMS) is a collection of symptoms that affect between one third and one half of women for the week or two before menstruation. You may feel irritable, tired, and depressed. Your breasts may be swollen and tender, and your back may ache. You may notice that you're retaining fluid and that you feel bloated as a result. You may crave certain foods and want to eat more than usual.

The cause of PMS is unclear. It probably has something to do with the hormonal changes that accompany the menstrual cycle. Both estrogen and progesterone are known to interact with brain chemicals. Some vitamin deficiencies also have been linked—inconclusively—to PMS.

You can try several things to ease PMS. Cutting down the amount of caffeine and salt in your diet during the two weeks before your period may help. Eating salty foods may worsen your tendency to retain water. Caffeine can worsen irritability and fatigue by stimulating you artificially and letting you down when its effects disappear. Some experts believe that sugar has the same effect and should also be avoided. It may also be a good idea to stay away from alcohol during this time. Alcohol, caffeine, and sugar can affect your mood.

Exercising regularly may help you combat PMS. It will probably help you feel more relaxed, and also may boost your mood. Studies have found that women with PMS may also have insomnia and may not sleep deeply when they do finally drift off.

Staying well rested can help you fight the fatigue that may come before your period.

Consult your health care provider to develop a PMS management strategy that works for you. He or she may prescribe medication if your symptoms are severe, or it may be enough to make a few dietary and other behavior changes. For tips on good sleep habits, see *Insomnia*, page 271.

Decision Guide for Bleeding Between Periods

Symptoms/Signs	Action
Occasional spotting or breakthrough bleeding	 Use self-care
Spotting or breakthrough bleeding recurring over 1 or 2 months	 Call provider's office
Bleeding between periods that lasts 3 or more days	 Call provider's office
Menstrual pattern that does not return to normal by the third month	Call provider's office
Very heavy bleeding (for example, bleeding enough to soak a pad or tampon every hour for 2 to 3 hours in a row)	 See provider
Bleeding between periods, and pain	 See provider
If you are over 40 years old: More than 6 months since your last period and irregular bleeding is now occurring	 See provider

For more about the symbols, see page 60.

Bleeding Between Periods

Bleeding between periods—also known as spotting or breakthrough bleeding—can be inconvenient and annoying. In most cases, it is nothing to worry about. But because bleeding between periods may be a sign of more serious problems, such as ectopic pregnancy or cancer, you should call or visit your health care provider if it happens more than two months in a row.

Spotting (light bleeding) or breakthrough bleeding (heavier bleeding) between periods usually lasts one or two days. About 10 percent of women regularly have spotting around the time they ovulate, or release an egg. Bleeding between periods is also common when hormones are rising and falling

Self-Care Steps for Bleeding Between Periods

- After a while, most women take their menstrual cycles in stride. Many find it difficult to remember the exact date of the first day of their last period, let alone dates a few months earlier. That's why it's important to keep a menstrual diary if you begin to have bleeding that is unusual for you. Keep a written record of the dates of your periods and any bleeding between periods. Also note how long the bleeding lasted and how heavy the flow was. This diary can help your health care provider find the possible cause and decide whether the bleeding between periods is anything to be concerned about.
- Wear a pad or tampon to protect your clothing while you are bleeding, just as you would during a regular period.
- Avoid aspirin while you are bleeding. It may increase the flow.
- Relax. In most instances, spotting and breakthrough bleeding are nothing to worry about.

the most—during the first few years of menstruation and again as women approach menopause.

Spotting is very common among women who have intrauterine devices (IUDs). It may also occur if the hormone levels in the birth control pills a woman takes are not well suited to her body. Women may also experience spotting if they take the pill for the first time, switch to a new pill, or start the pill again after having been off it. Your provider may prescribe a different pill or recommend another form of birth control. Spotting and breakthrough bleeding are also very common with Depo-Provera (a method of birth control given by injection), especially during the first three months.

If you are near menopause and breakthrough bleeding is often a problem, your health care provider may recommend an endometrial biopsy to check for cancer and other problems. Your provider may suggest a D and C (dilation and curettage), in which the uterine lining is gently scraped and cleaned away. For some women, this will end the problem.

See your health care provider if your breakthrough bleeding

- is accompanied by pain
- lasts three days or more
- is very heavy
- happens more than two months in a row

If you are spotting and there is a chance you are pregnant, you should see your health care provider.

Missed Periods

For most women, the first thing to come to mind when they miss a menstrual period is pregnancy. Although pregnancy is a common cause of missed periods (also called amenorrhea), many other factors can cause amenorrhea. Stress, being very overweight or underweight, birth control pills, an

Self-Care Steps for Missed Periods

- If you are in your 40s or 50s, a missed period may mean you are nearing menopause. Before your periods stop entirely, they may be irregular for a time (see *Menopause,* page 252).
- For some women, a bout of the flu or stress at work or home can throw their menstrual cycles off. If you are under stress, find ways to relieve it. Take time out daily to meditate, listen to soothing music, or read a book. Getting regular exercise and enough sleep each night can also reduce stress.
- Rapid weight loss or being very overweight or underweight can also cause amenorrhea (missed periods). If you are trying to lose weight, make sure to eat at least 1,200 calories a day from a well-balanced variety of foods. If you are underweight, eat a well-balanced diet that provides about 2,000 calories a day. Whether you are overweight, underweight, or dieting, your doctor, nurse practitioner, or a dietitian may be able to help you set up a healthy diet and exercise plan (see *A Healthy Lifestyle,* page 38).
- Intense athletic training and exercise can also cause amenorrhea. If you are in training and you miss periods, your periods may return to normal if you ease up. If you are an endurance athlete, ask your health care provider if hormone therapy or calcium supplements might be right for you, to help prevent osteoporosis.

intense exercise regimen, and the approach of menopause are all common causes of amenorrhea. Also, a woman's menstrual periods may not resume for several months after she gives birth or while she is breastfeeding. Diseases that affect the body's hormonal system can lead to missed periods, but this is rare.

The first thing to rule out if you miss a period is pregnancy. Home pregnancy tests on the market today are fairly accurate beginning about two weeks after the missed period was supposed to begin. More sensitive pregnancy tests, available through your health care provider's office, are accurate within days after your period should have started. If you are sure you are not pregnant, you should consider other possible causes, many of which you can do something about.

If a girl has not started to menstruate by age 16, she may have a type of amenorrhea. Hormone imbalances or problems with the ovaries, uterus, or vagina may be the cause. If menstruation hasn't begun by age 16, the girl should see her provider.

Birth control pills are sometimes prescribed to make periods regular. They can also have the opposite effect, causing periods to stop. If your periods stop while you are on the pill, talk with your health care provider. Switching to another birth control pill may solve the problem. Going off the pill after being on it for a while may also disrupt your menstrual cycle for a few months while your body adjusts to the change in hormones.

Decision Guide for Missed Periods

Symptoms/Signs	Action
Occasional missed period	Use self-care
Missed 1 or 2 periods, not pregnant but dieting, under stress, near menopause, or exercising heavily	Call provider's office
Missed 2 or more periods, not pregnant, and no obvious cause	See provider
Missed 2 or more periods, not pregnant and taking birth control pills	See provider
Age 16 or older and have never had a period	See provider
Missing periods and having irregular spotting or pain in lower abdomen	See provider

For more about the symbols, see page 60.

Endometriosis

Endometriosis is a puzzling condition in which tissue from the lining of the uterus, or endometrium, begins growing outside the uterus. This tissue most commonly grows in the abdomen, where it acts just like the normal uterine lining, responding to hormonal changes during the menstrual cycle: building up, breaking down, and bleeding. But because this tissue cannot leave the body through the vagina, it can cause internal bleeding, inflammation, and the buildup of scar tissue. The cause of this condition is unclear, and there is no definitive cure.

As many as 10 to 20 percent of women have endometriosis at some time during their childbearing years. Endometriosis can be very painful, and it causes infertility in 30 to 40 percent of women who suffer from it. Symptoms of endometriosis include increased pain during and before periods and sharp pain in the pelvis during intercourse. Lower back pain, and pain with bowel movements during periods, as well as heavy or irregular menstrual bleeding, can also indicate endometriosis.

If you suspect that you may have endometriosis, call your health care provider. If endometriosis is diagnosed, he or she may prescribe hormones, painkillers, or surgery. (Your health care provider may first check your condition with ultrasound, in which sound waves are used to create an image of structures within the body. A precise diagnosis is made by laparoscopy, in which an instrument is used to look inside the body through a small incision in the abdomen.)

Infections of the Reproductive Organs

Several conditions of the reproductive organs may cause pain, irritation, or other symptoms. Because some of these conditions could lead to infertility or present a serious health risk, all women should become familiar with these conditions and know how to prevent them.

Pelvic Inflammatory Disease

Pelvic inflammatory disease (PID) is an infection of the pelvic organs that affects one million women every year. It can strike the uterus, fallopian tubes (the passages through which eggs pass from the ovaries to the uterus) and/or the ovaries, but also may occur in the abdominal lining. PID is usually caused by a previous infection with a sexually transmitted disease, especially gonorrhea or chlamydia (see *AIDS and other Sexually Transmitted Diseases*, page 192).

According to the American College of Obstetricians and Gynecologists, symptoms of PID include:

- vaginal discharge that has an unpleasant odor
- painful urination
- pain in the lower abdomen
- abnormal uterine bleeding
- fever and chills
- nausea and vomiting

You may also experience pain during intercourse. About 75 percent of women diagnosed with PID are sexually active and under the age of 25. Other risk factors include the following:

- having more than one sexual partner
- having a partner with gonorrhea or nongonoccocal urethritis
- past gonorrhea or chlamydia infections
- previous cases of PID

As many as one quarter of women diagnosed with PID may develop complications such as becoming infertile or having an ectopic pregnancy, in which the embryo begins developing outside the uterus—a potentially fatal condition.

If you have any of the symptoms of PID, talk with your health care provider, who can usually determine if that is the cause. PID can often be treated with antibiotics. Severe cases may require hospitalization. It is crucial to take the full course of antibiotics your provider prescribes.

An estimated 1 in 4 women who have PID will develop it again. Other than sexual abstinence, the best way to prevent getting PID is to limit yourself to one lifetime sexual partner. If this isn't realistic, protect yourself against sexually transmitted diseases by having your partner use a condom with spermicide.

Vaginal Discharge and Irritation

Although makers of feminine hygiene sprays and douches would like you to believe otherwise, a healthy vagina cleans itself naturally. A clear or slightly cloudy vaginal discharge is part of this cleaning process.

But several conditions can cause irritation around the vagina and can change in the color, smell, amount, or consistency of the discharge. These include vaginal yeast infections, nonspecific vaginitis, trichomoniasis, and sexually transmitted diseases such as the herpes simplex virus type 2 (see *AIDS and Other Sexually Transmitted Diseases*, page 192).

Yeast Infections

Yeast infections are usually marked by a thick, white discharge that looks like cottage cheese, although sometimes the discharge is clear. The vagina and labia (the lips of the vagina) may be red and swollen.

Preventive Steps to Avoid Vaginal Discharge

- Clean the area around the vagina and the rectum daily with water.
- Wear cotton underwear.
- Avoid tight-fitting jeans and panty hose.
- Avoid douches and deodorant tampons.
- Use adequate lubrication during intercourse. (Try using a water-based lubricant. You can use this safely with a condom.)

Yeast infections also cause intense itching and burning in the genital area. An overgrowth of *Candida albicans*, a type of yeast normally found in the vagina, is the usual culprit. This type of infection is more likely during pregnancy, after taking antibiotics, when using birth control pills, or if you have diabetes. Spreading a yeast infection through sex is rare, but if your partner has genital itching, an over-the-counter antifungal cream may be used on the genitals.

Although other vaginal infections usually require examination and treatment by a doctor or nurse practitioner, you can usually treat yeast infections safely and effectively at home. But the first time you experience these symptoms, you must see your health care provider, because these symp-

Self-Care Steps for Irritating Vaginal Discharge

- Use an over-the-counter antifungal vaginal cream or suppository. Follow the directions and be sure to use all of the medicine. Don't stop treatment just because your symptoms are gone.
- Expose the area to air, and wear cotton underwear.
- Apply cool compresses to the area between the vagina and rectum, or add an oatmeal bath product to lukewarm water and soak in it.
- Avoid bubble baths, vaginal sprays, and douches. Soaking in a tub of plain, lukewarm water may help.
- To prevent further irritation, avoid sexual intercourse until you finish the medicine.
- If home treatment doesn't relieve your symptoms or if your symptoms get worse, call your health care provider.

toms can indicate other more serious conditions, such as pelvic inflammatory disease (PID). You may have heard of prescription drugs, such as Diflucan, that can be given by mouth to fight yeast infections. These medications are recommended only for very severe yeast infections and for patients who have no sexually transmitted diseases. The pills are considered too risky to use routinely, especially for women who might be pregnant.

Bacterial Vaginal Infections

Vaginal infections caused by bacteria include gardnerella. Symptoms include a yellow or white vaginal discharge, itching, burning during urination, and pain in the vaginal area following intercourse. If you think you might have gardnerella, see your health care provider. Treatments can keep the infection from spreading to the uterus and fallopian tubes. Bacterial vaginal infections are usually treated with prescription antibiotics. As with any antibiotic, be sure to finish the entire prescription.

Trichomoniasis

Trichomoniasis is caused by a tiny organism. Symptoms include a yellow-green frothy discharge from the vagina, itching, and sometimes pain. The discharge may have a bad odor, but not always. Because the *Trichomonas* parasite can live in the prostate gland, your partner should also be treated to prevent reinfection. See your health care provider if you have symptoms of trichomoniasis. He or she can prescribe drugs that you will need to take for the full time prescribed—even if your symptoms seem to be gone.

Other Disorders of the Reproductive Organs

Some menstrual problems are due to underlying disorders, such as noncancerous growths and cysts in the uterus or ovaries. But many women may experience other symptoms—or even no symptoms at all—as a result of these disorders. In fact, a woman may first find out she has a problem during a well-woman exam—another reason to make these visits a yearly habit. Just the same, you should become familiar with the signs and symptoms of these disorders. If you do have a concern, be sure to call your health care provider.

Endometrial Cancer

The endometrium is the lining of the uterus. Abnormal vaginal bleeding is a reliable early warning sign of endometrial cancer. Endometrial cancer accounts for 6 percent of all cancers among women. About 40,000 cases are diagnosed each year, with 4,000 women dying from the disease annually. Endometrial cancer occurs most commonly in menopausal or postmenopausal women. Use of estrogen replacement therapy for menopause has been linked to the disease. However, progesterone prescribed along with estrogen reduces the chance of a woman developing endometrial cancer.

Endometrial cancer is diagnosed by removing a sample of endometrial tissue and examining it for abnormal cells. If found early, endometrial cancer is extremely easy to treat. In most cases, treatment involves a total hysterectomy and possibly radiation therapy, depending on how much the cancer has spread. At later stages the disease is much more difficult to treat effectively.

Ovarian Cancer

Ovarian cancer is one of the most lethal cancers affecting women. Each year, about 24,000 new cases of the disease are diagnosed in this country, while nearly 14,000 women die from it. One of the reasons ovarian cancer is so deadly is that it's very hard to detect. Symptoms of ovarian cancer include abnormal bleeding, stomach pain or abdominal pain, and a swollen abdominal area, but symptoms don't usually appear until the cancer is fairly advanced. Risk factors for the disease include advancing age; never having children; North American or northern European descent; endometrial, colon, or breast cancer; and a family history of ovarian cancer.

If a pelvic exam and ultrasound indicate the presence of ovarian cancer, additional tests may be recommended to confirm a diagnosis. The disease is treated with surgery, followed by chemotherapy, and in some cases, radiation. As with all other cancers, the earlier it's caught, the better chance there is of a cure.

Fibroid Growths

Uterine fibroids are noncancerous growths that develop in the muscle of the uterus. About 20 to 25 percent of women have fibroids, which are most common in women ages 30 to 40. African-American women are more likely to develop them than Caucasian women.

Fibroids usually produce no symptoms. Symptoms that do occur include changes in the length and heaviness of your period, abdominal pain or pain during sex, feelings of pressure in the abdomen, and miscarriages and infertility.

The first signs of fibroids can be detected during a routine pelvic examination. Other tests used to confirm this diagnosis and reveal more about the fibroids include the following:

- ultrasound, a diagnostic method in which sound waves are used to create an image of structures within the body
- laparoscopy, in which an instrument is used to look inside the body through a small incision in the abdomen
- hysterosalpingography, an X-ray that can detect changes in the size and shape of the fallopian tubes and uterus
- hysteroscopy, in which the health care provider inserts an instrument through the vagina and cervix to see inside the uterus

Treatment is often not necessary. In some cases, hormonal treatment is prescribed to shrink the growths. Your provider may recommend surgery if you have any of the following symptoms:

- heavy or painful periods
- bleeding between periods
- infertility
- pelvic pain
- rapid growth of the fibroid

Surgical treatment of fibroids may involve removing the fibroids while leaving the uterus intact. In other cases, hysterectomy—the removal of the uterus—may be recommended.

Ovarian Cysts

Ovarian cysts are extremely common during a woman's childbearing years. A cyst is a fluid-filled sac, like a blister. There are many different types of cysts that develop on the ovaries, and most are benign (noncancerous). But because a cyst may occasionally indicate a more serious condition, see your health care provider if you have abdominal pain, pain during intercourse, swelling in the abdomen, or irregular or unusually heavy periods. Any of these may be a symptom of a cyst, although cysts may not cause symptoms at all.

Ovarian cysts are usually detected during a pelvic exam, and the diagnosis may be confirmed with ultrasound, in which sound waves are used to create an image of structures inside the body, or laparoscopy, in which an instrument is used to look inside the abdomen. Treatment may not be required, because cysts often disappear on their own after two or three menstrual cycles. Your health care provider may prescribe hormones to shrink the cyst. Surgery may be in order if a cyst

- doesn't go away after a few menstrual periods
- doesn't respond to hormonal treatment
- is very large
- appears after menopause
- causes severe plain or bleeding
- becomes twisted

Osteoporosis and Its Prevention

Osteoporosis is a disease in which the bones thin and become brittle. Bone is living tissue that continually rebuilds itself. Normally, after about age 35 you begin to lose more bone than you build. After menopause, bone loss speeds up. However, when bones become less dense quickly, or bone loss is severe, you may have osteoporosis, which means your bones could break more easily.

Women are more likely to suffer from osteoporosis (because men tend to have more bone mass to begin with), and Caucasian and Asian women are more likely to develop the disease than African-Americans. Several other factors can increase your chances of developing osteoporosis, including small bone structure, smoking, use of certain medications, and inactivity.

Osteoporosis has many disabling and even life-threatening consequences. Once the bones weaken, they fracture much more easily. Motions you could perform in your youth without a second thought can result in a fracture. When a brittle bone fractures, it can take longer to heal. Older people who break a hip may never have normal mobility again. In fact, 1 in 5 people who break a hip die within the year because their health can deteriorate rapidly after the injury. Osteoporosis also causes much of the shrinkage in height some older people experience and the "dowager's hump" many develop in the back. Although some loss in bone density is an inevitable part of aging, you can do a lot to help prevent osteoporosis. You can pave the way for an active, independent later life by building bones through good nutrition and regular exercise in your early years. And if you are older, such healthy lifestyle choices can help minimize additional bone loss.

Be sure to get enough calcium in your diet. The National Institutes of Health recommends that women begin consuming 1,000 to 1,500 mg of calcium each day well before menopause. Women from their teens to mid-20s and pregnant and breastfeeding women need 1,200 mg of calcium daily, according to the American College of Obstetricians and Gynecologists.

Dairy foods, leafy, green vegetables, and some shellfish are good sources of calcium; a cup of lowfat yogurt has more than 400 mg of calcium, while a glass of low-fat milk has about 300 mg. You may need to take calcium supplements to get the calcium you need. It's also important to get enough vitamin D, which aids in calcium absorption. But check with your provider before adding supplements to your diet. Regular weight-bearing exercise—exercise in which the legs carry the body's weight, such as walking and weight-lifting exercises—builds bones, while inactivity can result in loss of bone mass.

Once menopause occurs, you should be sure to consume 1,500 mg of calcium daily. This is the time to talk to your provider about hormone replacement therapy, which can counteract bone loss (see *Menopause*, page 252).

Preparing for a Healthy Pregnancy

Developing good habits before you get pregnant can give you a head start on having a healthy baby. If you're thinking about having a child, it's best to begin preparing for pregnancy long before you conceive. That way, you'll be sure that you're doing all you can for your baby in the earliest weeks of pregnancy, which is a crucial time in fetal development. The fact is, more than half of pregnancies aren't planned. Many women are pregnant for weeks—or even months—before they realize it. That's why it's important for all women to follow this advice during their childbearing years.

Eat right. You should eat a well-balanced diet, (see *Diet*, page 38) and drink plenty of liquids. One of the most important things you can do is get enough folic acid in your diet. Folic acid is a B vitamin that helps guard against birth defects of the brain and spinal cord. You should consume 0.4 mg of folic acid every day if you're of childbearing age. Citrus fruits and juices, whole grains, poultry, liver, and green, leafy vegetables are good sources of folic acid. Since it may be difficult to get all the folic acid you need from diet alone, check with your health care provider about taking a vitamin supplement to make up the difference.

Get healthy and fit. If you're thinking of becoming pregnant, schedule an appointment with your health care provider. Now is also the time to get any health problems you may have—such as high blood pressure or diabetes—under control. If you need a rubella vaccination, get it at least three months before you conceive (see *Preventive Care Recommendations*, pages 32 and 34). Beginning a regular exercise program now will make it easier for you to keep fit during pregnancy and can help ease delivery. Ideally, you should start a program at least three months before you get pregnant. This allows your body to adjust to exercise before the physical demands of pregnancy begin.

Kick the habit. You should quit smoking now. Women who smoke have a higher risk of miscarriage, premature labor, and delivery of a low-birthweight baby, which can lead to other health problems for your baby. If someone else in your household smokes, this is a good time for him or her to quit, too, since smoking affects the quality of the air you breathe.

Avoid alcohol and other substances. Since no amount of alcohol has been proven safe, and the unborn baby is vulnerable to damage during very early pregnancy, it's best to avoid alcohol if you're thinking of becoming pregnant. Avoid recreational drugs. They can cause serious health problems to the fetus.

Check out your risks. Ask your health care provider if any prescription or over-the-counter medications you take could be harmful to your baby if you become pregnant. Also, ask your provider if you or your baby face any risks from chemicals you may be exposed to at work or at home.

Now That You Are Pregnant

Due to the demands on your body and the needs of your developing baby, you should pay special attention to your health when you are pregnant.

Visiting Your Health Care Provider

When you first realize that you are pregnant, make an appointment with your health care provider. He or she will help you figure out your due date, which will be about 40 weeks after your last period began. You and your provider can discuss any special pregnancy risk factors you may have, so that you can make any changes that will help the health of you and your baby.

This is also the time that you and your health care provider will talk about a schedule for visits during your pregnancy. The standard timetable is once a month for about the first 28 weeks of pregnancy, then every two to three weeks from 28 to 36 weeks, then once a week from 36 weeks until delivery. Your provider may also schedule certain tests, depending on your pregnancy risk factors, such as diabetes, high blood pressure, or previous preterm delivery. In later months, you will also discuss delivery options and visit the labor and delivery suite.

If yours is a high-risk pregnancy—for example, if you have high blood pressure, develop gestational diabetes, or are expecting more than one child—your provider may refer you to a specialist. Your health care plan may have a special program for women with high-risk pregnancies.

Nutrition

Eating right is extremely important now. You will need about 300 more calories a day than you did before you were pregnant. If you're of average weight, you should gain 25 to 35 pounds while you are pregnant. Folic acid continues to be important. You should also be sure you're getting enough protein, calcium, and iron. (Review *The Food Guide Pyramid*, page 44, and talk with your health care provider about the number of servings you should be eating from each food group.) It is crucial that you get enough to drink now, too. You should be drinking at least eight 8-ounce glasses of water each day.

Exercise

Staying fit while you're pregnant will help you deal with the demands pregnancy places on your body, and it also may make labor and delivery a little easier. Swimming, brisk walking, and participating in prenatal exercise classes are excellent ways to stay fit. But don't overdo it. Working out too hard can affect blood and oxygen flow to your baby. Discuss your exercise plan with your health care provider before you begin. Avoid getting overheated, drink plenty of water, and make sure you wear comfortable shoes and a supportive bra.

Self-Care Steps for Discomfort During Pregnancy

BACKACHE

- Pay attention to your posture. Tilt your pelvis under slightly, and keep your spine straight.
- Avoid exercises that exaggerate the arch of your back.
- Avoid bending from the waist—bend at the knees instead.
- Wear comfortable, low-heeled shoes.
- Take warm, but not hot, baths.
- Apply a heating pad or an ice pack, or have your partner or a friend rub or gently apply pressure to the sore area.
- Sleep on a firm mattress.

CONSTIPATION

- Drink at least eight 8-ounce glasses of water every day.
- Exercise.
- Gradually add high-fiber foods to your diet such as bran, whole-grain cereals, vegetables, fruits, and dried fruits, or drink prune juice.
- Ask your provider to recommend a stool softener.

FAINTNESS

- Don't skip meals, and be sure to drink plenty of fluids without caffeine.
- Carry snacks such as fruit and whole wheat crackers to eat throughout the day.
- Change positions regularly, but don't rise suddenly.
- Lie down with your feet up, or put your head between your knees.
- Get some fresh air.

FATIGUE

- Get at least 6 hours of sleep per night. You may need more.
- Take a rest period or nap at least once during the day.
- Pace yourself during physical activity. Quit before you're tired.
- Check your diet to be sure you're getting enough iron and protein.

FREQUENT URINATION

- Relieve your bladder completely as soon as you feel the need.
- Drink most of your fluids early in the day.
- If you often feel like you have to urinate immediately or if urination is accompanied by a burning sensation, call your health care provider. You could have a bladder infection.

HEADACHE

- Take a warm bath.
- Minimize stess if possible.
- Practice relaxation techniques.
- Get enough rest.
- Eat frequent, healthy snacks.
- Drink warm milk, decaffeinated tea, or cocoa.
- Lie down with a cool, damp cloth on your forehead.
- Check with your provider to find out if you can take acetaminophen.

HEARTBURN

- Avoid clothing that's tight around the waist.
- Avoid bending at the waist to pick things up.
- Eat slowly.
- Eat small, frequent meals.
- Avoid rich, greasy foods, coffee, carbonated beverages, and snacking before bedtime.
- Ask your provider about antacids.
- Prop up the head of your bed by putting an object beneath the mattress.

(continued)

Self-Care Steps for Discomfort During Pregnancy (continued)

HEMORRHOIDS
- Follow recommendations above for avoiding constipation.
- Avoid sitting or standing too long in one position.
- Check with your provider before using any medications.

LEG CRAMPS
- Sleep on your left side to improve circulation. The major vein that takes blood from the heart to the lower body is on the right side. Use a pillow to support your abdomen, and place another between your knees.
- Stretch the cramped muscle by flexing your foot so your heel points, not your toe.
- Wear support hose.
- If they occur frequently or are severe, contact your provider.

MOOD SWINGS
- Talk about your feelings and your fears with your partner, your provider, and close friends.
- Recognize that mood swings are normal.
- Take a walk.
- Keep busy, but don't overdo it.
- Get plenty of rest.

NASAL CONGESTION
- Use a humidifier (clean the filter often).
- Apply petroleum jelly to your nostril openings.
- Drink plenty of water and other clear fluids.

NAUSEA AND VOMITING
- Avoid foods, beverages and smells that make you feel nauseous.
- Eat small meals frequently.
- Eat crackers before you get up in the morning.
- Sit on the side of the bed for a few minutes before you stand up.
- Move slowly in the morning.

PRETERM LABOR
You should call your health care provider immediately if you experience any of the symptoms below while you are pregnant. During your second and third trimester, the following symptoms may indicate preterm labor:
- changes in the type of vaginal discharge (watery, mucous, bloody)
- a sudden increase in amount of vaginal discharge
- pressure in the pelvic area or lower abdomen
- low, dull backache
- abdominal cramps, with or without diarrhea
- regular contractions or uterine tightening

SORE BREASTS
- Wear a comfortable, supportive bra.

SWELLING (FLUID RETENTION)
- Rest on your left side to improve circulation (see *Lower leg pain,* page 180).
- Continue to drink plenty of water.
- Check with your provider about limiting your salt intake.
- Don't sit or stand for long stretches of time.
- Elevate your legs when possible.
- Wear support hose and comfortable shoes.
- Avoid socks with elasticized cuffs.

VARICOSE VEINS
- Wear support hose.
- Avoid socks with elasticized cuffs.
- Avoid crossing your legs and standing with your knees locked.
- Lie on your side.
- Elevate your feet.
- Exercise regularly.
- Do ankle rolls: As you sit, circle one foot in each direction several times. Repeat with your other foot.

How Your Body Will Change

Your body will change dramatically during pregnancy. Some of these changes may be uncomfortable. Talk with your health care provider about the best ways to ease discomfort. You may have to try a few different methods before you discover ones that work best for you. While each woman's experience is different, the following symptoms are common during pregnancy.

First trimester (0 to 12 weeks). This is when most women experience morning sickness. You may need to urinate more often than usual, and you may feel tired and moody. Your breasts will begin to change now, and may be swollen and very tender. They may leak colostrum, a fluid the breasts produce as you prepare for lactation, although this is more common later in pregnancy. Any nipple discharge should be discussed with your provider.

Second trimester (13 to 28 weeks). Many women experience a return to normal energy levels, and morning sickness will often disapppear. Your breasts and belly will grow. You may experience leg cramps, constipation, and a faster heartbeat. During the fourth month of pregnancy, you may feel the baby move for the first time.

Third trimester (29 to 40 weeks). Since your baby is growing and your uterus is getting bigger, you may experience shortness of breath because the baby is crowding your lungs. You may have heartburn as your stomach is squeezed and hormones relax parts of your digestive system. Fatigue may return, mainly from the extra work your body is doing, carrying around a baby who is nearly fully grown. You may also have backaches. Your legs and feet may swell, and you may have a difficult time sleeping.

Labor and Delivery

To distinguish real labor from false labor, time the length of your contractions and the time between them. your partner can learn about how to watch for labor, when it's time to go to the hospital, and what to expect once you get there.

During the final weeks of pregnancy you may experience cramps that don't actually signal the start of labor. These cramps are called false labor, or Braxton Hicks contractions. To distinguish real labor from false labor, time the length of your contractions and the time between them. Call your health care provider if the contractions

- last at least 30 to 70 seconds
- occur at regular intervals
- don't go away if you move around

Also call your provider if your water breaks, even if you're not having contractions. Write down the time it happens. Go to the hospital if any of the following things happen:

- You are bleeding vaginally (more than spotting).
- Contractions are five minutes apart or closer (or as advised by your health care provider).
- You are in steady, severe pain.

Labor usually lasts 12 to 14 hours for the first child, and may be shorter for later births. It is divided into three stages. The first stage consists of the cervix beginning to open and reaching full dilation. In the second stage, you begin helping to push the baby out. This stage ends with the delivery of the baby. The third stage is the delivery of the placenta, the organ that develops along with the baby during pregnancy and allows oxygen and other nutrients to pass from the mother's blood to the baby.

There are several different methods available to ease the pain of labor, and you and your health care provider should talk about them in advance. Some women choose natural childbirth, and manage pain with relaxation techniques and special breathing patterns. Other women opt for pain relievers, or anesthesia that blocks pain in the pelvic area without putting you to sleep, such as a spinal or epidural block. Many women use a combination of techniques and medication.

Because of a difficult labor, a mother's medical condition, or the position of the fetus, it may be necessary to deliver a baby through a cut made in the abdomen and uterus. This is known as cesarean delivery. Recovery after cesarean delivery takes longer than after vaginal birth. You may still be able to deliver vaginally if you have another child.

The amount of time you spend in the hospital after your baby is born will vary, depending on your health plan and the health of you and your baby. Many plans are sending women home earlier and providing care at home with special nursing visits.

Self-Care Steps for Breast-Feeding Problems

For engorgement:

- Apply warm compresses to breasts for a few minutes to help the milk start to flow (called "letdown").
- Massage breast gently.
- Encourage frequent feedings (every 1 to 3 hours).
- Use cold compresses after feedings for up to 10 minutes for comfort and to reduce swelling.
- Acetaminophen or ibuprofen may be used for pain relief; follow the manufacturer's instructions.

For sore nipples:

- Do gentle breast massage to help bring milk down.
- Begin feedings on the least tender nipple.
- Encourage frequent feedings, limited to 10 to 15 minutes per breast.
- Apply 1 or 2 drops of breast milk to the nipples after feedings, to ease nipple discomfort.

Breast-Feeding

Breast milk has several advantages for newborn babies: It contains all the essential nutrients in the ideal proportions and provides natural protection against infection. Very few new mothers are unable to breast-feed. In many cases a lactation specialist will show you how to breast-feed while you're still in the hospital. Some of the more common problems—pain, engorged breasts, or a low milk supply—can be overcome with persistence and support from your health care provider and family.

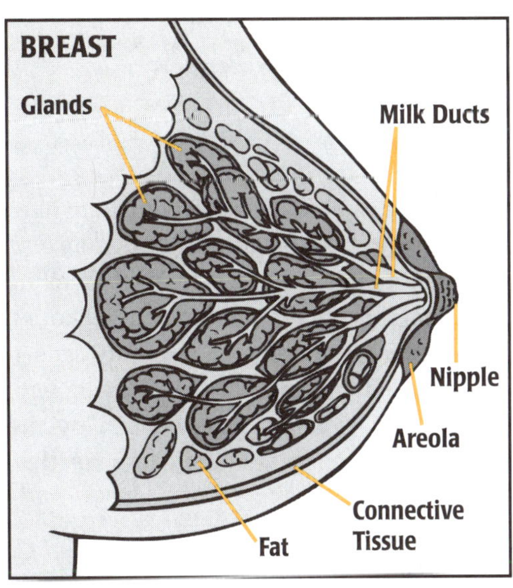

Decision Guide for Breast-Feeding

Symptoms/Signs	Action
Normal engorgement, short-term nipple pain	Use self-care
Engorgement that lasts longer than 48 hours	Call provider's office
Unable to get baby to nurse at least 8 times in 24 hours	Call provider's office
Nipple tenderness at latch-on that does not get better after the first minute when the baby begins to swallow	Call provider's office
Nipple pain lasts beyond 1 week; cracked or bleeding nipples	Call provider's office
Inflamed breast or part of one breast, or painful lump in one breast	Call provider's office
Temperature over 100.5 degrees and feeling ill	Call provider's office

For more about the symbols, see page 60.

Breasts can become overly full and hard when the milk first starts. Breasts may also feel sore between feedings. Mild swelling and tenderness is normal for 24 to 48 hours. More severe engorgement is usually caused by not feeding correctly or often enough. Nipple pain is most often caused by the baby latching on to the nipple incorrectly.

Proper Breast-Feeding

- Hold the baby close to your breast (nose and chin should lightly touch your breast) to reduce tugging.
- Encourage the milk to come down before feedings (called "letdown") by gently massaging the breasts from the fleshy part down to the nipple.
- Try to get the baby to open wide and take a portion of the areola (the darkened area around the nipple), not just the tip of the nipple.
- Make sure the baby eats at least 8 times in 24 hours.
- Vary the baby's nursing positions.
- Wear a supportive bra.

Menopause

Menopause is the time in your life when menstruation ends. Menopause occurs for most women between the ages of 45 and 55, and is considered complete when a woman hasn't had her period for one full year. However, the process leading up to the actual menopause may take several years. During this time the ovaries' production of estrogen and progesterone begins to slow Irregular periods are often one of the earliest signs that menopause is on its way. But the years leading up to menopause are different for every woman. Some women menstruate regularly until their periods suddenly stop. Others may see changes in the amount of menstrual flow or the length of time between periods. Still others miss periods or have bleeding between periods.

Irregular Periods

Although irregular periods are often a normal part of the years leading up to menopause, vaginal bleeding at odd times can also be a warning sign of other problems such as cancer. Check with your health care provider if you

- have a change in your menstrual cycle
- bleed very heavily
- bleed for longer than normal
- bleed more than once every three weeks
- bleed after intercourse

After discussing your symptoms with you, your provider may be able to rule out certain problems. If uterine cancer is suspected, he or she may recommend an endometrial biopsy (see *Missed Periods*, page 239, and *Bleeding Between Periods*, page 238).

Hot Flashes

As many as 80 percent of women have hot flashes as they near menopause—before their periods stop. A hot flash is a flushed feeling that usually begins around the chest and spreads to the neck, face, and arms. Hot flashes usually last three to four minutes, and can occur as often as once an hour. Hot flashes are often followed by sweating and then chills. They can happen at any time of day or night—when they're known as night sweats—and may last for up to five years, as a woman's body adjusts to the ovaries' much lower production of the hormone estrogen. If you are experiencing hot flashes, you may find it helpful to dress in light layers that you can remove.

Many researchers now believe that lack of sleep as a result of nighttime hot flashes is to blame for moodiness and other psychological symptoms linked with menopause. Scientific studies have yet to prove a relationship between lower estrogen levels and depression, moodiness, irritability, fatigue, or other psychological symptoms women commonly experience during menopause. Lack of adequate sleep, however, can cause any number of these symptoms, making nighttime hot flashes a likely culprit. Other life issues happening along with menopause may also add to depression or other problems. Examples include career issues, children leaving home, caring for aging parents, or possibly, struggling with what it means to be growing older or no longer being able to bear children.

Vaginal Dryness

Reduced estrogen levels in the body contribute to vaginal dryness and urinary problems, both of which can continue to be problems well beyond menopause. With less estrogen in the body, the vaginal walls lose elasticity, get thinner, and secrete less fluid. A drier, less elastic vagina can mean discomfort or pain during or after intercourse. Surprisingly, avoiding intercourse can make the problem worse, while continued sexual activity improves blood circulation and suppleness of the vagina, thus reducing or eliminating discomfort during intercourse. Vaginal suppositories and water-soluble lubricants sold over the counter and by prescription may also ease vaginal dryness.

Fitness and Nutrition

Good nutrition and regular exercise during menopause are extremely important. After menopause, be sure that you get 1,500 mg of calcium in your diet each day to prevent osteoporosis, a weakening of the bones that occurs when estrogen production drops off (see *Osteoporosis*, page 245).

Hormone Replacement Therapy

Hormone replacement therapy (HRT) can relieve vaginal dryness, reduce or end hot flashes, prevent osteoporosis, and may reduce heart disease risk. In the 1960s, estrogen was often given alone, and some women later developed a low-grade cancer of the endometrium, the lining of the uterus. However, when both estrogen and progestin (a synthetic form of progesterone) are given for HRT, the risk of endometrial cancer is actually less than if the woman is taking no estrogen at all. For this reason, a combination of estrogen and progestin is recommended for women who have not had a hysterectomy. Estrogen alone is recommended for those who have had a hysterectomy.

Many women and health care providers worry that HRT may increase the risk of breast cancer. The largest and most carefully done studies, however, show no conclusive evidence that this is true. Furthermore, estrogen has been shown to lower the risk of heart disease and osteoporosis. Postmenopausal women are more likely to die of heart disease than breast cancer. Most experts today agree that the benefits of HRT far outweigh any potential risks.

About 10 percent of women receiving HRT have minor side effects, such as breast tenderness, nausea, headaches, fluid retention, or irregular vaginal bleeding. These side effects may disappear after two or three months. If they don't, your health care provider may be able to adjust your medication to eliminate these problems.

Some women should not use HRT. The therapy may not be recommended if you

- have had a stroke or recent heart attack
- have had breast cancer or uterine cancer
- have a history of gallbladder disease
- have a history of blood clots
- have undiagnosed vaginal bleeding
- have pancreatic or acute liver disease
- are obese
- have severe varicose veins
- smoke

Other drugs may be available to help relieve menopausal symptoms if you cannot use HRT. The decision about whether to use HRT is best made by you and your health care provider.

Whether you choose to use HRT or not, there are some measures you can use that do not involve hormones to help relieve menopausal symptoms. (See the sections above on *Vaginal Dryness* and *Fitness and Nutrition.*)

Mental Health

You can do many things to take care of your mental health, just as you can tend to your physical health. Learning to handle stress is one important way to help you stay both mentally and physically healthy.

But you can't manage all mental health difficulties on your own. Some problems require professional help. Talking with your health care provider about mental health problems may feel awkward. Perhaps no illness has as much stigma attached to it as mental illness, and this stigma can prevent someone from seeking help. But if you have a problem with depression, anxiety, or with alcohol or other drugs, you are certainly not alone. An estimated 1 in 5 people will have a mental illness at some time in their lives, and 1 in 4 families has a member with some form of mental illness. The good news is that there are many qualified professionals who can help you.

Mental illness isn't just in your head. Depression, anxiety, and other problems often have physical causes that involve imbalances in the brain's chemistry. Mental illness is also highly curable; with treatment, 80 percent of people who have mental illness can lead happier, healthier lives. If you think you or a family member has a problem, call your health care provider for advice. The sooner you get help, the better.

Check with your employer to find out whether mental health benefits are part of your coverage. Your employer may also provide an Employee Assistance Program (EAP). EAPs offer free counseling for employees and sometimes their families. Any care you receive—whether for work-related stress, a family problem, or depression—will be kept confidential.

Alcohol and Drug Abuse

As with other mental health issues, people often find it difficult to get help when they are concerned about their use of alcohol or other drugs. The first step to getting help is recognizing the problem.

Alcohol abuse and dependence. These problems cost society tens of billions of dollars every year in medical bills, lost workdays, and early death, among other factors. More than 14 million Americans abuse alcohol or are dependent upon alcohol.

Addiction to alcohol often begins when a person drinks to relieve stress. Gradually, he or she may come to rely on drinking to relax. If you feel you need alcohol in order to enjoy certain activities or feel normal, you may be an alcoholic—or at risk of becoming one.

Alcohol dependence takes a physical and mental toll on the person who drinks as well as on his or her loved ones. Heavy drinkers can damage their liver, heart, and brain. A pregnant woman who drinks can also seriously damage the health and impair the development of her unborn child. Alcoholism often hurts the alcoholic's family and friends, and can even cause a person to lose his or her job.

Signs of addiction to alcohol include the following:

- failed attempts to stop drinking or cut down on drinking
- feeling annoyed when people mention how much you drink
- feeling guilty about drinking
- drinking alone or secretly
- drinking early in the day
- drinking more than you had planned
- drinking before going to a party
- drinking faster than your friends do
- experiencing blackouts (not remembering what happened while you were drinking)
- feeling that alcohol is causing problems in your life

What to do. If you have any of the signs of addiction to alcohol listed above, you may have a problem. Recognizing this is the first step toward getting help. Try to cut down or stop drinking completely. Call your health care provider, and he or she can discuss support groups and treatment options with you. If you think a family member or friend may have a problem with alcohol, talk with your provider about how to approach him or her.

Treatment of alcoholism generally involves quitting drinking and participating in a 12-step program (such as Alcoholics Anonymous) or other self-help support program. Counseling and medication to treat underlying problems, such as depression (see *Depression*, page 260), may also be a part of treatment.

Drug abuse. People can become addicted to prescription drugs, especially painkillers and tranquilizers, or they can come to rely on illegal drugs like marijuana, heroin, and cocaine. Many drugs require the user to take increasing amounts to experience their effects. A person who becomes addicted may need to take a drug in order to avoid the sickness of withdrawal.

What to do. Signs of addiction to illegal and prescription drugs include failed attempts to quit taking drugs or cut down on drug use, feeling guilty about drug use, and feeling that drugs are causing problems in your life. The first step toward getting help is recognizing that you may have a problem. Some people can stop taking drugs on their own. But if you are concerned that you may have a problem, you don't have to deal with it by yourself. Talk with your health care provider about treatment options and ways to help you stop using alcohol and other drugs. If you think a family member or friend may have a problem with drugs, talk with your doctor about how to approach him or her.

Treatment of drug addiction generally involves detoxification (making sure the drug has a chance to leave the body completely) and participating in a 12-step program (such as Narcotics Anonymous) or other self-help support program. If withdrawal from a drug is particularly difficult (such as with heroin), hospitalization may be necessary. Counseling and medication to treat underlying problems such as depression may also be a part of treatment.

Special Concerns for Children and Teenagers

If you think your child may be drinking or using other drugs, the sooner you do something, the better. Getting help for the child soon can help ensure that he or she avoids more serious problems down the road, such as criminal behavior, dropping out of school, or physical harm. However, many parents will choose to ignore alcohol or other drug use, because acknowledging such a problem can be painful. Warning signs of drug use can include the following:

- mood swings, such as angry outbursts
- loss of appetite
- state of stupor in which the child is unaware of what's going on around him or her
- change in friends; disinterest in socializing
- loss of interest in appearance
- falling grades
- withdrawal from family
- missing valuables, which may have been sold in order to buy drugs
- disappearance of liquor or medications
- frequent use of eyedrops or breath mints

It's important to realize that adolescence is a tough time for both parents and children, and many changes in behavior may just be a normal part of growing up and rebelling against authority. Strong family relationships and open lines of communication will make your child more likely to seek your help and guidance.

Decision Guide for Alcohol Problems

The signs listed below may indicate a drinking problem. Call your health care provider to talk about your concerns and discuss treatment options if you or a family member exhibits any of the following signs:

- drinking to calm nerves, forget worries, reduce depression
- losing interest in food
- gulping drinks and drinking too fast
- lying about drinking habits
- drinking alone with increased frequency
- injuring oneself or someone else while intoxicated
- getting drunk often or for extended periods of time
- needing to drink increasing amounts of alcohol to get the desired effect
- frequently acting irritable, resentful, or unreasonable
- experiencing medical, social, or financial problems caused by drinking

Anxiety

Anxiety disorders, which include phobias, obsessive-compulsive disorder, and panic attacks, are terrifying for the people who experience them.

Obsessive-compulsive disorder. People who have obsessive-compulsive disorder (OCD) find themselves obsessed with certain ideas or feelings, or are compelled to perform certain behaviors. They cannot stop unwelcome thoughts or certain actions. This condition may be inherited and may be related to imbalances in brain chemistry. OCD may be associated with certain personality traits, and often occurs along with depression.

Some people with OCD are obsessed with cleanliness. They must wash their hands dozens of times a day in order to feel clean, and may be unable to stop thinking about all the germs and dirt surrounding them. In some cases, a person with OCD will feel compelled to do certain things over and over again, such as checking to see that the oven is off, counting off steps from one place to another, or touching an object a certain number of times. These activities are the person's way of trying to relieve anxiety or keep fears at bay. A person may also become obsessed with certain thoughts, words, or problems.

What to do. If you find obsessions or compulsions interfering with your normal activities, you should call your health care provider. Treatment for OCD usually involves therapy, sometimes using a specific method in which the person is "desensitized" to the things or situations that set off anxiety. Medication may also be prescribed.

Panic attacks. A panic attack is a sudden episode of terror during which you may also experience the following symptoms:

- racing heartbeat
- chest pain
- dizziness
- nausea
- difficulty breathing
- sweating
- fear of death
- tingling or numbness in the hands
- a sense of dreaminess or distortions in perception
- fear of losing control

Attacks can be brought on by many types of situations, such as riding in an elevator, being in crowds, and driving over bridges. If you have frequent panic attacks and the fear of having another attack causes you to limit your activities, you may have a panic disorder.

No one is sure what causes panic disorder. However, most experts now believe that panic attacks probably have some physical cause involving the brain's chemistry.

What to do. Treatment for panic disorder is usually successful and works fairly quickly. Certain forms of psychotherapy are used, sometimes with medication. Since panic disorder may be associated with depression or drug or alcohol abuse, it may also be necessary to treat these conditions.

Phobias. Phobias are fears of certain things or situations that are out of balance with any actual danger. Common phobias include agoraphobia (the fear of open spaces) and claustrophobia (the fear of confined spaces).

What to do. If your fears are interfering with your daily life, call your health care provider, who may suggest that you see a psychotherapist. Treatment of phobias involves therapy and, sometimes, antidepressant medication.

Attention Deficit and Hyperactivity

Most children have times when they don't seem to pay attention, can't sit still, or just have more energy than they can burn. For some children, however, difficulty concentrating or very high physical energy levels (hyperactivity) interfere with their ability to fulfill social and academic tasks appropriate for their ages.

Self-Care Steps for Attention Deficit/Hyperactivity Disorder (ADHD)

- Stick to a routine and set firm limits at home and school.
- Make sure your child's schoolwork matches his or her abilities. A class that's either too easy or too hard can lead to inattention, boredom, and frustration.
- Provide outlets for your child's physical energy.
- Make sure you find ways to cope. Parenting a hyperactive child can be challenging. Avoid becoming very critical, controlling, or angry with your child. Remember—and let your child know—that you don't like the behavior, but you love the child.
- Use other resources. Ask your child's school or health care provider for information on help that is available in your community, including support groups.

A child who has true attention deficit/hyperactivity disorder (ADHD) may have problems paying attention, be impulsive, be hyperactive, or have some combination of these. Such a child may talk constantly, be unable to wait his or her turn in groups, and pay little attention to details. Schoolwork may be messy or filled with careless mistakes. The child may be easily distracted, act before thinking, or have trouble sitting still. The child may also have difficulty controlling anger.

In some ways, a diagnosis of ADHD is a relative diagnosis, meaning that a child with the disorder has far more difficulty with attention or controlling impulses or activity than do most other children. But not all children who have ADHD have major problems with hyperactivity and impulsiveness. For some, inattention is the primary problem. Likewise, some children who are clearly hyperactive are able to concentrate if they can just sit still long enough.

Because there is no scientific test for ADHD, the disorder can be difficult to tell from normal behavior in active children. Symptoms like those of ADHD may also be brought on by grief (over the death of a parent or a divorce); depression; post-traumatic stress (after physical or sexual abuse); or other physical, emotional, or psychological problems. Symptoms usually subside in late adolescence and early adulthood. But some teenagers and adults may continue to have feelings of restlessness or difficulty engaging in quiet, sedentary activities.

The exact cause of ADHD is unknown. Popular theories that sugar, food dyes, or other food additives contribute to hyperactivity or that the condition is caused by minute levels of brain damage have not been proven. But a controlled environment, special training for the child, and drugs—such as methylphenidate (Ritalin) or antidepressants—have been helpful in dealing with ADHD, but do not cure it.

What to do. Have your child evaluated. A careful evaluation will look at how your child functions intellectually, socially, emotionally, physically, and academically. Ideally, the professional(s) doing the evaluation should observe your child during normal daily activities in more than one setting (at home and at school) and at different times of the day. If your child is found to have ADHD, talk with your health care provider about how to treat this condition.

Depression

More than 11 million Americans suffer from depression. In fact, depression is called the common cold of mental illness. People who are depressed experience feelings of sadness, worthlessness, hopelessness, and irritability that can be disabling. This condition can appear at any age, often occurs in children and teenagers, and affects about twice as many women as men. Depression can last for weeks, months, or even years. About half of the people who experience major depression will have another episode later in life.

Depression is also one of the most treatable mental illnesses. However, many people do not seek help for depression, perhaps because of the stigma attached to this condition, and also because they may not know that they are depressed.

Symptoms of depression include the following:

- inability to enjoy life
- tiredness (see *Fatigue*, page 262)
- sleep disturbances (see *Insomnia*, page 271), early morning waking, or oversleeping
- eating disturbances (loss of appetite, weight loss, or weight gain)
- poor concentration
- feelings of guilt, worthlessness, or helplessness
- general irritability
- thoughts of death or suicide; suicide attempt
- problems such as headaches or stomachaches that have no obvious cause
- difficulty making decisions

The debate continues over whether depression is caused by life events, chemical imbalances in the brain, or both. Research shows the tendency to develop depression may be inherited, and that an uneven balance of mood-influencing chemicals in the brain can play a role. People who have a poor self-image, view themselves negatively, or are easily overwhelmed by life challenges may be more likely than others to experience depression. A serious loss, chronic illness, difficult relationship, or any unwelcome change can trigger depression.

What to do. Everyone goes through periods of feeling down. But if several of the above symptoms persist for more than two weeks, call your health care provider. He or she can help figure out whether you are depressed, and if you are, how to treat it. Treatment for depression can include psychotherapy, support groups, and antidepressant drugs. The aim of treatment is not just getting better, but staying well.

Eating Disorders

Eating disorders, in which food becomes not a source of nutrition but an enemy to be

Self-Care Steps for Depression

- Share your treatment plan with people close to you. Talk to friends and relatives and explain what you are going through.
- Take medication as instructed. You may be tempted to stop taking your drugs too soon. However, it is important to keep taking them until your health care provider says to stop, even if you begin feeling better. You may have to try several antidepressants before finding one that works. Also, you may have to take some antidepressant medications for a few weeks before you begin feeling better.
- Report any drug side effects to your provider, especially if the side effects interfere with your functioning.
- Keep all follow-up appointments with your health care provider and/or therapist. Do not miss an appointment, even if you are feeling better that day.
- Set realistic goals. Do not set hard goals for yourself or take on a great deal of responsibility.
- Divide your workload. Break large tasks into small ones, set priorities, and don't be hard on yourself if you are unable to get everything finished.
- Do activities that make you feel better. You might want to try moderate exercise, go to movies, or meet a friend for dessert at a cafe.
- Do not expect to "snap out of" your depression immediately. People rarely get better overnight. Instead, help yourself as much as you can, and do not blame yourself for not being up to par.
- If you find yourself thinking of killing or injuring yourself, call your health care provider or the local suicide hotline.

fought or an object of obsession, are most common among middle-class and upper-middle-class women. Approximately 1 in 10 people with eating disorders will die as a result of the condition, either by suicide or a heart attack due to starvation.

Anorexia nervosa. People who have anorexia nervosa, try to starve themselves thin. This condition usually begins in puberty, and tends to strike young people with perfectionist, obedient personalities. Some psychologists believe that people with anorexia nervosa are attempting to control their food intake and weight because they feel unable to control other aspects of their lives.

People with anorexia may also exercise obsessively, make themselves vomit, and use laxatives to purge themselves further. They may also go through phases of bulimia nervosa (see below). If the disease progresses far enough, all the symptoms of starvation show up: irregular heartbeat; brittle hair and nails; dry, yellowish skin; and symptoms of depression. Even though someone with anorexia may be extremely thin, the person will still think of themself as being too fat. People with this condition can literally starve themselves to death.

Bulimia nervosa. People who have bulimia nervosa will binge on food and then make themselves vomit, use a laxative, or take a diuretic. Bulimics may binge and purge several times a week or even several times a day. Unlike people with anorexia, people with bulimia are often at or near a normal weight.

Symptoms of bulimia include a sore throat, tooth decay (due to the teeth being exposed to stomach acid), swollen salivary glands in the neck and cheeks, and a puffy face. Serious cases of bulimia can cause dehydration and electrolyte imbalance (a proper balance of electrolytes is essential for the heart to function normally.)

Binge eating disorder. People with binge eating disorder eat large amounts of food without being hungry, and are often obese. This condition is similar to bulimia, except the person does not purge after bingeing. In men this disorder is more common than either anorexia or bulimia. People with this condition may abuse alcohol and other drugs, and may also have a history of losing and regaining weight. Binge eating disorder is also associated with depression.

What to do. People with these conditions usually have underlying emotional problems such as low self-esteem, depression, and a distorted body image, and must be treated by a therapist. Treatment must often be provided in the hospital for severe cases of these illnesses. People must be taught to eat normally again, which often requires careful supervision. Treatment includes individual therapy and, sometimes, family counseling. Antidepressant medications are sometimes prescribed as well. Treatment of these conditions is difficult, but people with eating disorders have a good chance of recovery, especially if the illness is caught early.

Fatigue

Fatigue is an overwhelming sense of tiredness that makes your body feel weak. What most people refer to as fatigue is brought on by hard work or exertion and can be remedied by sleep. However, when sleep and rest do not help, your body is sending you a signal that something else may be wrong.

Fatigue that lasts six weeks or longer can be an early symptom of many types of serious illness, although usually it is not. These conditions include anemia, cancer, diabetes, hepatitis, heart disease, hypoglycemia, hypothyroidism, mononucleosis, rheumatoid arthritis, obesity, alcoholism, sleep disorders, or low-grade urinary tract infection.

Depression (see *Depression*, page 260) and anxiety (see *Anxiety*, page 258) are common, treatable causes of fatigue. Symptoms of anxiety disorder or depression may include a depressed mood, feelings of apprehension, eating or sleeping disturbances, or not being able to enjoy life.

Fatigue may also be traced back to prescription drugs and other medications you are taking. Many of these can rob you of energy. Chief among the over-the-counter culprits are pain relievers, cough and cold medicines, antihistamines and allergy remedies, sleeping pills, and motion sickness pills. Prescription medicines that can sap your energy include tranquilizers, muscle relaxants, sedatives, and blood pressure reducers.

A pattern of serious fatigue could be a sign of a disabling condition known as chronic fatigue syndrome. Causing flulike symptoms such as fever, sore throat, and muscle pain, this debilitating illness affects more women than men. Confusion, sleep problems, and depression sometimes go hand in hand with chronic fatigue syndrome. In fact, more than two thirds of those with the illness also suffer from depression. Antidepressant drugs are often used in treatment. Researchers have not linked any virus or other disease to chronic fatigue syndrome and are investigating other possible causes, including infection, stress, and impaired hormone production.

What to do. If you feel fatigued and getting enough sleep hasn't helped, check with your health care provider to make sure there are no underlying causes for your tiredness.

Self-Care Steps for Fatigue

- **Organize your time.** Get up a few minutes earlier, so that you won't have to start your day feeling rushed and tired. Learn to delegate and how to say no when you have enough responsibilities and activities in your life.
- **Exercise regularly.** You should exercise 3 to 5 times a week for 20 to 30 minutes, and move around as much as possible during the day. Also, avoid late-night activities, as they can disrupt your regular sleeping habits and make you tired in the morning.
- **Get the right amount of sleep.** Most people need 6 to 8 hours of sleep each night. Short-changing yourself on sleep will leave you exhausted, and getting too much sleep will make you feel groggy. Older people who tend to sleep less soundly and younger people with hectic schedules may also need naps during the day (see *Self-Care Steps for Insomnia*, page 272).
- **Breathe deeply and slowly.** Shallow, rapid breathing often leads to fatigue because the body gets less oxygen.
- **Quit smoking.** Smoking steals some of your body's oxygen supply, replacing it with useless carbon dioxide. Because nicotine is a stimulant, going through the consequent withdrawal symptoms can cause temporary tiredness.
- **Lose weight.** Stick to well-balanced meals and avoid crash diets. When your calorie intake is too restricted, it's very stressful for the body. One of the many symptoms of this type of stress is fatigue.
- **Drink less caffeine and alcohol.** Alcohol is a depressant and will make you feel tired, not boost your energy. Likewise, caffeine will give you a temporary boost of energy, but when the effect wears off, your energy level drops drastically.
- **Figure out what kind of lunch suits you best.** Some people function best after eating a lighter lunch, while others need to eat their largest meal of the day at lunch. In either case, avoid high-fat foods. Because fats burn more slowly than carbohydrates, they will slow you down.
- **Interrupt your workday with periodic breaks.** And if you haven't gone on a vacation in a while, take that trip you've dreamed about, or unplug the phone and refresh at home.
- **Watch less TV.** If you depend on television to relax, you may find yourself relaxed into a state of lethargy. Try something more stimulating, such as reading or taking a walk.
- **Find ways to calm yourself.** Listen to music or relaxation tapes. Say a word, phrase, or prayer that gives you a sense of peace. Imagine yourself on a beach, at the mountains, or in your favorite spot.

Stress

"I'm all stressed out." "I need to go to a desert island and get away from all this stress." Sound familiar? All of us have had these thoughts, and we have all needed that desert island. But if we really lived where there was absolutely no stress—no competition, no risks to take, no inspiration to try just a little bit harder-we would be completely bored. Sometimes stress adds just the amount of challenge and motivation we need to have a happy life, in fact, to stay alive.

It's when there are too many good and bad challenges confronting us and we lose our ability to juggle them that the stresses in our lives cause us distress. Everyday hassles can cause as much stress as larger events, such as money worries, arguments, a divorce, a death in the family, losing a job, buying a house—or simply anticipating these things.

Stress is unavoidable, but that doesn't mean it's unmanageable. A walk around the block, a nutritious meal, and a good night's sleep will usually give you the energy and strength to face another day. However, taking these simple steps may not help when occasional stress turns into chronic stress.

Chronic stress cracks your emotional foundation, making you angry, apathetic, irritable, anxious, or even depressed. You may quit eating or eat too much. You find it hard to concentrate. You may start smoking. Too much stress may even make you more accident-prone, lead to alcohol or drug abuse, and weaken your body, increasing vulnerability to certain diseases.

So how do you regain control? Research has found that people who effectively manage the stress in their lives have three things in common:

- They consider life a challenge, not a series of hassles.
- They have a mission or purpose in life and are committed to fulfilling that mission.
- They do not feel victimized by life, but believe instead that despite temporary setbacks, they have control over their lives.

What to do. Anxiety is a normal part of life, but serious stress that depresses your mood or ruins your ability to experience joy may be the result of an anxiety disorder or depression. If you experience these feelings, see your health care provider for an evaluation. You may also want to take a stress management course. Check to see if your health plan, local hospital, employer or other community organization offers a class.

Self-Care Steps for Stress

- Identify the things in your life that bring you stress. Try to avoid them, but if you can't, have a Plan A and B for dealing with them. You may have to learn how to say no to things you don't want to do, or are too busy to handle.
- Share some of your responsibilities. A shared burden is lighter to carry, and you may develop a new friendship or learn another way of solving problems.
- Exercise regularly to relieve muscle tension and improve mental health. Stretching and walking are especially helpful.
- Find some crumb of humor (to the point of absurdity) in even the worst situation—even when you have to force yourself.
- Organize your time and don't procrastinate. Focus on the individual steps for getting a job done so that you don't feel overwhelmed.
- Take frequent breaks from tasks.
- Talk with a friend or family member. Sharing your thoughts and fears will make them less overwhelming and easier to handle.
- Practice deep breathing exercises to relax and to slow respiration. Take deep breaths through the nose while expanding the abdomen, and exhale slowly through your mouth.
- Learn progressive muscle relaxation to relieve tension throughout the body. Twice daily in a quiet room, tense and relax each muscle group starting with your face and ending with your feet.
- Use visualization to clear your mind. For 5 minutes, concentrate on a pleasant setting.
- Sit quietly and repeat to yourself a cue word that will make you feel calm, such as "peace."
- Listen to relaxation tapes or music.
- Relax in a warm bath.
- Avoid caffeine.
- Help other people. The sense of well-being you receive will help you put life's events in better perspective.
- Balance the different areas of your life (work, relationships, play, spirituality).
- Play. Join in athletics or take up a new hobby.
- Take time to focus on the spiritual (nature, religion).
- Follow a balanced diet to get the proper nutrients to keep you going.

Dizziness, Headaches, and Insomnia

Some ailments just don't fit into the categories used in this book. In fact, dizziness, headaches, and insomnia—the topics talked about here—can seem like whole-body problems. Occasionally, each of these conditions may be related to an underlying disease. However, in the great majority of cases, you can make yourself feel better by trying the self-care steps listed here.

Call your health care provider if self-care doesn't work; he or she may be able to prescribe medication that helps (for example, if you have migraines). Your provider will refer you to a specialist if necessary.

Dizziness

Dizziness is a feeling of light-headedness or faintness. This feeling can be caused by drugs, viral infections like colds and the flu, or stress and anxiety. Most dizziness is mild, temporary, and harmless. When coupled with other symptoms, however, it may be a sign of a serious health problem or even an emergency.

Postural Hypotension

This is the dizziness some people feel for a moment when they get up quickly from a sitting or reclining position. Postural hypotension is considered harmless unless it leads to fainting spells or blackouts. However, if you are taking drugs for high blood pressure, report dizziness to your health care provider. If you are dizzy and have black stools or any other illness, you should also call your provider's office.

Vertigo

This is another form of dizziness and may be a more serious condition. Vertigo is marked by a feeling of movement. You or the objects around you seem to be spinning. People who experience vertigo may be unable to walk in a straight line.

Vertigo can be caused by a condition called labyrinthitis, an inflammation of the inner ear. Nausea, vomiting, and involuntary movements of the eyes may accompany the vertigo. Sometimes symptoms appear only when the head is held in a specific position. Vertigo can signal as serious and rare a condition as a brain tumor or as benign a problem as earwax buildup.

Ménière's disease is another common cause of vertigo. Symptoms of this condition include attacks of vertigo, muffled hearing, a ringing in one or both ears, nausea, and vomiting. Ménière's disease may be related to excess fluid in the inner ear.

Self-Care Steps for Dizziness

- Avoid positions that you find cause dizziness.
- Take your time getting up if you have dizzy spells when you rise quickly from sitting or lying positions. Sit on the edge of the bed for a few minutes in the morning before standing up.
- When dizziness or vertigo strikes, slowly move to a sitting or reclining position. You'll be less likely to fall and injure yourself. If you feel faint or your vision begins to go dark, sit with your head between your knees.
- Drink more fluids.
- Avoid driving.
- Avoid caffeine, alcohol, smoking, and illegal drugs.
- Change positions slowly.
- Use relaxation techniques to combat anxiety. Breathe deeply and slowly.
- If you feel vertigo, keep your eyes open and focus on a stationary object; this may lessen your symptoms.
- Take aspirin, acetaminophen, or ibuprofen for pain or fever. (Do not give aspirin to children or teenagers due to the risk of Reye's syndrome.)

The disease can start and stop throughout life, and although there is no cure, symptoms can be relieved.

What to do. All dizziness should be discussed with and/or evaluated by your health care provider to find the cause. You can also do certain things to make dizziness less troublesome before treatment works; see the self-care steps above.

Decision Guide for Dizziness

Symptoms/Signs	Action
Occasional light-headedness or dizziness when first standing up or getting out of bed	 Use self-care
Dizziness or vertigo with vomiting, nausea, fainting, or black stools (see *Black or Bloody Stools,* page 95; *Vomiting,* page 113)	 See provider
Dizziness that lasts 3 or more days or is accompanied by ear pain, buzzing, or pounding sensation	 See provider
Dizziness with temperature of 101 degrees or higher	 See provider
Trauma, head injury (see page 79), or severe headache	 Seek help now
Weakness in extremities or tingling in any body part	 Seek help now
Sudden loss of hearing, sudden blurred or double vision, slurred speech, or difficulty swallowing	 Seek help now
Symptoms of shock (see page 88)	 Seek help now
Chest pain (see page 136) or pressure	 Seek help now
Loss of bladder control or bowel control	 Seek help now

For more about the symbols, see page 60.

Dizziness

Headaches

Headaches are one of the most common health complaints. Many different things can cause them, including tension, infection, injury, and changes in the flow of blood within the head. Most headaches occur when the muscles of the head or neck become tense and contract.

Contrary to popular belief, aspirin is not a cure-all for headaches. In fact, aspirin will occasionally mask symptoms that might help your health care provider uncover the underlying problem, and continued overuse can cause side effects. Fortunately, most headaches that occur without other symptoms respond well to self-care.

Nearly 90 percent of all headaches are caused by tension or stress and can be controlled. Unusual or very bad headaches can be a symptom of a serious health problem. If you suffer from these types of headaches, seek medical help.

Headaches are classified into three general categories: tension, cluster, and migraine.

Tension Headaches

These are also known as muscle contraction headaches and are often caused by the tightening of muscles of the back and shoulders in reaction to emotional and physical stress. A tension headache may occur as pain all over the head, a feeling of pressure, or a band around the head.

Tension headaches are believed to be the most common cause of head pain. Although they may be caused by poor pos-

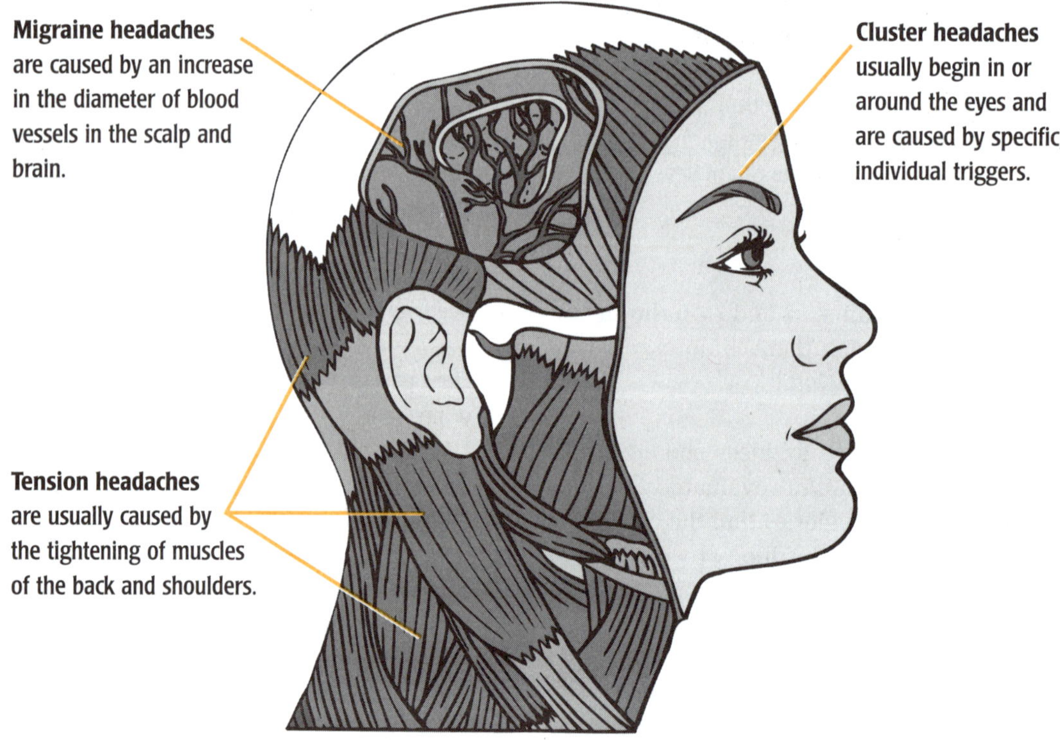

ture or working in awkward conditions, the most common triggers are stress, anxiety, and depression.

The symptoms of a tension headache include the following:

- steady pain that doesn't pulse
- a tightness, fullness, or pressure over the top of the head or back of the neck
- occasional nausea or vomiting

Tension headaches that occur two or more times weekly for several months are considered chronic, and you should consult your health care provider.

What to do. Home treatment of tension headaches is often successful. Aspirin or acetaminophen may relieve the pain; however, avoid frequent use. Read instructions and warnings on the labels of these medications. Taking a hot or cold shower, massaging the neck muscles, or lying down in a dark room may provide relief. Learning to relax using biofeedback, meditation, music, visualization, or hypnosis, or taking a stress management class may also be helpful (see *Stress*, page 264).

Cluster Headaches

These headaches are very painful and occur mainly in middle-aged men. A cluster headache lasts 30 minutes to two hours, and then recurs within a few hours. These groups or clusters of headaches can continue for several days, hence the name. There is no signal before a cluster headache begins, nor any sign that it is going to end. Lying down during an attack usually makes the pain worse.

Symptoms of a cluster headache include the following:

- a steady, boring pain in or around one eye, occurring in episodes that often begin at the same time each day or evening
- watering and redness of one eye, with nasal congestion on the same side of the face

What to do. Call your health care provider if you believe you are having cluster headaches. People who have cluster headaches are encouraged to keep a diary of patterns that may help identify a personal trigger. Due to the rapid start of cluster headaches, over-the-counter pain relievers are of little use because they take effect too slowly. Although prescription drugs can ease the pain, side effects may limit their use.

Self-Care Steps for Headaches

- Lifestyle plays an important role with headaches.
- Eating and sleeping habits, stress, and exercise can all be factors in triggering occasional and more frequent headaches. Over-the-counter pain relievers such as aspirin, acetaminophen, or ibuprofen can usually control a headache. Children and teenagers should not be given aspirin due to the risk of Reye's syndrome.
- For recurring headaches, a headache diary may help to identify possible triggers. This diary should record everything you eat, your sleep and exercise patterns, and work and home activities. Women should also record their menstrual cycles because headaches can be triggered by hormonal changes.

Migraine Headaches

These headaches have very specific symptoms and because the victim may become nauseated, are sometimes called sick headaches. The victim of a migraine will often see bright spots, flashes of light, or areas of blindness just before the headache strikes. These symptoms are called an aura. Some people have great bursts of energy and activity just before a migraine starts.

Symptoms of a migraine headache include the following:

- throbbing pain
- pain more often on one side of the head
- an aura, or preheadache phase, that may include flashes of light, bright spots, distorted vision, abdominal pain, and nausea

The pain of a migraine headache is caused by the increased dilation or widening of the blood vessels in the head. These headaches occur suddenly and often recur. Possible triggers of a migraine headache include hunger, fatigue, bright light, alcohol, caffeine, excitement or stress, birth control pills, and certain foods.

What to do. Most migraine headaches require diagnosis and treatment by a health care provider. See your provider to discuss appropriate treatment. He or she may prescribe medication.

Decision Guide for Headaches

Symptoms/Signs	Action
Occasional headaches that cause minor discomfort	Use self-care
Recurring headaches that cause loss of function	Call provider's office
Nausea and vomiting	See provider
Convulsions	Seek help now
Weakness, numbness, or tingling in arms or legs	Seek help now
Sudden, disabling pain	Seek help now

For more about the symbols, see page 60.

A mild migraine headache may pass quickly if you go immediately to a dark room and lie down. Place a cool, damp cloth on your forehead. Relax your entire body, focusing on the eyes, the forehead, the jaw and neck muscles, and working your way down to the toes.

Insomnia

For many people, insomnia—difficulty falling asleep—is an occasional response to excitement or anxiety from good and bad events in life that keeps them awake and thinking late at night. But insomnia is a chronic problem for 15 million to 20 million Americans. Improving your sleeping habits (by avoiding caffeine late in the day, relaxing before going to bed, sticking to a regular sleeping schedule) can usually take care of any problems you may have getting to sleep.

However, sleeplessness can be related to underlying health problems. For example, insomnia may be a symptom of depression. If you do not feel well, think you may be depressed (see *Depression*, page 260), or are waking unusually early, you should discuss these symptoms with your health care provider. There are helpful treatments for depression that may cure your insomnia if the two problems are related.

Trouble sleeping sends many people to see their health care provider, often to get sleeping pills. Yet most medical professionals believe that sleeping pills should be avoided whenever possible. Many nonprescription sleep aids rely on what is called the placebo effect, which means they work only if you think they are going to work. And prescription drugs are likely to knock you out rather than producing a natural, restful sleep.

In many cases, your insomnia may be related to a poor sleep schedule. Sleeping late into the morning or napping during the day makes sleep at night more difficult. Instead of taking sleeping pills, your best bet is to get your sleeping schedule back on track.

What to do. It may take several weeks or longer to establish a new, natural sleeping routine. If you are unable to make progress after trying the self-care steps on page 272, call your health care provider.

Self-Care Steps for Insomnia

- **Avoid drinking alcohol in the evening.** Although alcohol is a short-term sedative that may quickly bring on sleep, it interferes with deep sleep, so that you may wake up suddenly after its effects have worn off.
- **Avoid or reduce your intake of caffeine.** Caffeine stays in your system for as long as 12 to 24 hours. Remember that in addition to coffee, caffeine is present in chocolate, some prescription and over-the-counter medications, and many colas and teas. If you suspect that caffeine is contributing to your sleeplessness, don't use any caffeinated products for at least 12 hours before you go to bed.
- **Be aware of other drugs that may affect your sleeping patterns.** Many over-the-counter decongestants and products containing phenylpropanolamine can be as stimulating as caffeine. Before you start using a drug, ask your pharmacist if it might keep you awake and whether another product can be substituted.
- **Break your chain of thought before you turn in.** Try setting aside 30 minutes before bedtime to work on problems that might keep you up later. Make lists and diagram strategies to attack your problems. You may sleep better knowing you've taken steps to address those issues. You can also treat this time as an opportunity to wind down and do something you find relaxing, such as listening to music or reading.
- **Avoid eating large meals just before you go to bed.** The uncomfortable feeling of having a full stomach may delay sleep. Try a light snack instead. This will satisfy your hunger and won't interfere with your sleep. Many people swear by the virtues of a glass of warm or cold milk. Try adding a touch of honey, cinnamon, or vanilla to this bedtime standby.
- **Take a warm bath 1 or 2 hours before bedtime.** This can soothe tense muscles and help make you sleepy. However, taking a bath immediately before going to bed may be too stimulating and keep you awake. Experiment with the timing to see what works best for you.
- **Exercise regularly.** This will help relieve tension and clear your head. It will also tire you out, so you can sleep more soundly. Avoid strenuous physical activity for several hours before going to bed. It may stimulate you and interfere with falling asleep.
- **Keep your bedroom quiet and dark.** If noise is a problem, try earplugs or "white noise." Many people like the reassuring sound of a fan or air conditioner as they drift off to sleep. A cool room temperature—between 60 and 65 degrees—is best for sleeping. A firm, comfortable mattress is also important for a good night's sleep.
- **Avoid long, late afternoon naps.** Short catnaps, lasting no more than 20 minutes, can be surprisingly refreshing. Longer naps and those taken later than 4 P.M. may disrupt normal sleep patterns and contribute to insomnia.
- **Read in bed for a few minutes before you turn out the light.** This helps you relax and can make you feel drowsier.
- **Counting sheep is not recommended.** Counting requires focusing the brain on a specific activity. Instead, try picturing yourself in a pleasant place, and use your imagination to hear relaxing sounds as you drift off to sleep.
- **Ban stressful activities from your bedroom.** Don't spend time in your bed paying bills, finishing up extra work, or talking on the phone. Reserve your bed for sleep and sex.
- **Stick to a routine.** Your body's internal clock responds best to a regular schedule. Try going to bed and getting up at the same time each day, including weekends.

Section Five

Living With Chronic Health Problems

If you have a chronic health condition such as heart disease or asthma, you know the kind of physical and emotional demands a long-term disease can place on your life. But you may not realize that the changes you make in your behavior and the effort you bring to your therapy can have an impact on the course of your illness and your quality of life.

You can do many things that will help improve and manage a chronic condition. You need to work in close partnership with your health care provider to maintain your health. Learning how to control your illness should involve getting and staying fit. Whether you have diabetes, high cholesterol, or another condition, eating a healthy diet is a strategy that can do a world of good for anyone. A dietitian with special training in your disease can design a meal plan for you and help you improve your eating habits if necessary.

Living with a chronic health condition can also take its toll emotionally. Learning how to handle stress is a good idea for everyone. Chronic disease can cause stress within families. Family counseling or other approaches to good communication and conflict resolution can help you identify and manage such problems.

Angina

Angina is a heart condition that occurs when the coronary arteries that bring oxygen-rich blood to the heart are clogged with a fatty substance called plaque. A person with angina often experiences pressure or pain that comes and goes in the heart. Angina is a warning sign that the heart isn't getting the oxygen it needs.

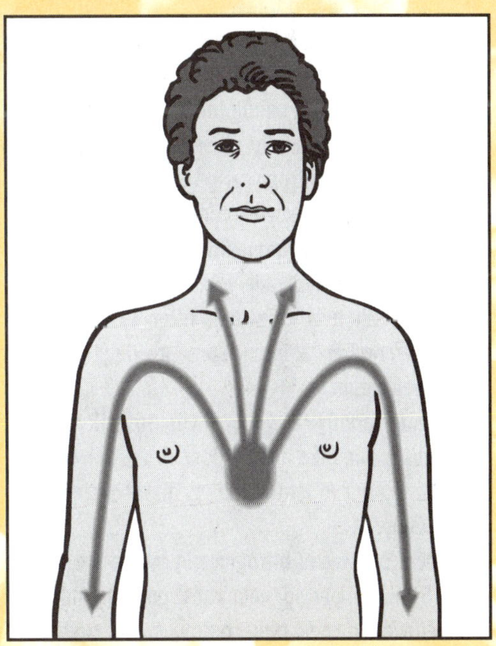

Angina can feel similar to a heart attack. However, unlike a heart attack, the pain from angina usually goes away in 15 minutes or less with rest or the use of nitroglycerin, a prescription medication that comes in tablets or as a spray. Angina may be brought on by exertion, a large meal, emotional upset, smoking, or other triggers. It can also strike when you're resting.

Know the signs of angina. Angina can cause any of the following symptoms:

- a crushing, squeezing, burning pain in the chest
- a feeling of pressure in the chest
- pain radiating to jaw, arms, neck, and/or back

Self-Care Steps for Angina

The following steps are usually recommended for angina. Keep in mind that your doctor knows you and understands your medical needs. Therefore, it is more important to follow your doctor's advice than these guidelines.

- Sit down before taking medicine—nitroglycerin can occasionally cause light-headedness. You must let nitroglycerin tablets dissolve completely under your tongue; do not swallow tablets. If you use nitroglycerine spray, take one spray inside your cheek.
- If you still have chest pain after 5 minutes, take another tablet, or spray inside your cheek again.
- If after another 5 minutes you are still having chest pain, take a third dose of nitroglycerin. Remember to let the tablets dissolve completely.
- After 3 doses of nitroglycerin over a 15-minute period, your chest pain should be relieved. If chest pain continues, you could be having a heart attack and should call 911.

If you feel any of these symptoms and the pain goes away within 15 minutes of rest, you may have angina. If you've never had this type of pain before, don't try to diagnose yourself. Call your health care provider for advice. If your provider wants to see you right away, ask a friend or relative to drive you there.

Call your provider's office if your attacks become more frequent, last longer, or feel different or more painful than normal, or if chest pain wakes you from sleep. Talk with your provider if you find you're having angina after expending less effort than usual.

Use medicine effectively. If you take medicine for angina, take it as directed and be sure you understand the possible side effects and what to do about them. Don't allow yourself to run out of medicine. Keep nitroglycerin tablets in their original container. Check the expiration date. If you have questions about medication, talk with your provider or pharmacist.

Asthma

Asthma is a disease of the lungs and the air tubes leading to them. When someone has asthma, the tiny airways in the lungs, called bronchioles, swell and produce extra mucus so that it's difficult to breathe. The bands of muscle around the outside of the bronchial tubes tighten, further blocking the flow of air and causing coughing, wheezing, and shortness of breath. Asthma attacks can be mild or life-threatening.

No one is sure what causes asthma, but it is clear that the bronchioles in people who have asthma are extra sensitive to stimuli such as allergens, irritants, and weather changes.

Medications can be used to treat an asthma attack after it begins, and medications are also available to help prevent asthma attacks.

Asthma symptoms fall into two categories: acute and chronic. Symptoms may last just a few minutes, several days, or even weeks. Asthma symptoms come on gradually in some patients, and quickly in others.

Asthma triggers. Managing your asthma involves finding out which stimuli can bring on an asthma attack for you, and avoiding them. These stimuli, called triggers, include the following:

- allergies to pollen, dust mites, mold spores, and dander (especially from animals with fur or feathers)
- infections and irritants including viral infections (such as colds and the flu), cigarette smoke, chemical fumes, smog, poor air quality, aspirin and other anti-inflammatory drugs, cold air, and weather changes
- exposure to certain materials at work such as grain dust, flour (commonly known as baker's asthma), or certain chemicals
- certain types of exertion or exercise, especially in cold weather
- intense emotions such as fear and worry

It is important to realize that emotional stress can trigger an asthma attack, but it doesn't cause asthma.

Managing asthma. Asthma treatment should give you the tools to control your condition so that you can do the activities you choose. Your health care provider will work with you first to control acute asthma and then to manage symptoms by finding out what triggers your attacks. Your provider may ask you to keep a daily record of symptoms, possible triggers, and medicine taken. Your provider may also ask you to monitor your lung function daily with an instrument called a peak flow meter. (A peak flow meter tells how well you are breathing.) This information will help your provider decide when to add the next level of medicine, if needed, to keep your symptoms under control. Through this treatment program, patients learn how triggers affect their asthma, how their lungs react to medicine, and how to control asthma.

Action plan. You and your provider should develop a written asthma action plan. Then you can recognize warning signs of an asthma attack early and take the right steps to treat it before it gets worse. You should also have an emergency plan to follow if an attack becomes severe.

Medicines. Many people need daily doses of prescription drugs to keep their symptoms under control. Medicines are most often taken by adults through an inhaler or nebulizer (a compressed air device for administering medication to the lungs). But medicine also comes in liquid, capsules, and tablets. Every medicine has its own set of possible side effects. Be sure to ask your provider or pharmacist what side effects you might have and what to do about them.

There are two general kinds of asthma drugs. Bronchodilators relax the muscles around the airways so they can open up and let air in more easily. The other type, anti-inflammatory drugs, reduces the swelling and mucus that lead to congestion. Inhaled steroids, which are anti-inflammatory agents, are commonly used to treat people who have moderate to severe asthma. If used at the recommended dosage, it will not cause side effects in most people because it goes directly to the lungs.

Oral corticosteroids (prednisone, prednisolone, and methylprednisolone) are stronger anti-inflammatory medications. Although these drugs may cause side effects, they are usually safe when taken according to instructions and are primarily used for short-term control of asthma.

Cromolyn sodium and nedocromil sodium are nonsteroidal anti-inflammatory drugs that can help prevent an asthma attack. They don't work during an attack. These medicines can be given with an inhaler or a nebulizer. Cromolyn and nedocromil have few side effects. Although cromolyn doesn't work for everyone and can require as much as a month of usage before any benefit is seen, it can be especially useful for children with allergies. Both drugs are most effective when taken on a regular, preventive basis. Inhaled steroids are occa-

Self-Care Steps for Asthma

- **Find out as much as you can about asthma.** Attend patient information sessions and asthma support groups.
- **Read books about asthma**. Contact the American Lung Association, Mothers of Asthmatics, Inc., the American Academy of Allergy and Immunology, or the National Heart, Lung, and Blood Institute for more information about asthma. (For addresses and phone numbers, see *Resources,* page 291.)
- **Follow your asthma action plan.** Know the warning signs of an asthma attack. Make sure you have written instructions for what to do in an asthma emergency. Keep an asthma diary, in which you record your episodes, drugs, peak flow readings, and responses to drugs. When an attack occurs, treat symptoms within minutes of their onset. It takes less medicine to stop an asthma attack in its early phase.
- **Manage your medicines.** Know the kinds of drugs you should take, how much, and how often. Know the possible side effects and what you can do to minimize them. Make sure you know which drugs to take first, and follow the instructions carefully. Also learn the correct use of an inhaler with a spacer. Don't run out of your medicines. Ask your provider or pharmacist to check any new drug for possible interactions with the asthma drugs you are taking. Keep good records of your drugs and dosages. Make sure someone else in your family knows where to find this information in an emergency.
- **Monitor your condition.** Learn how to use a peak flow meter. It can show a change in your lungs before an asthma attack starts, because lung capacity can drop as much as 24 hours before any symptoms appear. If you keep daily records of your symptoms and peak flow readings, you will be able to begin treatment soon enough to reduce the number and severity of asthma attacks.
- **Identify and avoid triggers.** Your record keeping will help you determine what brings on your asthma attacks. If things like dust and animal dander are high on your list, take steps to keep your living areas free of these triggers. Steer clear of irritants such as wood smoke and car exhaust fumes.
- **Don't smoke.** And stay away from areas where others are smoking.
- **Stay physically fit.** Most people can control their asthma so that they can exercise.
- **See your provider for regular follow-up exams.** Bring your asthma diary with you. Your record will help your provider determine whether your asthma is under control and if your medications are working effectively.

sionally prescribed along with cromolyn or nedocromil.

In partnership with your health care provider, you can use self-care techniques to manage your asthma, reduce the severity and frequency of your symptoms, and cut down on your trips to the clinic or hospital.

Home management recommendations assume that the patient has seen a health care provider and has both an asthma action plan and the right drugs for managing asthma attacks. People with undiagnosed coughing, wheezing, chest tightness, or other possible asthma symptoms should see their provider to set up a plan of care.

Special Concerns for Children

- Asthma causes more hospital and emergency room visits than any other chronic childhood disease. Children with well-controlled asthma, however, should be able to do any activity or sport they choose.
- About half of all children with asthma outgrow their symptoms by age 15, although the underlying condition—the extra-sensitive bronchial tubes—remains throughout life. Asthma can recur in the adult years. Smoking—or even breathing cigarette smoke—can trigger its return. When treating asthma in children, the education of both parent and child is key. Understanding the disease and the child's specific triggers and warning signs can help parents follow through with timely, effective treatment.
- Children who are too young to use an inhaler are often treated with a machine called a nebulizer. This device uses compressed air to turn a solution of liquid medication into a fine mist that the child breathes in through a mask or mouthpiece.

HOW TO USE AN INHALER

1. Stand up. Shake the container well. Remove the cap and hold the container upright.
2. Place a spacer (cardboard or plastic tube) on the end of the inhaler. A spacer is a holding chamber that allows you to use inhaled medications more effectively. If no spacer is available, hold the inhaler 1 to 2 inches from your mouth. Without a spacer, too much medication may end up in your mouth rather than in your lungs.
3. Breathe out normally, then position the spacer in your mouth. Place it on top of your tongue and close your lips around it.
4. As you start to breathe in slowly through your mouth, press down on the top of the inhaler container. It will let out a puff of medicine.
5. Continue breathing in slowly for 3 to 5 seconds, until your lungs are full.
6. Hold your breath for 10 seconds to allow the medicine to reach your lungs.
7. In some cases, depending upon the drugs used, you will need to wait 1 to 3 minutes before taking another puff on your inhaler. This allows your lungs to open up, and the second treatment works even better. Check with your health care provider for proper instructions.

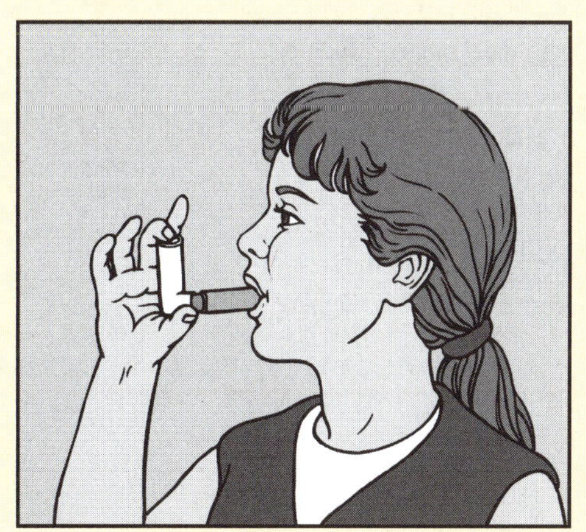

Decision Guide for Asthma

Symptoms/Signs	Action
Normal asthma symptoms that can be managed according to asthma action plan	Use self-care
Minor coughing after exercise	Use self-care
Wheezing when out in cold weather	Use self-care
Asthma symptoms that are worse with a cold or the flu	Use self-care
Severe asthma attack	Use self-care
Unsure about how to take medications	Call provider's office
Severe reaction to drugs	Call provider's office
Yellow, green, or bloody mucus, or mucus that thickens	Call provider's office
Temperature of 100 degrees or greater (101 degrees rectal) with wheezing or coughing	Call provider's office
A peak flow reading in the red danger area	Call provider's office
Inability to sleep because of wheezing and/or coughing	Call provider's office
Symptoms during exercise despite use of drugs	Call provider's office
Difficulty breathing, walking, or talking	See provider
Lips and/or fingernails that turn gray or bluish	Seek help now
Skin of the neck, chest, or rib area is sucked in with each breath; flaring nostrils	Seek help now
Peak flow less than 50 percent of your personal best	Seek help now
Symptoms that worsen despite drugs	Seek help now
Symptoms that rapidly get worse over a few hours	Seek help now
Severe wheezing and/or coughing; gasping for air; sweating; hunching forward	Emergency: call 911
Extreme anxiety due to shortness of breath	Emergency: call 911

For more about the symbols, see page 60.

Bronchitis and Emphysema

Chronic obstructive pulmonary disease (COPD) is the fifth leading cause of death in the United States. Although many people think first of emphysema when they hear COPD, chronic bronchitis is actually more common and equally serious because it can lead to emphysema, and can eventually cause death if not controlled.

Cigarette smoking is the number one cause of COPD, accounting for 82 percent of cases. Other causes include repeated exposure to lots of dust (such as in coal mines, granaries, or metal molding shops), chemical vapors, and possibly air pollution. A small percentage of emphysema cases are inherited.

Like acute bronchitis, chronic bronchitis is an inflammation of the lining of the bronchial tubes which lead to the lungs. This causes the lungs to produce too much mucus. As chronic bronchitis gets worse, the tiny hairs (called cilia) that sweep away irritants from the air passages can stop working or die. With acute bronchitis, otherwise healthy people have a one- to two-week bout after a cold or the flu. People with chronic bronchitis have inflammation and coughing with mucus for at least three months each year.

Emphysema occurs when the tiny air sacs (alveoli) in the lungs become larger and less elastic, making the lungs less able to pass oxygen into the blood. This leads to shortness of breath, eventually making even the most basic tasks—such as eating or getting dressed—difficult and tiring.

Neither disease appears overnight. Chronic bronchitis often begins as repeated cases of acute bronchitis after colds (see *Acute Bronchitis*, page 134). With chronic bronchitis, however, coughing and mucus

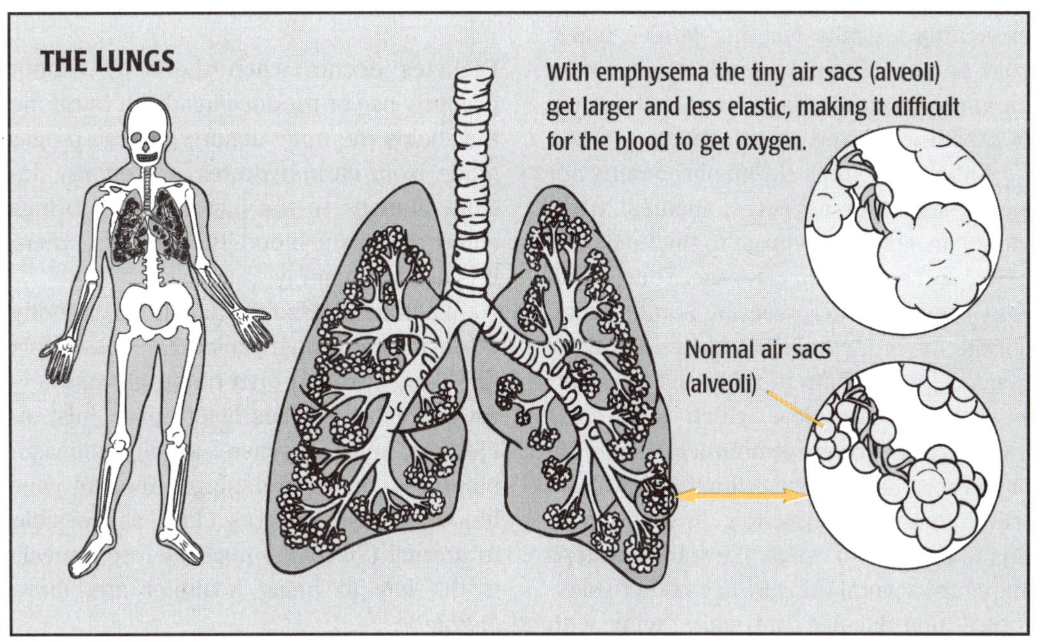

Self-Care Steps for Chronic Bronchitis and Emphysema

- Quit smoking! Read the information in this book on quitting smoking (see *Smoking,* pages 47-48) and talk with your health care provider. If you continue to smoke, it will only make your emphysema worse.
- Call your provider at the first signs of respiratory illness, such as a cold or the flu.
- Drink plenty of fluids. Drinking 6 to 8 glasses of clear fluids a day, such as juice or water, will help keep air passages clear of mucus, making it easier to breathe.
- Eat a well-balanced diet. If you have emphysema, spread your meals out. By eating 5 or 6 small meals a day, you avoid having a full stomach, which can interfere with your breathing.
- Strengthen your heart with aerobic exercise and build your upper-body strength. Strengthening the muscles in your upper body will make breathing easier. Moderate aerobic exercise, such as 15 minutes of daily walking, will make your heart less susceptible to complications of COPD. Exercise and a healthy diet will also build your resistance to illness and infection. Before beginning an exercise program, talk with your health care provider.
- Do breathing exercises. If you have emphysema, ask your provider about exercises to help you breathe better. Two common exercises are "pursed-lip" breathing (inhaling through your nose and exhaling twice as long through pursed lips) and breathing from the diaphragm (expanding your diaphragm and abdomen, rather than your chest, when you inhale).
- Get a flu shot each fall and a pneumococcal pneumonia vaccination at least once.

production occur more frequently and last longer after each cold. After a while, the bronchitis remains whether you've had a cold or not. Likewise, emphysema comes on gradually, often beginning as shortness of breath with exercise or activity.

Although neither chronic bronchitis nor emphysema can be cured, medical treatment can slow the damage to the lungs and heart, and symptoms can ease. Your health care provider may prescribe some combination of bronchodilator drugs (oral or inhaled), which help to relax and open airways; corticosteroids, which help clear away excess mucus; antibiotics, which kill bacteria; and exercise, which helps build and support lung function. In addition to taking prescribed drugs, the self-care steps above list several things you can do to slow future lung damage and make living with COPD easier.

Diabetes

Diabetes occurs when the body cannot properly use or produce insulin, a hormone that helps the body absorb glucose (sugar made from carbohydrates) for energy. Insulin is made in the pancreas and brings glucose from the blood into the cells, where it is used for energy.

When insulin isn't available or the body doesn't use it properly, blood glucose levels rise. Uncontrolled high blood glucose levels can cause serious health problems, including heart disease, kidney disease, blindness, or nerve damage. Keeping your blood glucose level as close as possible to normal (70 to 115 mg/dl before a meal) is the key to being healthier and more energetic.

Although there are different types of diabetes, the cause—the body's inability to use food properly—is the same. The major types of diabetes are type I (insulin-dependent), type II (non-insulin-dependent), and gestational diabetes.

Warning signs of diabetes. Call your health care provider if you have any of the following symptoms:

- extreme thirst
- unusual tiredness
- excessive appetite
- frequent urination
- tingling or numbness in legs or feet
- cuts or bruises that heal slowly
- blurred vision or any change in vision

Risk factors for developing diabetes. You are more likely to develop diabetes if you have any of the following risk factors:

- obesity
- over age 40
- a family history of diabetes
- race (diabetes is more common among American Indians, Hispanics, and African-Americans)
- history of impaired glucose tolerance
- high blood pressure or high levels of blood fats (cholesterol or triglycerides)
- history of gestational diabetes (for women)
- having given birth to a baby that weighed more than 9 pounds

Type I (insulin-dependent) diabetes. This type of diabetes may develop at any age, but occurs most often in children, teenagers, and young adults. Symptoms include being very thirsty, hungry, and tired, and needing to urinate often. Children with type I diabetes rarely have these symptoms for longer than a few weeks before it is diagnosed.

With type I diabetes, the pancreas stops producing enough insulin. To make up for this lack of insulin, people with type I diabetes control their blood sugar level through diet and exercise, and by giving themselves insulin injections.

Type II (non-insulin-dependent) diabetes. The most common form of diabetes, type II diabetes usually develops gradually with few, if any, symptoms. It most commonly occurs in people over the age of 40 and in those who are overweight. The pancreas keeps making insulin, but the body does not use it effectively. This leads to a buildup of glucose in the blood. Type II diabetes is often diagnosed by tracking a gradual increase in blood glucose levels. It can usually be controlled by diet and exercise, but sometimes oral medication is necessary as well.

Gestational diabetes. This type of diabetes is discovered through a routine blood test for glucose during a woman's pregnancy. Closely monitoring blood glucose levels helps women have safe pregnancies and healthy babies. Gestational diabetes usually disappears at the end of the pregnancy, but mothers may be at increased risk for developing diabetes in the future.

Once you have diabetes, you have it for life. There is no cure. The disease can be managed successfully by controlling your blood sugar through proper nutrition and exercise.

Self-Care Steps for Diabetes

NUTRITION

A good diet is important for everyone, especially people who have diabetes. Planning meals and watching the total amount of carbohydrates you eat is key to maintaining a blood glucose level that is as normal as possible. Your meal plans should be suited to your lifestyle and nutritional needs.

If you are overweight, it is important to reach a reasonable body weight. Ask your health care provider how much to lose. Weight loss can improve your body's ability to use glucose as well as reduce your risk of heart disease. For children, it is important to consume enough calories to provide for normal growth and development.

BLOOD GLUCOSE MONITORING

Whether you have type I, type II, or gestational diabetes, it is important to check blood glucose levels and keep them as close to normal as possible. Closely controlling your blood glucose helps you feel better and reduces the risk of problems associated with diabetes. Glucose levels are monitored by pricking a finger and testing a drop of blood using chemically treated plastic strips that indicate the glucose level in the blood. Color charts or small calculator-sized machines are used to analyze the blood glucose test strips. Your health care provider can teach you how to monitor your blood glucose correctly.

Many people with diabetes monitor their blood glucose up to 6 times daily, especially those taking insulin to help control type I or type II diabetes. Others who have type II diabetes and are not taking insulin may need to monitor their blood glucose only 2 or 3 days a week if the level remains within normal range, or close to it.

EXERCISE

People with diabetes enjoy the same benefits from exercise as everyone else: improved heart and lung efficiency, reduced body fat, increased muscle tone, and improved fitness. But people who have diabetes get more benefits; exercise combined with fewer calories will often control type II diabetes without the need for medication.

Exercise can lower blood glucose levels by making body cells more sensitive to insulin and improving their ability to use and store glucose. Your health care provider can help you determine the benefits of exercise and the type of exercise program that is best for you.

REGULAR MEDICAL CARE

People with diabetes are at higher risk for several illnesses. Although keeping your diabetes under control decreases your likeliness of developing complications, you still face the possibility of diabetic retinopathy, kidney damage, cataracts, and circulatory problems. Diabetic retinopathy is a condition in which the retina (a part of the eye) and the blood vessels nourishing it are damaged. This condition can lead to blindness.

If you have diabetes, it's important to have your eyes checked for retinopathy every year, because it is more easily treated if caught early. Also, talk with your provider about foot care and how to detect circulatory problems. Foot wounds in people with diabetes can develop into gangrene, but if you know how to care for your feet properly you should be able to prevent this from happening.

RESOURCES

The National Diabetes Information Clearinghouse and the American Diabetes Association offer more information with people with diabetes. (For addresses and phone numbers, see *Resources,* page 291.)

Heart Disease

The most common form of heart disease is atherosclerosis, or hardening of the arteries. Cholesterol joins with calcium and scar tissue and builds up in the arteries. When cholesterol levels are too high, the circulatory system becomes choked—and the result is a dam of plaque that narrows the channels the blood flows through.

You suffer a heart attack when blood can't flow to the heart. This could be caused by narrowing of your arteries due to plaque buildup, blood clots, or other heart-related problems such as a heart spasm. You may get a warning sign of a heart attack in the form of chest pain that moves to the left arm, jaw, or shoulder blade. *Don't ignore it.* American Heart Association research shows that hardening of the arteries is the leading cause of death that results from heart attack or stroke.

Stroke is another potentially deadly result of having heart disease. In a stroke, also known as a "brain attack," blood can't reach the brain because an artery is blocked or has ruptured. Cells in the blood-starved part of the brain begin to die. A stroke can cause paralysis, inability to talk, inability to understand speech, and other conditions brought on by brain damage.

Another form of heart disease is congestive heart failure. The heart is weakened by high blood pressure, previous heart attack, atherosclerosis, rheumatic fever, a congenital heart defect, or a muscle disease known as cardiomyopathy. Just as a weak hand can't squeeze all the water out of a dishcloth, a weak heart can't pump effectively, and fluid collects in the body and lungs.

CLOGGED ARTERIES

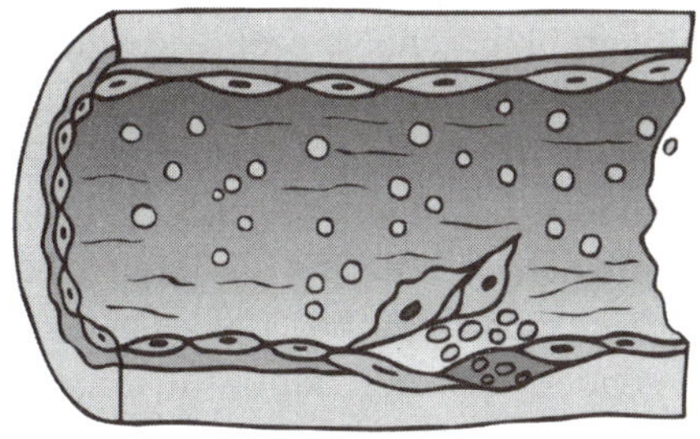

Atherosclerosis begins with a damaged spot in the artery. Cholesterol and other fats from the bloodstream build plaque on artery walls.

Macrophages (large white cells) and platelets (small blood cells that coagulate blood) contribute to the buildup of plaque. The macrophages fill up with cholesterol, and cholesterol packs the inside lining of the artery wall.

Plaque narrows the arteries. Sometimes a clot can form in an artery narrowed by plaque, causing angina or a heart attack. Blockage in an artery leading to the brain causes a stroke.

Risk Factors You Can Control

Three major risk factors for heart disease that you can control are high blood pressure, high blood cholesterol, and smoking. If you have even one of these risk factors, your risk for heart disease is doubled. If you have all three risk factors, your risk is eight times higher than if you had none. Other major risk factors for heart disease include age, gender, diabetes, family history, and your health history.

High cholesterol. Too much cholesterol in the bloodstream can contribute to the buildup in the arteries that causes atherosclerosis. High cholesterol can often be controlled with changes in diet, but some cases may require medication (see *High Blood Cholesterol*, page 286).

High blood pressure. The second leading risk factor for heart attacks and the major cause of stroke is high blood pressure, or hypertension (see *High Blood Pressure*, page 286).

Smoking. Smoking increases your risk of heart attack by lowering your level of "good" HDL cholesterol and raising your blood pressure. The HDL cholesterol level of a person who smokes can increase measurably when he or she stops smoking.

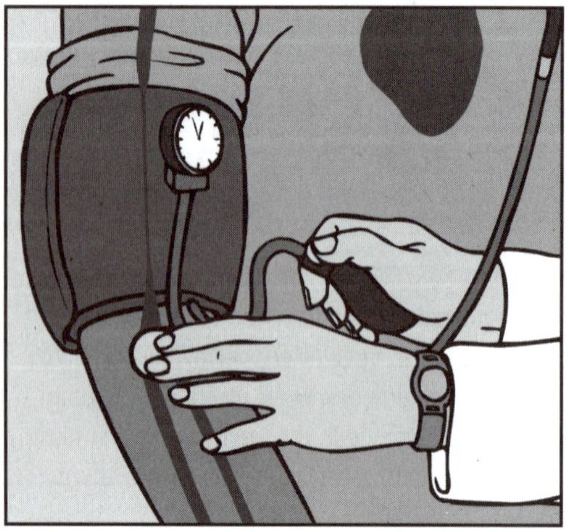

Lack of exercise. American Heart Association research shows that regular aerobic exercise actually strengthens the heart muscle, boosts HDL levels, lowers blood pressure, slows the progression of diabetes, and helps prevent obesity. Most organizations recommend about 30 to 40 minutes of moderate exercise four or more days a week.

Obesity. Research shows that obesity should be considered a major risk factor for heart disease, rather than one that just contributes to other risk factors—such as diabetes and high blood pressure. To learn more about losing and maintaining weight, see *Losing Weight*, page 42.

Diabetes. People who have diabetes are susceptible to heart disease. People with poorly controlled diabetes often have several health problems, including high cholesterol and other circulatory disorders that lead to atherosclerosis, hemorrhages of the tiny blood vessels in the eyes, and poor circulation to the feet and hands. Smoking makes these problems worse.

Uncontrollable Risk Factors

Some of the factors that contribute to heart disease cannot be controlled. These factors are the ones you are born with. Keep in mind that you can change the other risk factors, which are greater influences on whether or not you will have heart disease.

Age. Heart disease is more common among older people because it reflects the wear and tear on the body; however, it doesn't have to be part of aging. A healthy lifestyle can prevent it. It may take 20 to 30 years until the arteries are blocked enough to cause trouble. Atherosclerosis may be halted in its course if diagnosed in time for a person to make the needed changes.

Gender. Until the age of 55, men have more heart attacks than women of the same age. This changes after menopause because estrogen levels drop at this time. (Researchers believe that high estrogen levels protect women against heart disease.) After the age of 55, the incidence of heart disease in women is almost the same as men.

Heredity. High blood pressure and high cholesterol levels run in families. But don't use your genes as an excuse. Instead, take the steps necessary to offset this risk and control the risk factors you can control.

Getting More Help

Your family and friends can provide support and encouragement as you tackle each of your risk factors. Bring one of these people to your next doctor's appointment to help you take notes and ask questions.

If your arteries are already severely blocked, surgery may be your only option. The two most common surgeries are angioplasty and bypass surgery. Both are proven techniques. The success rate is 96 percent for angioplasty, the surgery doctors use to reopen a clogged blood vessel (balloon angioplasty and laser angioplasty). In addition, a procedure known as atherectomy shaves away plaque in a clogged artery and may be able to cut the reblockage rate in half. In a nonemergency bypass, the risk of fatality is usually less than 1 in 50.

You may need the expertise and help of a nurse or health educator to manage your heart disease, especially if you have surgery. He or she can give you written materials or information about classes, answer your day-to-day questions, and put you in touch with organizations and support groups that will help you even more. The American Heart Association and the National Heart, Lung, and Blood Institute can offer helpful information on managing heart disease. For addresses and phone numbers of these and other organizations, see *Resources*, page 294.

High Blood Cholesterol

High blood cholesterol is one of the biggest risk factors for heart attack, the leading cause of death in America. Cholesterol is a waxy substance your body produces to help it function properly. It combines with other substances to form "packages" that circulate through the body. Cholesterol found in low-density lipoproteins (LDL cholesterol) is considered most responsible for the formation of plaque that clogs the arteries, leading to stroke and heart attack. High-density lipoproteins (HDLs), known as "good cholesterol," are thought to be responsible for removing extra cholesterol from the blood and thereby cutting down the risk for coronary heart disease.

Eating too much saturated fat and cholesterol and consuming more calories than necessary can raise blood cholesterol levels. Saturated fats are usually solid at room temperature and tend to come from animal sources. Unsaturated fatty acids tend to come from plants and fish.

Classifying your cholesterol. Total blood cholesterol measurements below 200 mg/dl are classified as "desirable," 200 to 239 mg/dl as "borderline high," and 240 mg/dl and above are considered "high." Because cholesterol levels can go up and down from day to day, an average of two or more measurements should be used for classification.

Reducing your risk. Your chance of developing heart disease depends on more than just the amount of cholesterol in your blood. To get a better idea of what your total cholesterol number means and what action you should take, start by identifying and adding up your other risk factors for heart disease.

Such factors include:

- male (45 years and older)
- female (55 years and older or in early menopause without hormone replacement therapy)
- family history of early heart disease (men before the age of 55; women before the age of 65)
- cigarette smoking
- high blood pressure (140/90 or higher)
- low levels of HDL cholesterol (lower than 35 mg/dl)
- diabetes or impaired glucose tolerance

Just as these factors combine to increase your risk of heart disease, healthy habits such as eating a low-fat diet, getting regular exercise, and quitting smoking can reduce your risk. Many people can lower their blood cholesterol simply by increasing their level of physical activity, and changing the way they eat—avoiding foods high in fat, especially saturated fat and cholesterol. The higher your cholesterol level is, the greater the benefits if you lower it.

Along with changes in diet, there are drugs that can lower cholesterol in the bloodstream. These drugs can be costly and cause undesirable side effects for some people. For this reason, changes in diet are usually the first step in treatment, unless cholesterol levels are very high.

Dietary changes. A chart on dietary recommendations to reduce blood cholesterol begins on page 39. For additional information, see *Diet*, page 38.

Maintaining a Healthy Weight

For many people, taking in more calories than the body needs contributes to having a higher cholesterol level. Remember that your calorie needs are based on how many calories your body burns. People burn calories at different rates depending on many factors—activity, body size, heredity, age, health, and gender. Losing weight and increasing physical activity are important steps toward reducing blood cholesterol and other risks for heart disease.

Eat less fat. We all need some dietary fat to transport certain fat-soluble vitamins, to make hormones, and to regulate other body functions. (Vitamins A, D, E, and K are fat-soluble because they are stored for a longer time in fat tissue.) But the average American eats too much fat. Fats are the most concentrated form of calories. Ideally, you should get less than 30 percent of your calories from fat.

Eat less saturated fat. Animal products are a major source of saturated fat—and the only source of dietary cholesterol. So as you limit high-fat meat and dairy choices, you'll also cut down on saturated fat and dietary cholesterol. A few vegetable fats, such as palm and coconut oil, are also high in saturated fat. These fat sources are mainly found in commercially prepared foods. Less than one third of the total fat you eat should come from saturated fat. Use information on labels to help you limit your saturated fat intake.

Eat fewer high-cholesterol foods. Cholesterol in food can also raise your blood cholesterol level, but its effect is not as significant as that of saturated fat. Your liver makes the cholesterol your body needs.

Eat more carbohydrate-rich, high-fiber foods. Reducing calories from fat means you'll need to increase your carbohydrate-rich choices: legumes, breads, grains, pasta, rice, fruits, and vegetables. Carbohydrate sources include simple sugars and complex carbohydrates (starches and fibers). Most foods contain a combination of these carbohydrate sources. Eating more complex carbohydrates ensures a better balance of vitamins, minerals, and fiber.

Dietary fiber is found in all plant foods. Soluble fiber in particular can be an important factor in controlling blood cholesterol levels. It is found in certain fruits and vegetables; dried peas, beans, and other legumes; oats; and barley. Studies show that by eating more soluble fiber, you may lower your blood cholesterol level and reduce your risk of heart disease.

Make realistic changes. Once you recognize the health threat posed by high blood cholesterol levels, it may seem like an emergency. However, the heart disease caused by high blood cholesterol is a chronic condition that develops over many years. Just as it takes time to build up plaque in the arteries, it takes time to start eating better and exercising. You should adopt a cholesterol reduction diet gradually over four to six months.

The changes in eating and exercise you make are also likely to result in cholesterol changes that are slow but positive. If the response is not enough to meet your treatment goals, further reductions in fat, saturated fat, and cholesterol can help your progress. However, keep in mind that fat is necessary—in small amounts—for good health. Fat is needed to carry fat-soluble vitamins and to provide essential fatty acids. These functions require as little as 8 to 10 grams of fat per day.

High Blood Pressure

Everybody has blood pressure. When your heart beats, it pumps blood through your body. Blood leaves the heart through the arteries and returns to the heart through the veins. As the blood moves through the arteries, it pushes against the inside walls of the arteries. This force is called blood pressure. A normal blood pressure means that the heart is pumping the blood through the arteries with the right amount of force.

Think of your arteries as a garden hose. When anything clogs up the hose or makes the space inside the hose smaller, the water comes out at a higher pressure. The same thing happens in your body. Anything that clogs up the blood vessels (like cholesterol), causes them to become smaller (like nicotine), or fills them with too much fluid (as salt does), will cause blood pressure to rise.

High blood pressure or hypertension is referred to as the "silent killer." Since most people with high blood pressure don't have noticeable symptoms, and since it's not clear who will get it or when, it is important to have your blood pressure checked regularly. (See the table on page 289 to determine your blood pressure classification.) To confirm a diagnosis of hypertension, readings from two or more visits are needed.

Having high blood pressure for a long time can harm some of your most important organs. The brain, kidneys, eyes, and heart get oxygen and nutrients from very small blood vessels. When the pressure in these vessels rises, the organ may become damaged due to lack of blood flow and less oxygen to the organ. Left untreated, high blood pressure can cause strokes, heart attack, renal (kidney) failure, or vision problems. The damage can occur suddenly or, more likely, gradually.

How is blood pressure measured? Two numbers are used to measure your blood pressure, as follows:

132 (systolic)/84 (diastolic)

The higher number, the systolic pressure, refers to the pressure inside the artery when the heart squeezes to pump blood through the body. The lower number, the diastolic pressure, refers to the pressure inside the artery when the heart is relaxed and filling with blood. The numbers are recorded as "mm Hg" (millimeters of mercury)—meaning how high the column of mercury is raised by the pressure of your blood.

Your blood pressure is considered high when your readings are consistently 140 mm Hg or greater systolic and/or 90 mm Hg or greater diastolic. The term borderline is sometimes used to describe hypertension in which the blood pressure only occasionally rises above 140/90 mm Hg.

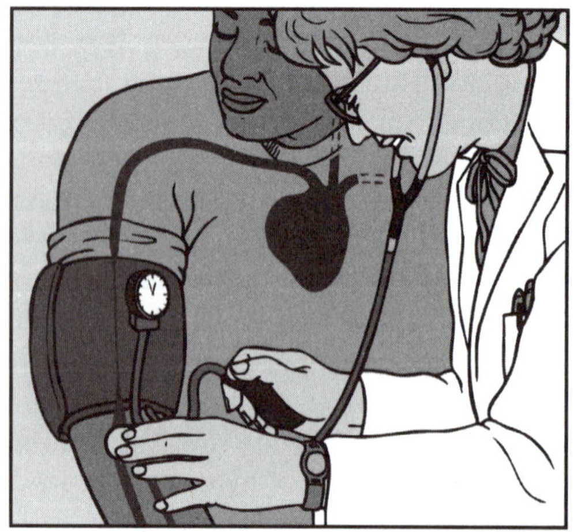

Getting an accurate reading. In addition to the normal minute-by-minute fluctuations in blood pressure, several biological factors such as anxiety, eating, and pain can also influence a blood pressure reading. If the people taking the readings don't use the same technique to measure blood pressure, the results may vary as well. Since blood pressure readings are an important test for diagnosing and treating high blood pressure, a standardized measurement technique is recommended to reduce as many of these variables as possible. To guard against incorrectly diagnosing high blood pressure on one elevated reading, readings from two or more separate visits should be used.

Your contribution to accuracy. Worry, poor eating habits, tobacco, air temperature changes, exertion, and pain can change your blood pressure temporarily and distort your blood pressure reading. To maximize the accuracy of your blood pressure measurement, follow these guidelines:

- Do not eat, smoke, drink caffeine, or exercise for at least 30 minutes before you have your blood pressure measured.
- Wear short sleeves or loose sleeves that can be pushed up easily when you have your blood pressure taken. For consistency, use the same arm for each reading.
- Sit quietly with your legs uncrossed for a few minutes before having your blood pressure measured.
- Bring along your blood pressure records and a list of any drugs you are currently taking.

Classification of Blood Pressure for Adults Age 18 Years and Older*

CATEGORY	SYSTOLIC** (top number)	DIASTOLIC** (bottom number)	WHAT TO DO
Normal	Less than 130	Less than 85	Recheck in 2 years.
High-Normal	130-139	85-89	Recheck in 1 year.
Hypertension			
Stage 1	140-159	90-99	Confirm within 2 months.
Stage 2	160-179	100-109	See provider within 1 month.
Stage 3	180-209	110-119	See provider within 1 week.
Stage 4	210 or higher	120 or higher	See provider immediately.

* If you are not taking antihypertensive drugs and are not acutely ill

** When systolic and diastolic pressures fall into different categories, the higher category should be used to classify your blood pressure status.

Source: 1993 Joint Committee on Detection, Evaluation, and Treatment of High Blood Pressure

Self-Care Steps for High Blood Pressure

To reduce high blood pressure and cardiovascular risks:

- **Lose weight.** Being overweight increases your risk of developing high blood pressure. Weight loss in even modest amounts can lower and help control blood pressure, blood cholesterol, triglyceride, and blood sugar levels. Of all the nondrug methods of hypertension control, weight loss is by far the most effective.
- **Exercise regularly.** Regular aerobic exercise such as walking, running, bicycling, or swimming laps can prevent and reduce high blood pressure. More activity can also help reduce weight and stress. Many experts recommend 30 to 45 minutes of aerobic exercise 3 to 5 times a week.
- **Control salt in your diet.** Not everyone is sensitive to the blood pressure-raising effects of too much sodium, but there is no simple way to find out whether you have such sensitivity. Since the amount of salt in the average American diet raises blood pressure for about half of those with high blood pressure and interferes with some blood pressure-lowering drugs, cutting down on salt is recommended for anyone with high blood pressure. Limit salt to less than 2,300 mg per day by not adding it to your food and by limiting processed, convenience, and fast foods, which are traditionally high in sodium.
- **Limit alcohol.** Drinking too much alcohol can raise blood pressure, add weight, and make it harder to control high blood pressure. Avoid alcohol or do not have more than 2 drinks a day. A drink is defined as 12 ounces of beer, 4 ounces of wine, or 1.5 ounces of 80-proof liquor.
- **Quit smoking.** Smoking cigarettes does not cause high blood pressure, but smoking is a major risk factor for cardiovascular disease. That is why everyone who smokes—especially people with high blood pressure—should quit.
- **Eat less fat.** Some evidence shows that a low-fat diet may reduce blood pressure and lower blood cholesterol. Eating less fat will also aid in weight loss.

- If using home blood pressure equipment, follow the manufacturer's instructions, and bring equipment in to your health care provider's office yearly to make sure it's accurate.

High blood pressure exam. If your blood pressure has been classified as higher than normal, you need an exam by your provider. He or she will check for any known causes for the elevated blood pressure and find out if there is any damage to your heart, kidneys, brain, or eyes. Your provider will also check for cardiovascular risk factors, such as smoking, diabetes, or high blood cholesterol. About 90 to 95 percent of patients have "primary" or "essential" hypertension, in which the cause is unknown. Only about 5 to 10 percent of patients have "secondary" hypertension (high blood pressure from a known cause such as diseases or organ problems).

During your exam, your provider will ask questions about your health and medication history and your family's health history. A physical exam and some lab tests will be done to look for possible causes of high blood pressure and to determine your risk of heart disease. Other lab tests will provide a baseline for comparison after treatment.

Treatment. Treatment decisions are based on your blood pressure stage, presence or absence of organ damage, and other risk factors. Your provider may give you drugs right away or may try a period of lifestyle changes (such as regular exercise or a change in your diet) for three to six months. Then he or she will tell you how often to have your blood pressure checked.

Lifestyle changes. Lifestyle and hereditary factors affect your risk of developing high blood pressure and cardiovascular disease. Changing health habits can help reduce health risks and control blood pressure. Lifestyle changes to prevent and manage high blood pressure include controlling weight, limiting salt, limiting alcohol, and exercising regularly. Be sure to read the sections on these topics for detailed recommendations on changes you can make to prevent and control high blood pressure.

Medications. Drugs have proven very effective in controlling high blood pressure. Your health care provider can help you determine whether you will need prescription medications in addition to changing your behavior. The goal of most drug treatment is to achieve and maintain regular blood pressure readings of less than 140/90 mm Hg with few or no side effects. Your provider will advise you if your treatment goals are different. Because it is still unclear why one type of drug works for a particular person while another is less effective or causes side effects, your medicine may need to be changed several times before you and your provider find the most effective one.

Continuing care. The goal of treatment is to lower and control your blood pressure to reduce your risk of stroke, heart attack, and kidney disease. The sooner your blood pressure is controlled, the lower your risk of future problems. After your blood pressure is controlled, you should continue to have your blood pressure checked at least once a year by your health care provider. Ask him or her to show you how to use equipment at home to monitor your blood pressure.

Resources

Want to learn more about a health topic you have read about in *Well Advised*? Here is a list of organizations and hotlines that can answer your questions, send you free information, and refer you to community resources.

AIDS (Acquired Immunodeficiency Syndrome)

Centers for Disease Control and Prevention
National AIDS Clearinghouse
P.O. Box 6003
Rockville, MD 20850
800-458-5231
National AIDS Hotline
800-342-AIDS (800-342-2437)
Spanish
800-344-SIDA (800-344-7432)
TTY
800-AIDS-889 (800-243-7889)

Aging

Administration on Aging
Department of Health and Human Services
330 Independence Ave. SW
Washington, DC 20201
202-619-0724 (general information)
202-619-0641 (publications)

American Association of Retired Persons
601 E St. NW
Washington, DC 20049

Children of Aging Parents
Woodbourne Office Campus
Suite 302-A
1609 Woodbourne Rd.
Levittown, PA 19057
215-945-6900
Eldercare Locator: 800-677-1116

National Institute on Aging
Information Center
P.O. Box 8057
Gaithersburg, MD 20898-8057
1-800-222-2225
1-800-222-4225 (TTY)

Alcohol and Other Drug Abuse

Al-Anon/Alateen Family Group Headquarters
P.O. Box 862
Midtown Station
New York, NY 10018-0862
800-356-9996

Alcoholics Anonymous General Service Office
Box 459
Grand Central Station
New York, NY 10163
212-661-5666
or check your local white pages

National Clearinghouse for Alcohol and Drug Information
P.O. Box 2345
Rockville, MD 20847-2345
800-729-6686

National Council on Alcoholism and Drug Dependence
12 West 21 St.
New York, NY 10010
800-NCA-CALL (800-622-2255)

Allergies and Asthma

Allergy and Asthma Network/Mothers of Asthmatics
Suite 200
3554 Chain Bridge Rd.
Fairfax, VA 22030
800-878-4403

American Academy of Allergy, Asthma and Immunology
611 East Wells St.
Milwaukee, WI 53202
800-822-2762

National Asthma Education Program
Suite 430
4733 Bethesda Ave.
Bethesda, MD 20814-4820
301-951-3260

National Institute of Allergy and Infectious Diseases
9000 Rockville Pike
Bethesda, MD 20892
301-496-5717

Alzheimer's Disease

Alzheimer's Disease Education and Referral Center (ADEAR Center)
P.O. Box 8250
Silver Spring, MD 20907-8250
800-438-4380

Arthritis

Arthritis Foundation
800-283-7800

National Institute of Arthritis and Musculoskeletal and Skin Diseases
Building 31, Room 4C05
Bethesda, MD 20892
301-496-8188

Back Pain

American College of Surgeons
55 East Erie St.
Chicago, IL 60611

Agency for Health Care Policy and Research
Publications Clearinghouse
P.O. Box 8547
Silver Spring, MD 20907
800-358-9295

American Physical Therapy Association
P.O. Box 37257
Washington, DC 20013

Texas Back Institute
3801 West 15th St.
Plano, TX 75075
800-247-BACK (800-247-2225)

Cancer

American Cancer Society
800-ACS-2345 (800-227-2345)

National Cancer Institute
Office of Cancer Communications
Building 31, Room 104A24
Bethesda, MD 20892
800-4-CANCER (800-422-6237)

Carpal Tunnel Syndrome

American Physical Therapy Association
APTA Brochures
P.O. Box 37257
Washington, DC 20013

Children

American Academy of Family Physicians
8880 Ward Pkwy.
Kansas City, MS 64114
800-274-2237

American Academy of Pediatrics
708-981-6757

National Maternal and Child Health Clearinghouse
703-821-8955, ext. 254

Diabetes

American Diabetes Association
1660 Duke St.
Alexandria, VA 22314
800-232-3472

National Diabetes Information Clearinghouse
Box NDIC
9000 Rockville Pike
Bethesda, MD 20892
301-468-2162

Eye, Ear, Nose, and Throat

American Academy of Ophthalmology
P.O. Box 7424
San Francisco, CA 94120-7424
800-222-EYES (800-222-3937)

American Academy of Otolaryngology, Head and Neck Surgery
One Prince St.
Alexandria, VA 22314

American Dental Association
Bureau of Health Education
211 East Chicago Ave.
Chicago, IL 60611
800-621-8099

American Speech-Language Hearing Association
10801 Rockville Pike
Rockville, MD 20852
301-897-5700 (voice and TDD)

National Eye Institute
Building 31, Room 6A32
Bethesda, MD 20892

National Institute on Deafness and Other Communication Disorders
Information Clearinghouse
P.O. Box 37777
Washington, DC 20013-7777

National Institute of Dental Research
Building 31, Room 2C
3531 Center Dr.
MSC2290
Bethesda, MD 20892-2290
301-496-4261

National Oral Health Information
Clearinghouse
1 NOHIC Way
Bethesda, MD 20892-3500
301-402-7364

National Society to Prevent Blindness
500 East Remington Rd.
Schaumburg, IL 60173
800-221-3004

Family Planning

Planned Parenthood
800-230-PLAN (800-230-7526)

Fitness

American Academy of Orthopaedic Surgeons
P.O. Box 1998
Des Plaines, IL 60017
800-824-BONE (800-824-2663)

American Association of Retired Persons
601 E St. NW
Washington, DC 20049

American College of Sports Medicine
P.O. Box 1440
Indianapolis, IN 46202-1440
317-637-9200

American Physical Therapy Association
P.O. Box 37257
Washington, DC 20013

National Handicapped Sports and Recreation Association
Suite 100
451 Hungerford Dr.
Rockville, MD 20850
301-217-0960

National Heart, Lung and Blood Institute
Education Programs Information Center
P.O. Box 30105
Bethesda, MD 20824-0105
301-951-3260

National Senior Sports Association
Suite 205
10560 Main St.
Fairfax, VA 22030
703-385-7540

President's Council on Physical Fitness and Sports
Suite 7103
450 5th St. NW
Washington, DC 20001

Foot Care

American Orthopedic Foot and Ankle Society
222 South Prospect
Park Ridge, IL 60068

American Podiatric Medical Association
9312 Old Georgetown Rd.
Bethesda, MD 20814

Heart

American Heart Association
National Center
7320 Greenville Ave.
Dallas, TX 75231
800-AHA-USA1 (800-242-8721)

National Cholesterol Education Programs
Information Center
Suite 530
4733 Bethesda Ave.
Bethesda, MD 20814-4820

National Heart, Lung and Blood Institute
Information Center
P.O. Box 30105
Bethesda, MD 20824-0105
301-251-1222 or 800-575-9355

Immunizations

Centers for Disease Control and Prevention
National Immunization Program
1600 Clifton Rd.
Atlanta, GA 30333
404-639-8225

Kidney and Urologic Diseases

Help for Incontinent People
P.O. Box 544A
Union, SC 29379
800-BLADDER (800-252-3337)

National Kidney and Urologic Diseases
Information Clearinghouse
P.O. Box NKUDIC
Bethesda, MD 20892
301-468-6345

National Kidney Foundation
800-622-9010

Lice

National Pediculosis Association
P.O. Box 610189
Newton, MA 02161
800-446-4NPA (800-446-4672)

Liver

American Liver Foundation
1425 Pompton Ave.
Cedar Grove, NJ 07009
800-223-0179 (Hepatitis Hotline)

Lungs

American Lung Association
1740 Broadway
New York, NY 10019-4374
800-LUNG-USA (800-586-4872)

Medication

U.S. Food and Drug Administration Center for Drug Evaluation and Research
Consumer and Professional Affairs (HFD-365)
5600 Fishers Lane
Rockville, MD 20857

National Council on Patient Information and Education
Suite 810
666 11th St. NW
Washington, DC 20001
202-347-6711

Mental Health/Illness

American Psychiatric Association
1400 K St. NW
Washington, DC 20005
202-682-6220

American Psychological Association
750 First St. NE
Washington, DC 20002-4242
202-336-5500 or 800-374-2721

Anxiety Disorders Association of America
Dept. A
6000 Executive Blvd.
Rockville, MD 20852

National Depressive and Manic Depressive Association
Suite 501
730 N. Franklin St.
Chicago, IL 60610
800-826-3632

National Institute of Mental Health
Room 7C-02
5600 Fishers Lane
Rockville, MD 20857

National Institute of Mental Health
Panic Disorder Education Program
800-64-PANIC (800-647-2642)

National Mental Health Association
1021 Prince St.
Alexandria, VA 22314-2971
800-969-NMHA (800-969-6642)

Obsessive Compulsive Foundation
P.O. Box 70
Milford, CT 06460
203-878-5669

Nutrition/Dieting

American Dietetic Association
216 West Jackson Blvd.
Chicago, IL 60606-6995
800-366-1655

Human Nutrition Information Service
U.S. Department of Agriculture
6505 Belcrest Rd.
Hyattsville, MD 20782
202-208-2417

National Cholesterol Education Programs
Information Center
4733 Bethesda Ave.
Suite 530
Bethesda, MD 20814-4820

National Heart, Lung and Blood Institute
Information Center
P.O. Box 30105
Bethesda, MD 20824-0105
301-251-1222

U.S. Department of Agriculture's Meat and Poultry Hotline
800-535-4555
202-720-3333 (Washington, DC area)

U.S. Food and Drug Administration
Information Office
Parklawn Building
5600 Fishers Lane
Rockville, MD 20857

Preventive Care

American Academy of Family Physicians
8880 Ward Pkwy.
Kansas City, MS 64114
800-274-2237

Put Prevention Into Practice
National Health Information Center
P.O. Box 1133
Washington, DC 20013-1131
800-336-4797

Safety and Injury Prevention

American College of Emergency Physicians
Suite 650
1111 19th St. NW
Washington, DC 20036
800-320-0610

American Red Cross
Check your local white pages.

Consumer Product Safety Commission
Washington, DC 20207
800-638-CPSC (800-638-2772)

Federal Emergency Management Agency
U.S. Fire Administration
16825 S. Seton Ave.
Emmitsburg, MD 21727
301-447-6771

National Highway Traffic Safety
Administration Hotline
Department of Transportation
400 Seventh Ave. SW
Washington, DC 20590
800-424-9393

Sexually Transmitted Diseases (also see *AIDS*)

Centers for Disease Control and Prevention
National STD Hotline
800-227-8922

American Social Health Association
P.O. Box 13827
Research Triangle Park, NC 27709

Skin Care

American Academy of Dermatology
P.O. Box 4041
Schaumburg, IL 60173-4965
847-330-0230

Sleep

Better Sleep Council
P.O. Box 13
Washington, DC 20044

National Sleep Foundation
Suite 200
1367 Connecticut Ave. NW
Washington, DC 20036

Smoking

American Cancer Society
1599 Clifton Rd. NE
Atlanta, GA 30329-4251
800-ACS-2345 (800-227-2345)

American Heart Association
National Center
7272 Greenville Ave.
Dallas, TX 75231
800-AHA-USA1 (800-242-8721)

American Lung Association
1740 Broadway
New York, NY 10019-4374
800-LUNG-USA (800-586-4872)

National Cancer Institute
Office of Cancer Communications
Building 31, Room 10A16
Bethesda, MD 20892
800-4-CANCER (800-422-6237)

National Heart, Lung and Blood Institute
Education Programs Information Center
P.O. Box 30105
Bethesda, MD 20824-0105
301-951-3260

Office on Smoking and Health
Center for Chronic Disease Prevention
and Health Promotion
Mail Stop K-50
Centers for Disease Control and Prevention
1600 Clifton Rd. NE
Atlanta, GA 30333
770-488-5705

Stomach and other Digestive Problems

National Digestive Diseases Information Clearinghouse
2 Information Way
Bethesda, MD 20892-3570
301-654-3810

Women

American College of Obstetricians and Gynecologists
409 12th St. SW
Washington, DC 20024-2188

The Endometriosis Association
P.O. Box 92187
Milwaukee, WI 92187
800-992-ENDO (800-992-3636)

La Leche League
Check your local white pages.

National Osteoporosis Foundation
Suite 500
1150 17th St. NW
Washington, DC 20036-4603
202-223-2226

Index

A

B

C

D

E

F

G

H

I

J

K

L

M

N

O

P

Q

R

S

T

U

V

W

Y

Z

Credits

Editor-in-Chief

Paul E. Terry, Ph.D., Park Nicollet Medical Foundation

Medical Editors

David Abelson, M.D., Park Nicollet Medical Center; Allan Kind, M.D., Park Nicollet Medical Foundation

Section Editors

Joseph Alfano, M.D., George Halvorson, HealthPartners Health Plans; Spencer Holmes, M.D., Park Nicollet Medical Center; Thomas Kottke, M.D., Mayo Clinic; Gordon Mosser, M.D., Institute for Clinical Systems Integration; Linda Peitzman, M.D., Park Nicollet Medical Center; James L. Reinertsen, M.D., HealthSystem Minnesota; Leif Solberg, M.D., Group Health Foundation; Steve Wetzell, Business Health Care Action Group

Writers/Contributing Editors

Paul E. Terry, Ph.D.; Lisa Bartels-Rabb, M.S.J.; Tom Brandes, M.A.; Scott Glickstein, M.D.; Robert Gorman, M.D.; Kathy Tingelstad

Contributors

Suzanne Bennett, M.P.H.; Joan Bissen, R.D.; Debra Boal, R.N.; Mark DePaolis, M.D.; Marion Franz, R.D.; Lisa Graham-Peterson; Susan Hanson, R.D.; Mary Kruse, M.A.; Judy Monn; Jane Norstrom, M.A.; Joan Nyberg; Linda Pietz, R.N.; Marta Simpson, R.N.; Susan Sullivan, Ph.D.

Medical Reviewers

Internal Medicine

Avis Baumann, R.N.; Jane Oh, M.D.; Jennifer Olson, M.D.; Barbara Steigauf, R.N.

Pulmonary Medicine

Kevin Komadina, M.D.; A. Stuart Hanson, M.D.; Kathleen Hornsby, R.N.; Richard Woellner, M.D.

Infectious Diseases

Pat Dahlman, R.N.; Paul Carson, M.D.

Family Practice

Donald Abrams, M.D.; Joseph Alfano, M.D.; Barbara Benjamin, M.D.; Alan Carter, M.D.; Susan Carter, M.D.; Michael Dukinfield, M.D.; Janet Frost, R.N.; John Haugen, M.D.; Mark Hench, M.D.; Jeanne Hesse, M.D.; Bonita Hill, M.D.; Julie Hudson, R.N.; John Kaintz, M.D.; Michael Lano, M.D.; Douglas Lowin, M.D.; Joseph Lukaska, M.D.; Alston Lundgren, M.D.; Jean Lundgren, M.D.; Donald Lynch, M.D.; Rosa Marroquin, M.D.; Charles McCoy, M.D.; Kenneth Olson, M.D.; Carolyn Torkelson, M.D.; David VonWeiss, M.D.

OB/GYN

Janet Claxton, N.P.; Barbara Davenport, N.P.; Deborah Meade, R.N.; Leslie Pratt, M.D.; Lois Satterberg, N.P.; Deborah Thorp, M.D.

Pediatrics

Renner Anderson, M.D.; Jayne Boche, M.D.; David Griffin, M.D.; Thomas Helm, M.D.; Robert Karasov, M.D.; Kristi Klett, M.D.; Beth Leneagh, R.N.; Douglas Martin, M.D.; John Meurer, M.D.; Michael Pryor, M.D.; Theresa Ryan, M.D.

Urgent Care
Shelly Barton, R.N.; Paul Bearmont, M.D.; Carol Manning, M.D.; Linda Peitzman, M.D.; Mary Ratz, M.D.; Suzanne Schaefer, M.D.; Omri Shochatovitz, M.D.; Susan Vitalis, M.D.

Allergy
David Graft, M.D.; William Schoenwetter, M.D.; Richard Sveum, M.D.

Cardiology
Steve Benton, M.D.; J. Mark Haugland, M.D.

Gastroenterology
Matthew Bagamery, M.D.; Michael Levy, M.D.

Dermatology
Spencer Holmes, M.D.; Michael McCormick, M.D.; Louis Rusin, M.D.; Victoria Vanroy, M.D.

Oncology
Steven Duane, M.D.; Charles Murray, M.D.

Neurology
Daniel Freking, M.D.; Sandra Hanson, M.D.; Debra Heros, M.D.; Eric Schenk, M.D.

Dental
David Buran, M.D

Orthopedics
Matthew Putman, M.D.; Gregg Strathy, M.D.; Thomas Youngren, M.D.

Ophthalmology
Robert Campbell, M.D.; Timothy Diegel, M.D.; Rodney Dueck, M.D.; Richard Freeman, M.D.; Anne Towey, M.D.; Anton Willerscheidt, M.D.

Rheumatology
Eric Schned, M.D.

Urology
Steven Bernstein, M.D.; Clyde Blackard, M.D.; William Borkon, M.D.; Sharon Reiter, R.N.; William Sharer, M.D.; Erol Uke, M.D.; Gang Zhang, M.D.

Senior Health
Sharon Marx, M.D.

Rehabilitation Medicine
Ann Brutlag, M.D.; Robert Gorman, M.D.; George Kramer, M.D.; Daniel Kurtti, M.D.

Occupational Medicine
David Parker, M.D.

Pharmacy
Richard Bleck R.Ph., Scott Bryngelson R.Ph., Roger Mickelson R.Ph.

Specialty Reviewers
Gail Amundson, M.D.; Dale Anderson, M.D.; Debra Boal, R.N.; Stephen Bonfilio, Ph.D.; Hyacinth Campbell-Roberts; Timothy Culbert, M.D.; Stacie Emberly; Mary Figueroa, M.D.; Jinnet Fowles, Ph.D.; Stanley Greenwald, M.D.; Carmen Gutterman, Ph.D.; Carol Hersman, R.N., M.A.; Rebecca Kajander, C.P.N.P., M.P.H.; Judy Kelloway, Ph.D.; James Li, M.D.; Janet Lima; Sheila McCormick, R.N.; Jeanne Nelson, M.D.; Joseph Nelson, L.P.; Stephen Olsen, Ph.D.; Anthony Pojman, M.D.; Stephen Powless, M.D.; Ira Rabinowitz, D.M.D.; Judson Reany, M.D.; Michael Rethwill, M.D.; Peter Smars, M.D.; Paul Spilseth, M.D.; Linda Strohmater, R.N.; Andrew Wood, R.P.T.

Editor-in-Chief
Delia Cabe

Managing Editor
Maria I. Hecht

Developmental and Copy Editor
Jules Verdone

Manuscript Revisions
Ann Harding

Production and Cover Design
Lynn Whittemore

Original Page Design
Mary Hom

Text Illustrations
Joan Orme, Karen Morgan

Cover Illustration
Jeanne Berg

Iconography
Bob James